Cell Companion 2022

EVERYONE'S GUIDE TO SERVING AND SURVIVING A PRISON SENTENCE

FIFTH EDITION

www.PrisonOracle.com

Cell Companion 2022

Fifth Edition

Mark Leech FRSA

Cell Companion
2022

Published December 2021 by
PRISONS.ORG.UK LTD,
PO BOX 679
BURY BL8 9RU
Tel: 0845 474 0013
Email: customer.services@prisons.org.uk
Web Site: www.prisons.org.uk

Copyright © Mark Leech 2021. All rights reserved. Formatting and design are the copyright of PRISONS.ORG.UK LTD to whom the exclusive reproduction rights in this edition have been licenced by Stephen Field. No part of this publication may be reproduced or stored in any retrieval system or transmitted by any means, including over the internet, without the express written permission of the publishers in writing. The right of Mark Leech to be identified as the author of this work has been asserted by him in accordance with the Copyright, Designs & Patents Act 1988.

Publication rights. All rights relating to publication of this edition reside with PRISONS.ORG.UK LTD, including the right to print and distribute copies of the work anywhere in the world. The edition must not be photographed, copied, reproduced, transmitted or recorded in any form or medium, or broadcast in any form or by any means, including over the internet, without the prior written permission of the publisher.

ISBN : 978-1-9160824-9-6
Printing & Binding: Hobbs The Printers, Brunel Road, Totton, Hants SO40 3WX.

Cover design: Mark Leech.

Photograph of Mark Leech
copyright © Mark Leech.

Setting & design: PRISONS.ORG.UK Ltd.

ABOUT THE EDITOR

MARK LEECH

From strip-cells and prison roof top protests at one end of the scale to being Editor of the definitive annual reference books on the prison system of England and Wales at the other, Mark Leech has travelled quite a distance. Though claiming no accolade for it, Mark served almost 20 years in 62 of Britain's jails, from Inverness in the north of Scotland to Parkhurst on the Isle of Wight, his prison career was characterised by riots, roof top protests and more than 40 successful legal battles against the prison service fought in every legal arena right the way to what is now known as the Supreme Court.

Once a tenacious thorn in the side of the prison authorities Mark, who was released in 1995, has risen to become the country's foremost ex-offender expert on the policy and practice of the penal system.

For the last 26 years Mark has been the Editor of the premier prison publications in England and Wales, including *The Prisons Handbook*, the definitive 1,600-page annual guide to the Prison System; The *Prison Oracle* the definitive UK prisons website, *Prison Law Index* the definitive annual A-Z on Prison Law and he is also the Editor of *Converse*, the highest circulation national monthly prisons newspaper edited and published entirely by ex-offenders. Mark is the Founder and former Chief Executive of the national ex-offenders charity UNLOCK, he is a regular prisons commentator on major UK television news outlets and writes on prison issues for The Guardian and The Independent newspapers.

In 2006 Mark was elected as a Fellow of the Royal Society of Arts.

Today Mark lives with his partner in Chiang Mai, northern Thailand, where they have a young son and daughter.

Outside of work, his interests are in aviation; Mark is a qualified Helicopter Pilot.

ACKNOWLEDGEMENTS

There are many people who have helped, inspired and contributed to bringing this book to reality, I can't name them all here, and someone of them would be horrified if I did - but they know who they are.

Thanks must go to Michael Jefferies, solicitor and senior partner with Jefferies Personal Injury Solicitors, not just for his support in delivering this book but his friendship too.

I am indebted to Paul Ferris 'The Wee Man' for his friendship over the last 25 years and his excellent foreword to this work.

The dozens of reformed offenders must also be mentioned for their excellent suggestions and contributions and I must also thank Sir Martin Narey the former Director General of HM Prison Service for his outstanding article on page 223, and also the excellent contribution by Steve Gillan, General Secretary of The Prison Officers' Association for his frank article on why his members have legitimate grievances about pay and pensions.

My thanks are due also to Andy Simpson for his ability to handle other work while this was in preparation, and while suffering from Covid-19, and of course to my partner Oui whose unswerving loyalty over the last 16 years has never missed a beat.

Mark Leech
Chiang Mai
Thailand
October 2021

www.prisons.org.uk

CONTENTS

About The Author, 5
Acknowledgements, 5
Contents, 6
Foreword, *Paul Ferris*, 9

The Prison Estate 2022, 10
Goverment Prison Estate Programmes, 10
Understanding the prison estate, 10
What are the different types of prison in HMPPS Estate, 11
Prisons and YOIs, 11
Adult Male Prisons, 11
Types of Prison, 11
Security Categories listed by Prisons, 12-13
Prisons listed by Security Categories, 12-13
Adult Female Prisons 14
Private Prisons, 14
Government Policy, 15
Age of the Prison Estate, 15
HMCIP Assessment of living conditions, 15
Measuring Accommodation Standards, 16
Maintenance of Prisons, 16
Recent Prison Estate Programmes, 17
The New Prisons Programme, 19
Sentencing Changes 2020, 21

SECTION 1. Prisons, *22-90*

* Prisons subject to Urgent Notifications

A-Z of Prison Establishments 2022, *22*

HMP ALTCOURSE
HMP ASHFIELD
HMP ASKHAM GRANGE
HMYOI AYLESBURY
HMP BEDFORD*
HMP BELMARSH
HMP BERWYN
HMP BIRMINGHAM*
HMP BRISTOL*
HMP BRONZEFIELD
HMP BUCKLEY HALL
HMP BULLINGDON
HMP BURE
HMP CARDIFF
HMP CHANNINGS WOOD
HMP CHELMSFORD
HMP COLDINGLEY
HMP DARTMOOR

HMP DONCASTER
HMP DOVEGATE
HMP DOWNVIEW
HMP DRAKE HALL
HMP DURHAM
HMP EAST SUTTON PARK
HMP EASTWOOD PARK
HMP ELMLEY
HMP ERLESTOKE
HMP EXETER*
HMP FEATHERSTONE
HMYOI FELTHAM*
HMP FIVE WELLS (Opens 1st Feb 2022)
HMP FORD
HMP FOREST BANK
HMP FOSTON HALL
HMP FRANKLAND
HMP FULL SUTTON
HMP GARTH
HMP GARTREE
HMP GRENDON
HMP GUYS MARSH
HMP HATFIELD
HMP HAVERIGG
HMP HEWELL
HMP HIGHDOWN
HMP HIGH POINT
HMP HINDLEY
HMP YOI HOLLESLEY BAY
HMP HOLME HOUSE
HMP HULL
HMP HUMBER
HMP HUNTERCOMBE
HMP ISIS
HMP ISLE OF WIGHT
HMP KIRKHAM
HMP KIRKLEVINGTON GRANGE
HMP LANCASTER FARMS
HMP LEEDS
HMP LEICESTER
HMP LEWES
HMP LEYHILL
HMP LINCOLN
HMP LINDHOLME
HMP LITTLEHEY
HMP LIVERPOOL
HMP LONG LARTIN
HMP LOW NEWTON\
HMP LOWDHAM GRANGE
HMP MAIDSTONE
HMP MANCHESTER

HMP MOORLAND
HMP MORTON HALL *(Opens December 2021)*
HMP THE MOUNT
HMP NEW HALL
HMP NORTH SEA CAMP
HMP NORTHUMBERLAND
HMP NORWICH
HMP NOTTINGHAM*
HMP OAKWOOD
HMP ONLEY
HMP PARC
HMYOI Parc Juvenile Unit
HMP PETERBOROUGH
HMP PORTLAND
HMP PRESCOED *See entry for HMP Usk*
HMP PRESTON
HMP RANBY
HMP RISLEY
HMP ROCHESTER
HMP RYE HILL
HMP SEND
HMP SPRINGHILL
HMP STAFFORD
HMP STANDFORD HILL
HMP STOCKEN
HMP STOKE HEATH
HMP STYAL
HMP SUDBURY
HMP SWALESIDE
HMP SWANSEA
HMYOI SWINFEN HALL
HMP THAMESIDE
HMP THORN CROSS
HMP USK / PRESCOED
HMP PRESCOED
HMP WAKEFIELD
HMP WANDSWORTH
HMP WARREN HILL
HMP WAYLAND
HMP WEALSTUN
HMYOI WERRINGTON
HMYOI WETHERBY
HMP WHATTON
HMP WHITEMOOR
HMP WINCHESTER
HMP WOODHILL
HMP WORMWOOD SCRUBS
HMP WYMOTT

HM Inspectorate of Prisons: List of Reports issued up to October 2021, 90

SECTION 2. ADVICE, 94

Before You Go To Prison, 95
• Before you go to Prison - *honestly, it's not the end of the world that it may seem right now.*
• The 'Bang Up Bag' - *what to pack.*
• What lays ahead - *Viewpoints from experienced voices who have been there.*

When You're In Prison, 100
• Adjudications - *Disciplinary charges and how to deal with them*, 100
• Applications & Complaints - *How to get things done in prison*, 103
• Bereavement - *when someone dies while you're inside, attending the funeral*, 107
• Block - *How to cope with segregation*, 108
• Categorisation - *male and female, what is it and getting a review*, 110
• Confiscation Orders - *what are they and what consequences do they bring*, 114
• Education - *how to apply/study and the new Education and Library Policy Framework and the rights it gives you*, 115
• Equality - *you have rights not to be discriminated against*, 117
• Extremism - *Recognising it, its dangers and how to avoid it*, 119
• Facilities List - *Explaining the national and local list of what you can have in prison*, 119, 242
• Family Matters - *Maintaining family contact with, letters, visits, and phone calls*, 120
• Getting out - *Pre-release check list*, 122
• Healthcare - *Your rights to healthcare in prison and how to complain*, 125
• Home Detention Curfew - *'On The Tag' what is it, how do I apply for it?* 127
• Incentives Earned Privileges - *Levels and keeping your privileges*, 129
• Keeping your home when in prison - *Steps you can take to keep accommodation*, 132
• **Legal Highs:** *Real Danger of DEATH*, 133
• Maintaining Innocence, 133
• Offending Behaviour Courses, 2022 what are they? 134

ACCREDITED FOR DELIVERY IN THE COMMUNITY

Becoming New Me + (BNM+)
Breaking Free: Health and Justice Package
Building Better Relationships (BBR)

www.prisons.org.uk

Building Skills for Recovery (BSR)
Drink Impaired Drivers Programme (DIDP)
Healthy Identity Intervention (HII)
Horizon
iHorizon
Identity Matters (IM)
Mentalization-based Treatment (MBT)
New Me Strengths (NMS)
Living as New Me (LNM)
Resolve
Thinking Skills Programme (TSP)

ACCREDITED FOR CUSTODY

Alcohol Dependence Treatment Programme
Becoming New Me + (BNM+)
Breaking Free: Health and Justice Package
Building Better Relationships (BBR)
Building Skills for Recovery (BSR)
Challenge to Change (C2C)
Choices, Actions, Relationships, Emotions
Control of Violence for Angry Impulsive Drinkers – Group Secure (COVAID-GS)
Control of Violence for Angry Impulsive Drinkers – Group Secure Women
Democratic Therapeutic Community Model
Therapeutic Communities Plus (TC+)
Healthy Identity Intervention (HII)
Healthy Sex Programme (HSP)
Horizon
Identity Matters (IM)
Kaizen
Living as New Me
New Me Strengths
Resolve
The Bridge Programme
Thinking Skills Programme

- Marriage in prison, 141
- Open Prisons - *how to prepare.* 142
- Pad Mates- sharing a cell without grief or friction, 144
- Parole New Review Mechanism. 154
- Prison Debt - why to avoid it, 146
- Property inside, 148
- Recall 2022 - your rights, 152
- ROTL 2022, 155
- Self-harm - how to cope, 156
- Sex in prison, 157
- Slang, 158
- Transfers, 159

- Veterans in Custody, 160
- VPUs, protection, 160
- Work & Pay, 162

SECTION 3. Personal Injury, 164
By Michael Jefferies, Senior Partner Jefferies Personal Injuries Solicitors, Chairman: Prison Injury Lawyers Association.

SECTION 4. Helpful Orgs, 170
Organisations that help people in prison, including charities that give grants to prisoners

SECTION 5. Legal, 195
PRISON RULES 1999 correct to November 2021

SECTION 6. Something To Say?
- *Rehabilitation has never been the primary purpose of prison - and rightly so too:* Sir Martin Narey 223

- *Do you know how to spot an Exit?* Mark Leech FRSA 228

ANNEXES, 229
- **Freedom of Information Act:** In prison you have Information rights - use them, 229
- **Full List of PSIs, PSOs, and Policy Frame works in force at 1st November 2021,** 231
- **List of Prison Groups and Directors,** 234
- **Annual Calendar January 2022 to January 2023,** 237
- **National Facilities List 2021,** 242
- **Map of the Prison Estate 2021,** 250.

FOREWORD

By Paul Ferris - 'The Wee Man'

I first met Mark Leech in the Secure Segregation Unit ('The Wendy House') of Barlinnie Prison in Glasgow in 1992 where I was on remand charged with murder - and in which Mark played a crucial part in justice being done and in securing my acquittal. Mark was in the Wendy House because he knew too much prison law.

Knowledge is power in a prison world where information is kept concealed, and that is why this book is so important - it tells prisoners of their rights, not so they can abuse the system, but so they comply with it, receive what they are entitled to receive and progress with safety towards release and a better life.

This book tackles serious prison issues head on, like the Gideon Bible in hospitals it should be on every bed, in every cell in the country. Prisons are dangerous places, never more so than now with almost 30,000 assaults last year - this book informs and empowers prisoners, it tells them who to follow in terms of leaders and achievers, and those to avoid such as those involved in drugs and violence.

Its nigh on impossible to get things done in prison without knowing your rights, I know I have been there, and being isolated can add to the misery of being in prison - 344 people died in English prisons last year, over 100 of them took their own lives because they reached such depths of despair they would rather take their own life than face the anguish of one more day. This book deals with how to cope with stress and depression in prison, telling prisoners and their families too where to get the help that is available and giving them hope for the future.

In many ways it is the simple things that make the most difference in prison, like making an application, understanding your rights to letters, visits and phone calls, what education courses are available and how to access them, how to deal with disciplinary charges, claim their right to compensation when through no fault of their own they are injured as a result of poor conditions, the lack of training when operating machinery in prison workshops, or are assaulted because the shortage of staff on the wings means less supervision.

This book has been needed for a long time, it should be on every bed, in every pad, in every prison in the country. Our prisons will be safer for it, prisoners will be better advised of their rights, and I am delighted to have been given this wonderful opportunity of writing this Foreword to it.

www.prisons.org.uk

KNOWLEDGE
— IS —
POWER

PRISON ESTATE 2022

Summary - October 2021

The prison estate in England and Wales contains 117 prisons holding people who have been sentenced or are on remand awaiting trial for a range of crimes. The prison estate has a mixture of publicly and privately-run institutions some of which are newly built, while others date back to the Victorian era.

Concerns about conditions

There has been growing concern that the prison estate is unfit for purpose. The estate includes many dilapidated and overcrowded prisons. There is a backlog of maintenance work in prisons that has been estimated at around £1 billion.

Reports from the Chief Inspector of Prisons in 2017-19 said that conditions in this period were some of the most disturbing and squalid the inspectorate had ever seen. The inspectorate reported that in 2019-20, prior to the Covid- 19 pandemic, some prisons had improved living conditions, but conditions remained poor and overcrowded for many prisoners. The current Chief Inspector of Prisons in his 2020-21 annual report stated that the pandemic had exacerbated some underlying problems and unacceptable conditions that inspections have previously criticised.

Government prison estate programmes

The Government ran a 'Prison Estate Transformation Programme' from 2016- 2019 with the aim of building 10,000 new prison places, investing in repairs and renovations and reorganising the functions of individual prisons.

In 2020 the National Audit Office and Public Accounts Committee published reports that were critical of the attempts made by the Ministry of Justice and HM Prison and Probation Service (HMPPS) to improve the prison estate. The Public Accounts Committee said that despite promises to create 10,000 new- for-old prison places by 2020, just 206 new places had been delivered, and prisoners continued to be held in unsafe, crowded conditions that did not meet their needs.

A New Prison Programme was created in 2019. In August 2019, the Government announced that it would spend up to £2.5 billion to create 10,000 prison places. In the 2020 Spending Review the Government stated it would spend more than £4 billion towards delivering 18,000 prison places across England and Wales by the mid-2020s. The 18,000 places would include the 10,000 places at four new prisons (announced in August 2019), the expansion of a further four prisons, the refurbishment of the existing prison estate and the completion of ongoing prison builds at Glen Parva and Five Wells (Wellingborough).

The 2020-21 Spending Review also included £315m capital funding which HMPPS said would be used to make a start on critical refurbishment projects. The Public Accounts Committee has said the £315 million is significantly below what is required to maintain the prison estate.

Responses to the Government's approach

Prison reform organisations have been critical of the Government's approach. They argue that instead of increasing prison places the Government should reduce the prison population thereby reducing overcrowding and freeing up resources for rehabilitation.

In January 2021, the Government announced that up to 500 prison places would be built in existing women's prisons. The plans have been criticised by prison reform organisations who have commented that they undermine the Government's commitments to reduce the women's prison population and go against the Government's own evidence that most women in prison do not need to be there.

Understanding the prison estate

England and Wales

Her Majesty's Prison & Probation Service (HMPPS) has responsibility for running prison services in England and Wales. It manages public sector prisons and the contracts for private sector prisons. HMPPS is an executive agency, sponsored by the Ministry of Justice. HMPPS operates a directorate in Wales which coordinates prison and probation services there.

Her Majesty's Inspectorate of

Prisons is the independent body which reports on conditions and the treatment of those in held in custody.

Scotland and Northern Ireland

Prisons in Scotland are managed by the Scottish Prison Service. Prisons in Northern Ireland are managed by the Northern Ireland Prison Service.

The HMPPS estate

HMPPS manages an estate of 117 prisons, an Immigration Removal Centre and two 'Secure Training Centres'. Outside the HMPPS estate, there are further immigration removal centres.

Prisons and Young Offenders Institutions

There are several different types of prisons which nominally serve different categories of prisoner (see section 1.2 below). Most prisons are managed directly by HMPPS, but some are run by private sector companies through contracts (see section 1.3 for more details).

Immigration Removal Centres

Separate from prisons, Immigration Removal Centres (IRCs) are used solely for the detention of people detained under the Immigration Act 1971 or under section 62 of the Nationality, Immigration and Asylum Act 2002. Prior to 2003, IRCs were called 'detention centres'.

Most IRCs are managed by private sector companies under contract to the Home Office. Only one, Morton Hall, is currently within the HMPPS estate. In July 2020 it was announced that Morton Hall would close as an IRC in 2021 and would revert to being used as a prison. The Verne was an IRC but was converted to a public-sector prison in 2018.

Secure Training Centres

Secure Training Centres (STCs) are institutions for children up to the age of 17. There are currently two STCs in England and Wales, Oakhill and Rainsbrook. Both are operated by private companies. In June 2021, the Government announced that all children would be removed from Rainsbrook due to serious ongoing concerns about safety and performance. The Ministry of Justice said negotiations were ongoing with the private provider MTC on the future of the contract and that options included bringing the STC back under public sector control and repurposing the site for alternative use.

In October 2018, the Government announced that Medway STC would be closed and reopened as a Secure School. Medway STC stopped accommodating children in January 2020 and closed at the end of March 2020. The Library briefing paper Youth Custody discusses STCs and Secure Schools.

Types of prison and young offender institutions

The PrisonOracle.com website contains an information page for each prison in the prison estate. The pages describe the types of prisoners that are held in each prison and the services which are provided to them.

On 1 October 2021 there were 78,780 people in prison in England & Wales - of these just 3,199 were female

Adult male prisons

Prisoner categories

Nominally, prisoners are assigned to a prison based on their personal security category. However, HMPPS may transfer a prisoner to another prison with a different security category at any time.

Adult male prisoners are assigned an alphabetical categorisation between A and D (where 'A' signifies highest risk and 'D' signifies lowest risk). The risk factors assessed when categorising an individual to a particular security category are the prisoner's risks of:

• escape or abscond;
• harm to the public;
• ongoing criminality in custody;
• violent or other behaviour that impacts the safety of those within the prison; and
• control issues that disrupt the security and good order of the prison.

Types of prison

There are four types of prison for adult males:
1. Training: Category 'C' and category 'B' 'training' prisons are designed to house offenders at their corresponding category.

www.prisons.org.uk

- 11 -

NAME	OPERATOR	FUNCTION	NAME	OPERATOR	FUNCTION
Altcourse	G4S	Local	Dovegate	Serco	Cat B Trainer
Ashfield	Serco	Cat C Trainer	Garth	Public	Cat B Trainer
Askham Gr	Public	Female	Gartree	Public	Cat B Trainer
Aylesbury	Public	YOI	Grendon	Public	Cat B Trainer
Bedford	Public	Local	Isle of Wight	Public	Cat B Trainer
Belmarsh	Public	LTHSE	Lowdham Gr	Serco	Cat B Trainer
Berwyn	Public	Cat C Trainer	Rye Hill	G4S	Cat B Trainer
Birmingham	Public	Local	Swaleside	Public	Cat B Trainer
Brinsford	Public	YOI	Woodhill	Public	Cat B Trainer
Bristol	Public	Local	Ashfield	Serco	Cat C Trainer
Brixton	Public	Cat C Trainer	Berwyn	Public	Cat C Trainer
Bronzefield	Sodexo	Female	Brixton	Public	Cat C Trainer
Buckley Hall	Public	Cat C Trainer	Buckley Hall	Public	Cat C Trainer
Bullingdon	Public	Local	Bure	Public	Cat C Trainer
Bure	Public	Cat C Trainer	Channings Wd	Public	Cat C Trainer
Cardiff	Public	Local	Coldingley	Public	Cat C Trainer
Channings Wd	Public	Cat C Trainer	Dartmoor	Public	Cat C Trainer
Chelmsford	Public	Local	Erlestoke	Public	Cat C Trainer
Coldingley	Public	Cat C Trainer	Featherstone	Public	Cat C Trainer
Cookham Wd	Public	YJB	Five Wells	G4S (2022)	Cat C Trainer
Dartmoor	Public	Cat C Trainer	Guys Marsh	Public	Cat C Trainer
Deerbolt	Public	YOI	Highpoint	Public	Cat C Trainer
Doncaster	Serco	Local	Hindley	Public	Cat C Trainer
Dovegate	Serco	Cat B Trainer	Holme House	Public	Cat C Trainer
Downview	Public	Female	Humber	Public	Cat C Trainer
Drake Hall	Public	Female	Huntercombe	Public	Cat C Trainer
Durham	Public	Local	Isis	Public	Cat C Trainer
East Sutton Park	Public	Female	Lancaster Fms	Public	Cat C Trainer
Eastwood Park	Public	Female	Lindholme	Public	Cat C Trainer
Elmley	Public	Local	Littlehey	Public	Cat C Trainer
Erlestoke	Public	Cat C Trainer	Maidstone	Public	Cat C Trainer
Exeter	Public	Local	Moorland	Public	Cat C Trainer
Featherstone	Public	Cat C Trainer	Morton Hall	Public	Cat C Trainer
Feltham	Public	YOI	Mount, The	Public	Cat C Trainer
Five Wells	G4S (2022)	Cat C Trainer	Northumberland	Sodexo	Cat C Trainer
Ford	Public	Open	Oakwood	G4S	Cat C Trainer
Forest Bank	Sodexo	Local	Onley	Public	Cat C Trainer
Foston Hall	Public	Female	Parc	G4S	Cat C Trainer
Frankland	Public	LTHSE	Portland	Public	Cat C Trainer
Full Sutton	Public	LTHSE	Ranby	Public	Cat C Trainer
Garth	Public	Cat B Trainer	Risley	Public	Cat C Trainer
Gartree	Public	Cat B Trainer	Rochester	Public	Cat C Trainer
Grendon	Public	Cat B Trainer	Stafford	Public	Cat C Trainer
Guys Marsh	Public	Cat C Trainer	Stocken	Public	Cat C Trainer
Hatfield	Public	Open	Stoke Heath	Public	Cat C Trainer
Haverigg	Public	Open	Swinfen Hall	Public	Cat C Trainer
Hewell	Public	Local	Usk	Public	Cat C Trainer
High Down	Public	Local	Verne, The	Public	Cat C Trainer
Highpoint	Public	Cat C Trainer	Warren Hill	Public	Cat C Trainer
Hindley	Public	Cat C Trainer	Wayland	Public	Cat C Trainer
Hollesley Bay	Public	Open	Wealstun	Public	Cat C Trainer
Holme House	Public	Cat C Trainer	Whatton	Public	Cat C Trainer
Hull	Public	Local	Wymott	Public	Cat C Trainer
Humber	Public	Cat C Trainer	Askham Gr	Public	Female
Huntercombe	Public	Cat C Trainer	Bronzefield	Sodexo	Female
Isis	Public	Cat C Trainer	Downview	Public	Female
Isle of Wight	Public	Cat B Trainer	Drake Hall	Public	Female
Kirkham	Public	Open	East Sutton Park	Public	Female
Kirklevington	Public	Open	Eastwood Park	Public	Female
Lancaster Fms	Public	Cat C Trainer	Foston Hall	Public	Female
Leeds	Public	Local	Low Newton	Public	Female
Leicester	Public	Local	New Hall	Public	Female
Lewes	Public	Local	Peterboro F	Sodexo	Female
Leyhill	Public	Open	Send	Public	Female
Lincoln	Public	Local	Styal	Public	Female
Lindholme	Public	Cat C Trainer	Belmarsh	Public	LTHSE
Littlehey	Public	Cat C Trainer	Frankland	Public	LTHSE
Liverpool	Public	Local	Full Sutton	Public	LTHSE
Long Lartin	Public	LTHSE	Long Lartin	Public	LTHSE
Low Newton	Public	Female	Manchester	Public	LTHSE

Lowdham Gr	Serco	Cat B Trainer	Wakefield	Public	LTHSE
Maidstone	Public	Cat C Trainer	Whitemoor	Public	LTHSE
Manchester	Public	LTHSE	Altcourse	G4S	Local
Moorland	Public	Cat C Trainer	Bedford	Public	Local
Morton Hall	Public	Cat C Trainer	Birmingham	Public	Local
Mount, The	Public	Cat C Trainer	Bristol	Public	Local
New Hall	Public	Female	Bullingdon	Public	Local
North Sea Camp	Public	Open	Cardiff	Public	Local
Northumberland	Sodexo	Cat C Trainer	Chelmsford	Public	Local
Norwich	Public	Local	Doncaster	Serco	Local
Nottingham	Public	Local	Durham	Public	Local
Oakhill	G4S	STC	Elmley	Public	Local
Oakwood	G4S	Cat C Trainer	Exeter	Public	Local
Onley	Public	Cat C Trainer	Forest Bank	Sodexo	Local
Parc	G4S	Cat C Trainer	Hewell	Public	Local
Pentonville	Public	Local	High Down	Public	Local
Peterboro F	Sodexo	Female	Hull	Public	Local
Peterboro M	Sodexo	Local	Leeds	Public	Local
Portland	Public	Cat C Trainer	Leicester	Public	Local
Prescoed	Public	Open	Lewes	Public	Local
Preston	Public	Local	Lincoln	Public	Local
Rainsbrook	MTCNovo	STC	Liverpool	Public	Local
Ranby	Public	Cat C Trainer	Norwich	Public	Local
Risley	Public	Cat C Trainer	Nottingham	Public	Local
Rochester	Public	Cat C Trainer	Pentonville	Public	Local
Rye Hill	G4S	Cat B Trainer	Peterboro M	Sodexo	Local
Send	Public	Female	Preston	Public	Local
Springhill	Public	Open	Swansea	Public	Local
Stafford	Public	Cat C Trainer	Thameside	Serco	Local
Standford Hill	Public	Open	Wandsworth	Public	Local
Stocken	Public	Cat C Trainer	Winchester	Public	Local
Stoke Heath	Public	Cat C Trainer	Wormwood	Public	Local
Styal	Public	Female	Ford	Public	Open
Sudbury	Public	Open	Hatfield	Public	Open
Swaleside	Public	Cat B Trainer	Haverigg	Public	Open
Swansea	Public	Local	Hollesley Bay	Public	Open
Swinfen Hall	Public	Cat C Trainer	Kirkham	Public	Open
Thameside	Serco	Local	Kirklevington	Public	Open
Thorn Cross	Public	Open	Leyhill	Public	Open
Usk	Public	Cat C Trainer	North Sea Camp	Public	Open
Verne, The	Public	Cat C Trainer	Prescoed	Public	Open
Wakefield	Public	LTHSE	Springhill	Public	Open
Wandsworth	Public	Local	Standford Hill	Public	Open
Warren Hill	Public	Cat C Trainer	Sudbury	Public	Open
Wayland	Public	Cat C Trainer	Thorn Cross	Public	Open
Wealstun	Public	Cat C Trainer	Oakhill	G4S	STC
Werrington	Public	YJB	Rainsbrook	MTCNovo	STC
Wetherby	Public	YJB	Cookham Wd	Public	YJB
Whatton	Public	Cat C Trainer	Werrington	Public	YJB
Whitemoor	Public	LTHSE	Wetherby	Public	YJB
Winchester	Public	Local	Aylesbury	Public	YOI
Woodhill	Public	Cat B Trainer	Brinsford	Public	YOI
Wormwood	Public	Local	Deerbolt	Public	YOI
Wymott	Public	Cat C Trainer	Feltham	Public	YOI

www.prisons.org.uk

Some category 'C' training prisons are "resettlement prisons" which hold prisoners on shorter sentences to prepare them for release.
2. Local: holding those on short sentences, those awaiting trial or sentencing, and those awaiting allocation to another establishment.
3. Open prisons: housing category 'D' prisoners, considered to be lowest risk. Sometimes these are prisoners who have worked their way down the prisoner categories coming to the end of their sentence.
4. High Security: There are two types of high security prison. 'Core locals' serve a population as described above under the 'Local' heading but can also hold category 'A' prisoners. 'Dispersals' spread category 'A' prisoners to ensure that the most dangerous prisoners are not held in a single establishment.

Reconfiguration

HMPPS is undertaking a project to reconfigure the adult male prison estate. HMPPS plans to reduce surplus local prison places and increase category B training places, category C capacity and access to resettlement places to ensure there is a sufficient supply of

suitable prison places to meet demand.
This project continues work started by the Prison Estates Transformation Programme (PETP, see below) which set out to simplify and reorganise the prison estate into three models: reception, training and resettlement.

Adult female prisons
There are 12 prisons in England and Wales which house adult female offenders. Two of the twelve operate as 'open' prisons (Askham Grange and East Sutton Park).

Prisons for children and young adults
Young offenders are housed in three types of institution: 'Young Offender Institutions' (YOIs), 'Secure Training Centres' (see Section 1.1 above) and 'Secure Children's Homes'. The Youth Custody Service (part of the Ministry of Justice) decides on the type of institution in which a young offender will be held.

YOIs house young male offenders aged between 15-17 and 18-20 in separate institutions. Secure Training Centres are institutions for children up to the age of 17. Secure Children's Homes are run by local authorities and house children aged 10-14. They are not part of the HMPPS estate, but places are commissioned by the Youth Custody Service.

The Prison Oracle pages on Youth Custody provides more information.

Private sector prisons
There has been private sector involvement in the prison system in England and Wales since 1992. The timeline below, taken from an Institute for Government research paper, details the early history of private sector involvement in the prison estate:
1987 Select Committee on Home Affairs report recommends that the Home Office should enable private sector companies to tender for the management of prisons.
1991 Criminal Justice Act introduces competition into offender management services.
1992 HMP Wolds first private prison opens.
1992 Conservative government announces its private finance initiative (PFI).
1997 New Labour government comes to power and adopts the PFI approach.

2000 Two privately run prisons are returned to the public sector.
2003 Carter Review recommends greater use of competition in the prisons sector.
2004 National Offender Management Service (NOMS) is established.
2010 Coalition Government comes to power and pushes ahead with a policy of privatisation.
2011 HMP Doncaster becomes the first prison to be run on a 'payment by results' (PBR) basis
2011 HMP Birmingham becomes the first public sector prison to be privatised
2011 Coalition Government announces competition for nine prisons.

Which prisons are operated by private sector companies?
There are thirteen prisons in England and Wales that are managed by private sector companies. Three different companies operate these prisons: G4S (Altcourse, Oakwood, Parc and Rye Hill), Serco (Ashfield, Doncaster, Dovegate, Lowdham Grange, and Thameside) and Sodexo (Bronzefield, Forest Bank, Northumberland and Peterborough).

Most privately managed prisons in England and Wales hold adult male prisoners. Only Bronzefield and Peterborough (female unit), which are both managed by Sodexo, are prisons for female prisoners.

Private sector prisons tend to be newly built and relatively large. There are no open or high security private sector prisons. This contrasts with public sector prisons which are a mix of prisons of different size, age and functions.

HMP Birmingham
HMP Birmingham was run under contract by G4S from April 2011 until it was moved back into the public sector from 1 July 2019. From August 2018 Birmingham was managed by the public sector as part of a 'step-in' plan. The 'step in' followed the Chief Inspector of Prisons triggering the urgent notification process. This process, introduced by the Secretary of State at the end of 2017, allows the Chief Inspector to bring urgent concerns to the attention of the Secretary of State who is then required to respond with an action plan. The

urgent notification from the Chief Inspector for Birmingham said the inspectorate had found a dramatic deterioration since the last inspection and concluded that the prison was in an appalling state.

Government policy

The Government has said it remains committed to a mixed market in custodial services. In October 2020 the Ministry of Justice announced that G4S had been successful in its bid to operate HMP Five Wells, a new build resettlement prison at Wellingborough. This followed the first mini competition under the Prison Operator Services Framework.

The framework was launched in November 2018 as a mechanism to choose private sector providers for new prisons and for current private sector prisons contracts when they expire. In June 2019 the Government announced that six bidders had been accepted onto the framework and were therefore eligible to bid in future mini-competitions to operate individual prisons. The six were: G4S Care and Custody Services UK Limited, Interserve Investments Limited, Management and Training Corporation Works Limited, Mitie Care & Custody, Serco Limited, and Sodexo Limited.

Comment

In its 2019 manifesto, the Labour Party opposed the use of private sector providers in the prison system and stated that there would be no new private prisons and PFI prisons would be brought back in-house.

Government. Similarly, the POA (the trade union for prison correctional and secure psychiatric workers) have opposed the privatisation of prisons. They supported a TUC call for an independent inquiry into private sector involvement in the estate.

Living conditions across much of the prison estate are poor. Many prison buildings are old and poorly designed. There are unresolved maintenance issues across much of the estate. Some prison accommodation has been found to be dirty and squalid.

Age of the prison estate

There have been three major periods of prison construction during which the vast majority of the current prison estate was built: the Victorian era, the mid- 20th century and the turn of the 21st century.

Around a third of the prison estate was built during the Victorian era. Victorian prisons tend to be 'purpose built'. Many Victorian prisons are located in town centres and many now function as 'local prisons'.

A little under a third of the prison estate dates from the mid-20th century (1940s-1970s). Whilst many of these buildings are 'purpose built', some have been repurposed, often from military bases or internment camps used during (or after) World War Two.

Around a quarter of the prison estate dates from the late 20th and early 21st century. These buildings tend to be 'purpose built'.

Chief Inspector of Prisons' assessment of living conditions

The then Chief Inspector of Prisons, Peter Clarke, in his 2017-18 and 2018-19 annual reports said that conditions in these periods were some of the most disturbing and squalid the inspectorate had ever seen.

In his 2019-20 annual report, which dealt mainly with the period before the Covid-19 pandemic, Peter Clarke said that while some prisons had improved living conditions, conditions remained poor and overcrowded for many prisoners. He said too many prisoners were spending much of their lives locked in shared, overcrowded, insanitary cells.

The current Chief Inspector of Prisons, Charlie Taylor, in his 2020-21 annual report stated that the pandemic exacerbated some underlying problems and unacceptable conditions that inspections have previously criticised. The Inspectorate reported:
With few exceptions, we found prisoners living together in cramped conditions in cells designed for one occupant. This was particularly a problem given the extended periods of lock-up under the COVID-19 restrictions. (…) Many shared cells were just too small and had unscreened washing and

www.prisons.org.uk

- 15 -

toilet facilities. Regime restrictions meant that there was little opportunity to alleviate these pressures and use communal facilities, which were often more private. The design of some single cells also meant that toilets were unscreened and sometimes next to beds.

We found the poorest accommodation in some of the older prisons, with Leicester, Pentonville and parts of Erlestoke among the worst. Cold, dark and shabby cells were often plagued by damp and cockroaches, leaking pipes and toilets, and broken or missing furniture and windows.

Measuring accommodation standards

There are international human rights standards for accommodation in prison. The UN Standard Minimum Rules for the Treatment of Prisoners and the European Prison Rules both include expectations that prisoners' accommodation should be clean, well ventilated, that prisons should have enough space and that they should have access to private WC facilities. Both sets of standards expect single occupancy cells to be the norm.

The European Committee for the Prevention of Torture and Inhuman Degrading Treatment or Punishment (CPT) has published minimum standards for living space per prisoner:
• 6m² of living space for a single-occupancy cell plus sanitary facility
• 4m² of living space per prisoner in a multiple-occupancy cell plus fully-partitioned sanitary facility
• at least 2m between the walls of the cell at least 2.5m between the floor and the ceiling of the cell.

Prison Service Instruction on Certified Prisoner Accommodation

Prison Service Instructions are non-statutory guidance to those who run prisons in England and Wales. Prison Service Instruction 17/2012 'Certified Prisoner Accommodation' advises on the minimum standards for the certification of prisoner accommodation in England and Wales. It states that each prisoner should have:
• A single bed (the establishment may choose between single beds and bunk beds for shared cells).
• Storage for personal possessions.
• A chair and table area (for dining and for personal pursuits).
• Circulation and movement

In uncrowded conditions, there is an expectation that prisoners should be able to use the WC in private. In crowded conditions the expectation is that prisoners should be able to use the WC with 'some privacy'.

Maintenance of prisons

History of private sector involvement in prison maintenance

Prior to 2012, prison maintenance of public sector prisons was managed by HMPPS (then NOMS). Private sector prisons have always managed their own maintenance contracts.

In 2012, Mitie was awarded the contract for prison facility management of HMP Brixton. Mitie later took over the provision of facilities management at two other sites. In June 2015, the facility management of the rest of the public-sector prison estate was contracted out. Amey won the contracts for the North of England, the Midlands and Wales; Carillion won the contracts for London and the South of England.

Following the liquidation of Carillion in January 2018 the Government set up 'Gov Facility Services Ltd', a government owned company, to manage the contracts in London and the South of England. This, in effect, brought the maintenance of these prisons back into the public sector.

Performance of maintenance contracts

The National Audit Office (NAO), in January 2020, reported that HMPPS had failed to achieve the expected savings of £79 million by contracting-out to Amey and Carillion. It also reported that providers' performance against targets had been below HMPPS's expectations. It said that for the two areas which have the biggest impact on prison maintenance – high-priority planned and reactive maintenance jobs – they did not meet HMPPS's expectations.

Andrea Albutt, the President of the Prison Governors Association, said in 2018 that maintenance contracts had "failed in their entirety, leaving accommodation and maintenance in a far worse state than when governors owned their own works departments".

HMPPS has recognised concerns regarding the quality of service being provided by facility management companies. Its 2019-20 annual report stated that it had acted to strengthen contract management arrangements for the facilities management contracts.

Costs

The Government in 2018 stated that prison service maintenance contracts had not delivered the savings they had anticipated owing to an underestimation of historical costs. The NAO said that HMPPS did not have a clear picture of facilities management services in prisons before outsourcing the service, commenting that its approach contained common mistakes made in first-generation outsourcing.

The Ministry of Justice in November 2019 estimated the size of the priority maintenance backlog as £900 million. The Ministry said that a figure for each individual establishment was not available and would represent disproportionate cost to obtain.

The cost of the backlog had increased from around £750m in 2018. The Ministry explained that the cost increases each year owing largely to degradation of an aging estate. The then Justice Secretary in October 2019 said that 500 places a year would be lost due to dilapidation if investment was not made.

In March 2021 the Public Accounts Committee described the backlog of maintenance work at an estimated £1 billion as 'eye-watering'.

Investment in maintenance

In July 2018 the Government committed £40 million of funding to improve the prison estate including £16 million for renovations and repairs to the estate. The Ministry of Justice said that this money would be targeted to "establishments with the most pressing maintenance issues". A further £30 million was committed in the Autumn 2018 budget to "improve security and decency across the prison estate". £100 million for prison security was announced in August 2019. In October 2019 the MOJ said it had secured an additional £156m on top of existing funding for 2020-21, which would be targeted at addressing the most urgent maintenance needs.

However, it acknowledged that even this enhanced level of funding would not, on its own, be sufficient to manage the existing backlog and so committed to seek further maintenance funding in future spending rounds.

In the 2020-21 Spending Review the Government included £315m capital funding to improve the prison estate. HMMPS provided an update to the Public Accounts Committee in February 2021. It said that the £315m would allow it to make a start on a number of critical refurbishment projects across the prison estate in the next year, including a programme of replacements which would allow HMPPS to bring previously decommissioned places back into use in better condition, helping it to address the issue of crowding.

The Public Accounts Committee said the £315 million was significantly below what was required to maintain the prison estate. The Ministry of Justice told the Committee that it was confident that HM Treasury understood the value for money implications of insufficiently funding the maintenance backlog and that they were in discussions to secure future funding to meet the challenge. The Committee said it remained concerned that the maintenance backlog poses a real threat to achieving a safe and secure prison estate able to accommodate future prison populations.

Recent prison estate programmes
The Prison Estate Transformation Programme (PETP) 2016-19
Background and objectives
The Government of 2015-2017 identified a need to transform the prison estate in its 2016 White Paper Prison Safety and Reform:
The physical environment that many staff and prisoners face on a daily basis is not fostering the kind of culture or regime needed for

prisoners to turn their lives around. For prisons to be places of safety and reform, there needs to be a fundamental shift in the way that the prison estate is organised and operates and a significant improvement in the overall quality of the buildings across the prison estate.

It committed £1.3 billion to create 10,000 new prison places, to replace old accommodation.

The PETP was set up with the following objectives:
• invest £1.3 billion to build up to 10,000 new adult prison places
• close prisons that are in poor condition and those that do not have a long-term future in the estate
• simplify the organisation of the estate, placing prisoners at the right level of security in prisons with appropriately tailored regimes
• build and open five new community prisons for women.

Response to the PETP
Prison reform groups were critical of the PETP. The Howard League for Penal Reform criticised the Government for focusing too heavily on expanding the operational capacity of the prison estate rather than reducing the size of the prison population. In their evidence to the House of Commons Justice Committee inquiry Prison Population 2022: planning for the future, the League said that there has been a failure of a plan which erroneously assumed that capital investment in expanding the prison estate could be a means of managing an ever-growing prison population. However, the answer to this rapidly worsening crisis is not to build more prisons, it is to reduce the prison population.

The Prison Reform Trust called for sentencing reform to ease pressure on prison numbers:
Limiting sentence inflation generally and curbing the growth in tariff length for indeterminate sentences would do more than any other measure to ease pressure on prison numbers, reduce overcrowding and free up resources to invest in rehabilitation.

New prison places
In March 2017, the Government announced a mix of building projects, including new prisons and projects to rebuild or expand existing prison buildings. The programme was to involve seven prisons:
• New prisons in Yorkshire (which would be adjacent to the existing Full Sutton prison) and Port Talbot, South Wales.
• The existing prisons at Rochester, Hindley, Wellingborough and Glen Parva to be redeveloped (in some cases completely rebuilt).
• A new house block to be built at Stocken.

The current status of the building projects is as follows:
• Outline planning permission has been given to build a prison at Full Sutton. This is now part of the new prisons programme (see below).
• Plans for a prison in Port Talbot were withdrawn in January 2019 following strong objections in the community.
• Construction began at Wellingborough in September 2019. The new prison will be known as HMP Five Wells. The building of the prison is being publicly financed and it will be contracted to private sector operators G4S. It is due to start accepting prisoners in early 2022.
• In June 2018, then Prisons Minister Rory Stewart confirmed that the Glen Parva project would be financed by a private finance initiative.67 However, following the announcement in the 2018 Budget that the Treasury will no longer undertake new PFI contracts, the Government stated that it would fund the construction of Glen Parva.68 Though the prison will be built with public capital it will be contracted to private sector operators. Works have started at Glen Parva and it is due to be completed in 2023.
• The new house block at Stocken was completed in 2019.

Closures
Plans to close old prisons in a poor condition were put on hold. In its 2017/2018 Annual Report HMPPS confirmed that the closure of Rochester and Hindley prisons had been put on hold. HMPPS said that a significant rise in the prison population had prevented them from closing the prisons.71 The then Justice

Secretary, Robert Buckland, in October 2019 told the Justice Committee that he did not intend to close any prisons in the near future. The then Prisons Minister, Lucy Frazer, said in her evidence to the Committee that Victorian prisons would need to be kept in operation to house the anticipated numbers of prisoners.

Simplifying and reorganising the estate
In the 2016 White Paper, the Government identified two problems with the way the prison estate was organised:
• that there was a mismatch between the types of places available and the composition of the offender population; and
• that the current system was too inflexible.

To simplify the estate, HMPPS developed three new 'operating models' for prisons: 'reception', 'training' and 'resettlement'.

As part of the PETP best practice tool kits were published to support Governors in creating purposeful regimes for reception, trainer and resettlement prisoners.

A new design for prisons
The PETP developed a new design for resettlement prisons following consultation to be a template for new prisons. The new design included smaller house blocks, majority single cells with a shower, digital technology and bar-less windows, functional rooms on each floor and a central services hub. In designing the new prison, HMPPS said that it had:
…invested significant efforts in researching, testing and refining the design based on international evidence on the built environment and the way in which it can facilitate meaningful interaction between staff and prisoners.

Community prisons for women
In the 2016 White paper, the Government committed to building five new 'Community Prisons' for women. However, in its 2018 Female Offender Strategy the Government confirmed its policy had changed, stating it wanted to reduce the female prison population and would therefore shift its emphasis from custody to the community, and so would not be building the five new prisons for women.

Ending of the PETP
In March 2018, the Ministry of Justice decided not to deliver the PETP in full due to budget pressures and removed around 6,500 places from the programme. In summer 2019 the PETP was retired and a new programme created (see below).

Criticism of the PETP
In February 2020 the National Audit Office published a report Improving the prison estate. It concluded that HMPPS's plans to provide a safe, secure and decent prison estate were failing, stating that the PETP's plans to create up to 10,000 new prison places had proved undeliverable.

The Public Accounts Committee's report on improving the prison estate, published in September 2020, was also critical.

It stated that the Ministry of Justice and HMPPS had failed in their attempts to improve the condition and suitability of the prison estate. It said that despite promises to create 10,000 new-for-old prison places by 2020, just 206 new places had been delivered, and prisoners continued to be held in unsafe, crowded conditions that did not meet their needs.

The New Prisons Programme
More new prison places
Adult male prisons
In August 2019 the Government announced that it would spend up to £2.5 billion to create 10,000 prison places. These 10,000 places, it said, would be in addition to the approximately 3,500 places being created at HMP Five Wells, Glen Parva, and Stocken, as part of the initial commitment to create 10,000 places made in the 2016 White Paper.

The Government said the first of the prisons to be built as part of the August 2019 commitment to 10,000 places would be at Full Sutton where outline planning permission has been given to build a 1,440 place prison.

The Government said in June 2020 that it was seeking to identify and secure sites for a further three new prisons, one in the North-West of England and two in the South-East. It anticipates each prison will have 1,680 places, subject to geographical and

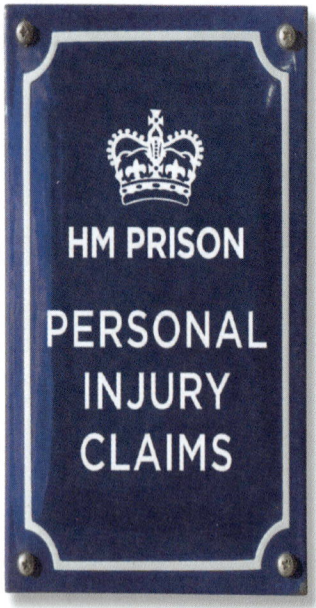

planning constraints.

Public consultations on proposed new prisons at the following sites have concluded this year:
• On land next to HMP Grendon/Springhill
• On land next to HMP Garth and Wymott
• On land next to HMP Gartree

A consultation on two new prisons on land at RAF Wethersfield, Braintree began in September 2020.

In addition to these four new prisons, the Government has said its programme includes expanding and refurbishing the current estate by building additional houseblocks and bringing decommissioned places back into use at the required standard. In October 2020 the Government announced that additional houseblocks would be built at Guys Marsh, Rye Hill and Stocken and that a new workshop would be built at High Down. The Government said these buildings would provide more than 930 places and would be ready from winter 2022 at Rye Hill, and throughout 2023 at the remaining sites.

In the 2020 Spending Review the Government stated it would spend more than £4 billion towards delivering 18,000 prison places across England and Wales by the mid-2020s. The 18,000 places would include:
• the 10,000 places at the four new prisons (announced in August 2019)
• the expansion of a further four prisons
• refurbishment of the existing prison estate
• the completion of ongoing prison builds at Glen Parva and Five Wells (Wellingborough).

Women's prisons
In January 2021 the Government announced that up to 500 prison places would be built in existing women's prisons.96 The Government said the new prison places would increase the availability of single cells and improve conditions. Then Prisons Minister, Alex Chalk, said in June 2021 that the initial sites under consideration for the building of the new places are: HMP Drake Hall, HMP Eastwood Park, HMP Foston Hall, HMP Send and HMP Styal.

The plans for more prison places for women have been criticised by organisations including the Howard League for Penal Reform, the Prison Reform Trust and Women in Prison. They argue that the plans to build 500 new prison places for women undermine the Government's commitments to reduce the women's prison population, "going against the Government's own evidence and published strategy which acknowledges most women in prison do not need to be there".

THE RELEASE OF PRISONERS (ALTERATION OF RELEVANT PROPORTION OF SENTENCE) ORDER 2019

As of 1st of April 2020, the **Release of Prisoners (Alteration of Relevant Proportion of Sentence) Order 2019** came into force - in a nutshell it means anyone sentenced to more than seven years for a 'specified' sexual or violent offence will now have to serve 2/3 of their sentence before release, rather than one half as at present.

This means that, having received a sentence of imprisonment **over 7 years** in length, offenders will serve two-thirds of their sentence in custody before release on licence instead of the usual half.

The prison must release them on licence at the two-thirds point - taking account of any additional days - as they would be at the conclusion of half of any other fixed-term sentence of imprisonment.

The new provisions raise two points worth noting.

Firstly sentences of less than seven years will **not** attract the modified application – therefore the difference in time served in custody by an offender who received a sentence of 6 years for a s18 assault (he would serve 3 years) and one who received a sentence of 7 and a half years (he would serve 5 years) means an extra two years in prison for a sentence that is only 18 months longer in length - the difference therefore is stark.

Secondly, the provisions relate to **individual sentences.** If an offender was sentenced to 10 years imprisonment for an offence of manslaughter (a relevant violent offence), and a **consecutive** sentence of 5 years imprisonment for a s18 wounding (also a relevant violent offence) the 2/3 release

www.prisons.org.uk

provisions only apply to the manslaughter sentence because it is only sentences over seven years that are relevant.

Therefore, the offender would serve a total of 9 years and 2 months in custody, comprising of 6 years 8 months for the kidnapping (2/3 of 10 years) and 2 and 6 months (half of five years) for the s18 assault.

The provisions do not apply:
To offenders who are under the age of 18 when they are sentenced; To offenders who are sentenced before 1st April 2020; To offenders who are sentenced under s236A of the CJA 2003 as an offender of particular concern.

The provisions apply to all relevant sentences passed after April 1st 2020. This means that a plea entered on March 15th but sentenced on April 15th would be sentenced in accordance with these provisions.

The relevant points are that section 244 of the 2003 Act (duty to release prisoners at the 'halfway' point of their sentence) will now, in cases where a prisoner is sentenced to a term of imprisonment of 7 years or more for a relevant violent or sexual offence, be changed to 'two-thirds'.

Also, in section 264 of the 2003 Act (consecutive terms), the reference to one-half of the sentence to be served in subsection (6)(d) is to be read, in relation to a sentence to a term of imprisonment of 7 years or more for a relevant offence, as a reference to two-thirds. A "relevant violent or sexual offence", is defined in Part 1 or Part 2 of Schedule 15 of the Criminal Justice Act 2003.

SECTION ONE. Prisons 2022. *A-Z of Prison Establishments*

HMP ALTCOURSE
FAZAKERLEY, LIVERPOOL L9 7LH
Tel: 0151 522 2000. Fax: 0151 522 2121
Task of the establishment Category B local prison holding sentenced and remanded adult and young adult male prisoners.
Prison status Managed by G4S Custodial.
Prison Service Area: Contracts Group.
Number held: 1,131
Certified normal accommodation 794
Operational capacity 1,133

Visits Telephone 0151 522 2196 / 2042.
Visiting Times Monday-Fri 13:30-1430 & 1515-1615 & 1815-1915. Sat 0915-1600, Sun 0915-1630
Last Inspection: July 2020 (SSV) - praised for creating a well-being room for staff; developing patient logs improving oversight of COVID-19 monitoring and an email system for family and friends to submit song requests to be dedicated to named prisoners on the prison radio - the request line was promoted

among prisoners and advertised externally via Twitter.
Brief history. Altcourse opened in December 1997 as a category A prison and restructured to a category B core local prison in June 2003. It expanded in 2007 with the opening of a further house block holding an additional 180 prisoners. There are seven house blocks divided into individual units, each holding between 60 and 90 prisoners.
Bechers remand and short-term sentenced prisoners; Canal medium to long-term sentenced prisoners on an enhanced regime. Furlong green: remand and short-term sentenced. Red: drug stabilisation unit; Melling induction unit; Reynoldstown vulnerable prisoner unit; Valentines medium- to long-term sentenced prisoners working in industries care suite; Foinavon red: mixture of prisoners taking part in vocational training. Green: prisoners over 50. Blue: mixture of prisoners taking part in vocational training.
Governor/Director Steve Williams
Escort contractor PECS
Healthcare Provider: G4S Health Services
Education Provider: Manchester College
IMB chair Eileen Darbyshire

HMP ASHFIELD
SHORTWOOD ROAD
PUCKLECHURCH
BRISTOL, BS16 9QJ
Tel: 0117 303 8000 Fax: 0117 303 8001
Task of the establishment Category C adult sex offenders treatment site.
Prison status Private - Serco
Region/Department South west
Number held 397
Certified normal accommodation 408
Visits: Mon - Sun: 13:30 - 16:30
Booking: Family and friends can contact the visits line to arrange a visit on 0117 303 8111
Brief history HMP Ashfield opened in November 1999, following the award of a contract to Premier Prison Services Ltd. It is built on the site of the former Pucklechurch remand centre. The establishment was re-roled in 2005 to accommodate juveniles after investment from the Youth Justice Board and has been run solely by Serco since July 2005. In July 2013 HMP Ashfield was re-roled again to accommodate category C adult male sex offenders.
Short description of residential units
There are two housing units, each divided into four wings. Each wing holds between 40 and 60 prisoners in single and double cells, which have integrated sanitation. There are seven dedicated cells for prisoners with disabilities. Each wing has a dining area, an association area, a servery, showers and cleaning facilities. There is no separate care and segregation unit and this is integrated on to Avon Delta wing. Avon Bravo wing has been a no smoking wing for about a year.
There is a small unit housing 16 prisoners changed to the first night centre in September 2015.
Governor/Director Martin Booth
Escort contractor GeoAmey
Health service provider NHS England commissioner; Bristol Community Health, Avon and Wiltshire Partnership; Somerset Partnership, Hanham Health; Lloyds Pharmacy

HMP ASKHAM GRANGE
ASKHAM RICHARD
YORK YO23 3FT
Tel: 01904 772000 Fax: 01904 772001
Task of the establishment Open prison for sentenced adult and young adult women.
Prison status Public
Region Yorkshire and the Humber
Certified normal accommodation 126
Operational capacity 128
Visits Mon-Fri 0915-1600
Sat & Sun 1400-1600
Booking line: 0300 060 6513
Brief history Askham Grange, which consists of a Victorian country house built in the 1880s, became the first open prison for women in January 1947. Extensions and annex buildings were later added and in the mid-1990s, a new mother and baby unit opened.
The prison is led by the same governing governor as at HMP New Hall, a closed women's prison near Wakefield, with which it is twinned. Although largely managed locally, some services were delivered across both sites. In 2013, the National Offender Management Service announced the closure of Askham Grange and the other women's open prison East Sutton Park as part of its review of the

women's estate. At the current time, October 2021, the prison remains open and there are no immediate plans to close the prison.

Short description of residential units Accommodation in the main house comprised a mix of single rooms and dormitories housing up to a maximum of six residents. The prison's Acorn House, a standalone building within the prison grounds, offered women and their families the opportunity to spend time together overnight in a domestic-like environment in single occupancy rooms. The two annexes for women eligible to work outside the prison or with specific reasons to be alone in a room and the mother and baby unit also offered single rooms. In total there were 45 single and 27 shared rooms but there was no integral sanitation.
Governor/Director Julia Spence
Escort contractor GEOAmey
Health: Spectrum Community Health
Learning and skills providers
The Manchester College
IMB chair Stephen Beyer

HMYOI AYLESBURY
BIERTON ROAD,
AYLESBURY, BUCKS HP20 1EH.
Tel: 01296 444000 Fax: 01296 444001
Task of the establishment Aylesbury holds long-term sentenced young adult males.
Prison status Public
Region South Central
Certified normal accommodation 410
Operational capacity 444
Visiting Times
Monday: 2pm to 4:15pm;
Tuesday: 2pm to 4:15pm;
Thursday: 2pm to 4:15pm;
Saturday: 9:30am to 11:30am
Booking Line: 01296 444302
Legal visit bookings lines: 01296 444302 or 01296 444312 Monday to Friday, 9am to 1:30pm Alternative booking lines: 01296 444207 or 01296 444097 Monday to Friday, 2pm to 3:30pm. Visiting times Wed, 0900-1100.
Brief history The prison opened as a county gaol in 1847 and in 1890 became a women's prison. Two new wings added in 1902 served initially as an 'inebriates' centre' and in the 1930s as a girl's Borstal. In 1959 the prison was converted to house adult male prisoners and in 1961 it changed again to house young male offenders aged between 17 and 21. In 1989, Aylesbury was designated as a long-term young offender institution, and now holds the longest sentenced young adult males in the English prison system.
Short description of residential units A to E wings and G wing are residential units. F wing holds vulnerable prisoners in an 'enabling environment'. There is also a segregation unit.
Governor/Director Mark Allen
Escort contractor GEOAmey
Health service providers: Care UK; Oxford Health NHS Trust
Education: Milton Keynes College
IMB chair Ian Wilkinson

HMP BEDFORD
ST LOYES STREET,
BEDFORD MK40 1HG.
Tel: 01234 373000.
Fax: 01234 273568
Task of the establishment HMP Bedford is a local category B and resettlement prison for young adult and adult males.
Prison status Public
Region/Department Eastern
Number held 493
Certified normal accommodation 322
Operational capacity 506
Visits Telephone 01234 373196
Visiting Times: Wed, Thurs, Sunday: 1:45pm to 2:45pm and 3:15pm to 4:15pm
Brief history HMP Bedford has been on its current site since 1801. It was enlarged in 1849 and a new gate lodge, house block and health care centre were added in the early 1990s. It accepts prisoners mainly from Luton Crown Court, St Albans Crown Court and the magistrates' courts in Bedfordshire and Hertfordshire, alongside a resettlement population.
Short description of residential units
A, B and C wings are gallery-style Victorian three-storey landings. B1 is the segregation unit. C2 is the first night centre but this was due to move to E wing at the end of June 2016. D wing is a more modern house block, on three storeys. E wing is a two-storey building

- 24 -

used as the drug recovery wing
F wing is a Victorian two-storey wing, with gallery landings accommodating vulnerable prisoners. The health centre is on a single landing of a new purpose-built building.
Governor/Director Patrick Butler
Escort contractor Serco Wincanton
Health service provider Northamptonshire Healthcare NHS Foundation Trust (NHFT) and the Westminster Drugs Project.
Learning and skills providers PeoplePlus
IMB chair Alexander Daye

HMP BELMARSH
WESTERN WAY,
THAMESMEAD,
LONDON SE28 OEB.
Tel: 020 8331 4400. Fax: 020 8331 4401.
Task of the establishment A local prison, holding men and young adults, some of whom require a high level of security.
Prison status Public
Group LTHSE
Number held 903 on 15 June 2020
Certified normal accommodation 781
Operational capacity 938
Visits Telephone: 0208 331 4750
Visiting Times: Tues-Thurs: 0915 - 1000, 1100-1145. Fri: 0915 - 1000.
Saturday: 0915 - 1000, 1100 - 1145
Brief history Belmarsh prison opened in 1991. It was the first adult prison to be built in London since Wormwood Scrubs in 1874.
Short description of residential units
House block 1 – London pathways progression unit (a resettlement service for prisoners with personality disorders released in London) and prisoners serving long sentences
House block 2 – prisoners serving short sentences or on remand
House block 3 – first night centre and new arrivals
House block 4 – prisoners undergoing detoxification and vulnerable prisoners
Main prison segregation unit – prisoners serving periods of punishment or needing to be separated from others. It also contained two designated prison rule 46 cells used for the temporary management of close supervision centre (CSC) system and/or managing challenging behaviour strategy (MCBS) prisoners (prisoners deemed to be some of the most dangerous in the prison system)
High security unit (HSU) – a self-contained unit holding prisoners who require a high level of security (including a small discreet segregation unit available for use with HSU prisoners only).
Governor/Director Jenny Louis
Escort contractor Serco
Health service provider Care UK
Learning skills provider Manchester College
IMB chair Hilary Powell

HMP BERWYN
BRIDGE ROAD
WREXHAM, LL13 9QS
Tel: 01978 523000
Opened: February 2017
CNA: 2106
Op. Cap: 2106
Cat: C Male Closed, resettlement and training prison with local remand function
Area: Wales
Task of the establishment. Berwyn opened in

February 2017 and is a category C prison providing a resettlement, training and remand function. It is the first public sector operated new build prison for thirty years. The accommodation is split across three houses called Alwen, Bala and Ceiriog, each holding 702 men. Each house is then separated into communities of 88 men so that the prison does not feel so big. Each house is managed by a senior manager with a Head of Operations and Head of OMU reporting to them. There is also a Care and Separation Unit (Ogwen).
Berwyn has three clear functions – a

resettlement element for men from North Wales, a training function for men from other parts of England and South Wales and a remand function for the North Wales courts. It is the biggest prison in the UK.

Governor/Director: Nick Leader

Visits

Booking line: 01978 523300

The booking line is open Monday to Friday, 8am to 5pm

Visiting times:
Tuesday: 1415-1500, 1545-1630
Wednesday: 0830-0915, 1000-1045, 1415-1500, and 1545-1630
Thursday: 0830-0915, 1000-1045,
Saturday: 0915-1000, 1045-1130, 1415-1500
Sunday: 1415-1500

Short description of residential units. Berwyn is a new build prison that has a clear focus on the rehabilitation of the men it looks after. All rooms have IT systems with a laptop issued to each man and there is a telephone in each room. There is also a shower in each room. Two thirds of the accommodation is double occupancy rooms.

There are facilities for disabled men and this includes purpose built rooms that are fully DDA compliant. They will have full access to the daily regime and all buildings have lifts to access all floors.

There will be more than 700 men working in industries on a daily basis and half of the workshops are operated by a private contractor. More than 750 men will be doing other activities such as working in the kitchen and cleaning with more than 500 men in education. College will be operated by Novus Cambria. The Novus Cambria partnership will play an important role within the Berwyn community, developing a clear, recognisable culture where innovative learning opportunities are embedded across the prison environment and the men encouraged and assisted to prepare for a fresh start in life.

Currently run by DHL. Shopping order forms are processed via the in room technology where the men submit their orders electronically.

Visits sessions were morning, afternoon and evening but as a result of the 2020/2021 Covid-19 pandemic evening visits have been curtailed to Monday to Thursday and morning and afternoon Friday to Sunday.

Berwyn is located on Wrexham Industrial Estate which is one of the biggest industrial estates in Europe. It is well sign posted from all routes into Wrexham. The nearest train station is Wrexham General and a bus service is available. A taxi costs approximately £9 each way.

All health and wellbeing services are provided by Betsi Cadwaladr University Health Board and the prison has a state of the art medical facility that provides the majority of services found in a minor injuries unit. There are no in-patient facilities.

The kitchen is operated by our in house team who prides themselves on the quality of its food. All diets are catered for and the menu choices are selected by the men using the in room technology.

A full chaplaincy provision is available to meet all faiths and denominations.

Drugs and Alcohol Treatment: by Betsi Cadwaladr University Health Board

Message from the Governor:

Berwyn has been designed and built using what we know works best in prison. The facilities here are modern and purpose built to give the men every chance to change their lives.

We are a big prison but our design principles and how we have trained our staff will result in a feeling of belong in each of the communities in the three houses.

The physical environment is important but what will make this prison a success is the staff. Our staff are dedicated to building a rehabilitative culture in which the men can have hope for a better future.

It will be their interactions with the men that will help them understand how to use the purpose built facilities at Berwyn to take responsibility for themselves and return to their communities as productive members of society. Our focus will be on giving them the chance to address the behaviour which caused them to offend, to build relationships with the families, to develop their skills and improve their chances of meaningful employment on release. This culture will mean our prison is a safe, decent and just place for the men to live in and the staff to work in.

HMP BIRMINGHAM
WINSON GREEN ROAD,
BIRMINGHAM, B18 4AS
Tel: 0121 598 8000
Fax: 0121 598 8111
Task of the establishment HMP Birmingham holds adult male convicted and unconvicted prisoners. The prison serves the Birmingham court circuit and its primary role is to hold remand and trial prisoners. The prison holds category B and C prisoners as well as a small population of retained category D prisoners.
Prison status Public (from July 2019)
Region West Midlands
Number held 1,443
Certified normal accommodation 1,093
Operational capacity 1,450
Booking a visit: Prisoners must book their own visits through the NForce system (kiosks) on the residential units. This will mean that the prisoner will have to inform you when he has booked the visit for. There is no longer the facility to book visits by e-mail or phone for domestic visits.
Visiting Times: Tuesday, Wednesday, Saturday and Sunday: 9am to 11am and 2pm to 4pm
Brief history Birmingham prison is a Victorian local prison that has been extended following the addition of modern units – K wing opened in 1992 and L, M, N, P wings and the health care, gym and education and work units opened in 2003. Housing adult male prisoners, the prison serves the Crown and Magistrates' Courts of Birmingham, Shrewsbury and Telford, along with the Magistrates' Courts of Burton, Cannock, Lichfield, Rugeley, Sutton Coldfield and Tamworth.
In 2004, a multi-million pound investment programme led to 450 additional prisoner places as well as new workshops and educational facilities and a new health care centre and gym. Existing facilities were also extended and improved.
G4S took over the prison on 1 October 2011. New initiatives since then have included reopening J wing as a social inclusion unit for older prisoners and those with similar needs.
Short description of residential units
A wing: Residential unit also holding a small population of prisoners at risk on the A1 landing and a mix of vulnerable and at-risk prisoners on the A2 landing
B wing: Detoxification unit, also housing the segregation unit on the B1 landing
C wing: Residential unit holding remand and non-sentenced prisoners
D wing: First night centre
G wing: Vulnerable prisoner unit holding sex offenders
HCC: Health care unit, with two inpatient wards: ward 1 for physical health and ward 2 for mental health
J wing: Social care unit
K wing: Cat C and enhanced regime category B prisoners
L wing: Residential mixed unit
M wing: Residential mixed unit
N wing: Residential mixed unit
P wing: Residential mixed unit
Governor/Director Paul Newton
Escort contractor GeoAmey
Health service provider Birmingham Mental Health Foundation Trust
Learning and skills providers Milton Keynes College

Get help with the cost of prison visits if you are on low income

Apply online from the Help with Prison Visits unit at www.gov.uk/helpwithprisonvisits

Nepacs' visitors' centre staff and volunteers will be pleased to offer you support and advice, and copies of the visit confirmation forms.

The quickest and easiest way to claim your costs is online.

But if you have difficulty applying online ring the Help with Prison Visits team for advice on 0300 063 2100, Monday to Friday, 9am to 5pm.
Paper application forms are available by ringing this number.

www.prisons.org.uk

South and City College, Birmingham N-ergy
IMB chair Roger Lawrence

No visits? Want someone to talk to?

Ask the Chaplaincy or a Prison Officer for a Prison Visitor

HMYOI BRINSFORD
NEW ROAD,
FEATHERSTONE,
WOLVERHAMPTON WV10 7PY
Tel: 01902 533450 Fax: 01902 533451
Task of the establishment A young offender institution and remand centre for young adult male prisoners aged 18 to 21.
Prison status Public
Region West Midlands
Number held 9.2.15: 393
Certified normal accommodation 545
Operational capacity 57
Visits: Brinsford is currently operating a limited visits schedule for family and friends. You can book your visit by telephone. There is no online booking service available.
Booking line: 0300 060 6500 open Monday to Friday, 0915-1200, 1300-1600
Visiting times: Mon, Tues, Thur, Sat & Sun: 2pm to 4pm
Brief history Brinsford opened as a young adult offender institution and remand centre in November 1991, and is on the same site as HMPs Featherstone and Oakwood.

Short description of residential units
Residential 1 first night unit
Residential 2,3,4 sentenced/remands
Residential 5 enhanced unit.
Health care centre 11 beds with inpatient accommodation (not included on CNA)
Drug and alcohol (DARS) 4 beds
First night care 15 beds
Care and separation unit 16 beds
Governor/Director Amanda Hughes
Escort contractor GEOAmey
Health service providers Staffordshire and Stoke-on-Trent Partnership NHS Trust
South Staffordshire and Shropshire Healthcare NHS Foundation Trust
Education provider Milton Keynes College
IMB chair Jo Chapman

HMP BRISTOL
CAMBRIDGE ROAD,
BRISTOL BS7 8PS
Tel: 0117 372 3100 Fax: 0117 372 3113
Task of the establishment HMP Bristol is a category B local prison holding male adults and young adults.
Prison status Public
Region/Department South-West
Number held 586
Certified normal accommodation 424
Operational capacity 614
Visits: Telephone booking line: 0300 060 6510
Visiting times: Monday to Sunday: 2pm to 4pm (except bank holidays)
Brief history The prison was built in 1883. B and C wings were added in the 1960s.
Short description of residential units
A wing is a 126-bed wing mainly for vulnerable prisoners.
B wing has 99 single cells and is the drug-free wing. It does not have in-cell sanitation.
C wing is a 148-bed wing, incorporating integrated drug treatment system/drug recovery and a dedicated detoxification unit on C3.
D wing (including the F wing annex) is a 116-bed wing and contains the dedicated first night and induction centre. This wing also holds Listeners and Insiders.
E wing is an 11-bed dedicated segregation wing, with two additional unfurnished cells.
G wing is a125-bed wing.

The prison no longer has a separate health centre unit; it has a reintegration unit, named the Brunel unit, holding prisoners with complex mental health and physical needs.
Governor/Director James Lucas
Escort contractor GEOAmey
Health service commissioner and providers
Physical health providers: Bristol Community Health and MedCo Secure Health Services
Mental health provider: Avon and Wiltshire NHS Partnership
Dental services: Somerset Partnership NHS Foundation Trust
Learning and skills providers Weston College
IMB chair Mike Flannery

HMP BRIXTON
JEBB AVENUE,
BRIXTON, LONDON, SW2 5XF
Tel: 020 8588 6000 Fax: 020 8588 6283
Task of the establishment HMP Brixton is a cat C and D resettlement prison.
Prison status Public
Region/Department London
Number held 741
Certified normal accommodation 530
Operational capacity 81
Visits Telephone 020 8678 1433
Visiting Times: Prisoners live in 5 wings which have different visiting times. This will be explained upon booking. Monday to Thursday: 2:15pm to 3:15pm and 4pm to 5pm Saturday and Sunday: 9:15am to 10:15am, 11am to midday and 2:45pm to 3:45pm
Brief history Opened in 1819 subsequently becoming a women's prison and a military prison. In 1898 it became an adult male local prison, serving the whole of the London area and particularly focusing on South London. In July 2012, it was re-roled again, becoming a category C and D resettlement prison for the local area.
Short description of residential units
A wing holds 240 category C prisoners
B wing holds 150 category C prisoners
C wing holds 133 category D prisoners
D wing is the drug recovery wing, with a capacity of 47
G wing which houses the first night accommodation holds a total of 240 category C prisoners.

Governor/Director Louise Ysart
Escort contractor Serco
Health service providers
Physical health service provider: Care UK
Mental health service provider: Barnet, Enfield and Haringey Trust
Learning and skills providers A4e Justice
IMB chair Amanda Williams

HMP BRONZEFIELD
WOODTHORPE ROAD
ASHFORD, MIDDLESEX TW15 3JZ
Tel: 01784 425690 Fax: 01784 425691
Task of the establishment Bronzefield is a designated resettlement prison, as are all women's prisons. It is also a high security prison for restricted status women (those considered to require specific management arrangements) as well as a local prison.
Prison status Private, run by Sodexo
Region Greater London
Number held 506
Certified normal accommodation 527
Operational capacity 527
Booking Residents make booking arrangements via the POD system on their house blocks.
Visiting Times - due to the Covid-19 pandemic visiting times are changing frequently so you will be advised when your visit is booked.
Brief history HMP & YOI Bronzefield opened in June 2004. Sodexo Justice Services was awarded a 25-year contract to run the prison, making it the first privately managed women's establishment in England and Wales. As a local prison, it accepted prisoners directly from the courts and had a high security function. In January 2010, an additional residential unit was opened bringing the total

number of units to four; in the same year, a smaller unit that acted as an intermediary between the main residential areas and health care was decommissioned.

Short description of residential units
HMP Bronzefield had three main residential units, holding approximately 135 women each on four separate spurs; a fourth residential unit held 77 women. The prison had 24-hour onsite nursing cover and inpatient facilities for 18 women, a separation and care unit (the segregation unit) and a mother and baby unit.
Residential units consisted of:
House block 1 – Convicted remand prisoners; the separate substance misuse recovery unit
House block 2 – Remand prisoners and separate induction unit
House block 3 – Convicted and sentenced
House block 4 – Enhanced and first stage lifer and long-term prisoners.
Director Vicky Robinson (Acting until January 2022 when Ian Whiteside returns)
Escort contractor Serco
Health service commissioner and providers Sodexo Justice Services (primary physical, mental health and clinical substance misuse services); Central and North West London NHS Foundation Trust (secondary mental health services)
Learning and skills provider Sodexo
IMB chair Alison Keightley

HMP BUCKLEY HALL
BUCKLEY HALL ROAD,
ROCHDALE, LANCS, OL12 9DP
Tel: 01706 514300 Fax: 01706 514399
Task of the establishment
Category C adult male training prison holding prisoners sentenced to four years and over.
Prison status Public
Region North West
Number held 450
Certified normal accommodation 409
Operational capacity 455
Visits Telephone 01706 514350
Visit Monday to Thursday: 2pm to 4pm. Fri: no visits. Sat/Sun: 9:30-11:30am and 2-4:30pm
Brief history Buckley Hall had been the first privately managed category C establishment holding medium-security prisoners. After tendering in June 2000, it reverted to Prison Service control. In April 2002 it reroled to a closed female training prison, but re-roled back to a male category C prison in September 2005 and is currently run under contract to the Prison Service until 30 October 2018. Under the 'Transforming rehabilitation' model, Buckley Hall was designated as an adult male category C training prison in 2015, holding men serving four years and over.
Short description of residential units
Four residential units.
Governor Robbie Durgan
Escort contractor GEOAmey
Health service provider
Manchester Mental Health Trust
Learning and skills provider Novus
IMB chair Kevin McKeogh

HMP BULLINGDON
PO BOX 50, BICESTER,
OXON, OX25 1PZ.
Tel: 01869 353100 Fax: 01869 353101
Task of the establishment
HMP Bullingdon is a designated local and resettlement prison for the Thames Valley and Hampshire areas. It serves the courts of Oxfordshire, Berkshire and Wiltshire.
Prison status Public
Region/Department South Central
Number held 1,102
Certified normal accommodation 869
Operational capacity 1,114
Visits Telephone 01869 353176 open Monday to Friday, 8:30am to 4pm
Every day except Friday: 1.45pm to 4pm
To cancel a visit, call 01869 353 176
Email: socialvisits.bullingdon@justice.gov.uk
Brief history HMP Bullingdon opened in April 1992, the first of a new design of prisons, which has since been copied elsewhere. It was

built with four cellular blocks based around the same T-shaped design of three spurs, each with three landings leading off a central office complex.
The Edgcott and Finmere units were added in 1997 and 2008, respectively.
Short description of residential units
A wing (Arncott) - Remand and short-term prisoners, including the support mentoring unit
B wing (Blackthorn) – Remand and short-term prisoners, including those detoxifying
C wing (Charndon) – Drug free unit
D wing (Dorton) – Convicted prisoners
E wing (Edgcott) – Sex offenders
F wing (Finmere) – Induction/first night and life-sentenced prisoners
Governor/Director Laura Sapwell
Escort contractor GeoAmey
Health service provider
Primary health services, pharmacy and mental health services: Virgin Care Services Ltd
GP services: Cotswold Medicare Ltd
Mental health in-reach team: Oxford Health Foundation Trust
Learning and skills providers
Milton Keynes College
CRC Thames Valley CRC
IMB chair Paul Miller

HMP BURE
JAGUAR DRIVE
BADERSFIELD
NORWICH, NR10 5GB
Tel: 01603 326000 Fax: 01603 326001
Task of the establishment HMP Bure is a category C prison. It is a sex offender treatment centre, which prioritises offenders from the East of England. The prison delivers a suite of nationally accredited offending behaviour programmes designed specifically to meet the needs of the establishment's sex offender population.
Prison status Public
Region East of England
Number held 520
Certified normal accommodation 503
Operational capacity 523
Visits Telephone 01603 326252
Visiting Times Sat 1:30pm to 2:30pm and 3pm to 4pm. Sun 1:30pm to 2:30pm, 3pm to 4pm
Brief history: HMP Bure is built on part of the former RAF Coltishall site, seven miles north of Norwich. Constructed in 2009, the prison is a mix of new buildings and converted RAF accommodation and service buildings.
Short description of residential units There are six residential units comprising mostly single cells. The seventh residential unit is currently under construction with a planned completion date of September 2013. This unit will house a further 101 single cells. Five units each have four double cells totalling 20 across the prison. All cells have a personal safe and integral sanitation. Each unit has communal showers.
Governor/Director Simon Rhoden
Escort contractor Serco Wincanton
Health service commissioner and providers
Commissioner: NHS England
Providers: Serco
Addenbrookes Hospital
Cromer and District Hospital
Norfolk and Norwich University Hospital
James Paget Hospital
Horizon Health
Learning and skills provider A4e
IMB chair Brian Blake

HMP CARDIFF
KNOX ROAD,
CARDIFF, CF24 0UG
Tel: 02920 923100 Fax: 02920 923318
Task of the establishment HMP & YOI Cardiff is a category B local training prison holding male adult prisoners serving the courts in south east Wales.
Prison status Public
Region/Department Wales
Number held 770
Certified normal accommodation 539

- 31 -

Operational capacity 820
Brief history HMP & YOI Cardiff dates back to 1827. Its main role was previously to hold unconvicted and short to medium-term sentenced prisoners. The accommodation was predominantly Victorian, with high levels of overcrowding.
Today the prison continues to hold unconvicted and trial prisoners from local courts and short-term prisoners serving up to two years. A new wing was built in 1996 to accommodate 218 additional men, including 96 lifers. Major refurbishment and modification of cellular accommodation has seen the capacity rise.
Visits telephone: 029 2092 3327
Visiting Times: Mon, Wed, Fri, Sat 1400-1500
A new health care centre was opened in May 2008. The facility provides 21 beds, mostly commissioned by the local health board.
Short description of residential units
A wing mainly convicted prisoners
A1 mainly kitchen workers
Care and separation unit separated men including R45
B wing mainly convicted prisoners
B1 vulnerable prisoners
C wing induction prisoners
D wing enhanced prisoners
E wing mainly convicted prisoners
F wing mainly remand prisoners
F1 prisoners undergoing detoxification
H health care unit
Governor/Director Helen Ryder
Escort contractor GeoAmey
Health service commissioner and providers: Cardiff and Vale NHS trust
Learning and skills providers: NOMS in Wales
IMB chair: Steve Cocks

HMP CHANNINGS WOOD
DENBURY,
NEWTON ABBOT,
DEVON, TQ12 6DW
TEL: 01803 814600 FAX: 01803 814601
Task of the establishment
HMP Channings Wood is a category C adult male resettlement prison.
Prison status Public
Region/Department South-West
Number held 706
Certified normal accommodation 698
Operational capacity 724
Visits Telephone 01803 812060
The booking line is open Monday to Friday (except Bank Holidays) 10am to 2:30pm
Visiting Times Wed, Fri, Sat, Sun: 14:00 – 16:00
Brief history
HMP Channings Wood was built on the site of a Ministry of Defence base in 1973 and the prison officially opened in July 1974. Further building programmes have taken place over the last two decades, with the addition of 104 prisoner places.
The establishment has eight residential units, known as 'living blocks' (LB). LB1 to LB5 are similar in layout, with two spurs of 56 cells over two floors. LB1 accommodates 138 prisoners and is the only unit with single cells that are 'doubled up' and holding two prisoners. LB2 to LB5 each accommodates 112 prisoners, and are designated as single occupancy. LB6 and LB7 accommodate prisoners on the highest level of privileges, holding 34 and 40 prisoners, respectively. LB8 accommodates 64 prisoners in double cells. LB1, LB5 and LB7 house vulnerable prisoners, and the remainder of the units house mainstream prisoners.
Video links: courts, probation, legal visits and inter-prison visits. For court and probation email OMU.channingswood@justice.gov.uk.
For legal visits and inter-prison visits, email legalvisits.channingswood@justice.gov.uk.
Governor/Director Huw Sullivan
Escort contractor GeoAmey
Health service provider
Dorset Healthcare Foundation Trust
Learning and skills providers Weston College
IMB chair Colin Stanley

HMP CHELMSFORD
200 SPRINGFIELD ROAD,
CHELMSFORD,
ESSEX, CM2 6LQ
Tel: 01245 552000 Fax: 01245 552001
Task of the establishment HMP/YOI Chelmsford is a category B local and resettlement prison for adult and young adult males.
Prison status Public
Region/Department Kent, Sussex and Essex
Number held 708
Certified normal accommodation 551
Operational capacity 745
Visits Phone 01245 552 265 and 01245 552 240 open Monday to Friday, 8:15am to 11am and 12:30pm to 3:30pm.
Visiting Times Monday to Thursday: 1:40pm to 3:40pm
Brief history HMP/YOI Chelmsford was built in the 1830s. Two new residential units were added in 1996 (E and F wings), and a third unit (G wing) was opened in 2006. The prison serves local courts and holds those who are sentenced, on remand or on trial. It holds adults, young adults and some foreign national prisoners.
Short description of residential units
The older part of the establishment has four wings, A, B, C and D, running off a central hub. The segregation unit is on A wing and vulnerable prisoners have separate accommodation on D wing.
The newer part of the prison has a 12-bed, 24-hour health care unit (known as the extra care unit). E wing provides the integrated drug treatment system. F wing is the first night and induction unit and G wing holds a mixed population, including older prisoners.
Governor/Director Penny Bartlett
Escort contractors Serco
Health service provider Care UK (H4H)
Learning and skills providers PeoplePlus
IMB chair Graham Finch

HMP COLDINGLEY
SHAFTESBURY RD,
BISLEY, WOKING
SURREY, GU24 9EX
Tel: 01483 344300 Fax: 01483 344427
Task of the establishment Coldingley is a category C working prison for adult males,

holding mostly long-term, including life-sentenced, prisoners.
Prison status Public
Region Greater London
Number held 512
Certified normal accommodation 494
Operational capacity 513
Visits are being led by prisoner application. There is no online or telephone booking service available.
Visiting times: Monday - Thursday: 10am to 11am and 2:30pm to 3:30pm Fri: 10am to 11am
Brief history Coldingley was opened in 1969 as a category B industrial training prison. It changed role to a category C prison in 1993. A new unit, E wing, was opened in 2009.
Short description of residential units The original four wings, A–D, hold 91 prisoners each, mainly in single cells. None of these cells has integral sanitation.
E wing has 115 single and eight double cells with integral sanitation. F wing, located in the old health care unit, is an enhanced wing. The 10 occupants are able to use communal toilets as needed.
Governor/Director Niall Bryant
Escort contractor SERCO and GEOAmey
Health service provider Virgin Care
Learning and skills provider A4E
IMB chair John Tilbury

HMP COOKHAM WOOD
SIR EVELYN ROAD
ROCHESTER
KENT ME1 3LU
Tel: 01634 202 500 Fax: 01634 202 501
Task of the establishment Young offender institution for boys aged 15 to 18 years.
Establishment status Public

Department Youth Justice Board
Number held 156
Certified normal accommodation 196
Operational capacity 196
Booking line: 01634 202 557
The booking line is open Mon-Fri 9am-3pm
Find out about call charges
Visiting times: Monday: 2:15pm to 3:15pm
Wednesday: 2:15pm to 4:15pm
Sat/Sun: 9:30-11:30am and 2:30pm to 4:30pm
Brief history HMYOI Cookham Wood was built in the 1970s, originally for young men, but its use was changed to meet the growing need for secure female accommodation at the time. In 2007-8, it changed its function to accommodate 15-17-year-old young men to reduce capacity pressures in London and the South East for this age group.
In January 2014, a new purpose-built residential unit was opened incorporating integrated facilities, and designed to meet the needs of the young people and improve safety.
Short description of residential units
179 single cells with integral telephone and showers, spread over six self-contained landings.
One room to accommodate a disabled young person.
Phoenix unit – seven-bed separation unit.
Cedar unit – 17-bed enhanced support unit.
Governor/Director Paul Durham
Escort contractor GEOAmey
Health service commissioner and providers Oxleas NHS Foundation Trust – primary care
Central & North-west London NHS Trust – child and adolescent mental health services
Learning and skills provider Novus
IMB chair Anne Finlayson

HMP DARTMOOR
PRINCETOWN
YELVERTON
DEVON, PL2O 6RR
Tel: 01822 322000 Fax: 01822 322001
Task of the establishment HMP Dartmoor is a category C training prison for adult males.
Prison status Public
Region/Department South-West
Number held 655
Certified normal accommodation 639
Operational capacity 659
Visits: No online booking service available.

Visits booking line: 01822 322 022 open: Mon: 12-3pm; Tues-Thurs: 10-1pm; Fri: 9-12pm
Visiting times: Friday: 9:30-11:30am
Sat 9:30-11:30am, and 24pm; Sunday 9:30-11:30am and 2-4pm
Brief history Built in 1809, Dartmoor is a category C prison.
Short description of residential units
A wing: vulnerable prisoner unit (holds 132)
B wing: vulnerable prisoner unit (holds 134)
D wing: integrated vulnerable prisoner and mainstream prisoner wing (holds 122)
E wing: resettlement unit (holds 49)
F wing: enhanced mainstream wing (holds 47)
G wing: mainstream wing (holds 157)
Governor/Director Bridie Oakes-Richards
Escort contractor GeoAmey
Health service provider Dorset Healthcare
Learning and skills provider Weston College
IMB chair Margaret Blake

HMYOI DEERBOLT
BOWES RD
BARNARD CASTLE
Co DURHAM, DL12 9BG
Tel: 01833 633200 Fax: 01833 633201
Task of the establishment A closed young offender institution holding convicted young male prisoners aged 18-21.
Prison status Public
Number held: 457
CNA 513. Operational capacity 513
Booking line: 01833 633 349 open Mon-Fri 0900 to 1200
Visiting times:
Tuesday to Thursday: 1:45pm to 4:05pm
Saturday and Sunday: 1:45pm to 4:05pm
Brief history The prison opened in 1973 on the site of a former military camp and was originally a borstal. It became a youth custody centre

and is currently a young offender institution.
Short description of residential units
The nine residential units include seven buildings constructed during the 1970s and early 1980s holding 60-66 young people in single cell accommodation, plus G wing, which holds 36, and J wing, with integral showers, which holds 39 young adults.
Governor/Director Andy Hudson
Escort contractor GEOAmey
Health service providers
Care UK Ltd
Tees, Esk and Wear Valley Mental Health Trust
Learning and skills provider
The Manchester College
IMB chair John Stoney

HMP DONCASTER
MARSHGATE,
DONCASTER,
SOUTH YORKS, DN5 8UX.
Tel: 01302 760870 Fax: 01302 760851
Task of the establishment A category B local prison accommodating both young and adult male prisoners.

Prison status Private, managed by Serco
Department
NOMS Director of Commissioning and Contract Management under the deputy director of custodial services contract management.
Certified normal accommodation 733
Operational capacity 1,145, reduced by 100 to 1,045 for approximately six-and-a-half months, ending 4 April 2016.
Prisoners book visits via ATM
Visits: Tues, Thurs, Sat, Sun: 0945-1145 for the main prison, and 1345-1515 for vulnerable prisoners. Mon, Wed, Fri are for Video Visits.

Under 18's can only visit if accompanied by a parent or legal guardian. If the adult is not the parent, they must prove guardianship by the child's birth certificate as proof of identity.
Brief history
Built by the Prison Service on the site of a former power station on an island in the town centre, the prison opened in June 1994.
Short description of residential units
Three house blocks made up of four wings each, with additional accommodation in the Annexe on the ground floor of the health centre building. The care and separation unit has 22 cells.
Governor/Director John Hewitson
Escort contractor GEOAmey
Health service provider
Nottinghamshire Healthcare NHS Trust
Learning and skills provider
Novus (based in The Manchester College Group)
IMB chair Lynne Hill MBE

HMP DOVEGATE
UTTOXETER
ST14 8XR
Tel: 01283 829400 Fax: 01283 820066
Task of the establishment Dovegate is a long-term category B men's training prison, which also provides some local prison accommodation.
Prison status Private – run by Serco
Region West Midlands
Number held 922
Certified normal accommodation 860
Operational capacity 933
Visits Telephone 0800 877 8951
Visiting Times everyday between
09:00 - 10:00 and 10:30 - 11:30
13:30 - 14:30 and 15:00 - 16:00
Brief history Dovegate opened in 2001. In September 2009 new accommodation opened to increase capacity, half of the 260 spaces were dedicated to local prisoners. In 2014 the population changed replacing a significant proportion of the prisoner sex offender population with an influx of more challenging, longer-sentenced, category B mainstream prisoners.
Short description of residential units
House block 1
A – E General wings.

House block 2
F and J General wings
G General wing for long-term prisoners
H Vulnerable prisoner unit
K Cellular confinement and accommodation for prisoners aged 50 and over.
House block 3
L and P General wings
M IDTS wing
N Remand prisoners and first night centre.
Governor/Director Clare Pearson
Escort contractor GEOAmey
Health service commissioner and providers NHS England (Shropshire and Staffordshire Area Team) (commissioner); Care UK (provider)
Learning and skills providers Serco
IMB chair John Dawson

HMP DOWNVIEW
SUTTON LANE
SUTTON
SURREY ÍSM2 5PD
Tel: 020 8196 6300 Fax: 020 8196 6301
The prison opened in 1989 as a category C Male Prison, converted from the former nurses' home of Banstead Hospital. In September 2001 Downview re-roled to a closed prison for adult women and in December 2004 a 16 bed juvenile unit (The Josephine Butler Unit) opened for young female offenders, this was then closed in 2013 following a national review of the female estate. In 2013 Downview closed for refurbishment and opened again in May 2016 continuing as a closed female establishment. The establishment is currently in the process of building up its population.
Operational capacity 355
Reception criteria: Adult Sentenced Female

Accommodation: Single cell accommodation with in-cell electricity. 5 Wings (A, B, C, D & E), all wings have in-cell electricity. D & E wings are currently out of use, when it opens D wing will serve as a resettlement unit, the function of E wing is currently being determined. There is also a Segregation unit on site.
HMP Downview is on the London Borough of Sutton / Surrey border close to the M25 and M23 and with good links to Sutton railway station. The characteristics of the population are varied and diverse with the majority of our prisoners originating from the London area or the South East of England.
There are clear links between the qualifications offered in the prison and the various progression routes to employment made available via Resettlement and National Careers Service.
The curriculum and training offer from August 2016 include: Catering, Business Administration, Beauty Therapy, Hairdressing, Customer Services, Functional Skills, ITQ, ESOL, peer mentoring, property maintenance and horticulture. All courses lead to nationally accredited qualifications.
We are developing our provision through partnerships with the London College of Fashion, Max Speilman Academy (specialists in reprographics), and a production kitchen with the Clink to improve employability and potential to gain qualifications. Opportunities will develop further with work and training places in the community, linked to our provision and as our population increases and based on the diverse needs and interests of the population. It is also anticipated that the TSP (OBP) Course will be introduced later this year.
Our developed gymnasium facilities including a full length astro - turf football field forms a key part of the promotion and development of health and well-being.
Healthcare is commissioned by NHS England (South) and provided by a number of specialist healthcare providers.
Primary care and mental health staff are provided by Central North West London NHS Trust and are on site every day of the week. Primary care staff will provide services similar to those provided in a GP Surgery and we offer access to screening programmes, health

living information and immunisations. The mental health services can offer a range of interventions which may be a brief conversation to signpost to services, therapy, psychosocial interventions, community mental health team case management and possible referral to more intensive services.

Substance Misuse services are provided by Addiction and RAPT and are on site seven days a week. Substance misuse maintenance and detoxification are available alongside psychosocial support.

GP services are provided by Cheam Family practice who are based locally and work across many other prison sites.

We do not provide access to 24 hour healthcare, therefore no inpatient beds. Women felt to need this level of input may be transferred to other establishments.

Mon-Thurs: Unlock 08.00 – 12.30, 13.50 – 17.15, 18.00 – 19.00; Friday: Unlock 08.00 – 12.30, association 13.50 – 16.30; Sat & Sun: Unlock 08.30 – 12.00, 13.20 – 16: 45

Visits Telephone 0300 303 0633.

Visiting Times Thu, Sat: 14.00 - 16:00

Sunday 0900 - 1100

Governor/Director Natasha Wilson

HMP DRAKE HALL
ECCLESHALL
STAFFS ST21 6LQ
Tel: 01785 774100 Fax: 01785 774010

Task of the establishment A resettlement prison and young offender institution for women and young adult women.

Prison status Public

Region Women's Estate

Number held 338

Certified normal accommodation 340

Operational capacity 340

Visits Telephone 0300 060 6501. Booking line open Monday to Friday 09:00-1600. Visiting Times Tue: 13:30-1545; Sat, Sun: 0930-1130 and 1330-1545; Sun 1330-1345

Date of last inspection 22nd May 2020

Brief history Drake Hall provided accommodation for women munitions workers during World War 11. It became a male open prison in the 1960s and was re-rolled as a semi-open prison for women in 1974. Some of the original accommodation was rebuilt in 1994–1995. In March 2009, Drake Hall was redesignated from a semi-open to a closed prison.

Short description of residential units There were 15 residential units within the perimeter fence, accommodating up to 315 women, with most units holding approximately 20 people.

Bristol, Canterbury, Norwich – general non-smoking units, some of which were double rooms

Durham, Exeter, Folkestone, Gloucester, Margate, Oxford – general units

Keele – a 19-room induction unit

Plymouth, Richmond – for women who had completed their induction

Ipswich – mostly accommodating women working outside the prison

Lancaster – mostly housing long-term prisoners and lifers

St David's – 16 single rooms for women with social care or mobility needs.

The new open unit located outside the prison gate could hold up to 25 women.

Governor/Director Carl Hardwick

Escort contractor GEOAmey

Health service provider: Care UK

Learning and skills provider

Milton Keynes College

CRC Ingeus

IMB chair John Townsley

HMP DURHAM
OLD ELVET
DURHAM DH1 3HU
Tel: 0191 332 3400 Fax: 0191 332 3401

Task of the establishment Category B local establishment for adult and young male prisoners.

Prison status Public

Region/Department North East

- 37 -

Number held 938
Certified normal accommodation 595
Operational capacity 996
Visits are booked by prisoner-led application. You will then be contacted your visit directly by the prison. You can also register to use the secure video calls service. There is no telephone or online booking service available. Visits happen everyday, including weekends at the following times:
10:45am to 11:30am, 2:00pm to 2:30pm
Brief history The prison opened in 1819 and was rebuilt in 1881. It has primarily been a local prison and now holds adult males over 21 and young adults, who are sentenced, convicted and remand prisoners from Tyneside, Durham and Cumbria courts.
Short description of residential units
A wing – remand, convicted and sentenced prisoners. Short and long term
B wing – landings 2,3,4 full-time workers. Landing 1 vulnerable prisoners attached to C wing
C wing – vulnerable prisoner wing
D wing – integrated drug treatment wing
E wing – integrated drug treatment wing
F wing – first night centre and induction unit
I wing – drug recovery unit
G wing – separation and care unit
M wing - health care inpatients
Governor/Director Phil Husband
Escort contractor GeoAmey
Health service commissioner and providers
Commissioner: NHS England (North East and Cumbria)
Providers: G4S (nursing and administration); Spectrum (pharmacy and GP); Tees Esk and Wear Valleys NHS Foundation Trust (mental health); Rethink (depression and anxiety services); MIND (counselling)
Learning and skills provider Novus
IMB chair Sarah Pearce

HMP EAST SUTTON PARK
SUTTON VALENCE
MAIDSTONE, KENT
ME17 3DF
Tel: 01622 785000 Fax: 01622 785001
Task of the establishment A women's open prison with a resettlement function.
Prison status Public

Region Kent
Number held 98 (on 5 August 2016)
Certified normal accommodation 103
Operational capacity 103
You can book your visit by telephone 0300 303 0630 -There is no online booking. Email bookings hmppsvisitsbooking@justice.gov.uk
Visiting times: Saturday: 9:30am to 11:30am and 2pm to 4pm. Sunday: 9:30am to 11:30am and 2pm to 4pm
Brief history East Sutton Park opened as a female borstal on 2 October 1946 and has been a women's establishment ever since. The prison was a 15th century listed manor house set in 80 acres of land, with a working farm. For almost ten years East Sutton Park has operated under the threat of closure in favour of smaller open units outside larger women's closed prisons.
The threat of closure remains but it is unsettling for staff and prisoners alike.
Short description of residential units.
There were 34 bedrooms, of which 15 were double rooms and one was a single; the largest room had seven beds. Bedrooms were all situated within the main house. The prison had a shower block and toilet facilities were located around the house.
Governor/Director Natasha Wilson
Escort contractor GeoAmey
Health service provider Oxleas NHS Foundation Trust
Learning and skills providers Manchester College

HMP EASTWOOD PARK
FALFIELD,
WOTTON-UNDER-EDGE,
GLOUC. GL12 8DB.
Tel: 01454 382100 Fax: 01454 382101

- 38 -

Task of the establishment Eastwood Park is a closed women's resettlement prison.
Prison status Public
Region Southwest
Number held 397
Certified normal accommodation 394
Operational capacity 442
Visits: You can book by telephone or email.
Booking line: 0300 303 0631, open Monday to Friday, 9am to 6pm
Email: socialvisits.eastwoodpark@hmps.gsi.gov.uk
Visiting times: Tues, Wed, Fri, Sat, Sun: 2pm to 3pm and 3:30pm to 4:30pm
Children can visit their mothers Mon-Fri 9:30am to 11:45am.
Date of last inspection 28 August 2019
Brief history Eastwood Park opened as a women's prison in March 1996, in 2019 the Prisons Inspectorate said Eastwood Park was found to have remained a safe, respectful and purposeful prison over the last three years.
HM Chief Inspector of Prisons said the latest inspection in May 2019 raised concerns about "completely inappropriate" conditions in the prison's three closed blocks – units 1, 2 and 3. Inspectors were also concerned about the number of women released homeless. In May 2019, Eastwood Park held just under 400 women.
Short description of residential units
1 – first night and induction unit
2 – general unit
3 – general unit
4 – complex needs unit for women with mental health problems.
5 – enhanced and drug recovery wing
6 – general unit
7 – low security enhanced unit for prison orderlies and women on release on temporary licence
8 – Kinnon Unit for those undergoing drug and alcohol detoxification, including a first night unit
9 – mother and baby unit, currently closed
10 – Nexus Programme Unit for women with personality disorders. Units 1, 2, 3, 4 and 8 were considered closed units, offering a restricted regime. Units 5, 6, 7, 9 and 10 were perceived as open units, where women had more freedom, although they were still contained within the prison's secure fence.

Governor/Director Suzy Dymond-White
Escort contractor GeoAmey
Health service providers
Inspire Better Health – a partnership made up of:
Bristol Community Health (lead provider)
Avon and Wiltshire Mental Health NHS Trust (mental health)
Hanham Health (GP service)
and other sub-contractors
Learning and skills providers Weston College

HMP ELMLEY
CHURCH ROAD
EASTCHURCH
SHEERNESS
KENT ME12 4DZ
Tel: 01795 802000 Fax: 01795 802001
Task of the establishment Category B local prison serving the courts of Kent
Number held 1,160
Certified normal accommodation 985
Operational capacity 1,252
You can book your visit by telephone. There is no online booking service available.
Booking line: 0300 060 6605 open Monday to Friday, 9am to 4pm
Visiting times: Monday to Friday: 2pm to 3pm
Brief history Elmley is a purpose-built local prison serving all courts in Kent. The establishment opened in 1992 and includes a category C unit of up to 240 prisoners built in 1997. Elmley is one of six Bullingdon design prisons in England and is the largest of the three prisons in the Sheppey group.
Short description of residential units
There are six residential units (house blocks) holding between 167 and 283 prisoners each in single or double cells.

- 39 -

House block 1: first night centre
House block 2: remand and convicted prisoners. B spur houses vulnerable (non sex-offender) prisoners
House block 3: substance recovery community working in partnership with RAPt
House block 4: remand and convicted prisoners
House block 5: category C prisoners.
House block 6: A spur houses foreign national prisoners and B spur houses prisoners with a current or historic sex offence
Governor/Director Dawn Mauldon
Escort contractor GeoAmey
Health service providers Integrated Care 24; Minster Medical Group; Rehabilitation of Addicted Prisoners Trust (RAPt); Oxleas NHS Foundation Trust
Learning and skills providers Novus
IMB chair Bob Duncan

HMP ERLESTOKE
ERLESTOKE
DEVIZES
WILTSHIRE, SN10 5TU
Tel: 01380 814250 Fax: 01380 814273
Task of the establishment HMP Erlestoke is a category C training prison for adult male sentenced prisoners. It has a focus on the rehabilitation of a longer-term population and is a national resource for high-intensity programmes on domestic violence, alcohol-related violence and substance abuse.
Prison status Public
Region/Department South-west
Number held 488
Certified normal accommodation 488
Operational capacity 488
Visits Booking line: 0300 303 0634

Monday to Friday, 9:15am to 5pm
Visiting times:
Monday to Thursday: 1:45pm to 2:45pm and 3:15pm to 4:15pm
Friday: no visits
Sat/Sunday: 1345-1445 and 1515-1615
How to book legal and professional visits
To book Legal visits please email: LegalVisits.Erlestoke@justice.gov.uk.
Date of last inspection 22nd September 2020 when Inspectors found a "very troubling" picture of violence, indiscipline and self-harm, with increased use of force by staff to get prisoners back into poor-quality cells in which they had been locked up for most of the day for more than five months.
Brief history HMP Erlestoke in 1977 became a young prisoners centre, and was converted to its current role as a category C adult male training prison in 1988. Life-sentenced prisoners were first received in the 1990s.
Short description of residential units
Marlborough unit 60-bed induction unit. All accommodation is in double cells.
Alfred unit 66-bed unit with standard and basic status prisoners and enhanced prisoners before successful progression to enhanced units.
Sarum unit 56-bed enhanced unit, which is the first progression unit for enhanced prisoners. All cells have courtesy locks and prisoners are locked behind end-of-landing doors, with a curfew compact.
Wessex unit 68-bed unit with standard and basic status prisoners and enhanced prisoners before successful progression to enhanced units.
Imber unit 40-bed enhanced unit, with similar arrangements to Sarum unit but with improved facilities, including integral sanitation and more association area and equipment.
Avebury unit 40-bed enhanced unit.
Kennet unit 40-bed enhanced unit, with similar arrangements to Sarum unit but with improved facilities, including integral sanitation and more association area and equipment.
Silbury unit 124-bed interventions unit.
Care & separation unit eight single cells and one special accommodation cell
Governor/Director Tim Knight
Escort contractor GEOAmey
Health provider Great Western Hospital
Learning and skills providers Weston College

HMP EXETER

30 NEW NORTH ROAD, EXETER. DEVON
EX4 4EX
Tel: 01392 415650 Fax: 01392 415691
Task of the establishment HMP Exeter is a male category B local and resettlement prison holding prisoners, including young adults, from Cornwall, Devon and Somerset.
Prison status Public
Region/Department South-West
Number held 482
Certified normal accommodation 326
Operational capacity 561
Exeter is currently operating a limited visits schedule for family and friends. You can book your visit by telephone. There is no online booking service available.
Booking line: 01392 415 833 open: Monday to Friday, 9:30am to 12pm and 1pm to 4:30pm
Visiting times:
Tues, Thurs, Fri: 2:15pm to 4:15pm
Date of last inspection May 2018 when an **Urgent Notification** was issued
Brief history Built in 1853, HMP Exeter is a Victorian prison, with three wings positioned around the centre. In the late 20th century, D wing was added and, more recently, education blocks were built. In the last few years, a refurbished reception, a new visits hall and a social care unit have been added
Short description of residential units
A wing – holds 194 remand or sentenced and convicted adults and young offenders.
B wing – is the vulnerable prisoner wing, holding 87 remand or sentenced and convicted adults and young offenders.
C wing – holds 189 remand or sentenced and convicted adults and young offenders. The C4 landing houses prisoners requiring integrated drug treatment.
D wing – is the enhanced living unit, holding 80 remand or sentenced and convicted adults and young offenders.
F wing – is a social care unit, holding 11 prisoners; it also contains the Jubilee Suite, a palliative care room for terminally ill prisoners.
Governor/Director Richard Luscombe
Escort contractor GeoAmey
Health service provider Dorset Healthcare University NHS Foundation Trust
Learning and skills providers Weston College

HMP FEATHERSTONE

NEW RD,
WOLVERHAMPTON
WV10 7PU
Tel: 01902 703000
Fax: 01902 703001
Task of the establishment HMP Featherstone is a male category C training and resettlement prison.
Prison status Public
CNA 621. Operational capacity 653
Visits Telephone: 0300 060 6502
Visiting Times: 14:00- 16:00 except Friday
Date of last inspection 7th February 2019
Peter Clarke, HM Chief Inspector of Prisons, said: "At this inspection we were pleased to find evidence of significant improvement. Across all four (healthy prison) tests we found measurable improvements, with outcomes in respect, purposeful activity and rehabilitation now all sufficiently good."
Brief history HMP Featherstone was opened in November 1976, and house units 5, 6 and 7 were added later. It was originally a long-term category C training prison but in 2014 became a designated training and resettlement prison for prisoners returning to Warwickshire and West Mercia.
Short description of residential units
House block 1: general residential
House block 2: general with one spur currently used for segregation
House blocks 3, 4: general residential
House block 5: induction
House block 6: enhanced
House block 7: general residential
Governor/Director Laura Whitehurst
Escort contractor GeoAmey
Health service provider Care UK
Education provider Milton Keynes College
IMB chair Ian Marks

HMYOI FELTHAM

BEDFONT RD, FELTHAM
MIDDLESEX, TW13 4ND
Tel: 020 8844 5000
Fax: 020 8844 5001

Feltham A (Urgent Notification issued)
Task of the establishment To hold young people aged 15 to 18 years and in **Feltham B**, young adults aged 18 to 21.
Establishment status Public
Group Young people's estate
Feltham A: Number held 180 - CNA 240
Feltham B: Number held 410 - CNA 522
Visits Booking line: 020 8844 5000 open: Mon-Sun 8am to 11:30am and 1pm to 4:30pm
Visiting times for Feltham A:
Monday: 2:00pm to 3:00pm, 3:30pm to 4:30pm
Tuesday: 2:00pm to 3:00pm, 3:30pm to 4:30pm
Wed: 2:00pm to 3:00pm, 3:30pm to 4:30pm
Thurs: 2:00pm to 3:00pm, 3:30pm to 4:30pm
Visiting times for Feltham B:
Mon: 2:00pm to 3:00pm and 3:30pm to 4:30pm
Wed: 2:00pm to 3:00pm and 3:30pm to 4:30pm
Saturday: 9:00am to 10:00am, 10:30 to 11:30am, 2:00pm to 3:00pm, and 3:30pm to 4:30pm
Sunday: 2:00pm to 3:00pm and 3:30pm to 4:30pm

Feltham A last inspection 23rd March 2021:
"Since our last inspection, progress had been made and, remarkably in the middle of a pandemic, outcomes in some areas had improved. Children were split into groups of four in which they accessed education and other activities. We found that being in small groups had improved the quality of relationships between children and staff, with more children than at the previous inspection reporting feeling cared for or being encouraged to attend education."

Feltham B last inspection 30th October 2019
"We found there had been improvements in safety and rehabilitation and release planning which were now reasonably good, but a decline in purposeful activity which was now poor.
Brief history The original Feltham was built in 1854 as an industrial school and was taken over in 1910 by the Prison Commissioners as their second Borstal institution. The existing building opened as a remand centre in March 1988. HMP/YOI Feltham was formed by the amalgamation of Ashford Remand Centre and Feltham Borstal in 1990. Feltham also has

Kepple Unit which is designed for young people who for a variety of reasons are not engaging or are unlikely to engage with the normal regime in a young offender institution. These young people are deemed to be highly vulnerable and invariably assessed as having complex needs across multiple domains including physical or mental health needs, learning difficulties, communication needs and substance misuse. The ethos of the unit is to increase their coping skills and self esteem to enable them return to normal location within the YOI estate at the earliest opportunity.

Feltham A: residential units:
There are eight units, each holding 30 young people, and a care and separation unit shared with Feltham B. Almost all cells are single occupation. All cells have sanitation & TV.
Bittern - first night and induction
Curlew - full-time workers' unit
Dunlin, Eagle, Falcon, Grebe, Heron - normal location. Jay - full-time education
Ibis – care and separation unit
Feltham B: residential units:
Kingfisher – induction unit, 53 beds
Lapwing – normal location, 46 beds
Mallard – normal location, 55 beds
Nightingale – normal location, 55 beds
Osprey – normal location, 55 beds
Partridge – normal location, 55 beds
Quail – normal location, 55 beds
Raven – normal location, 55 beds
Swallow – normal location, 55 beds
Teal – normal location, 38 beds
Ibis – segregation unit
Governor/Director Emily Martin
Health Provider: Care UK - now PPG

HMP FIVE WELLS Opens 2022)
HMP Five Wells Millers Park Wellingborough NN8 2NG.
CNA, 1680. OP Cap, 1680
Opens 4th February 2022
Director: John McLaughlin
Seven Houseblocks, with 4 spurs.
Healthcare provider, Practice Plus Group
Education provider Weston College
Because the prison is not yet open here are a few quick facts about the new mega prison.
How many inmates will it?
The prison is set to hold 1,680 inmates, and will be ran by security firm G4S who won the contract back in October 2020.
How much did it cost to build?
It has cost around £253,000,000 to build. It was constructed on the site of the old HM Prison Wellingborough; demolished in 2019.
What kind of prisoners will it hold?
The category C jail is seen as a flagship example of the Government's aim to create a "modern, efficient prison estate that is fit for the future" and will have a clear focus on rehabilitating offenders.
As a Category C prison its will not hold the most dangerous prisoners.
How has Northamptonshire reacted to the new mega prison?
Britain's biggest ever prison coming to the county has proven to be decisive among locals. Some believe that more needs to be done to keep offenders off of the street, and a prison like this is the perfect image of justice, deterrence and rehabilitation for the county. It's also created 700 jobs in the local area.
Others believe that the £253,000,000 spent could have been better used to combat the root causes of crime, like poverty and inequality.
Back in April 2021, protestors blocked delivery vehicles carrying construction materials to the prison, objecting to the privatisation and monetisation of the prison system.

HMP FORD
ARUNDEL, WEST SUSSEX BN18 0BX
Tel: 01903 663000 Fax: 01903 663001
Task of the establishment HMP Ford is a category D adult male prison.
Prison status Public

Region/Department Kent and Sussex
CNA 448, OpCap 448,, inmates May 2021 418
Visits Booking Line: 01903 663120 - there's no online booking - the booking line is open Monday-Saturday, 10-11 and 1-3pm
Visiting times: Wednesday: 6pm to 8pm
Friday to Sunday: 2pm to 4pm
Date of last inspection 19th May 2021 - Inspectors view: *"Urgent need to improve"*
Brief history Formerly a Royal Navy Fleet Air Arm station, Ford converted to an open prison in 1960. On 1 January 2011, a major disturbance at the establishment resulted in the loss of the induction unit, prisoner mailroom, association area, gym, offices and 36 prisoner rooms, including the first night billets. Following the rebuilding of some of these areas, with induction being moved to the 'P' units, the establishment also added a new kitchen, servery and anti-dash perimeter fencing, and refurbished the visits hall.
Short description of residential units
A mixture of shared-room billets, single room prefab pods and brick blocks. 'A' block with 11 landings of single rooms. 'B' block 22 billet modular units (pods). May 2021: 10 billet huts and 40 modular units were in full use in addition to the 214 single rooms on 'A' block.
Governor/Director Andrew Davy
Escort contractor GeoAmey
Health service provider
Sussex Partnership NHS Foundation Trust
Learning and skills providers Novus
IMB chair Ken Porter

HMP FOREST BANK
AGECROFT ROAD, PENDLEBURY, SALFORD M27 8FB
Tel: 0161 925 7000 Fax: 0161 925 7001
Task of the establishment HMP Forest Bank is a category B local prison for adult and young adult men.
Prison status Private – Sodexo Justice Services
Region/Department North-West
Number held 1,428
CNA 1,064. OpCap 1,460
Visits are booked by the resident on behalf of their visitors, on a month by month basis, max of 3 visitors, consisting of 2 adults and one child or 1 adult and 2 children.
Brief history The prison was opened in 2000

- 43 -

under a 25-year private finance initiative (PFI) contract to provide 800 places as a category B local prison. Spaces gradually increased to 1,160, and a 264-place extension was opened in November 2009. Following a further increase in prison places, the establishment now holds 1,460 remand and sentenced adult males, and remand and sentenced (up to 12 months) young adults (aged 18–21).
Short description of residential units
Residential wings A–H:
A1: Young adults
A2, B1, B2, C1, D1, F2, General
C2: Vulnerable prisoners
D2 Drug-free wing
E1: General and dispersal wing
F1: Basic, challenging behaviour wing
G1 Recovery wing
G2: First night and induction
H1: IDTS/induction
H2: Vulnerable prisoners
Health care inpatients (20)
Governor/Director Ian Whitehead
Escort contractor GEOAmey
Health service provider Sodexo Justice Services; Cimmaron (GP services); Greater Manchester West Mental Health NHS Foundation Trust
Learning and skills Sodexo Justice Services
IMB chair Barry Cave

HMP FOSTON HALL
FOSTON, DERBY
DERBYSHIRE DE65 5DN
Tel: 01283 584300 Fax: 01283 584301
Task of the establishment A women's local and resettlement prison.
Prison status Public
Group Women's estate
CNA 264 and OpCap 286
Visits: Book by phone - 0300 060 6516 open Mon-Fri 9am to 3pm - there is no online booking service available.
Visiting times: Wednesday and Friday: 1:45pm - 4.30pm. Sunday: 9am-4.30pm
Date of last inspection 19th June 2019:-
Most prisoners felt safe. Violence was rare and incidents minor. Work to investigate incidents when they did occur and the support offered to victims and perpetrators did, however, need to be better. The incentives scheme was not very effective and adjudications and use of force were both higher than we expected, although incidents when force was used were not normally very serious. Use of segregation was much reduced but conditions in the facility had yet to improve. Overall this is a good report about a good prison. Foston Hall is well led, with energy and creativity evident among the senior team. Themes that emerged from our inspection were the need to refine strategies so that initiatives were better coordinated and delivered more effectively, and to ensure that the staff group was more proactive in focusing on the needs of prisoners and their well-being.
Brief history Foston Hall was built in 1863 as a family home and was acquired by the Prison Service in 1953. Since then it has been used as a detention centre, an immigration centre and a satellite of nearby HMP Sudbury. Shut in 1996, it reopened on 31 July 1997 as a closed women's prison following major refurbishment and building work.
Short description of residential units
First night and induction unit for 63 prisoners
A wing – Cameo Unit accommodation for 42 prisoners with personality disorders B wing – mainstream accommodation for 42 prisoners
C wing – mainstream for 41 prisoners
D wing – mainstream for 29 prisoners
E wing – unit for 11 long-term and enhanced
F wing – mainstream for 63 prisoners
T wing – mainstream for 58 prisoners.
Governor/Director Andrea Black
Escort contractor GEOAmey
Health service provider Care UK
Learning and skills providers
Milton Keynes College
IMB chair Hilary Campbell

- 44 -

HMP FRANKLAND
BRASSIDE, DURHAM, DH1 5YD
Tel: 0191 376 5000 Fax: 0191 376 5001
Task of the establishment
A high security prison for category A and B convicted and category A remands.
Prisoners held January 2020: 841
CNA: 852. Operational capacity: 852
Visits: Book by phone - 0191 376 5048 open Mon-Fri 0830-1200.
Visiting times: Tues-Sun: 2pm to 4pm
Date of last inspection 5 May 2020 - high-risk secure prison maintaining strong standards.
Brief history
HMP Frankland, near Durham, is one of the country's most secure prisons. Holding 840 convicted adult men at the time of our inspection, over 250 were classified as category A, the highest security classification, and of these, nine were considered high-risk category A. Almost all those held were serving sentences in excess of ten years, with the majority serving indeterminate or life sentences. The majority had committed the most serious, and often violent, offences and posed very great risks to the public. The security measures applied at Frankland, as well the depth of custody experienced, reflected fully these risks.
Short description of residential units
A, B, C and D wings - the original wings, each holding 108 vulnerable prisoners:
A wing holds enhanced-status prisoners
A1 landing holds older prisoners and those with disabilities
D1 is for induction.
F, G and J wings - the newer wings, holding non-vulnerable prisoners:
F wing has 120 places
G wing has 88 places (including 18 beds on G4 for prisoners over 50)
J wing has 120 places.
Westgate unit has four units: 86 places:
Unit one: PIPE Unit
Unit two: induction for Westgate
Units three and four: treat prisoners with complex personality presentation.
Health care - nine places
Management and progression (segregation) unit - 28 places. The prison also has National Security Separation Unit.

HMP FULL SUTTON
FULL SUTTON,
YORK YO41 1PS
Tel: 01759 475100 Fax: 01759 371206
Brief history HMP Full Sutton opened in 1987 as a purpose-built high security establishment.
A high security prison for category A and B adult males. CNA: 597. OpCap: 586
Short description of residential units
A: Normal location; B, C, D: VPU.
E, F: Normal location
Close supervision centre
Visits: book by telephone 01759 475 355 open Mon-Fri 0830-1630 - no online booking -
Email: socialvisits.fullsutton@justice.gov.uk
Visiting times: Friday pm Sat am and pm
Date of last inspection 11 June 2020:
Overall, Full Sutton performs its important function well. A fundamentally safe and decent establishment, with energetic leadership and a staff group who interact well with the prisoners in their charge.
If the plans that are now in place to improve the provision of education, skills and work bear fruit, and a few key issues in other areas are addressed, there is no reason why Full Sutton could not aspire to be one of the best performing prisons in the country.
Governor/Director Gareth Sands
Escort contractor GeoAmey
Healthcare provider Spectrum Health CIC
Learning and skills providers Novus
IMB chair Sally Hobbs

HMP GARTH
ULNES WALTON, LEYLAND
PRESTON, PR26 8NE
Tel: 01772 443300 Fax: 01772 443301
Task of the establishment HMP Garth is a category B training prison.
Prison status Public
CNA: 810. Operational capacity: 830
Visits book by phone 01772 443 503, line open Mon-Thurs 9-12 & 2-4pm
Visiting times: Mon-Thurs: 2pm to 4pm
Garth is a Cat B trainer that opened in 1988
Residential units:
A: residential; B: The Beacon Support Unit; C: residential; D: The Building Hope Unit; E: residential & therapeutic community; F &G: VPU's. Plus Segregation unit
Last Inspection 9th May 2019: *"Although there was still too much violence, it had not risen in line with the overall trend across the prison estate, and credit is due to the staff at Garth for working hard to understand and contain it. There is absolutely no room for complacency, but there were some early encouraging signs of improvement. As with many other prisons, the ready availability of illicit drugs drove much of the violence, and the scale of the challenge in this respect at Garth was daunting. Sixty per cent of prisoners told us it was easy to obtain drugs, 30% were testing positive for drugs and around a quarter had developed a drug habit since entering the prison." Drugs and violence reduction strategies must be kept under constant review to maintain the progress.*
"The leadership of HMP Garth were keen to point out to me that there were early signs of improvement, and it was to their credit that what had been achieved was sufficient to raise our assessments in two of our healthy prison tests. Given the overall context in which establishments such as Garth have been operating over the past few years, this is an achievement that should not be underestimated. For the future, dealing with the twin scourges of drugs and violence will be the key to making further progress, and I hope that when we next inspect HMP Garth we will be able to report that the momentum we saw on this occasion will have been maintained."
Governor/Director Steve Pearson
Health Provider: Lancashire Care
Education: The Manchester College
IMB chair Peter Guy

HMP GARTREE
GALLOW FIELD ROAD
MARKET HARBOROUGH
LEICS, LE16 7RP
Tel: 01858 426600 Fax: 01858 426601
Task of the establishment Gartree is a category B training prison for adult male life-sentenced prisoners.
Prison status Public
Region East Midlands
Number held 698
Certified normal accommodation 708
Operational capacity 708
Visits Telephone: 01858 426 727
Visiting Times: Tues, Thurs, Sat, Sun: 2 – 4pm
Brief history The prison opened in 1966 as a category C prison, but was adapted in 1967 for use as a dispersal prison. In the early 1990s, it re-roled to a category B life-sentenced prisoner main centre, and now houses the largest group of life-sentenced prisoners in the UK. The operational capacity has increased significantly as new units opened.
Short description of residential units
A-D wings generic residential wings with single cells; part of the original 1960s build and since refurbished.
G wing drug recovery unit, all single cells, opened in 2005-06.
H wing older population unit and the psychologically informed planned environment
(PIPE) unit, all single cells, opened in 2005-06.
I wing stand-alone induction wing housing up to 30 prisoners in double cells.
Gartree therapeutic community (GTC) holds up to 24 in single cells.
TC+ designated unit for prisoners with learning difficulties or personality disorders

who require additional assistance and guidance, 12 single cells.
Segregation unit 12 beds.
Governor Babafemi Dada
Escort contractor GEOAmey
Health service provider
Leicester Partnership Trust
Learning and skills provider
Milton Keynes College
IMB chair Howard Witham

HMP GRENDON
GRENDON UNDERWOOD
AYLESBURY BUCKS, HP18 0TL
Tel: 01296 445000 Fax: 01296 445001
CNA: 193 Operational capacity: 233
Task of the establishment HMP Grendon is a category B training prison for adult males run on therapeutic community principles.
Prison status Public
Short description of residential units
A wing – TC for sex offenders
B wing – assessment and TC
C wing – TC: D wing – TC
F wing – closed 2021 for fire safety reasons
G wing – TC+ learning disabilities unit
Visits booked on 01296 445 243 - line open Mon-Fri: 1000-1200; no online booking.
Email: socialvisits.grendon@hmps.gsi.gov.uk
Visiting times: Wed & Sat 1:45pm to 3:15pm
Brief history Opened in 1962, Grendon adopted a model for addressing offending behaviour and psychological problems based on a model that grew out of attempts to treat what is now called post- traumatic stress.
Each therapeutic community had its own constitution and a prisoner chairman and vice chair. A democratic process was in place where staff and prisoners elected prisoners into these roles, and regulated behaviour standards. This included imposing sanctions where rules had been broken, implementing processes for selecting and deselecting prisoners for a place in the community, and discussing and resolving incidences of conflict or disagreement. With the backing of his small therapy group, a prisoner could initiate a discussion and a vote about any aspect of community life. This process had the potential to motivate prisoners to surrender their individual rights in the interests of peaceful community living. Prisoners were also expected to have a small job that supported the community. Each therapeutic community also had a range of specialist staff including therapists, trained specialist officers and offender supervisors. The therapeutic communities were accredited by the Correctional Services Accreditation and Advisory Panel. Their standards and performance were monitored by the Community of Communities (a quality improvement and accreditation programme for therapeutic communities) and they received annual assessments, which led to action plans and service improvements. End of therapy reports were required for all prisoners leaving therapy.
Last Inspection April 2021: *Leaders and staff at Grendon had responded well to the operational challenges presented by the pandemic and the prison remained a safe and respectful environment. However, while the prisoner therapeutic communities had weathered the necessary restrictions reasonably well, some outcomes were beginning to deteriorate. The longer the restrictions persist, the more the therapeutic culture will be at risk and the longer it will take Grendon to recover.*
It is important for HMPPS to support the governor and staff to implement a full recovery plan as soon as is practicable to enable a safe return to being a successful therapeutic community, particularly after the successful roll-out of the vaccine in the prison.
Governor/Director Becky Hayward
Escort contractor GEOAmey
Health service providers
Care UK – primary health care
Oxford Health – mental health in-reach team

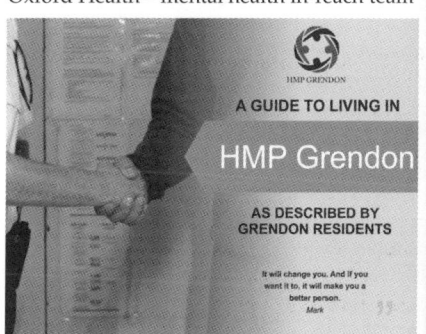

Haddenham Dental Centre
Howcroft and Selby – optometry
Lloyds – pharmacy
Learning and skills providers
Milton Keynes College
IMB chair Christoff Lewis

that enhanced, Gwent, main population wing holds 75 men, Mercia holds 80 men, Saxon is a main population wing and holds 75 men. Tarrant, Segregation holds 11, Wessex 66.
Governor/Director Ian Walters
Escort contractor GEOAmey
Health service provider CareUK PPG
Learning and skills provider Weston College
IMB chair Lesley Sim

HMP HATFIELD
THORNE ROAD
DONCASTER, DN7 6EL
Tel: 01405 746500 Fax: 01405 746501
Public Open resettlement prison for men.
Group Yorkshire
CNA 378. OpCap 378
Visits: book by phone 01405 746 611, open Mon-Fri 0900-1300.
Visiting: Wed, Fri, Sat, Sun, 2pm to 3:50pm
Last Inspection 9th January 2020: *HMP/YOI Hatfield is a category D resettlement prison for men near Doncaster in South Yorkshire. The prison is split across two sites: a main site, and a further site that used to form part of HMP Lindholme but is now used for receptions into the prison and is usually referred to as The Lakes site. Hatfield was a well-run and decent establishment, fulfilling its role in preparing men for their release. There was much to commend, and the leadership and staff should take pride in what they have achieved and how they have encouraged the prisoners to play an active role in making it a safe, decent and purposeful establishment.*
Brief History: Hatfield is an Open resettlement prison, formerly known as Moorland Open, as part of HMP Moorland. Hatfield officially separated from HMP Moorland in April 2014 and has also taken over the previous HMP Lindholme I wing, known as The Lakes site, which since June 2015 has been used to hold all new arrivals for an initial three-month period before moving to Hatfield.
There are currently eight residential units, A, B, C, D, E and F on the main site and G and H on The Lakes site (approximately four miles from the main site)
A, B and C units: 20 rooms per landing across three floors. D and E units: accommodate 40 prisoners across two floors. F unit: a self-contained six-bed unit that provides

HMP GUYS MARSH
SHAFTESBURY, DORSET SP7 0AH
Tel: 01747 856400 Fax: 01747 856401
Category C resettlement prison.
Prison status Public
Region South West
Last Inspection: January 2019 - *This inspection evidenced tangible progress for the first time in many years, there was still much to improve but managers were visible, there was good leadership, commitment and enthusiasm among those who worked there. The prison was far more settled and there was an underpinning commitment to promoting well-being among all those held.*
CNA 396. OpCap 396
Visits: Booking line: 01747 856 586, open Mon-Thurs 1pm to 3pm, Fri 1130-1pm
Visiting times: Fri/Sat/Sun: 2:15pm to 3:30pm
Brief history Opened in 1960 as a borstal, HMP Guys Marsh became a young offender institution (YOI) in 1984. In 1992 it became a closed establishment and started to accommodate adults. In 2008, the young offenders were moved out and Guys Marsh became an adult male category C prison holding both determinate and indeterminate sentence prisoners.
Short description of residential units
Anglia: Induction and First Night 70 men, Cambria 66 men, Dorset holds 66 men on progression, Fontmell, enhanced, 40 men. Jubilee, 60 men, is a progressive wing for those

independent living for six prisoners. G and H units: accommodate 56 men.
Governor/Director Mick Mills
Escort contractor GEOAmey
Healthcare: Nottinghamshire Healthcare
Education: The Manchester College
IMB chair Chris Hilley

HMP HAVERIGG
MILLOM, CUMBRIA, LA18 4NA
Tel: 01229 713000 Fax: 01229 713001
Category D male since December 2019.
Group Cumbria.
CNA 486. OpCap 488
HMP Haverigg was opened in 1967 on the site of a former RAF station and is the only prison in Cumbria. Originally, 350 prisoners were accommodated in the RAF billets, but the addition of new accommodation and the rebuilding of two units following incidents of concerted indiscipline in 1988 and 1999 increased the accommodation.
You can book your visit by telephone. There is no online booking service available.
Booking line: 01229 713 016 Monday to Friday, 1pm to 4pm
Visiting times:
Thursday: 1:45pm to 4:15pm
Friday: 1:45pm to 4:15pm
Saturday: 1:45pm to 4:15pm
Sunday: 1:45pm to 4:15pm
Short description of residential units
R1 Purpose-built house block split into two 60-cell wings. R2 Nine billets of 18 cells. R3 Seven billets of 16 cells. R5 Purpose-built house block split into six spurs across two landings. R6 Two billets of 16 cells. R4 and the segregation unit are closed.
Last Inspection: May 2021.

A prison with a troubled history and much criticism from the Inspectorate in recent years, significant change was introduced in late 2019 when Haverigg became an open prison which coincided with the COVID-19 pandemic. The prison's response to the pandemic, while maintaining the momentum behind the transition, has therefore been the main strategic challenge for the establishment over the last 16 months. It is greatly to the credit of the acting governor, her management team and the staff and prisoners of Haverigg, that they have progressed so well.
Name of governor Joanna Bailey
Prison Group Director John Illingsworth
IMB chair Lynne Chambers

HMP HEWELL
HEWELL LANE
REDDITCH WORCESTERSHIRE B97 6QQ
Tel: 01527 785000 Fax: 01527 785001
Category B local male prison and category D open male prison
Prison status Public
Group West Midlands
Number held 1,074 closed site, 204 open site
Certified normal accommodation 1,003
Operational capacity 1,278
Visits telephone: 0300 060 6503
Visiting Times: House blocks 1-6: Mon - Thurs: 14:00 - 16:45; Fri: 14:30 - 16:30; Sat & Sun: 09.30 - 11.30 & 14.30 - 16.30
Brief history HMP Hewell is a large category B local prison in Worcestershire, holding up to 900 adult male prisoners. The prison had a high churn and continued to serve the courts and manage many short-term sentences throughout the national restrictions. At the time of the last Inspection (August 2020) almost a quarter of prisoners had had their licences revoked, some of whom had been recalled for very short periods. This added to the challenges faced by the prison.
The six house blocks have single and double cells, all with in-cell sanitation. House blocks 1, 2 A&C spur, 3 B&C spur and 6 - Convicted and unconvicted prisoners House block 2 A&C spur 3 C Spur - Induction/first night unit. House block 4 - Prisoners with drug or alcohol issues. House block 5, 2B spur - Vulnerable prisoners. Segregation Unit. Inpatients' Unit for those with health issues.

Visits book online: gov.uk/prison-visits or by email or telephone
visitsbooking.westmidlands@noms.gsi.gov.uk
Booking line: 0300 060 6503 Mon-Fri 0915-1600
Visiting times:
Monday: 8:45am to 11am and 1:15pm to 4pm.
Wednesday: 8:45am to 11am and 1:15pm to 4pm. Friday: 8:45am to 11am and 1:15pm to 4pm. Saturday: 8:45am to 11am and 1:15pm to 4pm. Sunday: 8:45am to 11am and 1:15pm to 4pm
Governor/Director Ralph Lubkowski
Escort contractor GEOAmey
Health service provider Care UK
Education Milton Keynes College
IMB chair Rodger Lawrence

HMP HIGHDOWN
HIGHDOWN LANE
SUTTON, SURREY SM2 5PJ
Tel: 0207 147 6300 Fax: 0207 147 6301
Public sector male category B local prison
Prison status Public
Region Greater London
CNA 1001, OpCap 1153
Healthcare: Central and North-west London NHS Foundation Trust (CNWL)
Substance misuse: The Forward Trust
Prison education framework provider: Novus
Brief history
HMP High Down was built on the site of the former mental health hospital in Banstead and opened in 1992. Since 2009, two new residential houseblocks, a new gymnasium and an Educational Centre with 21 classrooms have been added to the site.
Short description of residential units
Each HB holds just under 200 prisoners
Houseblock 1 – general houseblock with protective isolation unit
Houseblock 2 – includes reverse cohort unit
Houseblock 3 – general houseblock
Houseblock 4 – substance misuse
Houseblock 5 – general houseblock
Houseblock 6 – VPU
Segregation unit: holding up to 21 prisoners
Inpatient unit holding up to 23 prisoners
Governor Jo Sims
IMB chair Sheila Souchard and Andrea Coady
Last Inspection 13th May 2021: *We found a troubled prison confronting difficult, long-term challenges. It is a serious indictment of HMPPS leadership that the governor and her team should have been asked to spend so much of the pandemic distracted by a change in function which was ultimately suspended. The prison leadership need an early, definite and final decision on the future direction of the establishment and category C prisoners who were brought to High Down deserve to know how their needs will be met to help them emerge from prison with less risk of reoffending.*
Visits - Booking line: 020 7147 6570 - open Monday to Wednesday 10am to midday and 2pm to 4pm, Thursday and Friday 10am to midday. No online booking service available.
Email: SocialVisits.HighDown@justice.gov.uk
Visiting times: Tuesday to Thursday: 9:30am to 10:30am and 2:30pm to 3:30pm. Monday and Friday: Video Visits only

HMP HIGH POINT
STRADISHALL
NEWMARKET SUFFOLK, CB8 9YG
Tel: 01440 743100 Fax: 01440 743092
Highpoint is a Cat C training and resettlement prison situated in Suffolk on the site of a former Royal Air Force base. It is a large establishment, holding a little under 1,300 prisoners and is spread over two sites, North and South, and uses many of the buildings from its days as an RAF facility.
CNA 1,287. OpCap 1,325
Visits: telephone booking - 01440 743 134 - no online booking service available. Booking line: Mon-Fri, 8am to 2pm
Highpoint North visiting times:
Friday: 3:30pm 4.30pm
Saturday: 3:30pm 4.30pm
Sunday: 3:30pm 4.30pm

Highpoint South visiting times:
Monday: 2:45pm to 3:45pm
Friday: 2:45pm to 3:45pm
Saturday: 2:45pm to 3:45pm
Sunday: 10am to 11am and 2:45pm to 3:45pm
Accommodation
South site
10 units (1-10) A number of units were reserved for prisoners on the enhanced level of the IEP scheme, others enabled prisoners to spend more time out of their cells. The integrated drug treatment system and drug recovery departments were also housed in two of these units.
A segregation unit was also included.
North site
6 units (11-16) A number of units were reserved for prisoners on the enhanced level of the IEP scheme, others enabled prisoners to spend more time out of their cells. Unit 16 accommodated a small number of prisoners involved in a pilot project providing them with additional support.
Name of governor - Nigel Smith
IMB chair Susan Feary
Last Inspection: August 2019
The strength of relationships between staff and prisoners had created a collaborative environment that was focused on establishing and maintaining a safe, decent and purposeful community. This marked Highpoint out from many of its comparator prisons, and there was much here from which others could learn. In particular, the visibility and active involvement of the senior leadership in checking and maintaining decent standards across the prison were notable. Within a three-week cycle, every one of the prison's 1,181 cells are checked by a member of the senior leadership team. Many prisoners commented positively to us about the leadership, and in our survey 58% of prisoners said they regularly saw senior leaders talking to prisoners. The figure for similar prisons is 10%.

HMP HINDLEY
GIBSON STREET
BICKERSHAW, WIGAN LANCS, WN2 5TH
Tel: 01942 663100 Fax: 01942 663101
Public Category C adult male prison and YOI
CNA 590. OpCap 590
Key providers
Physical and mental health provider: Greater Manchester Mental Health NHS Trust
Substance use treatment Phoenix Futures
Prison education framework provider: Novus
Prison group: Greater Manchester, Merseyside and Cheshire
Brief history
Hindley was originally opened in 1961 as a borstal and became a youth custody centre in 1983. In 1989, two additional wings – E and F – were built, and in 2019, the Acorn unit reopened as a preparation psychologically informed planned environment (PIPE), following refurbishment. The establishment has undergone a number of population changes and is now a young offender and adult male category C establishment. The two populations are housed separately.
Short description of residential units
A wing: up to 83 sentenced adult prisoners
B wing: up to 76 sentenced adult prisoners
C wing: up to 84 sentenced adult prisoners
D wing: up to 84 sentenced adult prisoners
E wing: up to 125 sentenced adult prisoners
F wing: up to 128 sentenced aged 18-21
Acorn PIPE unit: up to 10 adult and YO's
Willow unit: Segregation unit 11 cells
Name of governor Natalie McKee
IMB Chair Maggie Maudsley
 Last Inspection April 2021: *Staff and prisoners had managed well since the start of the pandemic, balancing the need for restrictions to remain COVID-19-safe with some creative adaptations, which allowed for support to be provided where needed. Positive relationships between staff and prisoners had been a strength, and the impetus to maintain decent living conditions had continued throughout the COVID-19 period. The challenge remains for the prison to understand better and tackle rising levels of violence as well as continue to implement positive practice developed during the pandemic in future recovery plans.*

HMP YOI HOLLESLEY BAY
WOODBRIDGE
SUFFOLK, IP12 3JW
Tel: 01394 412400 Fax: 01394 410115
Public: Hollesley Bay is a Cat D open prison for adult and young adult men.
CNA 482. OpCap 485
Book visits 01394 412 559 - open Mon-Thu 9am to midday and 1pm to 4pm-5pm there is no online booking service available.
Visiting times: Sat/Sun 2pm to 3:45pm
Last Inspection 5th March 2019
Physical/Mental health provider: PPG
Substance misuse: Phoenix Futures
Learning and skills provider: People Plus
Escort contractor: Serco Wincanton
Prison group Hertfordshire, Essex and Suffolk
Brief history
In the late 1800s, Hollesley Bay was a training camp for men being sent out to the colonies, predominantly Canada, teaching farming and husbandry skills. The first governor took post in 1938, and since then the prison has been a borstal, then a YOI it then underwent a merger with HMP Warren Hill, followed by an unmerging and today is Cat D Open prison.
Short description of residential units
There are nine residential units:
Blything – a 42-bed unit holding prisoners on their first night and during induction; it also contains medical use rooms for residents who need in-room toilets.
Hoxon 82-bed, Cosford 72-bed, Stow 76-bed, Bosmere 80-bed, Wilforde 72-bed all normal location units
Samforde 15-bed unit over 50's unit
Threadling a self-contained bungalow
Mutford 43-bed unit housing outworkers
Governor Gary Newnes
Escort contractor Serco
Healthcare: PPG
Learning and skills providers A4E
IMB chair Guy Baly

HMP HOLME HOUSE
HOLME HOUSE RD
STOCKTON- ON-TEES TS18 2QU
Tel: 01642 744000 Fax: 01642 744001
Public sector male Cat C trainer.
CNA 1036, OpCap 1210
Physical health provider: Spectrum

Mental health: Tees,Mental Health Trust
Substance misuse: G4S
Prison group Tees and Wear
Brief history The prison opened in May 1992. It expanded in the late 1990s with the building of two further house blocks, providing 235 additional places. Two new workshops opened in 1997 and an additional house block, with 224 places, opened in 2010, along with two further regimes buildings, providing activity places for around 200 prisoners. In June 2016, it was announced that HMP Holme House would be one of six reform prisons. In 2017, it re-roled from a purpose-built category B prison to its current Cat C trainer role.
Short description of residential units
House block 1A/ B wing Sentenced prisoners
House block1 C wing 'Own protection' unit
House block 2,3,4,5 Sentenced prisoners
House block 6 A Therapeutic community
House block 6 B wing Sentenced prisoners
House block 7 Unit Sex Offenders
Segregation unit
Name of governor Sean Ormerod
IMB Chair Brenda Kirby
Date of last inspection 17th June 2020:
Overall the prison was falling well short of a category C prison, it was still not safe enough. Reception of new prisoners were inadequate, much more could have been done to improve the safety and well-being of prisoners and reduce violence still further. More attention was also needed to ensure that the use of force was always fully accounted for, while both the regime and relationships between staff and prisoners in the segregation unit required improvement. There has been three Self-inflicted deaths since the last inspection and instances of self-harm had increased.

- 52 -

HMP HULL

HEDON ROAD, HULL, HU9 5LS
Tel: 01482 282200 Fax: 01482 282400
HMP Hull is a public male local prison.
CNA: 723. OpCap 1,044
Book your visit by telephone 01482 282 016, open Mon-Fri 0800-1230. No online booking.
Visiting times: Mon, Fri, Sat, Sun: 8:30am to 11:45am and 1:30pm to 4:45pm
Physical health, mental health and substance misuse provider: City Health Care
Learning and skills provider: Novus
Escort contractor: GEOAmey
Yorkshire Prisons Group
Brief history
Opened in 1870, HMP Hull originally held men and women. In 1939, it became a military prison and was later used as a civil defence depot. It reopened as a closed men's borstal in 1950 and in 1969, it became one of the first maximum security dispersal prisons. In 1986, HMP Hull assumed its role as a men's local prison and remand centre. In 2002, four wings as well as a new health care centre, sports hall and multi-faith centre were added, and other parts of the prison, including the kitchen, education and workshops, were refurbished.
Short description of residential units
A wing: General wing including the PIPE and drug recovery units
A, C and D wings: Sentenced and unsentenced adults and young offenders
F wing: Well-being unit
G wing: First night and induction wing
H, I and J wings: Vulnerable prisoners
K wing: VPU
Name of governor Shaun Mycroft
Date of last inspection April 2018: *HMP Hull is a prison doing its best and this is an encouraging report. Strong leadership and a positive staff culture underpinned, in our view, the maintenance of reasonably good outcomes during challenging times. There seemed to us to be a strong sense of community at the prison that combined the positive characteristics of a prison proud of its traditions, a culture of competence and an openness to new ideas and creativity. We saw plenty of evidence of managers and staff being keen to embrace new work. There is, as ever, more to do, but the governor and his staff should be commended for their hard work and achievements.*

HMP HUMBER

BROUGH, YORKSHIRE HU15 1RB
TEL: 01430 273000 FAX: 01430 428001
Public Male Category C Trainer prison
Yorkshire Group CNA 952. OpCap 1,062
Visits - book by phone only - 0300 060 6606 open Mon-Fri 9-11am and 1-3pm
Visiting time: Mon-Wed-Fri 1:30pm to 3:30pm
Last Inspection 8th December 2020: *Prisoners located on F and H wings had very little time unlocked. On most days, this was 50 minutes for showers, cell cleaning and outdoor exercise, and on Fridays this was only 20 minutes in total, with no time outside.*
The complaints system was not working well. In our survey, 26% of prisoners said that they could not make a complaint easily. Complaint forms were not readily available, and the arrangements for collecting complaints from the secure post boxes and dealing with allegations of discrimination were poor. Responses to complaints often failed to deal with all the issues raised, and some (including serious allegations about staff) were not investigated appropriately.
There was no reliable means of identifying prisoners with protected and minority characteristics, and their needs were not being systematically assessed or monitored, or their interests protected or promoted.
Healthcare: City Health; Education: Novus.
HMP Humber was formed in June 2013 by the amalgamation of two former prisons, HMP Everthorpe (originally opened as a borstal in 1958) and HMP Wolds (opened in 1992 as a category B establishment, and the first privately run prison in Europe).
Short description of residential units
Zone 1 comprises wings A to G. These are small, open-gallery units.

- 53 -

Zone 2 comprises wings H to N. Apart from a modern induction block, these are mostly older, tier-style units, and include the segregation unit.
Name of governor: Marcella Goligher
IMB Chair Paul Holland

HMP HUNTERCOMBE
NUFFIELD
HENLEY ON THAMES OXON, RG9 5SB
Tel: 01491 643100 Fax: 01491 643101
Public Category C foreign national prison
CNA 381. Opcap 480
Health provider: Practice Plus Group
Education: Milton Keynes College
Escort contractor: Serco/GeoAmey for serving prisoners; Mitie for immigration detainees
Prison group Foreign nationals IRC
Visits - book by phone only 01491 643195 open Tue,Wed,Thurs 10am-12pm
Visiting time: Sat/Sun 2-4pm
Brief history
The site was originally built as an internment camp. After World War II the site opened as a prison and was a Borstal until 1983. In 2000 Huntercombe became a prison for male juveniles aged 15 to 18. In November 2010 the establishment re-roled to an adult category C training prison and since March 2012 it has held solely category C foreign national prisoners, one of two prisons of this type.
Short description of residential units
The establishment has eight units. Patterson, Rich, Howard and Fry Units have an older style layout, with two levels and four closed spurs. Mountbatten A and B Units have a newer open layout on two levels and Mountbatten C comprises 26 portable cabins in a horseshoe formation. The segregation unit has five cells including one constant watch suite. Patterson Unit is the induction unit, Rich Unit is for enhanced prisoners and all other units consist of regular accommodation.
Name of governor David Redhouse
IMB Chair John Evans
Date of last inspection 19th January 2021: 33% *of prisoners said they had been victimised by staff; this by significantly more younger prisoners and BAME inmates saying staff were dismissive of their concerns about the time they spent locked up, worries about immigration cases, and concern* about inconsistent social distancing. The incentives scheme was being used inappropriately to sanction prisoners who were in dispute with the Home Office over immigration status claims. The prison's role of managing and caring for prisoners had become confused with Home Office procedures. Most prisoners were still locked in their cells for about 23 hours a day.

HMP ISIS
THAMESMEAD LONDON, SE28 0NZ
TEL: 0203 356 4000 FAX: 0203 356 4001
Public young adult and category C training prison for young adult and adult males
Group: London
CNA 478. OpCap 628
Visits - book by phone only on 020 3356 4034 open Mon-Fri 8-12pm, 1.30-5pm
Visiting time: Mon-Thurs 2-4.30pm
Healthcare: Oxleas NHS Foundation Trust
Learning and skills provider: Novus
Escort contractor: Serco
Brief history
HMP/YOI Isis in South East London was the first young adult and category C training prison for young men and adults in the London region. Constructed within the perimeter of HMP Belmarsh, it received its first prisoners on 26 July 2010. In December 2016, the age cap of 18–30 was lifted, allowing prisoners of all ages to be transferred to Isis.
Short description of residential units
The two house blocks, Thames and Meridian, are of a similar size, with four spurs radiating from a central hub and three landings on each spur. On average, there is accommodation for about 80 prisoners on each spur in a mixture of single and double cells. There are fully-equipped cells for prisoners with disabilities.

Governor Emily Thomas.
IMB Chair Peter Ward
Date of last inspection 2nd August 2018:
Prisoners still did not spend enough time in education or training, and those on vocational courses often did not have time to gain accredited qualifications. Poor attendance and punctuality contributed significantly to Ofsted's judgement that the overall effectiveness of education, skills and work required improvement. Prisoners were supported to build and maintain family ties, but a shortfall of offender assessment system (OASys) assessments impacted prisoners' ability to progress through their sentence. Offender management and the quality of supervision were mixed and there were weaknesses in public protection arrangements. Support for care leavers and resettlement planning were, however, better.

HMP ISLE OF WIGHT
NEWPORT, ISLE OF WIGHT PO30 5RS
Tel: 01983 634000 Fax: 01983 556345
Public Category B male training prison. It also has a small local remand function. The prison holds approximately 1,100 prisoners on two sites, Albany and Parkhurst.
Group South Central. CNA 1073. OpCap 1085
Visits - book by phone only on 01983 634 000 open Mon-Fri 10-12pm, pm-4pm
Visiting time: Mon,Fri,Sat,Sun 2.30-3.30pm (8th October 2021 visits were suspended due to a Covid outbreak so check with the prison.
Brief history HMP Isle of Wight opened in April 2009 with the merger of three prisons: HMP Albany, HMP Parkhurst and HMP Camp Hill. HMP Albany was constructed in the 1960s and occupies the site of a former military barracks. HMP Parkhurst was originally a military hospital and became a prison in 1863. HMP Camp Hill was built in 1912 using prisoner labour from HMP Parkhurst, but closed in April 2013.
Short description of residential units
Albany - the five original residential units (house blocks 11 to 17) on Albany are identical in design and located off one main corridor. In 2010 a new health care facility opened, replacing the former unit in Parkhurst. House block 15 is currently uninhabited following a fire in January 2015.
Albany has no internal sanitation in cells on house blocks 11 to 15. An electronic night sanitation system is in operation in these units. The remand unit on house block 16 has internal sanitation as does the assisted living unit on house block 17.
Parkhurst - comprises eight residential units, seven of which are Victorian galleried units and the eighth a small former health care unit. There is also a recently refurbished segregation and reintegration unit in a former special secure unit.
Governor/Director Dougie Graham
Escort contractor GeoAmey
Healthcare: Practice Plus Group
Education: Milton Keynes College
IMB chair Linda Johnson
Last Inspection: December 2019: *HMP Isle of Wight is a respectful place where good relationships between frontline staff and prisoners result in many positive outcomes. However, there needs to be a better operational grip on safety. Managers need to address the weaknesses in offender management to ensure the prison fulfils its purpose of reducing the risks these long-term prisoners pose, both within the prison and, importantly, when they are eventually released.*

HMP KIRKHAM
KIRKHAM, PRESTON PR4 2RN
Tel: 01772 675400 Fax: 01772 675401
Public Category D open prison
Group: Cumbria & Lancashire
CNA 589. OpCap 657
Visits are booked by the prisoner .
Enquiries only: kirkham@hmps.gsi.gov.uk
Visiting times: Thurs-Sun: 2.30pm to 3.15pm, 13.15 to 2pm
Healthcare: Spectrum Community Health
Learning and skills provider: Novus
Escort contractor: GEOAmey

Brief history
HMP Kirkham occupies the site of a former Royal Air Force technical training centre. The facility was taken over by the Home Office in the early 1960s and has been in use as a prison since 1962. Prisoner accommodation was built over the period 1990 –1999 but other parts of the prison date back to the 1940s.
Short description of residential units
25 small residential units, known as billets
77-bed admissions unit, including a reception and first night centre
Name of governor Derek Harrison
Date of last inspection 5 July 2018: *Despite the previous inspection report setting out serious concerns about staff – prisoner relationships, we found that prisoners' perceptions of their treatment by staff had deteriorated further. Far more prisoners than at other open prisons felt victimised, and fewer than at the time of the previous inspection said that staff treated them respectfully. During the inspection, many prisoners gave us examples of poor staff attitudes, which undermined the positive ethos of the prison.*

HMP KIRKLEVINGTON GRANGE
YARM, TEESSIDE TS15 9PA
Tel: 01642 792600 Fax: 01642 792601
Public male Category D resettlement prison
Group: Tees and Wear
CNA 283. OpCap 283
Visits: All social visits are booked by prisoners
Visiting times:
Tues, Thurs, Sat and Sun: 1:40pm to 2:40pm and 3:05pm to 4:05pm
How to book legal and professional visits
visitsbooking.kirklevington@hmps.gsi.gov.uk
Prisoners are allowed community visits after an initial risk assessment.
Physical healthcare: G4S Health Services (UK)
Learning and skills provider: Novus
Escort contractor: GEOAmey
Brief history
Kirklevington Grange was a detention centre for children before re-roling as a resettlement prison holding mostly category D adult male prisoners. It expanded more recently to include young adults to enable men between 18 to 21 to progress to open conditions in an area closer to their home.
Short description of residential units

A, B, C, J units have communal showers, toilets and a kitchenette with some cooking facilities F unit is the induction unit with communal showers, toilets and a kitchenette
G unit has a kitchenette but no showers toilets
H unit has a bath and toilets but no kitchenette
R unit has showers and toilets as well as a kitchenette.
D, E, K, L units all rooms are en-suite, there is a kitchenette.
Name of governor Rebecca Newby
IMB Chair Colin Stratton
Date of last inspection 23rd August 2019. *Kirklevington Grange was a safe, decent and purposeful place where prisoners ' needs were being met. The prison was well led, staff knew their prisoners well and the regime on offer was purposeful. Prisoners appeared to be responding positively to the opportunities they were being given. We left the prison with a small number of recommendations .*

HMP LANCASTER FARMS
LANCASTER,
LA1 3QZ. Tel: 01524 563450
Public Cat C Trainer.
Prison Group Cumbria and Lancashire
CNA 495. OpCap 560.
Book visits by phone only: 01524 563 636 open Mon-Fri 9am-12pm
Monday to Friday, 9am to midday
Email:lancasterfarmsdomesticvisitsbooking@hmps.gsi.gov.uk (enquiries only)
Visiting times:
Tues/Wed: 2pm to 3pm and 3.30pm to 4.30pm
Sunday: 1:45pm to 2:45pm and 3:15 to 4:15pm
Healthcare: Spectrum Community Health
Learning and skills provider: Novus
Brief history: The prison opened in 1993 as a remand centre and young offender institution

(YOI). In 2008–2009, it became the sole dedicated YOI for the north west. In 2011, the establishment changed its role from a category B YOI to a category C YOI training prison. In 2014, the prison became a category C resettlement prison for adults.
Short description of residential units
Grizedale – First night centre
Coniston 1 – Well-being unit
Coniston 2 – General population
Derwent – General population
Windermere – General population
Buttermere – General population
Ullswater – Segregation unit
Governor: Pete Francis
Date of last inspection 12th March 2019: *Lancaster Farms remained a competent prison enabled by a capable management team and a generally confident staff. There was a definite sense that if you were a motivated prisoner with a determination to improve your own life chances, there were opportunities and resources that were available for you in the prison. In contrast, if you were less motivated, you could easily opt out with too little challenge from the institution. This was a missed opportunity.*

HMP LEEDS
2 GLOUCESTER TERRACE
STANNINGLEY ROAD
LEEDS, WEST YORKS LS12 2TJ
Tel: 0113 203 2600 Fax: 0113 203 2601
Public male local prison.
Prison Group Yorkshire
CNA 687. OpCap 1131
Visits phone booking only 01132 032 995. open Mon-Fri 8-10am,12-2pm. Email Enquiries socialvisits.leeds@hmps.gsi.gov.uk
Visiting times: Thur-Sun 9-10:30am, 2- 3:30pm
Healthcare: PPG
Escort contractor: GEOAmey
Brief history
The establishment was built in 1847 and originally comprised four wings. Two further wings were added in 1993.
Short description of residential units
A, B, C, E wings hold adult male convicted prisoners and those on remand. A wing is an incentivised drug-free living unit, which accommodates those who wish to engage in therapeutic activities to support a substance free lifestyle. The segregation unit is on A1 landing. D wing accommodates adult male convicted prisoners and those on remand, along with those stabilising from the effects of drugs and alcohol. The first night D1 landing. F wing is the vulnerable prisoner unit
Governor Steve Robson
Date of last inspection 24th March 2020: *It is right to acknowledge again the challenges in running a prison like Leeds. The level of need among prisoners was great, the environment required constant work and attention in order that minimum standards could be maintained and the operational context required real grip. Overall, though, we were encouraged by what we saw. Leeds could not yet be described as cultivating a rehabilitative culture as aspired to by HM Prison and Probation Service (HMPPS), but we could see some very important work being done and improvements were evident. The Governor and his team deserve acknowledgement for what they have achieved so far. Priorities going forward, as we would see them, include further improvements in safety outcomes, notably safeguarding those at risk of self- harm, and getting prisoners out of cell and into purposeful activity with greater consistency.*

HMP LEICESTER
WELFORD ROAD
LEICESTER LE2 7AJ
Tel: 01162 283 000 Fax: 01162 283 001
Public male local prison
CNA 217. OpCap 300.
Healthcare provider: Nottinghamshire NHS
Education: People Plus
Prison group East Midlands
HMP Leicester is a Victorian prison built in 1874, behind a gatehouse dating back to 1825. It occupies a site of three acres, close to Leicester city centre. A visits and administration block was added in 1990.
HMP Leicester is predominantly made up of one large residential wing, separated into landings and units. Landing 1: (subterranean) the Parson's Unit (enhanced/workers'), Lambert Unit (re-integration) and segregation. Landing 2: mainstream population with the shielding unit attached. Landing 3: mainstream population and the reverse cohort unit. Landing 4: mainstream population, prisoner isolation unit and additional reverse

cohort unit spaces. Welford Unit: prisoners convicted of sexual offences and VPs.
Governor Jim Donaldson
IMB Chair Irene Peat
Date of last inspection 27th January 2021: *Managers, staff and prisoners had responded well to the early stages of the pandemic with a focus on reducing the risk of transmission and maintaining an environment safe from COVID-19. The continuing local community restrictions had understandably affected some aspects of recovery, but progress had been slow in re-introducing key strategic meetings and consultations with prisoners. More focus was needed on reducing the high levels of self-harm. The reduction in violence was welcome, but an emergency restricted regime is not a long-term solution to keeping prisoners safe and strategic planning will be needed to maintain any improvement when recovery from the pandemic gathers pace.*

HMP LEWES
BRIGHTON RD, LEWES
EAST SUSSEX, BN7 1EA
Tel: 01273 785100 Fax: 01273 785101
Public category B/C men's resettlement.
CNA 617. OpCap 692
Visits phone booking only: 01273 785 277 open everyday, 8am to 5pm
Visiting times
Monday to Wednesday: 2pm to 3:30pm
Friday: 9am to 10.30am
Saturday and Sunday: 2pm to 3:30pm
Health provider: Sussex NHS Foundation Trust
Substance misuse provider: The Forward Trust
Learning and skills provider: Novus
Escort contractor: GEOAmey
Prison group: Kent, Surrey and Sussex
Brief history
HMP Lewes was built in 1853 as the county prison for Sussex. It has a semi-radial design and is half a mile from the town centre of Lewes. In 2007, a new house block was completed, which created 174 places in two attached wings, plus a new workshop, gym, visits hall, multi-faith centre and several new classrooms. F wing was refurbished in 2012.
Short description of residential units
A wing: drug and alcohol support (recovery unit) for 134 prisoners C wing: 150 places. F wing: VPU. G wing: first night centre. K wing:

drug and alcohol stabilisation unit. L wing: 80 places. M wing: 94 places. Health care unit: 11 prisoners
Governor Hannah Lane,
IMB Chair Mary Bell
Date of last inspection January 2019: *Overall a very disappointing inspection that brings into question the utility of 'special measures' if a prison can decline so badly when supposedly benefiting from them for a full two years. It also validates the Inspectorate's new Independent Reviews of Progress, which are specifically designed to give ministers a report of progress against previous inspection reports at struggling prisons such as Lewes. The decline at HMP Lewes has to be arrested and reversed.*

HMP LEYHILL
WOTTON-UNDER-EDGE
GLOUC, GL12 8BT
Tel: 01454 264000 Fax: 01454 264001
Public male open prison
CNA: 492. OpCap: 497
Healthcare: Inspire Better Health
Education: Weston College
Prison group Avon and South Dorset
The prison first opened with hutted accommodation in 1946. It was then rebuilt in the late 1970s to early 1980s, and in 1986 residents were rehoused in new living accommodation. In 2002, again, new accommodation units were added, to create C unit. An expansion of two 60-bed units is expected to start later in 2021. At present, there is long-awaited refurbishment work ongoing to both the roofs of the industries building and washroom facilities.
Short description of residential units
• Ash unit holds 208 prisoners

- 58 -

- Beech unit holds 199 prisoners and has a facility for diables prisoners
- Cedar unit holds 108 enhanced prisoners. The establishment has a purpose-built end-of-life palliative unit.

Governor Steve Hodson
Date of last inspection 7th April 2021: *Staff–prisoner relationships had deteriorated since the inspection in 2016. Only 64% of prisoners said that they felt respected by staff, and almost a third that they had experienced bullying or victimisation by staff. Prisoners spoke negatively about their experience and staff were not visible on the residential units. Black and minority ethnic prisoners had even poorer perceptions of treatment; only 43% of these prisoners said that they felt respected by staff, and almost two-thirds that they were bullied or victimised by staff. Prisoners from this group were not engaged in equality focus groups and said that they felt targeted by staff because of their ethnicity, and were afraid to speak up for fear of repercussions.*
Video-call visits were proving increasingly popular but were not well enough resourced. Nearly 200 prisoners had signed up to the scheme, but only 36 prisoners could benefit each week and, when we arrived, there was a three-week wait for a visit.

HMP LINCOLN
GREETWELL ROAD
LINCOLN, LN2 4BD
Tel: 01522 663000 Fax: 01522 663001
Public Category B male local prison.
CNA 408. OpCap 664
Health provider: Nottinghamshire NHS
Prison group East Midlands Prison Group
Visits: book by phone only 01522 663 172 - open Mon-Fri: 9:30am to midday
Visiting times Thur, Sat, Sun: 9am to 11am and 2pm to 4pm
Brief history
Lincoln opened in 1872. Parts of the prison are grade II listed buildings, and three of the four main residential units are the original Victorian design. E wing was opened in 1992.
Short description of residential units
All wings hold a mixture of remand, convicted and sentenced adult and young adult prisoners.
A wing up to 216 prisoners (currently 196); includes the first night centre and induction landing. B wing up to 150 prisoners. C wing up to 198 prisoners. E wing up to 165 VPs
Governor Andy Burton (A)
IMB Chairs Norma Krawiec/Jeremy Taylor
Date of last inspection 15th April 2020: *The Governor should be commended for the work they have done at Lincoln. Progress at the prison was predicated on the quality of staff-prisoner relationships and very constructive partnerships. There was attention to getting the basics right in most areas but also space for innovation and creativity. There was lots still to be done and many of the problems like overcrowding had an intractability that required HMPPS intervention to support the prison. We were confident, however, that the Governor and staff were committed to ensuring continuous improvement.*

HMP LINDHOLME
BAWTRY ROAD
HATFIELD WOODHOUSE
DONCASTER, DN7 6EE
TEL: 01302 524700 FAX: 01302 524750
Public Category C adult male prison
CNA 935, OpCap 935
Visits book by phone only on 01302 524 980 open Mon-Fri 9-11am and 1:30-3:30pm
Visiting times everyday except Tues & Thurs 2:15pm to 3:15pm
Health provider: Practice Plus Group
Escort contractor: GEOAmey
Prison group Yorkshire
Brief history
HMP Lindholme was previously an RAF camp and opened as a prison in 1985. It currently holds category C convicted males over 21, including life sentence prisoners.
Short description of residential units
Ten wings with single and multi-occupancy

- 59 -

rooms. Six of the wings are of a dormitory design and have single and multi-occupancy rooms on lockable spurs.
Governor Rob Kellett
Date of last inspection 1st December 2020: *Prisoners were frustrated at the lack of contact with their prison offender manager and the inability to progress with their sentence plan. The measures for public protection were a concern, with five high-risk prisoners released during the pandemic restrictions without confirmation of their MAPPA. Although not a designated resettlement prison, Lindholme had released about 20 prisoners a month. Despite this, 10 prisoners released in the previous three months had no accommodation to go to on their day of release. Since the previous inspection there had clearly been progress, with significant improvements in prison safety. It was especially disappointing, therefore, to find such an excessively poor regime exacerbating mounting frustration, and the deterioration of well-being for many prisoners. There was a clear need for managers and local staff associations to come to an agreement about safe and credible plans that would allow the prison regime to develop and ensure outcomes for those detained improved.*

HMP LITTLEHEY
PERRY, HUNTINGDON
CAMBS, PE28 0SR
Tel: 01480 335000 Fax: 01480 335070
Public Cat C for sex offenders.
CNA: 1,154. OpCap: 1,220
Healthcare: Northamptonshire NHS Trust
Learning and skills provider: PeoplePlus
Prison group Beds Cambs Norfolk
In 1988, the prison opened as a male category C. In January 2010, there was an extensive expansion to the current site, to accommodate a population of up to 480 young offenders. In 2014, the prison re-roled to an all adult male category C establishment holding residents convicted of sexual offences.
A, B, D, K, L wings General Population
E wing Induction unit
F, G wings Enhanced
H wing Accredited enabling environment
I & J Elderly unit with support
M wing IPP Unit
Wings A–H are on the original site and are referred to locally as Lakeside. Wings I–M are on the newer site and are referred to locally as Woodlands.
Governor Olivia Phelps
IMB Chair - Harry Chandler
Date of last inspection 2–13 March 2015: *The area where outcomes were weakest was in rehabilitation and release planning. The promotion of family ties needed improvement. About half of prisoners did not have an up-to-date OASys assessment which was concerning given the high risk population. Contact between offender supervisors and prisoners was inconsistent and often reactive, with very little one-to-one sentence planning work taking place. Overall and despite some criticisms, this report reflects some very good findings and some excellent outcomes for prisoners.*

HMP LIVERPOOL
68 HORNBY ROAD
WALTON, LIVERPOOL L9 3DF
Tel: 0151 530 4000 Fax No. 0151 530 4001
Public male local category B.
CNA 1,173. OPCap 700
Healthcare provider: Spectrum
Education provider: Novus
Escort contractor: GeoAmey
Prison group GMMC
Visits must be booked by phone on 0151 530 4050 open Mon-Fri: 8:30am to 4:30pm
Visiting: Mon-Fri sessions 1.30pm-4.30pm
HMP Liverpool was constructed in 1855 to replace a much older establishment. The prison holds remand and convicted men in addition to a vulnerable prisoner population. There are eight wings, two of which have been refurbished. One wing is currently closed for refurbishment. There is also an inpatient facility located in the health care unit.
Short description of residential units

A Wing: Drug dependency unit
B Wing: First night centre - B1 Seg Unit
F, G, H, I, Wings: General wings
J Wing: Wellbeing unit
K Wing: VPU
Governor: Mark Livingston
IMB Chair John Hudson
Date of last inspection January 2020: *I hope both the words of this report and the grades awarded by the inspection recognise the work done - but there was still a huge amount of work to do. As we have seen in other prisons improvements can prove to be fragile, and I very much hope this will not prove to be the case at Liverpool, with the necessary support continuing from HMPPS. Encouragingly, despite all that has been achieved, I saw no signs of complacency within the establishment. It was very clear to me that senior managers were operating as a cohesive team in support of enormously energetic and respected leadership, and not as a group of individuals focusing only on their functional responsibilities. I am sure this has been the key to their success so far and will need to be maintained into the future if the work of transforming HMP Liverpool is to be completed.*

HMP LONG LARTIN
SOUTH LITTLETON
EVESHAM, WORCS WR11 8TZ
Tel: 01386 295100 Fax: 01386 295101
Public Maximum Security Dispersal prison.
CNA: 609. OpCap: 609
Health provider: Practice Plus Group
Education provider: Milton Keynes College
Escort contractor: GEOAmey
Prison group Long term high security estate
Long Lartin was built in the 1960s as a war department ordnance depot and opened as a prison in 1971.
Originally a category C prison, it was upgraded to provide dispersal-level security in 1973. Further improvements in security were made between 1995 and 1997 and an additional wing, Perrie, was opened in June 1999. In 2009, a new purpose-built unit, Atherton (E and F wings), replaced older-style wings, increasing the capacity of the prison.
Short description of residential units
A and B Older-style wings without in-cell sanitation, currently holding vulnerable prisoners. C and D Older-style wings without in-cell sanitation, currently holding mainstream prisoners. E and F Two wings in a modern unit with accommodation for 184 mainstream prisoners. Perrie A Modern unit with accommodation for up to 112 mainstream prisoners. Perrie Red has 74 single cells. Segregation Unit for 40 prisoners. Two cells are R46/close supervision centre.
Healthcare: 7 beds and one end of life cell. PIPE unit providing for 14 prisoners, both vulnerable and mainstream, who mix subject to risk assessment.
Governor Steve Cross, July 2019
Last Inspection February 2021: *HMP Long Lartin is part of the long term and high security prison estate. It holds some of the country's most dangerous and serious offenders, with two-thirds of the population serving life sentences and almost all of the rest serving more than 10 years. At the time of our visit, over 20% of those held were category A, the highest security classification, indicative of the risk being managed. This report outlines weaknesses in areas of prison life. The segregation unit subjected prisoners to a very austere regime for long periods without any reintegration planning. Planned use of force was very high, largely because of excessive use of handcuffs in the segregation unit, much of which went unrecorded. The prison's investigations into prisoner complaints were poor and sometimes carried out by the member of staff about whom the prisoner had complained. The system for investigating complaints into discrimination was in disarray and nearly half of allegations made in the previous three months had not received a response. Health care waiting lists were undermanaged, resulting in some waits of over a year to see the GP. There had been long delays in telephone monitoring of prisoner calls for public protection reasons.*

www.prisons.org.uk

Our concerns about these practices was compounded by the failure of leaders to establish effective oversight to identify or address any of them. We had little confidence that sustained progress was possible without a major improvement to governance and management.

HMP LOW NEWTON
BRASSIDE, DURHAM DH1 5YA.
Tel: 0191 376 4000 Fax: 0191 376 4001
HMP & YOI Low Newton is a women's local and resettlement prison in County Durham.
CNA 304. OpCat 344
Healthcare: Spectrum Community Health
Prison education provider: Novus
Escort contractor: GEOAmey
Prison department Women's estate
Low Newton was built in 1965 as a small remand centre for men and women. Additional accommodation was added in 1975 and the prison changed its role to a male young offender institute in 1976 with a small self-contained unit holding remand women. The prison became a women's prison in 1998.
Visits booked by phone only on 0300 303 0632 open Mon-Fri 0915-1600.
Visiting time: Tues, Thurs, Fri, Sun 2.30-3.30pm
Short description of residential units
A wing – 30; B wing – 31; C wing – 51; D wing – 52; E wing – 59 spaces; early days in custody unit; F wing – 40 long-term, lifers restricted status and Primrose unit (high-risk women)
G wing – recently decommissioned
D wing – 39 spaces PIPE unit.
Governor Rob Young
Prison Group Director Pia Sinha
Date of last inspection 2-18 June 2021: *It was very concerning the prison is being used as a 'place of safety' for women with acute mental health difficulties. The consequence of this policy designed to prevent seriously mentally ill women from languishing in police cells, has led to the problem being passed onto prisons, which are themselves an equally unsuitable environment. These women should be in hospital where they can be treated, not left in prison where they put an additional burden on already stretched resources. Women attending the health care department for their GP appointments could hear the constant screaming of one of the women. Despite the many examples of good practice we saw at the prison, women* continue to be locked in their cells for far too long and leaders must urgently begin to extend significantly the amount of time women are unlocked. There was very limited education provision, meaning that women who need to improve their basic learning, earn qualifications and acquire the skills that will help them to get work when they are released are not getting the help that they need to live safe, crime-free lives.

HMP LOWDHAM GRANGE

HMP LOWDHAM GRANGE
OLD EPPERSTONE ROAD
LOWDHAM NOTTINGHAM NG14 7DA
Tel: 0115 966 9200 Fax: 0115 966 9220
Category B training prison for adult men
Prison status Private Serco
CNA 884. OpCap 888.
All visits are booked by prisoners only.
Visiting Times: Mon, Tues, Weds, Thurs: 0930-1130, 1330-1530
Healthcare: Nottinghamshire NHS Trust
Education provider: Serco
Prison group Long term high security estate
The prison opened in February 1998 as an 'industrial prison' employing 300 prisoners in workshops with commercial partner companies. New house blocks of 128 places in 2007 and 260 places in 2010.
Short description of residential units
House blocks 1 & 2 Four residential wings
House blocks 3,4 & 5 Two residential wings
Director Mark Hanson
Date of last inspection February 2021: *Prisoners' access to the library was poor and the prison did not promote it enough as a resource, which was concerning given the need to promote in-cell activity to improve their well-being. Education staff were directly employed by Serco and had remained on site since March. Education leaders recognised that they had been too slow to*

- 62 -

reinstate a broad curriculum and, while it was good that the proportion of prisoners engaging in education had increased during this period, too few had had their new skills and knowledge accredited. The prison had taken far too long to introduce some critical aspects of prison life, such as family contact through Purple Visits video calling. Lack of staffing had limited the contact between prisoners and their prison offender manager for several months, and over half of the population had not received a review of their risk and sentence plan in the previous year. Recategorisation reviews were timely, but population pressures in other prisons often affected moves of prisoners to lower category prisons. Overall this is an encouraging report.

HMP MAIDSTONE
COUNTY ROAD MAIDSTONE, ME14 1UZ
Tel: 01622 775300 Fax: 01622 775301
Public Category C foreign national male prison.
CNA 565. OpCap 600.
Books visits by phone only on 01622 775 621, open Mon-Fri 0900-1230.
Visiting times: Tues, Thurs 2pm to 3:30pm
Healthcare: Oxleas NHS Foundation Trust
Substance misuse provider: Forward Trust
Education provider: Novus
Prison group FNP IRC
Brief history
Maidstone prison was originally built in 1819. The prison underwent a re-role in 2013 and is now a designated foreign national prison.
Short description of residential units
Kent unit - built in 1850, holds up to 178 prisoners in single cells. Medway unit - built in 1966, holds 101 prisoners in single cells. Thanet unit - built in 1909 and extended in the 1970s to hold 174 prisoners in single cells
Weald unit - built in 2009, holds 149 prisoners in single and double cells
Name of governor and date in post
Dave Atkinson, May 2013
Governor: Judith Feline
Date of last inspection February 2019: *Although the problems with education and employment needed to be taken very seriously and resolved as soon as possible, it was good to see that there had been improvements in two of our healthy prison tests. The prison was completely aware of the distinct needs of their population, although more needed to be done to understand the more* negative *perceptions of their treatment and conditions held by prisoners with protected characteristics. The establishment also needed support in terms of investment to get the fabric of the buildings back to an acceptable standard and facilities such as the sports hall restored.*

HMP MANCHESTER
SOUTHALL ST
MANCHESTER, M60 9AH
Tel: 0161 817 5600 Fax: 0161 817 5601
Public male core local with a discrete close supervision centre. Prison Group LTHSE
CNA 943. OpCap 1,136
Reception visits booking line: 0161 817 5655 open Mon-Fri 8am to 4pm. All other visits must be booked by the prisoner and all visiting times will be advised once booked.
Manchester Prison opened in June 1868.
A wing: first night/induction unit
B, D, G wings: general population
C wing long term and lifers and VDT
E wing inner: Category A unit
E wing outer: VPU and Seg
H wing: post-detoxification stabilisation unit
I wing: drug detoxification prescribing unit
K wing: VPU
M wing: health care inpatients' unit
Governor Rob Young
Date of last inspection July 2018: *During the inspection we found 40%, locked up during the working day, despite there being sufficient activity for all. Improvements were required in the quality of education and teaching practice, including the quality of some resources used in teaching. Too few learners made satisfactory progress and Ofsted judged all aspects of the provision as 'requires improvement'. Outcomes were undermined by gaps in strategy but offender management practice, while inconsistent, was good in many cases. Public protection work was generally good.*

HMP MOORLAND
BAWTRY ROAD
HATFIELD WOODHOUSE
DONCASTER, DN7 6BW
Tel: 01302 523000 Fax: 01302 523001
Public Category C resettlement prison.
CNA 957. OpCap 1006
Visits phone booking only on 01302 523 289.
Visiting times: Tues, Thurs, Sat 2-2.45pm
Healthcare: Practice Plus Group
Prison group Yorkshire
HMP Moorland opened in 1991 and today is a Cat C resettlement prison.
House block 1 – substance misuse treatment
House block 2 – first night centre
House blocks 3 and 4 – sexual offenders
House block 5 – includes the reintegration unit
House block 6 – drug-free environment
House block 7 – unit for older prisoners and integrated general population
Governor Jennifer Willis
Date of last inspection June 2019: *Overall this was a reassuring inspection, and shows what can be achieved even in difficult and testing times, but it would be unduly complacent not to acknowledge that improvement is necessary and achievable.*

HMP MORTON HALL
SWINDERBY, LINCOLN LN6 9PT
TEL: 01522 666700
Public category C **opens December 2021**
Brief history
Originally a Royal Air Force base, Morton Hall opened as a prison in 1985. New accommodation was added in 1996 and it was refitted in 2001 to provide facilities for women prisoners. Two more residential units were added in July 2002. In March 2009, Morton Hall, then a semi-open establishment, was turned into a closed prison, with a specialist role in managing foreign nationals, who comprised most of the population. In 2011, it became an immigration removal centre. In July 2021 the Immigration Centre closed and Morton Hall is due to reopen as a male Category Training prison in December 2021.
Short description of residential units
Morton Hall has five units in use, all with single cells.
Units
Fry and Windsor – 160 prisoners over two floors; each cell has a toilet and shower.
Johnson and Sharman – 145 prisoners in ground-floor accommodation with communal toilets and showers. Sharman has a purpose-built room for prisoners with reduced mobility.
Torr – 48 prisoners in ground-floor accommodation with communal toilets and showers. Torr houses the induction unit and a supported living area.
Governor: Karen Head
Last inspection (as an IRC): November 2019: *A real strength of the centre was its staff-detainee relationships. In our confidential interviews, most detainees were very positive about the way staff treated them. Consultation arrangements were good. Equality work was reasonably good and interpreters were used very regularly. Health services, including mental health provision, were good. Accommodation was in an adequate condition, but the centre still looked and felt far too much like the prison it was before it was designated an IRC. This was reinforced by large quantities of razor wire, which managers themselves acknowledged was out of keeping with the generally calm environment in the centre. Detainees were also locked in cells or on landings from 8.30pm. At other times, detainees could move freely around the centre and, unlike in most other IRCs, they could go outside easily during the day and walk around a fairly large and open site.*

HMP THE MOUNT
MOLYNEAUX AVENUE
BOVINGDON
HEMEL HEMPSTEAD HERTS, HP3 0NZ
Tel: 01442 836300 Fax: 01442 836301
Public male Cat C Training Prison
CNA 1008. OpCap 1028.
Visits phone booking line 01442 836 352 open

Mon-Fri 10:30am to 4pm. Online booking service email address: socialvisits.themount@justice.gov.uk
Visiting times:
Monday to Friday: 5:45pm to 6:45pm
Saturday and Sunday 2:30pm to 3:30pm
Healthcare provider: Hertfordshire NHS Trust
Group: Hertfordshire, Essex and Suffolk
The Mount opened in 1987 as a young offender institution. It changed to a category C training prison in 1989 and the large Nash wing was added in 2015. It is now a training and resettlement prison.
The Annexe – a 'super-enhanced' wing, cell doors never locked. 36 prisoners
Brister – Induction wing holding 110 prisoners
Dixon – Enhanced wing holding 120 prisoners
Ellis – Standard wing holding 117 prisoners
Howard – Enhanced wing 110 prisoners
Lakes – Well-being unit for men needing support, including substance misuse
Narey – Over 50's prisoner wing)
Nash – Standard wing holding 250 prisoners
Governor Katie Price
Date of last inspection September 2018: *The Mount was a prison undergoing significant difficulties. Across a broad range there had been deterioration not helped by crippling staff shortages. The prison was neither safe enough nor sufficiently respectful. In terms of its key mission to train and rehabilitate, it was absolutely failing. There needed to be some deep and joined-up thinking at The Mount about priorities.*

HMP NEW HALL
DIAL WOOD, WAKEFIELD, WEST YORKSHIRE, WF4 4XX
Tel: 01924 803000 Fax: 01924 803001
Public closed female local prison. It can also accommodate nine mothers and 10 babies in the MBU.
Group: Women's Estate Director Pia Sinha
CNA 416, OpCap 425.
Visits book by phone only 0300 060 6515 open: Mon-Fri 9:15am to 4pm
Visiting times:Tues, Thurs, Sat 1:45pm to 4pm
Healthcare: Practice Plus Group
Learning and skills provider: Novus
New Hall, which opened in 1933, was originally populated by prisoners from HMP Wakefield who were soon due to be released.

In 1961, it became a senior detention centre for male young offenders. It became a young offender institution in the 1980s, and in 1987, a women's prison.
Sycamore House Segregation with 12 cells
Holly House 12 prisoners with complex issues
Rivendell House 30 en-suite rooms for women with personality disorders and those on the enhanced regime
Larch House A 40-bed, semi-open unit for those aiming to progress to open conditions
Maple House Mother and baby unit for up to nine women and 10 babies
Oak House Mainstream residential unit and detoxification unit for some prisoners
Poplar House First night centre (Poplar 1) and mainstream residential unit (Poplar 2)
Willow House A and B wings – mainstream residential accommodation;
C wing for residents serving life and long-term sentences.
Governor Julia Spence
Date of last full inspection June 2019: *The environment in the prison was good but the quality of accommodation was more variable, although reasonable overall. Staff-prisoner relationships were good although some prisoners expressed frustration at their inability to get some simple tasks done by staff. The prison would have benefited from greater visibility and support from managers. It was also our observation that the proportion of female staff was too low and was something that was a very stark and particular feature of the senior team. Work to promote equality was limited despite the best efforts of the equalities officer who was too often redeployed. Outcomes for minorities despite this, remained broadly consistent with others, and the mother and baby unit was excellent. Health care was similarly*

good but mental health provision was undermined by staff shortages among the mental health team. Substance misuse services were reasonable. Prisoners experienced good time out of their cells, including association on Friday evenings which we now rarely see.
The provision of learning, skills and work was improving with plans for a new curriculum and strong partnership working evident. Our colleagues in Ofsted assessed the overall effectiveness of provision as 'good', but undermined in part by quite poor levels of attendance. The coordination of resettlement work had improved greatly and offender management was clearly focused on risk reduction. Work in support of the resettlement pathways was also effective, including a range of offending behaviour initiatives – most notably Rivendell House, a self-contained unit that catered for women with a personality disorder.

HMP NORTH SEA CAMP
CROPPERS LANE
FREISTON, BOSTON LINCS, PE22 0QX
Tel: 01205 769300 Fax: 01205 769301
Public open male category D prison holding a large proportion of indeterminate sentence prisoners and those convicted of sexual offences.
CNA 420. OpCap 420
Visits booked by phone only: 01205 769 368
Visit times Wed: 1:30pm to 3:30pm; Sat/Sun: 9:30am to 11:30am and 1:30pm to 3:30pm
Healthcare: Nottinghamshire NHS Trust
HMP North Sea Camp, which opened in 1935, was originally a Borstal. A tented camp was established at the site while the permanent buildings were constructed. A new sea bank was also built, to reclaim land from The Wash. The work was completed in 1979. In 1988, NSC became an adult male open prison.
• North unit holds general prisoners and also those with mobility issues or disabilities.
• South 1 unit is the induction unit which holds general prisoners and new receptions.
• South 2 unit holds general prisoners, but 4 and 5 landings are a protective isolation unit.
• Llewellin unit holds general prisoners
• Harrison unit holds general prisoners.
• Selby unit 66 self-contained single bed units.
• Jubilee holds long-term prisoners living

independently and prisoners working outside of the establishment on ROTL.
Governor: Colin Hussey, 4 April 2021
Date of last inspection June 2021: *Overall, this like many other open prisons had been hit hard by the restrictions imposed nationally throughout much of the last year. However, the pace of recovery at the establishment needed review, to make sure that every possible step was being taken, at the earliest opportunity, to reinstate its focus on progression, engagement and rehabilitation.*

HMP NORTHUMBERLAND
MORPETH
NORTHUMBERLAND NE65 9XG
Tel: 01670 383100 Fax: 01670 383101
Private Sodexo Male Category C Working. Group: Contracted
CNA 1,348. OpCap 1368.
Healthcare provider: Spectrum Health
Escort contractor: GEOAmey
Brief history
HMP Northumberland was formed from the merger of HMP Acklington and HMP/YOI Castington, completed in October 2011. It became part of the private prison sector on 1 December 2013.
Short description of residential units
There are 16 house blocks, five holding vulnerable prisoners, including sex offenders. House blocks range from 40 to 240 beds and are of differing layouts and ages.
There are two induction house blocks (one for vulnerable prisoners), dedicated integrated drug treatment systems house blocks, a drug recovery house block, a drug-free house block, and an older vulnerable prisoner house block.
Director: Samantha Pariser.
IMB Chair Lesley Craig
Visits operate Wed-Sun and must be booked by residents via the Kiosk. Residents must book their visit 48 hours prior to the visit so we can contact visitors to explain the COVID-19 safety measures. All visitors must be a family member and live at the same address. Friends are not permitted to visit yet and any adjustments to this arrangement will be communicated with residents.
https://www.hmpnorthumberland.co.uk/home/visiting-the-prison.html
Date of last inspection September 2020: *There*

was an air of positivity and confidence across many aspects of the prison's life and its management; many departments had risen to the challenges of the pandemic situation well. However, in some specific areas of work, management grip was lacking; and while the regime had in many respects moved forward, the prison still needed to seek out and pursue further opportunities to provide as full a regime as possible within the current restraints.

HMP NORWICH
KNOX ROAD, NORWICH
NORFOLK, NR1 4LU
Tel 01603 708600 Fax 01603 708601
Public multifunctional local prison holding remand and sentenced category B, C and D adult prisoners as well as remand and sentenced young adults.
CNA 770, OpCap 773
Visits booked by phone only on 01603 708790 open Mon-Fri 10am-noon, 2pm-4pm.
Visiting times will be advised on booking due to location of prisoner in the prison
Healthcare: Virgin Care Limited
Education framework provider: People Plus
Escort contractor: Serco
Prison group Beds, Cambs and Norfolk
Brief history
Norwich prison was built in 1887 on the site of the Britannia barracks home of the Royal Norfolk Regiment. The establishment has a mixture of buildings dating from 1887 to 2010, when the new A wing and activity centre was built. The prison is a complex site – it is split into three areas, each serving different functions: the main prison (a local prison), the local discharge unit (LDU) (a category C unit) and Britannia House (which holds category D prisoners).
Short description of residential units
Main prison site (local prison)
A wing – induction, 1st night, IDTS.
B wing – 119 remands, convicted, adults, YOs
C wing – 123 remands, convicted, adults, YOs
E wing – 26 remands, convicted, adults, YO
M wing – Cat C unit for 40 prisoners.
U wing – segregation unit 10 prisoners.
LDU (unit for category C prisoners)
F and G wings – 178 category C prisoners.
L wing – 15 prisoners with palliative care.
Britannia House D wing resettlement unit.

Governor: Declan Moore
Date of last inspection February 2020: *There was a growing backlog of OASys reports and basic screening often did not take place. There were no structured offending behaviour courses and while Britannia House provided some useful resettlement opportunities, some recent disruption had limited the availability of outside work. Reintegration work was organised and effective, but finding suitable accommodation for those being released remained a challenge. The findings of this inspection indicated that local managers were right that there were improvements to be seen at Norwich. Much of this improvement was, however, recent, inconsistent and not particularly well coordinated. It was also hard to discern a coherent and considered plan for the prison, a plan consistent with the development of a rehabilitative culture. In addition, there remained a number of safety risks that needed to be addressed, prisoners needed to be supported and incentivised to engage purposefully with the regime and there was much to do in ensuring that an inexperienced staff group received the support they needed.*

HMP NOTTINGHAM
PERRY ROAD, SHERWOOD
NOTTINGHAM, NG5 3AG
Tel: 0115 872 4000 Fax: 0115 872 4001
Public Category B local.
Group North Midlands
CNA 718. OpCap 1060
Visits phone booking 0115 962 8980 open Mon & Thurs 1-4pm. Tues, Fri, Sat 9am to midday
Email: socialvisits.nottingham@justice.gov.uk
Visiting times: Mon: 2pm to 4.30pm. Tues, Thu, Fri Sat/Sun: 9am to 11.30am, 2pm to 4.30pm. Wednesday: no visits
Healthcare: Nottinghamshire NHS Trust

Education provider: PeoplePlus
Escort contractor: GEOAmey
Brief history: Nottingham opened in 1890, but the original Victorian buildings were demolished in 2008. The new prison opened in February 2010.
Short description of residential units
A wing – integrated drug treatment service
B,C,D,E wings normal location
F wing – first night centre and induction unit
G wing – vulnerable prisoner unit
Governor Phil Novis
IMB chair Janet White
Last Inspection April 2020: *I hope this inspection can at long last mark a watershed in the troubled history of Nottingham. For many years it had a well-deserved reputation for being an unsafe prison. There is still a huge amount to do, but it would be wrong not to recognise the impressive progress that has been made since the poor findings of the IRP in November 2018.*
When a previously poorly performing prison improves, I have seen how it is possible for a new and optimistic culture, offering real care for prisoners and a better chance for them to rehabilitate, can take hold. I hope that can be achieved at Nottingham, as it could underpin future progress. All too often we have seen improvements in prisons prove to be fragile. The greatest risks have come from complacency or lack of consistency in leadership. I hope that neither will be the case at Nottingham, and that the highly creditable progress at this complex and challenging prison can be sustained into the future.

HMP OAKWOOD
FEATHERSTONE
WEST MIDLANDS WV10 7QD
Tel: 01902 799700
Private, G4S, Category C training prison.
CNA 1600. OpCap 2106
Visits: Prisoners book visits and you'll be told of the date and time when to arrive.
Healthcare: Practice Plus Group
Education provider: Novus
Escort contractors: GEOAmey
Prison group Contracted
Brief history
HMP Oakwood opened on 24 April 2012, as a Cat C men's prison for up to 1,605 prisoners. In 2017 it increased its capacity to 2,106.

Short description of residential units
Ash: VPU; Beech: Normal location, including Willow and accommodation for long-term prisoners; Cedar: Normal location, including Chestnut an enhanced level unit and an over-40s enhanced level unit; Douglas: Lifer and long-term population; Elm: Drug support unit; Fir: Segregation unit; Oaks: 80 temporary single occupancy units.
Director Sean Oliver
Date of last inspection 17-28 May 2021. *The prison has a friendly and positive atmosphere in which people are treated with respect and expectations are high. The governor and his staff are determined to maintain the levels of trust and responsibility that are given to prisoners, because they are committed to the rehabilitation of the men in their care. Staff and prisoners should be proud of what they have achieved.*

HMP ONLEY
WILLOUGHBY, RUGBY
WARKS, CV23 8AP
Tel: 01788 523400 Fax: 01788 523401
Public Category C training and resettlement prison for men. CNA: 742. OpCap 742
Visits. Book by phone 01788 523 402 or email socialvisits.onley@justice.gov.uk
Visiting every day except Tues: 2pm to 3:30pm
Healthcare: Northamptonshire NHS Trust
Learning and skills provider: Novus
Escort contractor: GEOAmey
Brief history
Built as a Borstal in 1968, Onley had various roles until in 2013 Onley was designated as a resettlement prison for Greater London.
A to H wings were the older original wings. A, B, C, D and E wings each provide general accommodation for 60 prisoners. F wing is the

- 68 -

segregation unit, G wing is the resettlement wing, H wing is the first night unit. I wing holds 100 prisoners. J wing and K wings each hold 76 prisoners, L wing enhanced.
Governor Matthew Tilt
Date of last inspection March 2019: *At the last inspection we found that the prison was unsafe, and judged the area of safety to be 'poor', our lowest assessment. Making this judgement is not something we do lightly, and is a reflection of the depths of our concerns when we do so. It was particularly disappointing, therefore, to find that at this latest inspection, two and a half years later, the prison was still fundamentally unsafe, and for the second time attracted our lowest assessment. Inexplicably, of the 18 recommendations we made in 2016 in the area of safety, only five had been achieved. Time and again we find that prisons which are unsafe will struggle to make progress in other areas, and HMP Onley was no exception. On this occasion we found that the prison was offering less respectful detention than at the last inspection, and had failed to make progress in the areas of purposeful activity and resettlement and release planning.*

HMP PARC
HEOL HOPCYN JOHN
BRIDGEND, CF35 6AP
Tel: 01656 300200 Fax: 01656 300316
Private, G4S, Category B local prison
CNA 1612: OpCap 1699.
Visits: Prisoners are responsible for booking their own visits. Once a visit has been approved it is up the individual prisoner to inform his family and friends of the date and time of the visit.
Health provider: G4S Health
Learning and skills provider: G4S Education
Prison group Contracted.

Brief history: Located in Bridgend, South Wales, Parc opened in November 1997. G4S has a 25- year contract expiring in 2022.
Parc holds a complex mix of young people aged 15–17 years, young adults, life-sentenced prisoners and those who have committed sexual offences, making it one of the largest prisons in the UK.
A2 is the induction/early days in custody
A4 (Dewis unit) post induction.
Cynnwys unit provides assisted living.
B3 is the young adults unit.
D unit is the substance misuse support unit.
T1 first time in custody/college unit.
T3 first time in custody and military vet unit.
T4 is the families and significant others unit.
T5 the thinking skills programme/Resolve.
Coed VPU unit. X1 is the induction/early days in custody unit for vulnerable prisoners.
X3 and T6 are assisted living units.
Director Janet Wallsgrove
Date of last inspection March 2020: *Although there is a body of opinion that large prisons are inferior to smaller establishments, Parc shows that this need not be the case. In fact, I gained a clear impression of how Parc has avoided being inflexible or monolithic in its service provision, and has, in fact, used its size and breadth of resources to provide a range of services to different groups that simply could not be made available in smaller establishments. For instance, there were bespoke services for prisoners with learning disabilities or autism. There was an excellent unit focusing on veterans, and young adults had specialist provision, as did vulnerable prisoners and those with assisted living needs. Parc has, of course, also retained its international reputation for the work carried out with children and families. The result is that it does not feel like a huge establishment for the prisoners held there, and it certainly did not merit the pejorative description of a 'warehouse' that is sometimes aimed at large establishments.*
Parc has benefitted from consistency of leadership over many years, and it was clear during my meetings with the governor, senior management and staff at Parc that they were rightly proud of what has been achieved. Of course, as with every prison, there was room for improvement, some of it urgent and in key areas, but overall this was a prison that, as we considered it, was fulfilling its core purposes and performing well.

At Parc, some 100 prisoners were released on average each month, and 17% of them did not have an address to go to. We saw a great deal of effort going into rehabilitation and release planning at Parc, and indeed our overall judgement in this area was that the outcomes for prisoners warranted our highest grading. However, there is a serious risk that much of this good work could be undone by prisoners not having appropriate accommodation on their release. We have therefore made a recommendation directly to HMPPS that it should work with the Welsh Government to ensure that accommodation is available for prisoners on release.

HMYOI Parc Juvenile Unit
Children's unit within a category B training prison with capacity for up to 64 remanded and convicted young people.
Establishment status Private G4S
Group: Contracted. Number held 39
CNA 64. OpCap 64
The children's unit houses 64 children aged 15-18, from a large catchment area including Bristol, Swindon and Wiltshire.
The children's unit is located in the main establishment and consists of two separate accommodation units. Echo One has an operational capacity of 24 with cells split over two separate levels. The unit consists of 16 single and six double cells. The living accommodation of Golf One is slightly different with rooms all located on one level.
HMIP 2020: *Overall, Parc is easily the best performing YOI in England and Wales. It has the advantage of being smaller in size than some of its comparators, but that should not be used by others as an excuse for not taking full and proper notice of what has been achieved. In recent times we have had to publish some troubling findings from our inspections at other YOIs. I would suggest that there is much to learn from Parc, and that practitioners and others involved in the development of policy and delivery of operations in children's custody should pay close attention to this report.*

HMP PENTONVILLE
CALEDONIAN ROAD
LONDON, N7 8TT
Tel: 020 7023 7000 Fax: 020 7023 7001
Public, local category B resettlement prison

CNA 906. OpCap 1310
Health provider: Practice Plus Group
Learning and skills provider: Novus
Escort contractor: Serco
Prison group: London
Visits booked by phone on 0300 060 6504 open Mon-Fri 9:15am to 4pm. Visiting times: Mon-Fri: 1:45pm-2:40pm, 3:20pm to 4:15pm.
HMP Pentonville is a very large Victorian local prison for remand and convicted prisoners, with four wings unchanged since it was built in 1842. It is one of the busiest prisons in the country with approximately 33,000 men through its reception a year.
Short description of residential units
General remand and convicted prisoners: A wing 226 spaces; C wing 154 spaces; D wing – 180 spaces; E2-5 wings 136 spaces; F wing 389 spaces. C1 wing segregation unit, 12 spaces; E 1-3 wings 127 spaces for detox; F4-5 wing 66 VPU spaces; J wing 64 space first night centre.
Governor: Ian Blakeman
Date of last inspection August 2019: *This inspection found a prison that was delivering weak outcomes for prisoners in most areas and unacceptably poor outcomes in safety. We found no denial of the gravity of the prison's situation, and there was a clear recognition of the scale of the work to be done. Managers and many staff at all levels throughout the prison told us they were committed to the changes that were underway and expressed confidence in the leadership of the establishment. Importantly, HM Prison and Probation Service (HMPPS) had ensured a recent influx of new staff to bring the prison close to its full complement – this is self-evidently critical to decent outcomes and, like many other establishments, Pentonville has suffered the consequences of inadequate staffing for far too long.*

HMP PETERBOROUGH - MALE
SAVILLE ROAD
PETERBOROUGH, PE3 7PD
Tel: 01733 217500 Fax: 01733 217501
Private, Sodexo, local and resettlement prison for category B prisoners with an extension for category C men serving between 1-4 years.
Group Contracted
CNA 759. OpCap 868
Visits are booked by prisoners and visitors will be advised of the date and time to visit once the booking has been accepted.
Brief history The prison was run by Peterborough Prison Management Ltd, which sub-contracted Sodexo Justice Services. It was established on 28 March 2005.
In January 2015, it opened a resettlement unit in house block 5, providing spaces for an additional 292 men. House blocks 3 and 4 were part of the original prison and accommodated 582 men. A women's prison in separate buildings on the same site was inspected independently in 2014.
Short description of residential units
12 wings, four each on three house blocks.
House block 3
W1– first night and induction unit
X1 – integrated drug treatment system and first night centre for those requiring detoxification or stabilisation
Y1 and Z1 – remand prisoners.
House block 4
W2, X2 and Y2 – convicted prisoners
Z2 – convicted prisoners on the enhanced level of the incentives and earned privileges scheme.
House block 5
Burghley wing – convicted prisoners on the enhanced level, veterans, over 50s and those participating in release on temporary licence.
Cavell and Nene wings – convicted category C men whom the prison aimed to progress to Burghley wing.
Royce wing – safeguarding unit for vulnerable prisoners.
Director Damian Evans
Escort contractors Wincanton; Serco
Healthcare provider Sodexo Justice Services Cimmaron UK (GP 24-hour medical care)
Education: Sodexo Justice Services

HMP PETERBOROUGH - FEMALE
Private, Sodexo, the women's prison serves the East Midlands, East of England and Essex. The operating capacity is 372 including 12 additional prisoner places (APP). There are two modern house blocks containing 10 wings including a young offenders and young adults unit for women aged 18 – 25, a life and long sentence unit and a foreign national unit for residents awaiting deportation. There is also a 12- bed, 13-cot mother and baby unit (MBU). Facilities include classrooms, workshops, a gym, a chapel, library and gardens. The prison also holds some restricted status women.
Visits are booked by prisoners and visitors will be advised of the date and time to visit once the booking has been accepted.
Houseblock 1: A1–YPs (18-25 years); B1-detox; C1–at risk prisoners; D1– long termers; E1–first night. Houseblock 2: A2 – remands; B2/D2 – sentenced; C2–enhanced; E2–foreign nationals.
Director Damian Evans
Last Inspection November 2018: **Male**: *HMP Peterborough still had much work to do to reduce the violence that had flowed from the influx of drugs into the establishment. Nevertheless, at the time of this inspection the signs were promising that further progress could be made. It is essential that the prison is restored to being a safe place, so that all the good work that was being delivered in so many areas is not put in jeopardy.*

Last Inspection November 2018: **Female:** *Overall, this is a more mixed report than when we last inspected this prison. We were particularly concerned about safety, and this is the first women's prison in several years to have been assessed as 'not sufficiently good' in this area. The prison remained basically respectful, but serious deficits in health care meant that the assessment in this area was not as positive as at our previous visit. On the other hand, outcomes in purposeful activity had improved and resettlement remained very strong.*

The leadership team at Peterborough were motivated to provide good outcomes for the women, but told us they were distracted by some significant challenges in the male prison. A renewed focus on the female prison is now needed to ensure the concerns we have raised at this inspection are addressed.

www.prisons.org.uk

HMP PORTLAND
104 THE GROVE, EASTON
PORTLAND, DORSET DT5 1DL
Tel: 01305 715600 Fax: 01305 715601
Public, Male closed young offender institution and male category C adults
CNA 463. OpCap 530
Visits must be booked by phone on 01305 715 775 open Mon-Fri 8:30am-12pm, 1:30-3pm
Visiting times: Wednesday, Saturday, and Sunday: 2pm to 3pm and 3:30pm to 4:30pm
Healthcare: Practice Plus Group
Education provider: Weston College
Prison group Avon and South Dorset
Brief history
HMP/YOI Portland is a category C prison located on Portland Bill, Dorset. It is a historic prison, originally built in 1848. It houses around 500 adult male and young adult male prisoners. Collingwood; Induction; Nelson, Grenville YO wings; Benbow, Raleigh and Drake mixed adults YOs. Beaufort is an enabled environment
Governor Rob Luxford
Last Inspection Report: 16 January 2020: *Portland is a category C closed facility holding up to 530 adult and young adult male prisoners. Originally built in 1848. The population as a whole are relatively young, with 25% aged under 21 and nearly 58% between 21 and 39. Overall, our findings at this inspection were troubling. Outcomes had not declined and there was some recent evidence that the impetus and initiative provided by the Prison Group Director was having some beneficial effect. This, however, was not enough. We had concerns about whether local managers had realistic, grounded plans to meet the challenges the prison faced. The prison's approach to safety was lacklustre, basic standards were not maintained and staff generally needed to have greater expectations of the prisoners they supervised. The prison also needed to re-focus on its primary function as a training and resettlement prison and ensure first that it did the basics right. It urgently needed to ensure that an active and purposeful regime was being delivered and that this met fully the needs of the men held.*

HMP PRESCOED
See entry for HMP Usk

HMP PRESTON
2 RIBBLETON LANE
PRESTON, LANCASHIRE PR1 5AB
Tel: 01772 444550 Fax: 01772 444566
HMP Preston opened in 1895 and operates as a category B male local and resettlement prison. It holds male remands, and those serving sentences of 12 months or less. Its location allows good access links for visitors. In March 2021 the prison roll averages around 675, with an operational capacity of 680, against a certified accommodation of 433.
Visits booking line: 01772 444 777, open 8am to 4pm Mon-Fri. Visiting times Mon-Fri: 2pm to 2:45pm and 3:45pm to 4:30pm
In addition to the core residential accommodation and prison facilities, the following are available to the prisoners:
• a 30-bed healthcare centre
• a 28 bed detox unit
• a dental surgery meeting current
• an education department which includes an information technology (IT) centre (with 48 computers) and an art suite
• well-equipped PE facilities
• a textile workshop
• a horticulture centre
• a waste management unit
• clothing exchange and laundry
Education and training
The education function is run by Novus, part of The Manchester College. The training function is run by HMP Preston.
The establishment operates a regional hospital facility, which includes a general medical ward with 12 beds, as well as a mental health ward with 18 beds. It takes prisoners from other prisons who have serious conditions or who are recovering from operations, and it has a palliative care role run by Spectrum Community Health CIC.
Amey has the prison's maintenance contract.
IMB Report 2020/2021: *It is difficult to recommend areas for development when the main wish must be "to get back to normal", which is outside the Governor's control. The pandemic has seen the introduction of some innovative uses of technology; Purple Visits, tablets for socially important meetings with families and Christmas photos. It is hoped that these will continue and be developed. The pandemic has also seen the*

reduction in some functions such as key workers. It is to be hoped that this function can be reinstated as soon as possible.

The prison does not meet modern standards being built in the Victorian era. Particular areas of concern are reception and the size of the cells. The personal relationship between the staff and the prisoners is good. This is in part due to good communications in keeping the prisoners informed of all regime changes.

HMP RANBY
RETFORD, NOTTS DN22 8EU
Tel: 01777 862000 Fax: 01777 862001
Public category C male adult trainer.
CNA 892. OpCap 1038
Visits booked by phone on 01234 373196, open Mon-Fri 8:30am to 4pm. Visiting times:
Mon & Fri: 2pm to 4pm
Sat/Sun: 9am to 11am and 2pm to 4pm
Healthcare: Nottinghamshire NHS Trust
Education provider: Milton Keynes College Group North Midlands
Brief history
Since opening as a prison in 1972, Ranby has regularly had its capacity increased, most recently in 2008 when further accommodation workshops, health care, kitchen, library and education facilities were added.
HB1 1: induction. HB2 North: a general wing; HB2 South: detox. HB3 North: a general wing; HB3 South: the 'enabling environment', where the regime was more relaxed and prisoners living there were expected to live more autonomously; HB4 general wing; HB5: Single cells for 192 lower risk, older, and night shifts. HB6&7 Single and double occupancy cells with integral sanitation and showers for 60 enhanced and elderly prisoners on each wing.
Governor: Nigel Hirst.
Date of last inspection October 2018: *Staff-prisoner relationships were good and most prisoners felt respected. It was clear that prisoners*

held on the prison's smaller units were receiving better attention than those on the busier, larger wings, where the lack of any form of key worker arrangement was an omission. The development of collaborative 'enabling environments' on some of the wings seemed to us to be a useful and encouraging initiative, although their effectiveness had yet to be fully assessed.
Living conditions and the general environment remained good. There was some overcrowding in some cells. Prisoners were more positive about the food, and the ability to access the prison shop on the day of arrival mitigated the risk of debt with all its consequences for intimidation. The apps and complaints system needed improvement. The prison was well led by a competent and effective governor. We observed much good practice, and an openness to innovative ideas as well as an attention to detail. The governor had sought to attend to getting the basics right and in our view the prison had unquestionably improved. It is to be hoped that, if the team stay focused on this agenda, their hard work will soon begin to realise more clearly improved outcomes for prisoners.

HMP RISLEY
WARRINGTON ROAD
RISLEY, WARRINGTON WA3 6BP
Tel: 01925 733000 Fax: 01925 733001
Public Category C resettlement prison
CNA 1,061. OpCap 1,115
Visits booked by phone on 01925 733284 open Mon-Fri: 9am to 4pm. Also email booking on SocialVisitsRisley@justice.gov.uk
Visiting times dependent on wing location to be advised on booking.
Healthcare: Gtr Manchester NHS Trust
Substance use provider: Change Grow Live
Education provider: Novus

Group: Gtr Manchester, Merseyside Cheshire
Risley opened in 1964 as a remand centre and in 1989 it became a training prison. The training prison was expanded further and refurbished in 2003 with the addition of a new wing (G). The population of prisoners convicted of a sexual offence was relocated to separate residential areas in 2020. Risley has become a hub for up to 200 foreign national prisoners (FNP).

Short description of residential units
A wing – Cat C plus FNPs
B wing – induction, first night unit
C wing – drug free unit
D wing – Cat C prisoners
E wing – sex offenders
F wing – sexoffenders
G wing – sex offenders, including older prisoners and those with a disability
R1 – Enhanced wing

Governor Dan Cooper (Acting Oct 2021)

Last Inspection Report: January 2021: *We found a well-led prison that had continued to progress despite the pandemic. The management team had worked effectively, in partnership with health care staff and Public Health England, to control a COVID-19 outbreak at the start of the pandemic and to contain a later outbreak on G wing in September. Quarantine arrangements for those in their first 14 days at the prison and shielding arrangements for those vulnerable to the virus had been implemented in accordance with national directives. For most prisoners, the regime was severely limited to around one hour a day unlocked, which was a serious concern. Although a larger proportion (30%) than we have seen in some other prisons had jobs, a lack of in-cell telephony placed further pressure on prisoners to make their calls during the short time available out of their cell. Prisoners now had weekly access to the gyms, but the sessions took place during their hour of unlock. In conclusion, we found strong leadership and a motivated management team that had risen to the challenges of the pandemic. Despite the lack of some basic facilities, such as in-cell telephones and decent showers, there were ongoing efforts to improve the environment and to build on work already done to make Risley a safer place. However, the impact of lack of time unlocked for most prisoners some eight months since the start of the pandemic was a serious concern.*

HMP ROCHESTER

1 FORT ROAD ROCHESTER KENT, ME1 3QS
Tel: 01634 803100 Fax: 01634 803101
Public, Category C resettlement prison
CNA 695. OpCap 695
Visits booked by phone on 01634 803 237 open Mon-Fri 8:30am to 11:30am
Visiting times: Monday to Thursday: 2pm to 2:45pm and 3:30pm to 4:15pm. Friday: 9:15am to 10am and 10:45am to 11:30am
Healthcare provider: Oxleas NHS Trust
Mental health provider: Oxleas NHS
Learning and skills provider: Novus
Group Kent Surrey and Sussex

IMB Report 2021: Rochester is a Category C Resettlement prison for both adult male and young offenders; it has an operational capacity of 695. Prisoners are held in eight residential units: one is a dedicated drug reduction unit, six are general accommodation, and one caters for prisoners with enhanced privilege status, and has improved cell facilities. There is a separate Care and Separation Unit (CSU). One wing has been allocated for first night accommodation and induction into the prison. During the pandemic, this has changed to another wing being used as a Reverse Cohort Unit for all incoming prisoners to prevent spread of the Covid-19 virus.

The prison has four Edwardian built wings and 4 modern blocks. The older wings are challenging to maintain. The newer wings have continual ventilation and heating problems. Maintenance is provided by GFSL. The majority of cells are twin bedded. The grounds are spacious with each wing being a separate location. The open location of the prison gives plenty of opportunity for fresh air

and outdoor activity. Outside of the pandemic regime, as a resettlement prison, the regime is intended to give prisoners training through a structured sentence plan.
Governor Dean Gardiner
Date of last inspection November 2017

HMP RYE HILL
WILLOUGHBY, NR RUGBY
WARKS, CV23 8SZ
Tel: 01788 523300 Fax: 01788 523311
Private, G4S, Category B for adults male sex offenders serving over four years.
CNA 600. OpCap 664.
Physical and mental health provider: G4S
Prison education framework provider: Novus
Prison group Contracted
HMP Rye Hill opened in 2001. In 2014 it was re-rolled to hold an entire population of prisoners convicted of sexual offences.
Short description of residential units
One unit (Andrews wing) was the induction unit and all the other seven units held sentenced prisoners.
Director Peter Small.
Last Inspection Report: February 2020: *Rye Hill had become a more respectful prison. Relationships between staff and prisoners were constructive and supportive, encouraged further by well managed key worker and very useful peer worker schemes. Consultation was wide ranging and although we were concerned that not all formal complaints were properly recorded, those that were, as well as general requests and applications, were mostly properly dealt with. The prison was doing some useful and encouraging work to promote diversity, including providing good support for older prisoners and those with disabilities, but despite this there was clear evidence that perceptions among some protected groups continued to be more negative. Faith provision was a strength of the prison and the quality of health provision was reasonably good.*

HMP SEND
RIPLEY ROAD, WOKING
SURREY, GU23 7LJ
Tel: 01483 471000 Fax: 01483 471001
Public, Closed women's prison.
CNA 202. OpCap 192 temp Covid cap
Visits telephone booking only on 0300 060 6514 open Monday to Friday, 9am to 4pm
Visiting times: Thu, Sat, Sun 2pm-3.30pm
Population of the prison August2021
• 17 foreign national prisoners
• 28% of prisoners from BAME backgrounds
• 80 prisoners on support for substance use
Healthcare provider: Central and North West London NHS Foundation Trust
Prison education provider: Weston College
Community rehabilitation companies (CRCs):
Prison group Women's Estate
Brief history
Originally an isolation hospital, Send first opened as a prison in 1962 when it was a junior detention centre. In 1987, it was reclassified as a category C adult men's training prison. Re-roled in 1998 and completely rebuilt by 1999, Send currently operates as a closed women's prison. It houses a PIPE unit with a capacity of 35 and a therapeutic community with a capacity of 24.
Short description of residential units
A wing PIPE (including pre and progression)
B wing general population
C wing enhanced prisoners
D wing enhanced prisoners and ROTL unit
E and F wings currently closed
J wing induction; TC
Governor Amy Frost, 2 November 2020
Prison Group Director Pia Sinha
Date of last inspection 26 August 2021: *The governor had a very positive vision for the prison and a clear set of priorities that included restoring education, release on temporary licence (ROTL), visits and the therapeutic interventions. Inspectors agreed with her analysis that sentence progression, particularly for women on longer sentences, was not as good as it should be. There was a strong, deep culture of respect and support that had been*

www.prisons.org.uk

established in the prison, maintained by the visible and accessible leadership team and a dedicated staff. This perhaps explains why some women who had achieved category D status decided to stay at Send rather than transfer to open conditions. This culture had sustained the prison through the last, challenging year and inspectors were confident the prison will continue to make good progress.

HMP SPRINGHILL
GRENDON UNDERWOOD
AYLESBURY BUCKS, HP18 0TL
Tel: 01296 445000 Fax: 01296 445001
Public, adult male Cat D open.
Group South Central
CNA 335. OpCap 335
Visits booked by phone only on 01296 445 082 open Mon-Fri 10am to 12pm.
Visiting times: Sat and Sun 1:45pm to 3:15pm
All prisoners who are not serving a short sentence are encouraged to join a resettlement scheme that allows them to carry out work for the local community, and to seek work experience and full-time work for the last months of their sentence.
Residents live in 13 huts. In 10 of these, they live two to a room. Huts have a communal lounge, kitchen, showers and separate toilets. There are three huts with 40 single rooms, which are allocated according to a structured incentive system and for medical, wellbeing or vulnerability concerns.
There is a single 16-bed unit, which is dedicated to those with substance misuse support needs.
Certain facilities – for example, the dental suite in Grendon, offender management unit (OMU), business hub and security department – serve both prisons.
However, the two prisons cater for different categories of prisoner and have quite different regimes.
The following health services are provided:
• Primary healthcare Practice Plus Group
• Drug and alcohol recovery team (DART)
• Podiatry and physiotherapy
• Dental (Time for Teeth)
• Audiology (Specsavers)
• Optician (Pen Optical Ltd)
• Education: Milton Keynes College.
• Maintenance:Gov Facility Services

HMP STAFFORD
54 GOAL ROAD STAFFORD, ST16 3AW
Tel: 01785 773000 Fax: 01785 773001
Public, Category C prison for sex offenders
CNA: 751. OpCap 751
Visits booked by phone only on 0300 060 6505 open Monday to Friday 9:15am to 4pm.
Visiting times: Wed, Thurs, Sat, Sun: 2 to 4pm
Healthcare providers Practice Plus Group
Education framework provider: Novus
Escort contractor: GEOAmey
Prison group West Midlands
Brief history
There has been a prison in Stafford since the end of the 12th century. In 1793, the prison opened as the new Staffordshire Gaol but, although some of the original building remains, the present establishment is mainly Victorian, notably the main hall and crescent wings. The present prison was built in 1794 and, apart from the period 1916 to 1940, has been in continuous use. The prison was closed between 1916 and 1940, reopening at the outbreak of the Second World War as an establishment holding both men and women. The women's section of the prison closed within a few years of reopening, and for many years afterwards HMP Stafford held young offenders as well as adult prisoners.
The prison re-roled in August 2014 from a category C adult male prison to a category C prison for sex offenders.
Short description of residential units
The modern buildings include the reception area, visits hall, education department, kitchen, a 40-bed house block and the sports hall. A site adjacent to the prison was purchased and developed as an industrial workshop complex in 1986. There are seven

- 76 -

wings: A, B, C, D, E, F and G.
Governor Mark Greenhaf
Date of last inspection report: May 2020: *HMP Stafford is a settled establishment where, to an extent, the nature of the prisoner population is such that it contributes to their own positive outcomes. When this is combined with a positive inspection report, as this most certainly is, there can sometimes be a risk of complacency on the part of management. This has not been the case to date at Stafford, and my sense was that the leadership were aware of the risk, and were determined to avoid it and continue to make the positive progress that has been achieved to date.*

HMP STANDFORD HILL
EASTCHURCH SHEERNESS
KENT, ME12 4AA
Tel: 01795 884500 Fax: 01795 884638
Public Category D male open prison.
Group Kent Surrey and Sussex
CNA 464. OpCap 464
Visits booked by phone only on 0300 060 6603 open Monday-Friday, 9am to 4pm
Visiting times: Wed, Thurs, Sat, Sun 1345-1545
Health provider: Practice Plus Group
Substance misuse provider: Forward Trust
Education provider: Weston College
Prison group Kent, Surrey and Sussex
The buildings were redeveloped in 1986 and are on the site of a World War 1 Royal Air Force station.
A wing – 192 bed 1st night/ induction unit
B wing – 192 bed-unit normal location
C wing – 80 bed-unit normal location.
Governor Dawn Mauldon
Date of last inspection Report: February 2020: *Despite a few criticisms and the identification of a small number of areas for improvement, highlighted throughout the report, the prison fulfilled its resettlement function well. The prison's calm atmosphere, the good staff-prisoner relationships, its impressive education, training and work opportunities and the solid rehabilitative work clearly motivated and incentivised prisoners and gave them a good chance of a successful return to the community on their release.*

HMP STOCKEN
STOCKEN HALL ROAD
OAKHAM, RUTLAND, LEICS LE15 7RD

Tel: 01780 795100 Fax: 01780 410767
Public, adult male category C training prison
CNA 768. OpCap 853
Healthcare: Practice Plus Group
Education provider: Milton Keynes College
Prison group North Midlands
Built in 1985 as a young offender institution, HMP Stocken then re-roled as a category C closed training prison. It has since expanded, with new accommodation added in 1990, 1997, 1998, 2003, 2008 and 2011, which significantly expanded the roll.
Short description of wings
F wing – General population
H wing – Induction unit
I wing – Drug recovery unit
K wing – Integrated drug treatment system
wing L wing – General population
M wing – General population
N wing – General population
Governor Neil Thomas (30 January 2017)
Date of last inspection report: May 2019: *Overall, we found a mixed picture of progress since 2015, with improvements in one area and declines in performance in two – purposeful activity and rehabilitation and release planning.*
The approach to implementing our previous recommendations was reasonable, and better than we sometimes see.
Some 48% had been fully achieved, and a further 7% partially achieved, and it was clear that the leadership of the prison was fully committed to maintaining and improving performance.
There was also a very clear commitment from the governor to promulgating the values he wished all his staff to adhere to when going about their work.
In conclusion, I would recommend that this report is read very carefully to appreciate the evidence which sits behind our judgements, both those that were positive and those that were less so.
Some of those judgements were finely balanced, but the main concerns we have identified will, I hope, give a clear steer for where the undoubted energy and commitment of the leadership and staff at Stocken can best be focused.

HMP STOKE HEATH
MARKET DRAYTON
SHROPSHIRE, TF9 2JL
Tel: 01630 636000 Fax: 01630 636001
Public, male Category C prison

Group West Midlands
CNA 662. OpCap 782
Visits booked by phone only on 0300 060 6506 open Monday to Friday, 9.15am to 4.00pm
Visiting times: Tue, Thur, Sat, Sun: 1430-1530
Health provider: Shropshire NHS Trust
Learning and skills provider: Novus
Prison group West Midlands
Stoke Heath was built in 1964 as a category C adult prison, holding both adults and young adults since July 2011. In November 2014, it began reconfiguration as a designated resettlement prison for Wales. The resettlement function was reviewed in 2017 and the prison now serves the West Midlands.
A–E wings – residential units
F wing – designated drug treatment/ active citizenship unit G wing – induction and longer-term prisoners
I wing – progression & ROTL unit
Clive unit – external unit holding up to 16 category D prisoners
Governor John Huntingdon - 2009
Date of last inspection report: March 2019: *The prison remained an overwhelmingly safe institution. Stoke Heath has benefitted from stable and competent leadership that has attended to trying to get the basics right. This is not to argue that there aren't further improvements that can be made – there are many. But Stoke Heath was dealing with the same risks and challenges that other less successful training prisons face and yet it remained a largely well-ordered place where the prisoners, for the most part, trusted the staff. The challenge going forward is to maintain these successes and build on them.*

HMP STYAL
STYAL ROAD, WILMSLOW
CHESHIRE, SK9 4HR
Tel: 01625 553000 Fax: 01625 553001
Public closed female prison.
CNA: 471. OpCap 486
Prison Group Women's Estate Pia Sinha
Visits booked by phone only on 0300 060 6512 open Mon-Fri 9.30am to 5pm
Visiting times: Mon-Thurs and Sat -Sun 2pm to 4pm. Friday: no visits
Health provider: Spectrum Health
Learning and skills provider: Novus
Group Women's Estate - Pia Sinha
There are 16 detached Victorian houses, with mainly shared accommodation for approximately 20 women each. Some have specialist functions. Oak house - first night centre; Fox house - drug recovery unit; Waite wing - a mixture of single and double cells on two spurs holding 140 women needing greater supervision, including those on the basic regime or requiring regular observations as part of suicide and self-harm prevention management; Dove unit - complex needs centre, a 10-bed unit offering therapeutic support to women with complex needs
Bollinwood house - an open unit outside the gate holding 25 women; Bruce house - holds 22 women in semi-open conditions; Mother and baby unit - spaces for nine mothers and 10 babies; CSU unit - holds up to 10 women.
Name of governor Michelle Quirke
Date of last full inspection Report: September 2018. *Most women felt safe, and there was some excellent work to manage poor and problematic behaviour. Levels of self- harm were very high, involving a small number of prolific self-harmers, but the care and support provided was good, particularly for the most vulnerable women. There had been one self-inflicted death since our last inspection, and the prison had an ongoing action plan addressing the recommendations of the Prisons and Probation Ombudsman (PPO). Security was proportionate and helped to facilitate safe movement around the site, and to address the supply of illegal drugs. Most behavioural issues were dealt with at an interpersonal level and formal disciplinary processes were well managed, and only used as a last resort. The regime in the segregation unit needed to be improved.*

HMP SUDBURY
ASHBOURNE
DERBYSHIRE, DE6 5HW
Tel: 01283 584000 Fax: 01283 584001
Public, Category D male adult prison.
Group North Midlands. CNA 581. OpCap 581
Visits phone booking only on 01283 584 175 open Mon-Fri 9am to 11am and 1.30pm-3pm
Visiting times: Wed & Thu 2pm to 3pm and 4pm to 5pm. Sat &Sun: 9am to 10am, 11am to 12 noon, 2pm to 3pm and 4pm to 5pm
IMB 2021: Prisoners leave during the day, to work and support the local community, or are temporarily released at weekends to reintegrate into family life. Owing to the COVID-19 pandemic the average population is 460. The prison is in a rural location. The long perimeter fence present a number of challenges for the safety and security of the prison but the installation of CCTV has helped mitigate some of these problems.
The prison holds a complex group of people, including older and disabled prisoners, as well as an increasing number of young adult prisoners. It carefully manages the risk associated with such prisoners being held in an open prison, with risk assessment being a core part of day-to-day management.
The buildings were originally a United States Air Force hospital for D-Day landing casualties during World War II. Most of the original single-storey accommodation is still in use but has been converted and refurbished, and in some instances replaced, to provide single and double rooms.
There is a small secure office.
Healthcare: Practice Plus Group.
Governor Craig Smith
Education: Milton Keynes College
Last Inspection Report April 2017

HMP SWALESIDE
ISLE OF SHEPPEY KENT, ME12 4AX
Tel: 01795 804100 Fax: 01795 804200
Public, Category B men's training prison.
Group: Kent Surrey and Sussex
Number held 1,107
CNA 1,111. OpCap 1,111
Visits phone booking only on 0300 060 6604 open Mon-Fri 0830-1600.
Visiting times: Tues-Thurs 1400-1600
Health provider: Integrated Care 24
Prison group: Long-term high security estate
Brief history
Swaleside prison, which opened in 1988, first opened with four wings, adding four further wings – E, F, G and H – between 1998 and 2010. In 2010, a PIPE unit was built, along with a pre-PIPE unit for prisoners with personality disorders and very challenging behaviour.
Short description of residential units
A wing – 126 places; general population
B wing – 126 places; VPU for debt
C wing – 126 places; prisoners in crisis
D wing – 126 places; the induction wing
E wing – 120 places; the drug recovery unit
F wing – 120 places; the PIPE unit
G wing – 178 places; lifers on one spur
H wing – 178 places for sex offenders
Segregation unit – 25-bed unit
Health care unit – 17-bed in-patient unit
Governor Mark Icke.
Date of last inspection May 2019: *Our findings suggested to us that there had been a significant amount of effort to improve the safety of Swaleside. Arrangements to receive new prisoners generally worked well, with very good induction procedures for mainstream prisoners. They were not as good for the vulnerable population. Violence had risen considerably since the last inspection, and although the number of assaults had reduced in recent months, many assaults were serious.*
Of the 204 assaults that had taken place in the preceding six months, well over a third were against staff and during that same period the number of prisoner-on-prisoner assaults was higher than at other similar prisons.
In our survey, some 35% of prisoners told us they felt unsafe.
The vital task of reducing violence remained a priority and is therefore the subject of one of our main recommendations.

HMP SWANSEA
200 OYSTERMOUTH ROAD
SWANSEA. SA1 3SR
Tel: 01792 485300 Fax: 01792 485430
Public, Category B local prison
CNA 255. OpCap 499
Visits by phone booking on 01792 485 322 open Mon-Fri, 8:45am to 3:45pm or by email: socvisswansea@justice.gov.uk
Visiting times:
Mon-Thurs & Sat-Sun: 2:30pm to 3:30pm
Health provider: Swansea Bay Health Board
Education provider: HMPPS
Prison group HMPPS in Wales
The prison is situated about half a mile from the city centre on the coast road. Today it is operated as a local prison, holding prisoners up to and including category B in five wings.
Governor: Amanda Corrigan November 2019
Date of last inspection Report October 2020:
We found a well led establishment that had made good progress since the start of the pandemic. There was good partnership work with the local health care provider, Public Health Wales, and the Welsh Government to ensure that every symptomatic prisoner was tested. There had not been a confirmed case of COVID-19 at Swansea since April 2020. The governor ensured that staff and prisoners were well informed and acted on concerns. Appropriate priority was given to keeping prisoners in work, maintaining some limited face-to-face education and continuing sentence and risk management. Outcomes for many prisoners at Swansea were better than at other local prisons. As the prison continues to progress, the management team need to establish appropriate oversight in the areas of self-harm prevention, equality and diversity and health care to ensure that outcomes continue to improve.

HMYOI SWINFEN HALL
LICHFIELD, STAFFS WS14 9QS
Tel: 01543 484000 Fax: 01543 484001
Public, Cat C, for males aged 18-28 serving 16 months to life. CNA 604. OpCap 624
Visits booked by phone (01543 484000 Mon-Fri 9:15am to 4pm) or email visitsbooking.westmidlands@noms.gsi.gov.uk
Visiting times:
Tues, Wed, Thu, Sat, Sunday: 2pm to 4pm - note visits on Thursdays will be facilitated on the 1st and 3rd Thursday of the month only.
Healthcare: Practice Plus Group
Education provider: Novus
Prison group - West Midlands
Prisoners are housed in nine wings:
A 64 places; B 60 places; C 60 places; D 68 places; E 60 places; F 90 places; G 90 places; I - 72 places; J - 60 places; CSU - 15 cells
Governor Ian West
Prison Group Director Teresa Clarke CBE
Date of last inspection Report October 2021:
An excellent custody manager on the induction wing had made this a safe and positive place for new arrivals who were helped by more established peers to settle into the prison. On the specialist units, we saw prisoners with complex needs making good progress in a supportive environment. Elsewhere, some less experienced staff did not have high enough expectations of prisoners' behaviour and lacked the skills and confidence to create a stable and safe environment. Though inspectors saw some positive interactions between officers and prisoners, they also witnessed staff members who were ineffectual, dismissive or rude. In a prison like Swinfen Hall, the incentives scheme should be a key tool in improving behaviour and helping leaders and staff to raise standards. It was, therefore, disappointing to hear how ineffective prisoners felt it was in motivating them, with those on an enhanced level often not getting the rewards that they had earned.

HMP THAMESIDE
GRIFFIN MANOR WAY THAMESMEAD, LONDON SE28 0FJ
Tel: 0208 317 9777
Private, Serco, Cat B local.
CNA 600. OpCap 1232.
Visits are booked by prisoners and visitors will be advised of the date and time to visit

once the booking is accepted. Online information about visiting however is here: serco.com/uk/sector-expertise/justice/hmp-thameside An industries building provides classrooms and workshops for print finishing and textiles. The prison was purpose built. All cells have integrated toilets and showers, a telephone and in-cell information technology (IT) for communication within the prison. Using the in-cell technology, prisoners can book their own visits, choose menu options, book healthcare appointments and send messages to departments in the prison. Eligible prisoners can opt to pay for access to a limited number of television channels. There is a well-equipped gym with outdoor sports area, a library, an education centre and multi-faith centre. The prison is managed under contract by Serco Group plc with two partner agencies, Catch 22 and Turning Point (focusing on issues arising from drug and alcohol misuse).

Short description of residential units

There are five wings, each divided into two units (upper and lower), with an average unit capacity of 110 prisoners. The first night centre is on A wing (upper unit) and the IDTS wing is on A wing (lower unit). The prison has a dedicated health care unit with inpatient facilities for 20 prisoners, and a care and separation unit which has a capacity for 18 prisoners.

Director Dave Bamford

Health service provider Practice Plus Group

Learning and skills providers A4e

IMB 2020: *HMP Thameside went into lockdown on 23 March 2020 as a response to the COVID-19 pandemic. The year has also suffered from a chaotically planned and implemented email systems upgrade by Serco IT in July and August 2020, which left many without access to email and many of the IMB monitoring records for over a month, without warning.*

However prisoner representatives were unlocked for most of the day to help resolve minor issues and the library had a successful outreach service that gave prisoners regular access to books this was noted on 23 June 2020 when a team from Her Majesty's Inspectorate of Prisons (HMIP) conducted a one-day scrutiny inspection on the prison's handling of the pandemic. A new Director and Deputy Director both took up their posts in April 2020.

HMP THORN CROSS
APPLETON THORN
WARRINGTON CHESHIRE, WA4 4RL
Tel: 01925 805100 Fax: 01925 805101
Public, Cat D open resettlement.
Group: Gtr Manchester, Merseyside Cheshire
CNA 327. OpCap 325 - temp reduction
Visits: Prisoners book visits and visitors advised of date and time once the booking has been accepted.
Healthcare: GMMH NHS Trust
Education provider: Novus

Thorn Cross was purpose built in 1985 as an open establishment for male juvenile and young prisoners. It was re-roled in 2008 to become a prison for 18- to 25-year-old men but, due to the decrease in prisoners under 25, this upper age limit was removed in 2013.

Short description of residential units

Units 1-5 Each unit has 60 single rooms. Unit 4 is closed for fire safety work.

Unit 6 An enhanced unit with 10 single rooms

Unit 7 has 33 single rooms and Unit 8 has 44 self-contained outworker living units

Governor Dan Cooper, February 2019

Date of last inspection Report: April 2021: *Thorn Cross remained an impressive establishment with a culture and physical environment that supported rehabilitative endeavour and delivered positive outcomes for prisoners. Relationships between staff and prisoners were mature and respectful. Complaints were managed well and leaders had continued to undertake a good level of prisoner consultation. Leaders were aware of prisoners' main concerns and tangible actions were usually being taken to address them. Security was proportionate and it was encouraging that relatively few prisoners were returned to closed conditions. There was little violence, use of force or self-harm, but governance of segregation and use of force was weak.*

HMP USK / PRESCOED
47 MARYPORT ST, USK NP15 1XP
Tel: 01291 671600 Fax: 01291 671752
Public, **Usk** is an adult men's category C national sex offender treatment provider and resettlement prison. **Prescoed** is a public adult and young adult men's open prison.
Usk CNA 159. OpCaP 254
Prescoed CNA 260. OpCaP 260
Population of the prisons June 2021.
Usk
• 45% of the population was aged over 50.
• 10.45% were from BAME backgrounds.
• 10 prisoners were foreign nationals.
• 12 prisoners had under 8 weeks left to serve.
• 78.18% were sentenced to five years or more.
• 99.09% were sex offenders.
• 8.63% working with the substance use team.
Prescoed
• 21.05% were aged over 50.
• 14.91% were from BAME backgrounds.
• There were no foreign national prisoners.
• 27 (11.84%) had under 8 weeks to serve.
• 72.26% were sentenced to five years or more.
• 8.33% were sex offenders.
• 13.15% working with the substance team.
Prisons' status and key providers
Physical and mental health provider: Aneurin Bevan University Health Board Substance use treatment provider: Dyfodol
Education provider: HMPPS
Prison Group: Wales
Brief history
Usk opened in 1844 as a house of correction. In 1870, it became the county gaol for Monmouthshire and remained in that role until 1922, when it closed. It reopened in 1939 as a closed borstal and became a detention centre in 1964. In 1983, it was turned into a youth custody centre, and from 1988 to 1990 a young offender institution. Since May 1990, it has been an adult category C establishment largely holding sex offenders. It became a resettlement prison in 2019.
Prescoed opened in 1939 as an open borstal. It became a detention centre in 1964, an open youth custody centre in 1983 and an open young offender institution in 1988. Some years

later it also started holding category D adult men. Since 2004, it has been exclusively an open prison for adult males, including young adult men aged 18 to 21.
Short description of residential units
Usk accommodation consisted of four wings:
• A, B and C – each with two-storey landings. A1 landing was used as protective isolation units (PIUs) (accommodation for known or probably COVID-19 cases) and reverse cohort units during the height of the pandemic.
• D wing – a single-storey shielding unit.
At **Prescoed**, there were 10 residential units; all except the Lester unit were single storey, and a mixture of single and double rooms:
• The Mitchell unit – larger single room for prisoners working in the community.
• Two semi-detached houses for up to eight longer term men, preparing for release.
• Forty temporary pods with their own en-suite facilities, 20 of which had been used as PIUs and RCUs during COVID-19, and the remainder for outworkers.
Governor of both prisons Giles Mason
Prison group director Kenny Brown
Date of last inspection Report October 2021.

HMP THE VERNE
PORTLAND
DORSET, DT5 1EQ
Tel: 01305 825000 Fax: 01305 825001
Public, a male category C training prison, for those convicted of sexual offences.
CNA: 570. OpCap: 580
Visits are booked by prisoner led application.
Visits enquiry-only line: 01305 825 014 - open Mon-Fri 2pm to 4pm (Friday closes at 3:30pm)
Tues, Sat, Sun: 1:45pm to 4pm.
Physical health provider: Practice Plus Group
Education provider: Weston College
Prison group Avon and South Dorset
The citadel, on which HMP The Verne is built, was built by convicts from Portland Prison between 1860 and 1872. In September 2013, it became an immigration removal centre until in July 2018 when it became a prison for sex offenders. The residential structure consists of three standard residential buildings, a dormitory unit and a segregation unit.
Each residential building is divided into two units, giving a total of six separate residential

units (named Arne, Abbotsbury, Bincombe, Blandford, Corfe and Chesil), each with 80 rooms spread across their second and third floors. New receptions are accommodated on Corfe while they undergo an induction programme.

The ground floor of each residential unit consists of an association room, a dining area, office spaces and a communal foyer.

'The dormitories ' (named Dorset unit) consists of 10 ground-floor dormitories and is largely used to house residents with mobility issues or other social care needs.

Governor David Bourne (July 2016)

Date of last inspection report June 2020: *Overall this was a positive inspection of a well-run institution. Since The Verne reopened as a training prison, the Governor has established a culture where staff and prisoners treat each other with respect and legitimate concerns are responded to. However, there needs to be better partnership work and robust challenge of key partners in order to improve healthcare and activities provision.*

HMP WAKEFIELD
WAKEFIELD WF2 9AG
Tel: 01924 612000 Fax: 01924 612001
Public, high security prison for Cat A & B.
CNA 750. OpCap 750.
Visits by phone booking only on 01924 612274.
Health provider: Practice Plus Group
Learning and skills provider: Novus
Group: LTHSE
Wakefield became a dispersal prison in 1996 and held those posing the highest security risk. It is now a lifer centre with a focus on serious sex offenders.
Wings A-D: residential units. F: segregation and CSC, Health care centre: inpatient unit.
Governor Tom Wheatley
Latest Inspection Report: November 2018: *An essentially respectful prison, with many examples of good relationships and interactions between staff and prisoners. However, as in so many establishments, our survey revealed that black and minority ethnic prisoners had a poorer perception of their treatment and conditions than their white counterparts. These negative perceptions needed to be understood. Until this happened there would be no way of knowing whether the negative perceptions were justified or not, and even if they were not, the negative perceptions themselves needed to be taken seriously and addressed. There was still a need to provide sufficient activity places for all inmates that would complement the adequate time out of cell that was already available to those who were employed. The introduction of key workers was a highly significant development, and once it was fully embedded could well offer the opportunity for further improvement in the area of rehabilitation and release planning. By any standards this was a good inspection, which was highly creditable given the complexity of the prison. The high standards, good practice and improvements that have been achieved were the result of hard work and dedication on the part of those who clearly took very seriously their responsibilities for the safe, secure and purposeful imprisonment of inmates.*

HMP WANDSWORTH
PO BOX 757
WANDSWORTH LONDON, SW18 3HU
Tel: 020 8588 4000 Fax: 020 8588 4001
Task of the establishment HMP Wandsworth is a category B local male prison with a category C resettlement unit.
Group London. CNA 963. OpCap 1452.
Visits by phone booking only on 03000 606 508 open, Mon-Fri 0915 to 1700.
Visiting times
Mon-Fri: 1:30pm-2:30pm, 3:30-4:30pm.
Healthcare: St George's NHS Trust
Learning and skills provider: Novus
Brief history
HMP Wandsworth is a large Victorian prison serving the courts of south-west London. The category B local prison function is fulfilled by Heathfield unit, while Trinity unit holds category C prisoners.
A and B wings – general population
C wing – half is VPU, D wing – drug recovery unit. E wing – first night and induction unit, and seg unit. G, H & K wings Category C unit
Governor Graham Barratt
Date of last inspection report: July 2018. IMB 2020: *"The Board cannot describe the prison as 'safe' when 270 prisoner-on-officer assaults were reported, 352 prisoner on prisoner assaults and 774 self-harm incidents.*
Wandsworth might feel safer if:
• *all prisoners were housed in single cells*

- 83 -

- the prison had fully staffed hospital wing
- all prisoners received the support, education and activities they needed every day
- a phone blocker was installed, to render illegal mobiles useless
- a body scanner was used to greatly reduce drug trafficking.

How fairly and humanely are prisoners treated? Prisoners were as well treated as possible, despite the unacceptable living conditions in the prison's overcrowded 169-year-old buildings. The age, decay and physical limitations of the buildings created conditions for the prisoners which the Board considered inhumane."

HMP WARREN HILL
WOODBRIDGE
SUFFOLK, IP12 3BF
Tel: 01394 633400 Fax: 01394 633438
Public, category C adult male closed prison
CNA 258. OpCap 264
Visit by phone booking on 01394 633 633 open Mon-Thurs: 9am to midday or book by email: socialvisits.warrenhill@justice.gov.uk
Visiting times: Wed, Sat, Sun: 2pm to 4pm.
Healthcare provider: Practice Plus Group
Prison group Hertfordshire, Essex, Suffolk
Previously an establishment holding boys aged 15 to 18, in 2014 the prison became a category C establishment holding adult men in a developing progression regime, a therapeutic community and a psychologically informed planned environment.

The progression regime was initially established in response to the decision by the Secretary of State for Justice on prisoners' suitability to transfer to open conditions, and it excluded a number of prisoners on indeterminate sentences (ISPs), both on life sentences and indeterminate sentence for public protection (IPP). The progression regime was established to ensure that ISPs excluded from open conditions could evidence that they had reduced their risk of serious harm sufficiently to enable them to be released from custody. Since then, additional groups of prisoners are now also considered for the progression regime. The PIPE has places for up to 20, primarily to offer transitional support for prisoners who have completed therapy. The TC accommodates up to 40 prisoners and provides intensive group-based therapy under the guidance of psychologists and trained officers.

Short description of residential units
Alder: 89 beds (progression regime)
Oak: 90 beds (progression regime)
Elm: 40 beds (therapeutic community)
Maple: 20 beds (PIPE)
Sycamore: 19 beds (over 50's)
Governor David Nicholson.

Date of last inspection Report March 2020: *The overwhelmingly positive aspects of the prison were such that we have made very few recommendations. There was one key concern which focused on expanding and improving the education provision, and ensuring that attendance was encouraged on a consistent basis. Otherwise, we made only 11 recommendations. Among these, we have commented on the need to improve the response to complaints, to help staff with their understanding of diversity issues, to do more for prisoners with disabilities and to more carefully monitor the timing at which medication is administered. Yet again, we have found ourselves looking at the issue of how to improve prisoners' ability to contact their families through the use of video-enabled social media. We are well aware of the potential risks associated with this, but would encourage Her Majesty's Prison and Probation Service (HMPPS) to think innovatively as to how these risks could be managed and trials conducted in appropriate circumstances. It is surely inevitable that at some point in the future this will be seen as an entirely normal feature of prison life, and Warren Hill could well be the type of environment in which the possibilities and benefits could be usefully explored.*

HMP WAYLAND
GRISTON, THETFORD
NORFOLK, IP25 6RL
Tel: 01953 804100 Fax: 01953 804220
Public, Category C male training prison.
Group Beds Cambs & Norfolk
CNA 264877 OpCap 1,003
Visits book by phone on: 01953 804152 or by email Socialvisits.wayland@hmps.gsi.gov.uk
Visiting times: Mon-Wed, Sat-Sun 2pm to 4pm
IMB 2020: Wayland is a category C male training and resettlement prison, with an operational capacity of 1,003. The original

building units - four H blocks, a segregation unit, a healthcare unit, and a kitchen - were built over 35 years ago. There have since been four expansions, and there are now five ready-to-use wings, a first night centre, a second kitchen and four individually designed accommodation units, which has resulted in a very spread-out site. A new segregation unit was extensively damaged by prisoners, after refurb it reopened successfully as a first night centre. The original wings have double and single cells, each with an integral toilet, and a shower block on each spur. Two of these units have been designated for enhanced prisoners, with a more relaxed internal regime.

The older buildings had ongoing problems with leaking flat roofs, resulting in puddles in the corridors. These have been repaired, but more work is likely to be needed, especially as the cell construction in these buildings includes inward-opening doors, which are easy to barricade and potentially a source of difficulty for staff in such a situation.

There have also been severe problems with the fabric and construction of the newer builds. An ongoing refurbishment programme has been in place throughout the year, but the design and construction of these units mean that further work will be needed for many of them; they are already beyond their original design life.

Governor Steve Garvie

HMP WEALSTUN
WETHERBY YORKSHIRE, LS23 7AZ
Tel: 01937 444400 Fax: 01937 444401
Public, Cat C adult training and resettlement.
CNA 820. OpCap 812
Group Yorkshire
Visits booked by phone on 01937 444 599 open Monday, Tuesday and Thursday 8am to midday and 1pm to 4pm, and Wednesday and Friday 8am to 12pm.
Visiting times:
Mon-Tue: 9:30-11am, 2:15-4pm, Wed 2:15pm to 4pm. Thurs 9:30-11am, 2:15pm-4pm, Sat 9:30am-11:30am, 1:45pm-3:45pm, Sun 9:30am-11:30am,1:45pm-3:45pm
Health provider: Practice Plus group
Education framework provider: Novus

On 1 April 1995, HM Prisons Thorp Arch and Rudgate amalgamated to form HMP Wealstun. This created a category C (closed) side and category D (open) side within one establishment. In 2008, the open prison closed and the prison underwent a conversion to an entirely category C prison, which was fully operational in May 2010. Since May 2015, it has served a resettlement function for the West Yorkshire area.

There are 10 residential units and a 13-bed segregation unit.

A and B wings are the original 1960 remand centre buildings, which between them hold 230 prisoners in a combination of single and double cells. A wing is split in to two units, a standard residential unit and a residential support unit (RSU). The purpose of the RSU is to support prisoners who struggle to cope until they can be successfully reintegrated back onto one of the main residential units.

C wing holds 180 prisoners in single cells, and includes two safer cells. This wing also accommodates the majority of prisoners on the integrated drug treatment system programme (90 spaces). D wing is a prefabricated single-cell accommodation unit, holding 120 prisoners. Half of D wing supports the incentivised substance-free living initiative. E, F, G, H, I and J wings were converted from open category D accommodation to closed category C accommodation. Between them, they hold 300 prisoners, with approximately 50 on each unit, in single-cell accommodation. I wing supports prisoners on induction/first night but also holds some of the older population.

Governor : Diane Lewis (October 2015)
Date of last inspection February 2020

HMYOI WERRINGTON
STOKE-ON-TRENT
STAFFS, ST9 0DX
Tel: 01782 463300 Fax: 01782 463301
Public establishment to hold sentenced and remanded boys aged 15 to 18 years.
CNA 115. OpCap 118
Visits Booking line: 0300 060 6508 open Monday-Friday, 9am to 6pm
Visiting times: Tues-Sun 1330-1615
Group: Youth Custody Service

The establishment became a youth custody centre in 1985 and in 1988 became a dedicated juvenile centre (15-18-year olds) with secure accommodation for those serving a detention and training order.
Doulton unit: main accommodation
Denby unit: induction and enhanced unit.
Care and support unit: segregation
Health provider: Practice Plus Group
Education: Novus
Date of last full inspection June 2019: *Time out of cell was reasonably good for most children but 'keep apart' issues meant there were often delays in moving them to education, health care or other appointments. This meant that resource was wasted as teachers, clinicians and other professionals waited for children to arrive. Support for children with additional learning needs was very good but there was too little outreach provision to meet the needs of children who were unable to attend mainstream education.*

There was some good work in support of resettlement but a lack of coordination, and caseworkers and sentence plans were not driving the care of children at Werrington.

There are many positives in this report but weaknesses in behaviour management have led to deterioration of outcomes in some areas. Managers need to make a concerted effort to support frontline staff in the challenging task of implementing behaviour management schemes, with the principal aim of reducing the number of violent incidents at Werrington.

HMYOI WETHERBY
YORK ROAD, WETHERBY LS22 5ED
Tel: 01937 544200 Fax: 01937 544201
Public sector. Wetherby holds in custody boys between the ages of 15 to 18 committed by the courts.
Group Youth Custody Service
CNA 336. OpCap 336
Visits are led by prisoner application, visitors will be advised of dates and times once the booking has been accepted by the prison.
Visiting times: Mon-Fri: 6.45pm – 7.45pm
Wetherby became a borstal in 1958, and is now a dedicated centre for males under 18.
Short description of residential units
Anson – care and separation unit
Benbow – long-term determinate and lifers
Frobisher – first night facility and standard
Collingwood – standard accommodation
Drake – standard accommodation
Exmouth – standard accommodation
Keppel – specialist complex issues unit
Governor/Director Peter Gormley
Health service Leeds NHS Trust
Learning and skills providers: Novus
Latest Inspection Report July 2019: *Overall Wetherby continues to be a well-led institution, run by a confident staff group delivering useful outcomes for children. We observed considerable initiative and energy and a very evident commitment to ongoing improvement. We have made a small number of recommendations which we hope will assist this process.*

HMP WHATTON
NEW LANE, WHATTON NOTTS, NG13 9FQ
Tel: 01949 803200 Fax: 01949 803201
Public, adult male category C training prison holding exclusively sex offenders.
Visits are booked by phone on 01949 803 200 open Mon-Fri 9am-noon and 1pm to 5pm.
Visiting times: Mon, Thu, Fri 1:45-3:45pm
Saturday: 9am to 11am and 1:45pm to 3:45pm
Sunday: 9am to 11am and 1:45pm to 3:45pm
CNA 775. OpCap 841.
Healthcare: Practice Plus Group
Education provider: PeoplePlus
Prison group East Midlands
Brief history
HMP Whatton was built in 1966 as a detention centre for boys. During the 1990s, it developed as a prison for people convicted of sex offences. Its population doubled in early 2006 with the building of eight new units.
A1–8 Newer residential wings with modern cells. The care and separation (segregation) unit is attached to A3.
B1 and B2 The original accommodation,

mostly former dormitories with cubicles. B3 landing 35 cells C1-3 Modular units: C2 is low security, C3 is doubled accommodation. Palliative care unit. Governor Dr Lynn Saunders OBE008 Date of last inspection report: September 2020: *Almost one in four prisoners reported feeling unsafe. We were concerned that some of the systems in place to identify vulnerable prisoners, such as first night safety interviews and good quality key work, were not sufficiently robust, and there was no formal system to identify those who were isolating themselves from staff and peers. During a normal regime at Whatton these prisoners would possibly stand out, but at a time when prisoners spent most of their day locked up there was an increased risk that some vulnerable prisoners could be overlooked.*

HMP WHITEMOOR
LONGHILL ROAD, MARCH
CAMBS, PE15 0PR
Tel: 01354 602350 Fax: 01354 602351
Public maximum security prison for category A and B male prisoners.
Group LTHSE. CNA 514. OpCap 459.
Visits booked by phone only on 01354 602 800 open Mon-Fri 9.30am to 1.30pm
Visiting times: Wednesday: 1:30pm to 3:30pm
Thursday: 1:30pm to 3:30pm
Healthcare: Northamptonshire NHS Trust
Mental health provider: Northamptonshire Healthcare NHS Foundation Trust
Education provider: Milton Keynes College
Prison group: LTHSE
HMP Whitemoor opened in 1991 as part of the high-security estate. The main establishment supported two regimes: a mainstream prisoner population and a population with personality disorders. Most prisoners were younger than those in other maximum-security prisons, and those who needed to be separated from others because of their offence were not held. One wing was specifically designated for prisoners with personality disorders.
A close supervision centre, which opened in October 2004, was part of a centrally managed national strategy administered by the directorate of high security at Prison Service headquarters. It aimed to provide the most dangerous, disturbed and disruptive prisoners with a controlled environment, to help them develop a more settled and acceptable pattern of behaviour.
Short description of residential units
A wing – has three spurs, with one spur designated as the psychologically informed planned environment (PIPE) unit
B wing and C wing – residential units with three spurs each
D wing – the Fens unit, with 70 cells for prisoners on a personality disorder programme Segregation unit – 30 cells (12 of these spaces are designated as Bridge unit accommodation) Health unit – 9 bed spaces
Governor Ruth Stephens,
Date of last inspection report: September 2020
The prison was largely safe and decent however establishing in-cell education provision had taken too long. Managers needed to buy more telephones, improve the quality of the food and implement a safe way for prisoners to cook for themselves. In addition, managers needed to address and redress shortfalls in the areas of segregation, equality and diversity.

HMP WINCHESTER
ROMSEY ROAD
WINCHESTER, SO22 5DF
Tel: 01962 723000. Fax: 01962 723001
Public, category B local men's prison, with a separate category C unit.
CNA 486. OpCap 500
Visits booked by phone only on 0345 223 5514 open Mon-Friday 10-11:30am, 2pm to 3:30pm
Visiting times: Tue, Thu, Sat 1:30-4:30pm
Healthcare provider: CNWL NHS Trust.
Education provider: Milton Keynes College
Prison group South Central
HMP Winchester was built in 1849 and

radial design, typical of Victorian prisons. The prison covers an area of approximately six acres. In 1908, the health care centre was built, and in 1964 another unit was added for use as a remand centre holding young offenders. The unit, known as Westhill, continued to be used until 1991 when it housed women prisoners. In 2004, its role changed to a category C resettlement unit.

Short description of residential units
On the local prison site:
A wing: remand and convicted VP's.
B wing: remand and convicted prisoners
C wing: detoxification and the integrated drug treatment system; induction and first night.
D wing: remand and convicted prisoners, including the induction and first night unit.
On the category C site:
Two units accommodating category C and a small number of category D prisoners.
Name of governor/director and date in post
Jim Bourke – September 2018
Date of last inspection report January 2020.
Overall this was a disappointing inspection. In the local prison we found significant deterioration compared with findings at our previous 2016 inspection. Decline was evident in three of our four tests of a healthy prison. Outcomes in safety and purposeful activity were now poor, and not sufficiently good in rehabilitation and release planning. In respect they remained insufficiently good. On the category C unit, outcomes remained reasonably good in safety and respect but had deteriorated in purposeful activity and rehabilitation and release planning. Despite this concerning picture, there was some evidence that the decline had been arrested and some tentative improvements made.

HMP WOODHILL
TATTENHOE ST
MILTON KEYNES MK4 4DA
Tel: 01908 722000 Fax: 01908 722320
Public, core local prison, which means that the bulk of its population comprises a mixture of short-sentenced men with the substance misuse and other local prisons; it also has a high on for a small number of oners. The prison also has a n centre (CSC), which is part of a national system for managing some of the most high-risk prisoners in the system; this is inspected separately.
CNA 626. OpCap 637.
Group LTHSE
Visits booked by telephone on 01908 722 329 open Mon-Fri: 8-11:30am and 1-3:30pm
Visiting times:
Mon-Tue:: 9:30-10:30am and 2:15-3:15pm
Wednesday: 9:30am to 10:30am
Thur-Fri: 9:30-10:30am and 2:15-3:15pm
Healthcare provider: CNWL NHS Trust
Group: LTHSE
Brief history
HMP Woodhill was opened in 1992. It started as a local prison but in the late 1990s took on a high- security role as a core local prison.
Short description of residential units
Each house unit, except units 5 and 6, is divided into two wings, A and B. Each wing on the main house units is designed to hold 60 prisoners in single cells. Some cells have been converted into doubles. All units hold a cross-section of prisoners, including category A and YPs following a risk assessment.
House unit 1A a mix of remand and convicted prisoners; 1B is the induction wing.
House unit 2A a mix of remand and convicted prisoners; 2B is the drug rehabilitation unit
House unit 3 a mix of remand and convicted prisoners; House unit 4A a mix of remand and convicted prisoners; 4B is the vulnerable prisoner unit House unit 5, 51 cells, all purpose built for two prisoners. House unit 6 – national CSC and protected witness unit.
Governor Nicola Marfleet, September 2017.
Underpinning nearly all the concerns raised in this report, including issues of safety and well-being,

were chronic staff shortages and inexperience. This led to poor time out of cell, unpredictable daily routines and limited access to activity. Most interaction we saw between staff and prisoners was polite but reactive, and many prisoners expressed frustration at the apparent inability of staff to help them. A restricted daily routine had been in place for three years and there was little challenge and encouragement to help prisoners to engage constructively with activity. During the working day we found half the population locked in their cells. Our colleagues in Ofsted judged the overall effectiveness of learning and skills provision to be 'inadequate', their lowest assessment, and caused mainly by the underuse of available training and education resources owing to staff shortages.

HMP WORMWOOD SCRUBS
PO BOX 757
DU CANE ROAD LONDON, W12 0AE
Tel: 020 8588 3200 Fax: 020 8588 3201
Public Cat B Local reception and resettlement.
CNA 1175. OpCap 1273.
Visits are booked by phone on 0300 060 6511 open Mon-Fri 9am to 6pm
Visiting times: Mon, Wed, Thu: 9am to 11am and 2pm to 4pm. Tues, Fri: 9am to 11am
Healthcare: Practice Plus Group.
Education provider: Novus;
Prison group London
Brief history
Wormwood Scrubs was built by prisoners from Millbank Gaol between 1875 and 1891. In 1902, the last female prisoner was transferred to HMP Holloway. In 1922, one wing became a borstal. During World War II, the prison was used by the War Department. In 1994, a new hospital wing was completed, and in 1996 a fifth wing was completed.
Short description of residential units
• A wing: Workers, remand and sentenced prisoners. Protective isolation unit.
• B wing: Induction, reverse cohort unit that holds 167 prisoners. Jan Wilcox unit: Induction workers. It holds 17 prisoners, in double rooms and a dormitory.
• C wing: Workers, remand and sentenced prisoners. It holds 138 prisoners. Second-stage integrated drug treatment system. It holds a maximum of 165 prisoners.
D wing: Workers, remand and sentenced prisoners. It holds a maximum of 180 prisoners. Incentivised substance-free living unit. It holds a maximum of 64 prisoners, all in single rooms. E wing: Workers, remand and sentenced prisoners. It holds a maximum of 91 prisoners. E wing: Elizabeth Fry unit and off-wing workers. It holds a maximum of 55 prisoners. The EFU supports those with learning difficulties and those engaging with in-reach. Health care unit: Holds a maximum of 17 inpatients. Conibeere unit: Detoxification stabilisation unit and RCU. It holds a maximum of 55 prisoners. First night centre: Holds a maximum of 36 prisoners. Segregation unit: 18 single cells.
Governor: Jonathan French, June 2020
Prison Group Director Ian Bickers
Date of last inspection report September 2021.
Overall, the prison was a much safer, cleaner and better organised prison than it had been in the past, but prisoners were locked in their cells for too long. The most important challenge facing leaders is to maintain and improve on the levels of safety, while significantly increasing the amount of time prisoners are spending out of their cells in education, training, work, leisure and rehabilitation activity.

HMP WYMOTT
LEYLAND, PRESTON PR26 8LW
Tel: 01772 442000 Fax: 01772 442001
Public, complex, category C training prison, with half of the population convicted of sexual offences and others being convicted of a wide range of offences, including violence.
CNA 1077. OpCap 1020.
Visits booked by phone on 01772 442 234 open Mon-Fri 9am to 3pm. Visiting times: Mon-Fri 2:30pm to 3:30pm. Saturday and Sunday: 9:30am to 10:30am and 2:30pm to 3:30pm.
Health provider: GMMH NHS Trust
Education provider: Novus
Prison group Cumbria and Lancashire
Wymott opened in 1979 as a short-term category C prison. There was extensive damage to the prison following a disturbance in 1993, after which part of it was rebuilt, and it was redesignated to hold prisoners convicted of sexual offences. The prison population increased in 2003/04, with the addition of two new wings, and again in 2008, when the therapeutic community opened. On

learning of the restrictions to prison regimes at the start of the COVID-19 pandemic, the prison entered command mode in March 2020; it adopted a temporary regime and reduced its population by about 100.
Short description of residential units
K wing (category C)
I wing MCOSOs / older prisoners / social care
B wing MCOSOs non-cellular accommodation
 G wing MCOSOs, cellular accommodation
Reverse cohort units:
D wing (category C) (1 landing)
H wing PIPE unit, MCOSOs cellular
Prisoner isolation unit:
D wing (category C) (1 landing)
H wing MCOSOs, cellular accommodation
Workers units (essential workers):
A wing (MCOSOs)
C wing (category C)
F wing (PIPE unit)
J wing (mixed MCOSOs and category Cs)
E wing (category C)
Governor Graham Beck (January 2018)

HM INSPECTORATE OF PRISONS REPORTS Published to October 2021

The Inspectorate reports on all prisons in England and Wales available online at:
www.prisonoracle.com.

Prisoners can get a FREE copy of any Inspectorate Report by post from the Inspectorate, just by writing or phoning and asking them for a copy.

**HM Inspectorate of Prisons
3rd floor, 10 South Colonnade
London. E14 4PU. Tel: 020 7340 050**

In March 2020, in response to the Covid-19 pandemic, the then HM Chief Inspector of Prisons, Peter Clarke, announced the suspension of full inspections of prisons.

On June 1st 2020 Peter Clarke issued the following statement:

"On 17 March 2020, I announced a suspension of full inspections until the end of May 2020. This reflected government public health guidance and recognised that it would be wrong to burden prison staff with the rigours of full inspections as they dealt with the rapidly-unfolding COVID-19 crisis. I also emphasised that I have an ongoing statutory duty to report on treatment and conditions for those detained.

"On 21 April 2020, we published information about our model of short scrutiny visits (SSVs), which would enable HM Inspectorate of Prisons to fulfil this duty.

"The suspension of full inspections will remain in place for the time being. However, the Inspectorate will continue to carry out short scrutiny visits, and is also currently working to enhance and develop the SSV methodology.

"The SSV model developed in April, focusing on short visits to groups of similar establishments, has been successfully implemented and well received – both in principle, reflecting the importance of independent scrutiny, and in practice, in locations we have visited. Governing teams have reported that they have found an independent perspective to be useful and we have seen some positive changes as a result of our visits.

"Since 21 April, we have visited 19 establishments – men's local, training and long-term/high-security prisons, women's prisons, young offender institutions and immigration removal centres. We have a schedule of further visits over the coming weeks.

"You can read findings from our published reports here. It is clear from our visits that swift action by the prison service appears to have prevented widespread transmission of the virus and averted the potentially disastrous consequences that some had feared. There have been fewer cases of COVID-19 than was initially predicted. However, we have also noted the extreme impact of these measures on regimes, time out of cell, and the risks created by the reduction in support services provided to prisoners, particularly the most vulnerable.

"Our initial SSV model was designed for a prison system navigating its way through a crisis. However, as we know, the COVID-19 pandemic picture has changed significantly. We have also noted that the prisons we have visited have been stable, and there have been enough staff.

"In light of this, development of our methodology in this next phase will be guided by the core considerations of whether the restrictions in place

are proportionate to the health risks facing places of detention and balanced against the negative impact of those restrictions on prisoners and detainees. "We do not in any way underestimate the continuing challenges facing those who run these establishments. As with our initial SSV model, we will work constructively with HM Prison and Probation Service (HMPPS) and other agencies in refining our model.

"We will continue to follow national public health advice, and seek to ensure that our visits and reports make a positive and valuable contribution as establishments move from severe restrictions towards regimes which reflect the easing of those restrictions in the wider community.

"We will publish further detail on our enhanced SSV model in the coming weeks."

Following on from this the following different types of Inspection were introduced:

Short scrutiny visits (SSVs) were introduced in April 2020 as a response to the COVID-19 pandemic.

In August 2020, we replaced them with **Scrutiny Visits (SVs),** which reflected our updated approach to inspection in light of the changing circumstances around COVID-19.

As of May 2021, HMI Prisons has returned to a programme of full inspections.

• HMP/YOI Swinfen Hall Report on an unannounced inspection of HMP/YOI Swinfen Hall by HM Chief Inspector of Prisons (28 June – 9 July 2021) Published: 06 October 2021

• HMP Usk and HMP and YOI Prescoed Report on an unannounced inspection of HMP Usk and HMP and YOI Prescoed by HM Chief Inspector of Prisons (14-25 June 2021) Published: 01 October 2021

• HMP Wormwood Scrubs Report on an unannounced inspection of HMP Wormwood Scrubs by HM Chief Inspector of Prisons (7-17 June 2021) Published: 09 September 2021

• HMP & YOI Low Newton Report on an unannounced inspection of HMP & YOI Low Newton by HM Chief Inspector of Prisons (2-18 June 2021) Published: 07 September 2021

• HMP Oakwood Report on an unannounced inspection of HMP Oakwood by HM Chief Inspector of Prisons (17-28 May 2021) Published: 03 September 2021

• HMP Haverigg Report on an unannounced inspection of HMP Haverigg by HM Chief Inspector of Prisons (17-28 May 2021) Published: 01 September 2021

• HMP & YOI Chelmsford Urgent Notification letter, issued on 26 August 2021, and inspection debriefing paper Published: 27 August 2021

• HMP Send Report on an unannounced inspection of HMP Send by HM Chief Inspector of Prisons (10-21 May 2021) Published: 26 August 2021

• HM Prisons Inspectorate Annual Report 2020-21 In his Annual Report, for 2020–21, HM Chief Inspector of Prisons Charlie Taylor reports on the Prison Service's success in preventing large-scale deaths as a result of COVID-19, but describes how severe and prolonged daily lock-up have harmed prisoners' physical and mental welfare. Published: 20 July 2021

• Neurodiversity in the criminal justice system. This review, produced by HMI Prisons with HMI Probation and HMICFRS, explores how the needs of neurodivergent people are being identified and met within the criminal justice system. Published: 15 July 2021

• HMP & YOI Sudbury Report on a scrutiny visit to HMP & YOI Sudbury by HM Chief Inspector of Prisons (27–28 April and 11-12 May 2021) Published: 17 June 2021

• HMYOI Parc Report on a scrutiny visit to HMYOI Parc by HM Chief Inspector of Prisons (20 and 27–28 April 2021) Published: 02 June 2021

• HMP North Sea Camp Report on a scrutiny visit to HMP North Sea Camp by HM Chief Inspector of Prisons (19 and 27–28 April 2021) Published: 02 June 2021

• HMP/YOI East Sutton Park Report on a scrutiny visit to HMP/YOI East Sutton Park by HM Chief Inspector of Prisons (12–13 and 20–21 April 2021) Published: 27 May 2021

• HMP/YOI Thorn Cross Report on a scrutiny visit to HMP/YOI Thorn Cross by

HM Chief Inspector of Prisons (12–13 and 20–21 April 2021) Published: 25 May 2021
• HMP Ford Report on a scrutiny visit to HMP Ford by HM Chief Inspector of Prisons (29–30 March and 13–14 April 2021) Published: 19 May 2021
• HMP High Down Report on a scrutiny visit to HMP High Down by HM Chief Inspector of Prisons (23 March and 7 – 8 April 2021) Published: 13 May 2021
• HMP Bure Report on a scrutiny visit to HMP Bure by HM Chief Inspector of Prisons (16 and 23–24 March 2021) Published: 30 April 2021
• HMP Exeter Report on a scrutiny visit to HMP Exeter by HM Chief Inspector of Prisons (9 and 16–17 March 2021) Published: 27 April 2021
• HMP Bedford Report on a scrutiny visit to HMP Bedford by HM Chief Inspector of Prisons (2 February and 16–17 March 2021) Published: 21 April 2021
• HMP & YOI Peterborough (women) Report on a scrutiny visit to HMP & YOI Peterborough (women) by HM Chief Inspector of Prisons (2 and 9–10 March 2021) Published: 20 April 2021
• HMP Grendon Report on a scrutiny visit to HMP Grendon (2 and 9–10 March 2021) Published: 13 April 2021
• HMP Leyhill Report on a scrutiny visit to HMP Leyhill by HM Chief Inspector of Prisons (23 February and 2–3 March 2021) Published: 07 April 2021
• HMYOI Feltham A Report on a scrutiny visit to HMYOI Feltham A by HM Chief Inspector of Prisons (9 and 17 February 2021) Published: 23 March 2021
• HMP Long Lartin Report on a scrutiny visit to HMP Long Lartin by HM Chief Inspector of Prisons (2 and 9 February 2021) Published: 16 March 2021
• HMP Lowdham Grange Report on a scrutiny visit to Lowdham Grange by HM Chief Inspector of Prisons (12 January and 2 February 2021) Published: 05 March 2021
• HMYOI Wetherby and Keppel Report on a scrutiny visit to HMYOI Wetherby and the Keppel unit by HM Chief Inspector of Prisons (19 and 26–27 January 2021) Published: 26 February 2021

• HMP Birmingham Report on a scrutiny visit to Birmingham by HM Chief Inspector of Prisons (24 November 2020 and 5–6 January 2021) Published: 16 February 2021
• HMP Leicester Report on a scrutiny visit to HMP Leicester by HM Chief Inspector of Prisons (8 and 15-16 December 2020) Published: 27 January 2021
• HMP/YOI Hindley Report on a scrutiny visit to HMP/YOI Hindley by HM Chief Inspector of Prisons (8 and 15–16 December 2020). Published: 26 January 2021
• HMP Huntercombe. Report on a scrutiny visit to HMP Huntercombe by HM Chief Inspector of Prisons (1 and 8–9 December 2020). Published: 19 January 2021
• HMP Risley. Report on a scrutiny visit to HMP Risley by HM Chief Inspector of Prisons (17 and 24–25 November 2020) Published: 12 January 2021
• HMP Peterborough (male). Report on a scrutiny visit to HMP Peterborough (male) by HM Chief Inspector of Prisons (17 and 24–25 November 2020) Published: 06 January 2021
• HMP Humber. Report on a scrutiny visit to HMP Humber by HM Chief Inspector of Prisons (27 October and 3–4 November 2020) Published: 08 December 2020
• HMP Pentonville. Report on a scrutiny visit to HMP Pentonville by HM Chief Inspector of Prisons (27 October and 3-4 November 2020) Published: 04 December 2020
• HMP Lindholme. Report on a scrutiny visit to HMP Lindholme by HM Chief Inspector of Prisons 13 and 27-28 October 2020 Published: 01 December 2020
• HMP Dartmoor. Report on a scrutiny visit to HMP Dartmoor by HM Chief Inspector of Prisons (22 and 29-30 September 2020) Published: 03 November 2020
• HMP Gartree. Report on a scrutiny visit to HMP Gartree by HM Chief Inspector of Prisons (22 and 29-30 September 2020) Published: 30 October 2020
• HMP Bristol. Report on a scrutiny visit to HMP Bristol by HM Chief Inspector of Prisons (14 and 22-23 September 2020) Published: 23 October 2020
• HMP Northumberland. Report on a scrutiny visit to HMP Northumberland by

HM Chief Inspector of Prisons (8 and 15–16 September 2020) Published: 16 October 2020
- HMP Swansea. Report on a scrutiny visit to HMP Swansea by HM Chief Inspector of Prisons (25 August and 2-3 September 2020) Published: 06 October 2020
- HMP Whatton. Report on a scrutiny visit to HMP Whatton by HM Chief Inspector of Prisons (18 and 25–26 August 2020) Published: 29 September 2020
- HMP Wymott. Report on a scrutiny visit to HMP Wymott by HM Chief Inspector of Prisons (18 and 25–26 August 2020) Published: 29 September 2020
- HMP Erlestoke. Report on a scrutiny visit to HMP Erlestoke by HM Chief Inspector of Prisons (11 and 18-19 August 2020) Published: 22 September 2020
- HMP Hewell scrutiny visit. Report on a scrutiny visit to HMP Hewell by HM Chief Inspector of Prisons (4 and 11 – 12 August 2020) Published: 15 September 2020.
- HMP Preston scrutiny visit. Report on a scrutiny visit to HMP Preston by HM Chief Inspector of Prisons (4 and 11–12 August 2020). Published: 15 September 2020
- HMP Whitemoor scrutiny visit. Report on a scrutiny visit to HMP Whitemoor by HM Chief Inspector of Prisons (28 July and 4–5 August 2020) Published: 08 September 2020
- Report on short scrutiny visits to Prisons holding prisoners convicted of sexual offences by HM Chief Inspector of Prisons (2 June 2020) Published: 22 June 2020
- Report on short scrutiny visits to long-term and high security prisons by HM Chief Inspector of Prisons (26 May 2020) Published: 15 June 2020
- Report on short scrutiny visits to long-term and high security prisons by HM Chief Inspector of Prisons (26 May 2020) Published: 15 June 2020
- Report on short scrutiny visits to prisons holding women by HM Chief Inspector of Prisons (19 May 2020) Published: 05 June 2020
- Report on short scrutiny visits to immigration removal centres by HM Chief Inspector of Prisons (12 May 2020) Published: 02 June 2020
- Report on short scrutiny visits to category C training prisons by HM Chief Inspector of Prisons (5 May 2020) Published: 22 May 2020
- Local prisons short scrutiny visit Report on short scrutiny visits to local prisons by HM Chief Inspector of Prisons (28 April 2020) Published: 18 May 2020
- Young offender institutions holding children Report on short scrutiny visits to young offender institutions (21 April 2020) Published: 07 May 2020

THE 2022 PRISONS HANDBOOK

For over 25 years it has been the definitive 1,600-page annual guide to the prison system of England and Wales.

Buy it online at HALF PRICE for prisoners at:
WWW.PRISONS.ORG.UK
Tel: 0845 474 0013

www.prisons.org.uk

SECTION TWO. ADVICE
A-Z of Advice Subjects

Before You Go To Prison, 95
- Before you go to Prison - *honestly, it's not the end of the world that it may seem right now.*
- The 'Bang Up Bag' - *what to pack.*
- What lays ahead - *Viewpoints from experienced voices who have been there.*

When You're In Prison, 100
- Adjudications - *Disciplinary charges and how to deal with them,* 100
- Applications & Complaints - *How to get things done in prison,* 103
- Bereavement - *when someone dies while you're inside, attending the funeral,* 106
- Block - *How to cope with segregation,* 107
- Categorisation - *male and female, what is it and getting a review,* 110
- Confiscation Orders - *what are they and what consequences do they bring,* 113
- Early Release Scheme - *Foreign nationals, how to return home early,* 114
- Education - *how to apply/study,* 114
- Equality - *you have rights not to be discriminated against,* 117
- Extremism - *Recognising it, its dangers and how to avoid it,* 118
- Facilities List - *Explaining the national and local list of what you can have in prison,* 119, 226
- Family Matters - *Maintaining family contact with, letters, visits, and phone calls,* 120
- Getting out - *Pre-release check list and how not to come back again; Licence, Supervising Officer, Discharge Grant, Rail Warrants, Accommodation, Benefits, Pensions, Work,* 122
- Healthcare - *Your rights to healthcare in prison and how to complain,* 125
- Home Detention Curfew - *'On The Tag' what is it, how do I apply for it?* 127
- Incentives Earned Privileges - *Levels and keeping your privileges - new 2019 scheme,* 128
- Keeping your home when in prison - *Steps you can take to keep accommodation,* 132
- Legal Highs: *Real Danger of DEATH,* 132
- Maintaining Innocence after conviction - *consequences of saying you didn't do it,* 133
- Marriage - *getting married while in prison, including civil partnerships,* 141
- Offending Behaviour Courses* what are they? 134

Currently Accredited Programmes 2022

ACCREDITED FOR COMMUNITY
Becoming New Me + (BNM+)
Breaking Free: Health and Justice Package
Building Better Relationships (BBR)
Building Skills for Recovery (BSR)
Drink Impaired Drivers Programme (DIDP)
Healthy Identity Intervention (HII)
Horizon
iHorizon
Identity Matters (IM)
Mentalisation based treatment (MBT)
New Me Strengths (NMS)
Living As New Me (LNM)
Resolve
Thinking Skills Programme (TSP)

ACCREDITED FOR CUSTODY 2022
Dependence Treatment Programme (ADTP)
Becoming New Me + (BNM+)
Breaking Free: Health and Justice Package (Custody)
Building Better Relationships (BBR)
Building Skills for Recovery (BSR)
Challenge to Change (C2C)
Choices, Actions, Relationships, Emotions (CARE)
Control of Violence for Angry Impulsive Drinkers – Group Secure (COVAID-GS)
Control of Violence for Angry Impulsive Drinkers – Group Secure Women (COVAID-GSW)
Democratic Therapeutic Community Model (DTC)
Democratic Therapeutic Community Model Plus (TC+)
Healthy Identity Intervention (HII)
Healthy Sex Programme (HSP)
Horizon
Identity Matters (IM)
Kaizen
Living as New Me
New Me Strengths
Resolve
The Bridge Programme
Thinking Skills Programme (TSP)

- Open Prisons - *how to prepare.* 141
- Pad Mates- sharing a cell without grief or friction, 143

- 94 -

- Parole New Review Mechanism, 154
- Prison Debt - why to avoid it, 144
- Property inside, 148
- Recall 2019 - your rights, 152
- ROTL 2019, 155
- Self-harm - how to cope, 156
- Sex in prison, 157
- Slang, 158
- Transfers, 159
- Veterans in Custody, 160
- VPUs, protection, 161

BEFORE YOU GO TO PRISON

If you're facing the possibility of a prison sentence, it probably feels like its the end of the world right now - but, honestly, it isn't.
In 2020 almost 47,000 people went to prison and 70,000 were released from it, and every single one of them, at one time or another, was feeling exactly the same as you feel right now. They came through it - and so can you.
But it's important to remain focused.

Surviving a prison sentence is made easier with forward planning, be realistic, expect the worst, hope for the best, and educate yourself about what lays ahead - you've started to do that already by buying this book.

THE 'BANG UP BAG'
A question that will probably have crossed your mind is 'what should I take in with me?' There's a 'National Facilities List' **(see page 242)** of what prisoners may have in their cell, from which each Governor selects items for a 'Local Facilities List' that apply to their own prison; you'll find Local Facility Lists for every prison on the **prisonoracle.com** prison entries.

Remember, just because it states in the National Facilities List that you may be allowed an item, it doesn't automatically mean will be able to have it at every prison.

Also, sometimes court dock officers will tell you that you can't have a packed bag ready with you during the trial and this can vary from court to court.

However, it is definitely worth packing a bang-up bag just in case.

Until August 2019 when the new Policy Framework on Incentives was issued **(see page 234)**, all adult male prisoners had to wear prison-issue uniform for the first two weeks - but this has now been abolished. The following are the basic things to take with you when you first go to prison.

• Cash. Take as much money with you as you can reasonably afford. This should be logged on your valuable property card (along with any bank cards, watch, jewellery etc) by the desk officer in the area underneath the courtroom. Any cash that you take in with you will be credited to your prison account and this will allow you to order goods from the prison canteen when you arrive at your destination prison. Your family and friends can top this account up once you are settled - they can top up your private cash account online at https://www.gov.uk/ send-prisoner-money Its free, it can only be used to send money to prisoners in public sector prisons – not private prisons – and it takes around three days to reach your account.

• Comfortable footwear. Shiny shoes are fine for the courtroom, but useless on prison wings, so make sure you have a decent pair of trainers in your bang-up bag. You can have two pairs (one for the gym).

• Shower flip flops. Anyone who has been in a prison shower knows why a decent pair of flip flops is absolutely essential. You do not want to wade barefoot through other people's filth, including blood, urine, faeces or semen. Our prisons are rife with infectious diseases, some of which – such as hepatitis or scabies – are highly infectious. Verruca's are the least of most prisoners' problems.

• Underwear and socks. Prisons do issue these items but they can be in short supply and may have been used by dozens of prisoners before you.

• Foam earplugs. Some prisons do sell these via the canteen list, but better not to take any chances. Almost all blokes snore and since it is highly likely that you'll end up sharing a cell in our seriously overcrowded jails, getting some sleep can be difficult if the stranger you are bunking with has rattles like a freight train. Earplugs also help deaden the worst of the shouting and banging that you get on most prison landings. Anything other than foam may be confiscated, so no silicon ones.

• Make sure you have a small address book containing all the addresses and phone numbers of family, friends and your legal team – basically anyone you want to stay in touch with, including your bank and/or landlord if you have one. You could also include your local MP's contact details in case you need their help.

• Prisoners can write and receive letters, as well as calling pre-approved numbers on the wing payphones, so having a book of stamps and your own ball-point pen (clear plastic type) will mean you avoid having to borrow in your first few days. Borrowing anything is against prison rules and can lead to debt where the interest rates make the worst payday lenders look like Father Christmas.

• You should be able to take in a radio or CD player (no iPods or similar devices, nor anything rechargeable), but they should have in-the-ear type headphones. Remember, your choice of music may not be the same as your new roommate's. Your own headphones let you drift away into your own little private world for a while.

• Make sure you have a watch with you, but not a flashy one that you would be devastated to lose in prison. Strangely enough jails are full of thieves. A small basic battery-operated alarm clock is also worth taking in with you, as is a cheap calculator that would be helpful when placing orders on your canteen sheet.

• Most toiletries are likely to be confiscated by reception officers (especially all aerosols), but you should be allowed to keep your toothbrush, comb or hairbrush and nail clippers (no files for obvious reasons).

• Add a few little luxuries. These could include a dressing gown (not black in colour and no hood) and a decent-sized towel from home. Prison-issue towels are tiny and can be as rough as sandpaper. In a world where comfort and privacy are lacking, these little things can make a big difference.

• *Prisonoracle.com* has a great online book store, they're approved MOJ Book Retailers so buy books from there at discount prisoner prices - your greatest enemy in prison is boredom and you'll spend days, or even weeks, just sitting around in your cell – **The Prisons Handbook 2022** is the 'bible' for prisons in England and Wales and has been for over 25 years – this 1600-page annual reference book can be bought online (50% off to serving prisoners) from **prisons.org.uk** It could also be weeks before you finally get a chance to visit the prison library. Having a few good books to read might just help you keep your sanity, especially if the alternative is endless daytime TV.

• Pack a few unframed photos of your loved ones, even if it's just the cat or dog. Prison can be a very lonely place and just having something familiar from home can make all the difference.

Even if you can't take a bang-up bag into the dock with you, you will be entitled to what is called a 'reception parcel' during your first month in custody. This will be limited mainly to clothing and footwear, so try to take any small electronic items with you from court.

You should be allowed to keep and wear wedding rings, most types of personal jewellery, including small earrings and other body piercings and small religious symbols on neck chains. Large, heavy or very valuable jewellery, however, is best left at home. Anything you are allowed in possession is held at your own risk. The prison is responsible for anything placed in storage during the reception process.

WHAT LAYS AHEAD? *Viewpoints*

Its important to get things clear right from the start - before you even arrive in jail.

The advice that is set out below is generally applicable to all prisons to which you will be sent either on remand or when you have been sentenced - but it is a guide only and you should check with the prison itself a week or so before you go to court expecting to be remanded or sentenced.

Not sure which prison you will go to? Phone the court, ask to speak to the Listings Officer, explain your age and ask if sentenced or remanded what prisons they transfer to.

When you first arrive in prison it can be confusing, you will be unsure of your surroundings, what to do, what to expect, so here are some experienced views to give you a general idea of how to make the best of what may seem like the end of the world - but isn't.

Female ex-offender:
Coming into prison for the first time is, needless to say, a daunting experience. For remand prisoners, not knowing how long you may be staying there makes it even worse. All that is running through your mind (if it is not so numb that it can't function) is the family you have left behind. How will your children cope without their mother?

How will you cope without your partner for comfort? Depression, anger and resentment each take their turn to roll through you until you feel emotionally and physically drained.

Reception is the first point of call once you are off-loaded from the 'sweatbox'. The reception staff can appear quite solemn and somewhat regimental in manner, but this is mainly because they want to get you processed and accommodated as quickly as possible.

It is a national routine procedure to be strip-searched.

Not a pleasant experience, but they need to check that you have not concealed any weapons, drugs, or other prohibited items on your person. In some prisons you are then given a 'prison issue' towel, soap, shampoo, toothbrush and dressing gown, and made to take a shower. The nurse comes to take your height and weight and will ask you about your general fitness, you are also usually questioned as to whether you have any suicidal tendencies. They then send you back to the care of the reception staff to have your property logged. Finally you are permitted to put your clothes back on and collect your belongings to take with you to your allocated cell.

If you had started to gain comfort from getting to know the other new prisoners who came in with you, then it is soon lost as you are all split up and locked in separate cells.

I remember walking down the wing hearing the prisoners shouting 'New meat!' to each other, and having to take deep breaths to steady my rapidly beating heart. The harsh sound of steel-on-steel as your cell door is slammed and locked behind you is enough to send your already delicate nerves over, or at least close to, the edge. Then you are completely alone to adjust to and take in your new surroundings.

You will be given an induction on the prison's facilities, including what the gym, library and education have to offer. These can all be used to vent your pent-up emotions and feelings through the right channels, giving you a modest sense of release. Keeping yourself to yourself is best, at least until you have studied and observed how your fellow prisoners profile. For those who have been sentenced it is a good idea to 'plan' how to spend your time inside constructively. Offending behaviour courses are always beneficial and, depending on the length of your sentence, there is usually a range of educational courses available.

It does not generally take long to adjust to prison life. I am, not saying that it is enjoyable, far from it, but you learn to cope. For anyone who is finding it exceptionally difficult to settle, and becoming quite desperate, do not be afraid to talk to someone. If you feel that you cannot do so to an officer or any other member of the prison staff, there is a 'Listener's Scheme' in every prison, which is a group of inmates trained by the Samaritans.

You do not need to be told who to hang around or socialise with, this is simply a matter of common sense.

The main thing always to remember is that you have to look out for yourself at all times as, believe me, no one will be doing it for you. All you need to know is that a focused mind is the key to survival!

Female ex-offender:
Here are my bullet points on survival
• The shock, chaos and disarray of what has happened to you will lead to a range of emotions starting with denial, then anger, blame, bargaining and, finally, acceptance.
• People with you in the reception queue will be sharing your emotions of fear, doubt and insecurity too.
• You must look at the amount of possessions you are allowed in the light of the entitlement depending on your sentence.
• Reception staff may appear intimidating, but they are merely people doing a job and seeing that your needs are attended to.

• Strip-searching is part of the procedure, to ensure that nothing is being smuggled into the prison. Officers are not interested in your size or shape.
• If you are sentenced to four or more years you are likely to be allocated to the hospital wing for observation, a necessary step to keep a check that you are not going to attempt suicide or self-harm.
• If you appear to officers to be at risk of self harm/injury, you will be either placed in designated accommodation or placed in the prison and made subject to continual observation.
• Medication will be prescribed if the doctor is concerned about your mental state.
• There is nothing to be ashamed of in asking for a sedative or a mild sleeping tablet for the first few days, to help you cope.
• Everything is strange and different at first, but you will soon adapt.
• Prison gives you the option of bettering yourself. Life is what you make it, whether you are free or in jail: the choice is yours.
• The best approach to avoiding intimidating people, or being bullied by them, is to be constructive, well-informed, intelligent, confident and prepared for the worst case scenario.
• Stay away from drugs; you are only inviting trouble to your door.
• Feel people out. Don't reveal too much of your business and get to like your own company. It's healthy not to depend on other people, as you'll find most individuals will come and go.
• Observe and follow in the footsteps of the winners, achievers, leaders and survivors.
• Forgive yourself for whatever you have done wrong and strive to make the most of a bad situation. Be kind to you and realise that you too are a human being, not a human doing.

IMB Member:
Well, I just feel sad I can't give watertight advice on this. Only qualified advice... follow it and hope it works; it's the best I can do. If my son (or daughter) were going into prison I'd be terrified, frankly. I'd say get yourself onto a work or education program that will keep you occupied and in a community of others who want to get on... something secure ... and engage with it.

Don't do something that will make you lose it. I say that knowing there aren't enough spaces for everyone and there are delays getting allocated and if you're on a short sentence it won't help.

I say it knowing lock downs and staff shortages cause cancellations.

Get to the library (but access is limited).

Read. If you can't, try to learn, there are chances to do that.

Try to keep fit.

Use your gym sessions.

Look at Cell Workout. I say this knowing the food doesn't help. The chaplaincy do some good work and are in more of a position than most to be able to engage with prisoners on a human level. I'm not religious and so am uneasy you'd have to engage on that level to have that access, but there it is and maybe that's fine with you.

There are some good people involved.

Some prisons have mindfulness available through the chaplaincy. Anything that helps you feel calm and balanced...grab it.

There are sometimes some worthwhile behaviour programs on offer also. Some IMB members are really happy to listen if you want to talk. Others you have to approach through the app system which skews the relationship somewhat.

You'll get told they're useless, and it's true they get almost as frustrated by the system as you do - but they want to highlight and improve conditions and can have some general influence (they have the ear of the governor once a month), so chat to them.

If nothing else it can feel good to be listened to. There are really good staff members. They should be easy to spot but are not necessarily the most immediately accommodating ones. I believe! prisons are introducing a "key worker" system - there used to be a very imperfect "personal officer" system which gave you a particular officer you knew you could engage and take your concerns to, but it kind of fizzled out - maybe this will work in giving a go-to person??

I hope so; if so try to get on with him/her! Don't get into debt.

Debt is the main cause of bullying. I say that knowing some of the pressures to do so. Chances are if someone's particularly nice to you, you could be on a slippery slope - don't take things you're "given", borrow things, accept things on credit.

On the other hand, be aware of things you might have that are desirable and could make you a target. Nicotine patches are a current example.

Getting involved in gangs can make you feel safe but actually make you anything but.

This is hard isn't it?

You need friends but you have to be canny. I'd say don't do drugs, don't smash up, avoid getting red marks or put on basic, you don't want to get into a round of seg stays and adjudications and get a reputation with staff which means they may pre-judge you and treat you in a certain way, it can be hard to get out of that cycle.

But I know that's all simplistic.

It's hard to control your life when you've had your agency taken away.

If you feel really awful use the Listener system and/or Samaritans phone and get help through the Mental Health Trust MHT.

You need resilience in prison.

I say that knowing a lot of people going into prison are already vulnerable.

I want to say, I'm so sorry you're in this situation.

I fervently hope for you to get through it, get out as soon as you can, and wake up and smile each day knowing that when you do get out, you won't be coming back.

Male ex-offender:
Interesting. Firstly hold your head up and never stare at anybody until you know the lay of the land. Always try to be pleasant but if someone is trying to intimidate you by staring or walking aggressively towards you move away but never turn your back.

A smile can go a long way defusing a potential situation but be prepared to stand your ground.

Try not to become a whiner most prisoners are generally pleasant and will go to your defence.

Don't get into any form of debt and keep and valuables on your person - there are thieves in prison.

Finally the food is crap just grin and put up with it. Write letters and use the phone buy extra snacks on your canteen to make yourself feel better.

Use the library and gym and keep yourself clean nobody likes a smelly cell mate.

It's going to be a culture shock but never be afraid to ask for help see the screws they don't mind you having a rant or asking for advice.

However pick the right officer many are lazy

Hope this helps.

WHEN YOU'RE IN PRISON

ADJUDICATIONS:
HOW TO DEAL WITH THEM

In the strange parallel universe that is a prison an inmate can be charged ('nicked') by prison staff for breaches of the Prison Rules. Sometimes these alleged actions would constitute criminal offences outside the prison (eg assault or possession of illegal drugs), but many nickings are for breaking rules that wouldn't be criminal outside the prison environment – for example having alcohol or unauthorised possession of a wide range of odd contraband items including chewing gum, Blu-tack (useful for copying keys), aftershave (may contain alcohol) or even wearing flip flops on the landing or borrowing a book from another prisoner.

Prison law doesn't really follow the normal pattern of what passes as justice on the outside. Assuming that the alleged offence isn't serious enough to merit police charges and a criminal trial, a prison nicking usually leads to an adjudication (internal hearing) with procedures conducted according to Prison Service Instruction (PSI) 05/2018 – Prison Discipline Manual.

A prison officer lays the charge and is essentially the prosecutor, as well as the lead prosecution witness. A governor is the 'judge', but also serves as the jury and usually acts as a lead prosecutor. In more serious cases an external judge may be brought in to hold a so-called 'independent adjudication' or a case can be referred to the outside courts for trial. This is common in cases of serious assault, prison mutiny, drug smuggling or possessing a contraband mobile phone.

You might conclude that the accused – you the prisoner – doesn't really stand a chance, and you'd be right. Most adjudications lead to guilty verdicts, pretty much whatever the actual evidence may be – as one long-since forgotten Governor once said to me on an adjudication when I had the cheek to question the officer's evidence: *"Look, if my officer told me he saw you riding a fucking motor bike around my exercise yard at three in the morning, the only question I'd ask is where you got the petrol – clear?"*

Crystal.

To be fair, some governors do make a stab at getting to the truth, but by and large in most cases the inmate has been found guilty long before the actual adjudication takes place. Governors – even fair-minded ones - just can't afford to upset officers by dismissing too many of their nickings, they need to carry their staff with them if they are to have any hope of running the jail and you are just fodder in that process - so avoid nickings!

Although the IEP system is supposed to be separate from disciplinary adjudications, in some prisons the very fact of getting charged can be sufficient to get a prisoner placed straight on Basic level regime (effectively solitary confinement, with no rented TV set, dressed in dirty old prison kit and deprived of virtually all personal possessions) before any hearing had even taken place. Although on paper there is a right of prior representation and then a right of appeal against an administrative IEP penalty, in practice wing managers have wide-ranging powers decisions.

Although the vast majority of

prisoners opt to plead guilty at adjudications (and, to be honest, a good many of them are!) at least part of the reason for this is that the average inmate probably has literacy problems and isn't articulate or confident enough to speak in his or her own defence. A fair proportion of prisoners also have varying types of mental health conditions and this can make presenting a defence case an uphill struggle. Add to that the fact that it is now almost impossible to get any kind of legal representation for internal adjudications and you have a one-sided 'justice' system, to say the least.

How to Prepare for Adjudication

So you've been nicked. What happens next?
• You should be handed a charge sheet (DIS1 or 'nicking form') within 48 hours of an alleged offence. This should state clearly which rule you are supposed to have broken and the name of the officer bringing the charge against you.
• You should be notified of the date and time of the adjudication and given at least two hours notice to prepare your case. In practice this will not be long enough to get any advice except from other prisoners, so PSI 05/2018 allows you to ask the governor grade who is in charge of the hearing to adjourn the case until you have had a chance to get legal advice.
• If you are planning to go 'not guilty', then it is best to make written representations giving your side of the story. This doesn't have to be long or complicated. Just stick to the facts.
• Generally speaking, it's best not to accuse anyone else of an offence. That's not your job. Just make it clear it wasn't you who did something or that you didn't have an unauthorised item in your possession – you can't be found guilty of an unauthorised item in possession unless it can be proved beyond reasonable doubt that you knew it was there, often difficult in cells where people come and go.
• If an unauthorised item has been found in a shared cell, it is often standard practice to charge both prisoners unless it is clear who had control of the item.
• If you are planning to call other prisoners or members of staff as witnesses, it is best to ask them whether they are willing to give evidence for you before calling them.
• It is also worth checking dates and times if stated in the nicking form – there have been cases where officers have given evidence that the same offence occurred, on the same date, at the same time, in three different cells at once. Sometimes charges can be dismissed if factual information is wrong or if adjudications have been adjourned for too long (especially if staff are absent on holiday or sick leave).

Although the same general rules apply to both, there are two types of adjudication:

Governors' adjudications are presided over by a senior member of prison staff – governor, director or operational manager, who can impose a range of punishments, including loss of earnings or privileges and cellular confinement. Except under very exceptional circumstances there is no right to be legally represented at these hearings, although you may seek legal advice via telephone or letter on their conduct. Since December 2013 there is no legal aid for such advice, meaning that many solicitors no longer provide it.

Independent adjudications that are for the more serious offences, possession of drugs or mobile phones and these are dealt with by visiting judges who, unlike governors, have power to impose up to 42 additional days' imprisonment for each finding of guilt. You have a right to be legally represented at these hearings.

If you do not or cannot have a solicitor to represent you but feel you will need someone to support you during a hearing you should ask the governor to let

> Between January and March 2021 there were 37,226 adjudications, 84% of them resulted in guilty verdicts and 11,959 days were added to sentences - that is 32.7 YEARS of additional imprisonment imposed in just one three month period in 2021.
> *HMPPS Offender Management Statistics Published July 2021*

- 101 -

you bring what is called a 'McKenzie Friend' with you which is explained below.

McKenzie Friends
An adjudication can be a daunting process, especially for prisoners who have literacy problems or mental health conditions, so PSI 05/2018 does allow prisoners facing a charge to get help or support with an adjudication (the so-called Tarrant Principles). In practice, this often means finding another inmate willing to sit next to you during the hearing to give you advice, although not normally speak for you during the adjudication. This is called being a 'McKenzie Friend'.

I think that it's a fair bet that the vast majority of people outside prisons (other than lawyers and law students) are unlikely to have come across the case of McKenzie v. McKenzie [1970]. This case is of relevance to prisoners facing charges for breaking prison rules.

McKenzie v. McKenzie was a contested divorce action in which Mr McKenzie had lost the services of his lawyers when his Legal Aid was withdrawn. Since he no longer had legal representation, he wanted to have the advice and support during the hearing of an Australian barrister – who was not permitted to practice at the English bar. This request was refused by the judge and Mr McKenzie appeared on his own without assistance. Perhaps unsurprisingly, he lost the case, but then took the matter to the Court of Appeal. Their Lordships were obviously unimpressed by the original trial judge's ruling and granted Mr McKenzie a retrial on the grounds that the interests of justice had not been served.

The appeal judgment, McKenzie v McKenzie [1970] 3 WLR 47 expressly supports the right of a litigant in person to have the support and advice of another individual (professional or lay) to assist them during the case by taking notes, helping with documents and giving advice (although not usually speaking in court). And this is the origin of the 'McKenzie Friend', although, of course, it's not a requirement that the people concerned are actually friends!

That is where the McKenzie Friend comes in. PSI 05/2018 makes specific provision for such support: "A McKenzie friend is a person who attends the hearing to advise and support, but may not normally actively 'represent' the accused prisoner by addressing the adjudicator or questioning witnesses." Although a McKenzie Friend can be a social friend, an unpaid solicitor or a member of the public, in practice behind bars it is usually another prisoner.

Being Found Guilty
Although some charges do get dropped due to technical flaws (especially when long adjournments mean that the case has run out of time – usually when the case has taken over six weeks due to staff absences), most prison nickings do end with a guilty verdict. If the governor hearing your case finds the charge proven, then you can expect to receive a penalty. How harsh this punishment will be can also depend on whether this was a first offence, your overall disciplinary record etc.

At an adjudication heard by a governor grade you can be awarded time in the Block (Segregation), as well as 'losses' of privileges (eg canteen, association, gym access, wages etc). In some cases the penalty can be suspended. However, a governor cannot add extra days to your sentence. Only an external adjudicator – a judge – has that power.

Remember that any adjudication finding against you will be recorded in you P-Nomis prison record and may have an impact on recategorisation or, if you are a lifer or on an IPP sentence, your chances of being recommended for parole by the Parole Board.

Appealing the Outcome of an Adjudication
It is possible to appeal the outcome of an adjudication if you don't think you have been treated fairly or if you still dispute the original charge. You can request a review of the adjudication within six weeks of the hearing by completing a DIS8 form (or a legal advisor can help you with this). This will be undertaken by the Briefing and Casework Unit (BCU) at the Ministry of Justice. If you are still unhappy after a review has taken place you can then take your case to the Prisons and Probation Ombudsman.

Offences Against Discipline
There are 25 Offences Against Discipline - these are set out in Prison Rule 51:
You are guilty of an offence if you –
(1) commits any assault;
(1A) commits any racially aggravated assault;
(2) detains any person against his will;
(3) denies access to any part of the prison to any officer or any person (other than a prisoner) who is at the prison for the purpose of working there;
(4) fights with any person;
(5) intentionally endangers the health or personal safety of others or, by his conduct, is reckless whether such health or personal safety is endangered;
(6) intentionally obstructs an officer in the execution of his duty, or any person (other than a prisoner) who is at the prison for the purpose of working there, in the performance of his work;
(7) escapes or absconds from prison or from legal custody;
(8) fails to comply with any condition upon which he is temporarily released under rule 9;
(9) is found with any substance in his urine which demonstrates that a controlled drug has, whether in prison or while on temporary release under rule 9, been administered to him by himself or by another person (but subject to rule 52);
(10) is intoxicated as a consequence of consuming any alcoholic beverage (but subject to rule 52A);
(11) consumes any alcoholic beverage whether or not provided to him by another person (but subject to rule 52A);
(12) has in his possession –
(a) any unauthorised article, or
(b) a greater quantity of any article than he is authorised to have;
(13) sells or delivers to any person any unauthorised article;
(14) sells or, without permission, delivers to any person any article which he is allowed to have only for his own use;
(15) takes improperly any article belonging to another person or to a prison;
(16) intentionally or recklessly sets fire to any part of a prison or any other property, whether or not his own;
(17) destroys or damages any part of a prison or any other property, other than his own;
(17A) causes racially aggravated damage to, or destruction of, any part of a prison or any other property, other than his own;
(18) absents himself from any place he is required to be or is present at any place where he is not authorised to be;
(19) is disrespectful to any officer, or any person (other than a prisoner) who is at the prison for the purpose of working there, or any person visiting a prison;
(20) uses threatening, abusive or insulting words or behaviour;
(20A) uses threatening, abusive or insulting racist words or behaviour;
(21) intentionally fails to work properly or, being required to work, refuses to do so;
(22) disobeys any lawful order;
(23) disobeys or fails to comply with any rule or regulation applying to him;
(24) receives any controlled drug or specified drugs or, without the consent of an officer, any other article, during the course of a visit (not being an interview such as is mentioned in rule 38);
(24A) displays, attaches or draws on any part of a prison, or on any other property, threatening, abusive or insulting racist words, drawings, symbols or other material;
(25)
(a) attempts to commit,
(b) incites another prisoner to commit, or
(c) assists another prisoner to commit or to attempt to commit, any of the foregoing offences.

The best way of dealing with an adjudication is not to get nicked in the first place. Comply with the rules, orders and instructions you are given, once you start to get involved in nickings it will have effects throughout your sentence, staff will make assumptions about you so avoid trouble if you can.

APPLICATIONS & COMPLAINTS
The latest version of the **Prisoner Complaints Policy Framework** is dated September 2021 and you can access a copy of this through the

Library. The first thing that most prisoners discover is that prison is very bureaucratic and almost everything requires you to fill in an application form - known simply as ' apps'.

The most common forms on prison wings are:
- General applications ('general apps')
- Comp 1
- Comp 1a
- Comp 2 ('confidential complaints')

General apps can be neutral forms. They can include requests for almost anything, from a prison transfer or a replacement mattress for a bed to an application for a prison job or education course.

Once completed, in some establishments they are handed to wing staff at a set time of day – usually in the morning after unlock – or else they can be submitted at the wing office. Apps are supposed to be logged in a ledger by the duty officer and then passed on via internal post to the correct person or department.

Although there is usually only one type of general app form, there are three types of complaint form available on prison wings.

These can be paper documents which you fill in but the prison service has started to move towards digital technology where apps can be made via a laptop in a cell via in-cell technology or via an electronic kiosk on the wing.

If being completed by hand, the complaint forms are posted in metal post boxes (usually yellow) on each wing. These boxes are locked and the post is supposed to be collected and sorted daily, Monday to Friday.

The Comp 1 is the usual starting point for most complaints, although prisoners are also sometimes advised by staff to use them for enquiries involving off-wing issues.

Once a response has been received to a Comp 1, if the prisoner isn't happy with what has been written in reply, then he or she can fill in a Comp 1a. This takes the issue to the next management level for a review and a further response.

The pink Comp 2 form is something rather more weighty (at least in theory). It is supposed to come with its own official brown envelope addressed either to the governor or to the deputy director of custody (the regional boss), depending on the issue. This system is known officially as the 'confidential complaint' and is primarily intended to give any prisoner direct access to the top levels of management when they wish to allege assault, bullying or victimisation by members of staff, uniformed or civilian, or they wish to raise a serious issue that they don't feel able to with their own wing officers.

Again, in theory at least, these sealed envelopes are supposed to go directly to the governor's complaints clerk in his or her office. This is aimed at preventing wing staff from intercepting them, reading them or even destroying them before they get up to the governor or the deputy director. Of course it doesn't necessarily always work as intended.

The critical issue is often which member of staff is designated to open the boxes on each wing daily.

The Independent Monitoring Board (IMB), which operates in every prison, also has its own post box – usually dark blue – and a yellow complaint form. However in general the IMB members will only initiate an investigation into a grievance once other channels, such as the Comp 1 and Comp 1a routes have been tried and exhausted. The IMB are pretty useless these days, they exist now to 'monitor' what happens and they have no power over the prison Governor. The one thing they do have that is valuable is the ability to go direct to the Governor and get a response so for that reason alone it is worth having this extra string to your bow – just don't expect too much of them that's all.

The Prisons and Probation Ombudsman (PPO) will only investigate complaints once a prisoner has already been through all the stages of the internal complaint process. For this reason, it is important to keep all your comps and the replies in case you need to take things further.

You can also write to your local MP (the one responsible for the area in which your last home address was) or the MP in the constituency where the prison is located. You should be able to get their name and address from the prison library.

Other points to note.
There are time limits for complaints to the PPO and these are as follows:
• If you have received a final response from the prison you must submit your complaint to the PPO within 3 months
• If you have not received a final response within 6 weeks of the final stage of the complaint you can contact the PPO (in practice they will rarely take the complaint at this point but should contact the prison to see why they have not replied to you).
• Unless there are exceptional circumstances your complaint must be submitted within 12 months of the actual events complained of.

Reserved Subjects
The following are known as Reserved Subjects and complaints about them cannot be considered internally in the prison.
You should still use a COMP1 form but it will be sent to the Ministry of Justice, or in the case of parole, the Parole Board. You should expect a reply within about 6 weeks.
• Allegations against the governor
• Requests for artificial insemination
• Category A prisoners' categorisation, approved visitors, change of name, marriage, transfer and allocation
• Early release on compassionate grounds
• Litigation against the Prison Service
• Mother and Baby unit placement appeals
• Parole
• Repatriation
• Section 90/91 juvenile allocations
• Special remission
• Transfer to other parts of the UK

Confidential access complaints
Using form COMP2 (a pink form). These forms should be available as freely as the other forms. Read the notes on the form carefully. If you think your complaint is suitable then fill in your details accordingly. Place the complaint in the envelope and seal it.
Then address it to the person who you want to read it. This must be: the Governor; the Deputy Director of Custody; or the Chairman of the Independent Monitoring Board. Then post the envelope in the complaints box. The envelope will only be opened by the person to whom it is addressed. You should receive a response within about 6 weeks. Written submissions may be sealed in an envelope, marked Confidential Access and posted in the complaints box.
It should be noted that filling in a pink COMP 2 confidential access form is not the next stage in the complaints procedure after using the COMP1 and COMP1A forms. If confidential access is used for complaints that are not suitable, your complaint may be returned unanswered.

Complaints about adjudications
To appeal against adjudication by a prison governor, director or controller you need to complete a DIS8 form, which should be posted in the complaints box. It will then be passed to the Offender Management and Public Protection Group (OMPPG) and you should receive the reply within six weeks. Appeals against decisions by independent adjudicators cannot be made through the complaints procedure, but must be made in writing via the governor to a senior district judge at Westminster Magistrates Court. There is currently no mechanism, other than judicial review, for appealing the finding of guilt in these cases and the appeals can only address the level of punishment.

If You Need Help
If you need help filling in a general app or a comp form you should ask someone you trust for assistance. This could include:
• An Insider
• A wing rep
• A fellow prisoner that you trust
• Your OMiC Keyworker
• A member of staff

Thoughts About Apps and Comps by an ex-prisoner
It has often been noted that there is a serious disconnect between the mechanics of the present app and comp system as operated in our prisons and the literacy levels among a majority of prisoners since around half of all of adult inmates have literacy skills at or below Level 1 (what would normally be

expected of an 11-year old child), with as many of 75 percent having some problems with writing ranging from poor spelling right through to functional illiteracy.

For these reasons a written app and comp system is always going to seriously disadvantage the average prisoner who lacks either the ability to write fluently or the confidence to put pen to paper when it comes to approaching officialdom. In many respects, this reflects the prison bureaucracy, which is top-heavy with internal memos and reports of every kind. Most of our modern communications systems are completely dependent on users being literate. Illiteracy, by its very nature, tends to exclude those who are already marginalised socially and economically. In prison this experience of exclusion often continues.

It is also important not to overlook the exclusion of those for whom English is not a first language, or who perhaps don't even speak English at all. How can we expect someone who has never written (or perhaps spoken) a word of English to cope with the prison apps and comps system? This becomes even more acute when it is almost impossible to communicate verbally with staff or fellow inmates.

Even for prisoners who have a reasonable level of literacy in English, there are other factors to consider. There is a widespread perception that many apps or comps never get further than wing offices, especially if it involves a complaint against staff. Prisoners fear that these apps never get logged in the system and just end up in the office waste bin.

Most governors would like to believe that all their uniformed staff would be above such petty and vindictive behaviour. However, most also know that this sort of practice does take place on occasion.

Another key problem is that more than a few uniformed staff, at least in the lower operational grades, aren't all that good at writing themselves. Again and again, prisoners receive apps back covered with unintelligible scrawl and an anonymous squiggle as a signature. A response that can't be read from someone who can't be identified is yet another fatal flaw in the app system.

Prisons are institutions largely built on mutual mistrust, both between staff and inmates, as well as between prisoners. Many prisoners genuinely believe that their comps will be intercepted and read (and often destroyed) by wing staff, particularly when the complaint is about staff misconduct or bullying. This widespread perception is enough to severely impact on the functioning of the entire system.

This lack of trust extends to Comp 2 forms, despite the provision of dedicated envelopes. Many prisoners are wary or even fearful of making complaints because they fear retribution or victimisation as a result.

Most prisoners are fairly reasonable if they understand the reason for operational decisions. If activities have to be suspended or cancelled because of staff shortages or some specific emergency situation, then as long as that is explained clearly, tensions and resentments can usually be managed. It's when inmates feel that they are being kept in the dark and not treated like reasonable adults that they start to feel justified in behaving unreasonably, if only to get their message across.

In relation to apps and comps, clear, timely and fair responses can defuse potential conflicts. However, telling a prisoner that he can't attend his father's funeral a day after it has actually taken place really doesn't do anyone any favours.

It could be argued that the current written apps and comps system really isn't fit for purpose, particularly in view of the large proportion of prisoners who have problems with literacy, language or, indeed, with mental health conditions that impact on their ability to communicate in writing. These inmates are effectively silenced and their voices often go unheard, leading to frustration, anger and even self-harm and, in extreme cases, suicide.

If our prisons had sufficient frontline staff and the personal officer system actually functioned, then prisoners who are currently marginalised or excluded from the written bureaucracy might stand a fair chance as they could make requests verbally or with the assistance of staff who have time to spend listening and assisting them. Sadly, given staff shortages, this may still be some way off.

BEREAVEMENT WHEN YOU ARE IN PRISON

One of the most difficult aspects of imprisonment is being separated from your family and friends. This becomes even more stressful if a loved one is ill or elderly or if there has been an accident. Prisoners' family members can also be victims of crime. Suffering a bereavement while serving a prison sentence can be extremely distressing and prisoners can feel especially helpless, as well as frustrated and sometimes angry with themselves or others.

In some cases, the prison authorities may know about a death in a prisoner's family before the prisoner does. Family members may contact the prison to inform them of the situation and it will then fall to a member of staff, often a member of the chaplaincy team, to break the bad news.

Being locked in your cell while your family is experiencing a traumatic loss at home can affect individuals very differently. However, there are some practical ways in which a prisoner can ask for assistance.

- Ask a member of staff, particularly a member of the chaplaincy team, if you can make an urgent compassionate phone call to a family member. This contact may provide an opportunity for you to discuss what has happened and to let your family know how you are feeling about the sad news. Such a call should be possible even if you have no credit on your PIN phone account.
- Many prisoners feel very angry with themselves for being in prison when a loved one has just died. Try not to bottle up your feelings. You may find talking to others may help. Members of the chaplaincy team will speak to you even if you are not religious.
- If you are distressed and feel you'd benefit from speaking to a specially trained prisoner, ask to speak to a Listener. If you don't want to seek support inside the prison, you can also telephone the Samaritans. This should be possible via your PIN phone and is without charge.
- Otherwise try to speak to another prisoner who you think may be a good listener or who is a friend. Quite a few prisoners have experienced bereavement for themselves and may be in a position to support you.
- It may help to write down your feelings about your loved one who has died. Some people find that writing a final 'goodbye' letter can be helpful because it can offer a chance to say things that you didn't get to say while they were still alive.
- If you want to request permission to attend the funeral of a member of your immediate family (usually defined as partner/spouse, parent, child or brother/sister or fiancé/fiancée, although other close relationships should be considered) put in an immediate app to the No 1 governor even if you don't yet know the date of the funeral. Explain why it is so important for you to attend the ceremony. Don't leave things until the last minute.
- The rules about attending a funeral can be found in section 7 of PSI 33/2015 - latest update 1st October 2021. Prisoners who are not suitable for ROTL must be escorted. There is no absolute ban on prisoners in any security category attending the funeral of a close relative. A close relative is defined (in PSI 16/2011)

All prison governors will at least carry out a security and risk assessment upon receiving a request for **compassionate escorted leave.** However, it is best to be prepared for a refusal (knock back) owing to staff shortages at many prisons. If an escorted leave is granted, you may need to request that suitable clothing is delivered to the prison ahead of the funeral. Depending on the security assessment, you are likely to be required to be handcuffed to an escorting officer throughout the time you are outside the prison, including in the church and at the graveside or crematorium, but they could be removed if risk assessment permits.

BLOCK: HOW TO SURVIVE TIME IN THE SEGREGATION UNIT

For those who haven't spent any time inside as a guest of Her Majesty, the segregation unit is a kind of prison within a prison. Officially known as a Care and Separation Unit (CSU), prisoners refer to being 'sent down the Block', although it's also called 'the Seg'. Seg Rules are contained in PSO 1700.

It's a separate unit or wing inside a prison where prisoners can be sent for extra punishment over and beyond the usual, although a quite a few prisoners do get sent there for their own protection – often if they've run up substantial drug debts or are suspected of 'grassing' (informing) on other cons. Usually, however, prisoners get sent to Seg as a result of being involved in some form of serious disorder (such as a fight or participating in a riot) or because they have been found guilty of a disciplinary offence, for which they might get 7 days, 14 days or 28 days in solitary.

Life down the Block can be pretty austere. No rented TV, no personal possessions to speak of. You get to wear dirty old prison kit (sometimes the oldest, most stained specimens available) and you get a coarse prison towel. Unless it's actually a 'strip-cell' in which case you are kept naked, but with an anti-suicide blanket you can wrap round yourself.

The bed is either a solid concrete slab with a very thin mattress on it (if you don't have back pain when you arrive down the Block, you will have by the time you leave), or in the older type of Seg it can be a metal-framed single bunk bolted to the floor. In fact, pretty much everything in the segregation unit is fixed to the wall or the floor in order to prevent irate prisoners from either throwing anything at staff or trying to barricade themselves in.

Windows can't usually be opened, but are fixed units with a small grill to one side that can be opened for fresh air using a knob. However, some of these window mechanisms aren't working – so either the cold air blows through in winter, or it's jammed shut in the heat of the summer. Either way, the environment can be pretty grim.

After all, what's the point of having a prison within a prison if it isn't made even nastier than a normal jail cell?

Although Block cells vary in design, most have some form of table fixed to the floor and wall, a similarly fixed bench to sit on, a stainless steel sink and WC and… that's about it. Apparently they used to make you roll up the mattress during the day and leave it outside the door to discourage cons from lying on their beds. This practice seems to have stopped.

In theory, you are supposed to be able to request the loan of a radio (or use your own if in possession). However, it's unlikely that there will be one available, so don't get your hopes up. Prisoners considered at heightened risk of suicide or self-harm are also supposed to be assessed and can be issued with a TV set to keep them occupied, but this is pretty rare.

It's well documented that extended periods of isolation have a negative impact on mental and physical health. Some prisoners in UK prisons experience solitary confinement for months or even years resulting in the inevitable deterioration of their minds.

If you are spending time in the Block you should get various visitors throughout the day. These will probably include:
• A Seg officer
• A governor grade
• A nurse

You might also receive a visit from a member of the chaplaincy team and a member of the local Independent Monitoring Board (IMB), although not every day. The usual limit of most exchanges with members of staff consist of the question "Any complaints?"

Each day you should also be asked if you want exercise on the Seg yard, a shower or access to the payphone, although you might not actually get all (or any) of these extras.

There should be periodic reviews by governor grades of the decision to place you in Seg. According to the Mandela Rules, placing a prisoner in solitary should only be as a last resort and for as short a time as possible. Prolonged confinement in the Seg is defined as being anything over 15 consecutive days.

PUNISHMENT

- 108 -

How Survive in the Seg
Each prisoner copes with segregation differently, often depending on the state of their mental health. Some welcome time away from their usual wing, especially since the Block tends to be much quieter, at least most of the time. All cells in Seg are singles, so if you are padded up with someone on normal location, then you can find it provides a break from having to live in close proximity to another person for a while.

On the other hand, life down the Block can be boring, lonely – especially if you have some good mates on your usual wing or house block – and you are very unlikely to get any privileges such as gym time or a TV to watch. If you like reading you can try to take a few books with you, but otherwise there won't be much to do.

Some prisoners take advantage of the time alone to catch up on sleep or even a little 'personal' recreation time. One lad used to refer to his time in the Block as his *'long wank to freedom'* (a nod in the direction of Nelson Mandela).

Boredom can take its toll, however and too many prisoners end up self-harming or even taking their own lives when in Seg. You can still request a visit from a Listener or from a member of the mental health team while down the Block.

My experience of the Block (by an ex-prisoner)
During my stay in the Block (seven days) I was allowed the following personal possessions: a cheap wrist watch (mainly because I think the Seg staff forgot to confiscate it), my reading glasses with plastic lenses, one paperback book and a toothbrush (prison issue). I also had the usual plastic prison-issue mug, plate and bowl, plus plastic knife, fork and spoon. Add in a towel, some toothpaste and half a bar of prison soap and that was the lot. Absolutely nothing else other than bedding.

Meals were served on the floor. Literally. You had to stand back from the door as soon as a screw opened it. Then place your empty utensils on the floor by the door. They were then collected by a fellow con who had the enviable job of 'Seg orderly' while the two officers on duty watched you like a hawk. Next a tray with food (no choices down the Block other than like it or lump it) and two slices of dry bread was placed in the same place, along with a plastic flask containing hot water – enough to make three mugs of prison tea. When ordered to do so, you stepped forward, bent over and picked these things up, then stepped back. The door was slammed, locked and bolted.

During the course of the day, three people would invariably come and look in your cell. One was a medic, another was from the chaplaincy team and the third was a governor grade. Occasionally the senior officer responsible for the Block would also check up on you. That was the extent of the human contact permitted.

Exercise consisted of being allowed to walk on your own around an entirely enclosed concrete yard with high walls on all four sides topped with rolls of razor wire and what I later discovered were anti-helicopter nets, just in case any of us were sufficiently well-connected to have associates willing to fly over and rescue us, James Bond-style. Every move was monitored by two screws and by CCTV cameras mounted on high poles around the yard.

So what else is there to do in the Seg unit? Another activity was to pace out the cell in each direction. My cell was around 8 feet by 10 feet, so I paced it out a couple of hundred times each day. I also did some rudimentary exercises (sit-ups, press-ups etc).

What struck me most about being down the Block was the almost total lack of human interaction. Prison staff would simply ask "Any complaints?", although the chaplains usually managed at least to enquire how we were doing. We weren't allowed to speak to the Seg orderly and although we could hear that there were other prisoners held in the Block, we never actually saw them. Sometimes you did hear cons screaming or shouting, but the screws quickly put a stop to any disturbances. At least it was usually pretty quiet down the Block.

I'm very fortunate that I don't get claustrophobic. For any con who is, a normal cell must be torture, but a Seg cell must be their very worst nightmare. While I was down there I often heard the alarm sounding because one of my unseen fellow residents had managed to smuggle in a razor blade and cut his wrists, arms or neck. For this reason, razors are forbidden in Block cells. Instead they are issued each morning as you are locked in the shower cubicle and are then collected by the member of staff who also stands and watches as you wash. Self-harm or suicide is always a constant problem in the Seg unit.

A few other prisoners have spent 20 years or more in similar conditions down the Block. All pretty shocking in 21st century Britain, especially when the British government is so quick to criticise human rights violations elsewhere in the world. Perhaps we should sort out our own backyard first.

I'm not sure how I would have been able to cope if I had served my entire sentence down the Block. Although I'm pretty strong-minded and haven't lived with any form of mental illness, I'm certain that extended solitary confinement would have impacted on my personality, perhaps even led me to consider self-harm or suicide.

For those prisoners who are already vulnerable, or suffering from mental health problems, or have addictions, a stint down the Block could prove to be a life or death situation, especially when healthcare resources and staffing are at critical levels in many prisons. In such cases, perhaps the best we can hope for is that they actually survive the experience. Sadly, some don't.

CATEGORISATION
Male
In February 2020 HMPPS issued a new **Security Categorisation Policy Framework** - you have the right of access to it via the library.
It was updated on **17th August 2021** in respect of terrorist and terrorist connected offences.

Prisons exist to keep you locked up until its time to let you out, and the amount of security needed to keep you locked up as an individual is called security categorisation.

Security Categorisation is a risk management process, its purpose is to ensure that you are put in the lowest category appropriate to managing your risk of:
• escape or abscond;
• harm to the public;
• ongoing criminality in custody;
• violent or other behaviour that impacts the safety of those within the prison; and
• control issues that disrupt the security and good order of the prison.

All of the above things affect your security categorisation, so it's not just about preventing you from escaping and harming the public - though that is a large part of it - it is also about your behaviour in prison and harming prisoners or staff inside too.

You need to aim to get the lowest possible security categorisation to ensure that you progress through your sentence as quickly as possible - so be careful who you associate with; if they are dealing in criminality inside the chances are you will suffer as a result of your association with them.

So, what are the different security categories and what do they mean?

The official definition of prisoner security categories is as follows:
Cat A – Prisoners whose escape would be highly dangerous to the public or the police or the security of the state and for whom the aim must be to make escape impossible.

Within Cat A there are three sub-categories, Standard Risk, High Risk and Exceptional Risk.
Standard risk Cat A applies to all, but for those who are known to have the resources and contacts to effect an escape they can be classified as **High Risk**.

Where there is creditable intelligence available that a Cat A prisoner is actively planning an escape, they will be categorised as **Exceptional Risk** with additional security around them.
Cat B – Prisoners for whom the very highest conditions of security are not necessary, but for who escape must be made very difficult.
Cat C – Prisoners who cannot be trusted in open conditions, but who do not have the resources and will to make a determined escape attempt.
Cat D – Prisoners who present a low risk; can be reasonably trusted in open conditions and

for whom open conditions are appropriate.

Initial Categorisation

All newly sentenced individuals, other than those who are Provisional Category A/Restricted Status or where the time left to serve to earliest release at the point of categorisation is 28 days or less, must have an initial categorisation in line with the new Policy Framework - including those brought back from abroad.

The initial security category assessment must be completed within 10 working days of sentencing and it must take account of your current identified risks, available information, including information about your capability to cause harm or to continue with criminality while inside.

Category C will be the most appropriate security category for adults in the majority of cases. Where Category C is not appropriate then Category B will be assigned (unless Category A is deemed necessary having followed PSI 9/2015).

Where risk is assessed as low, an individual may be assigned to Category D. In all cases staff must weigh up all of the available information and to arrive at a security categorisation outcome that reflects your individual circumstances.

Effective security categorisation is fundamental to risk management and ensuring good order is maintained by making sure that those who need higher levels of security receive it and so it supports HMPPS's duty to implement the sentences of the courts; protect the public; and provide a safe, secure and ordered environment that keeps everyone safe inside and allows rehabilitative services, training, treatment and progression through the prison system to take place.

Allocation is a separate process from categorisation, the purpose of which is to assign an individual to a suitably secure establishment which effectively meets their needs insofar as pressures on the estate allow.

Categorisation is an independent process, so someone may be assessed as a particular category even if it will not be possible to allocate them immediately to a prison of that category.

Allocation decisions should take into account the individual's offending behaviour and resettlement needs (such as access to suitable training and interventions and closeness to home at the end of their sentence), their individual circumstances (e.g. medical requirements), and control issues (e.g. danger to particular staff or other prisoners). This may result in an individual being held in a prison of a higher category than their own.

What determines my initial security Categorisation?
Guidance on **Category A** prisoners is given in PSI 9/2015

Guidance on categorisation of other adult male prisoners is in the Policy Framework - according to this you will be initially considered as **Category B** if any one of the following applies:
- Current fixed sentence of 10 years or over
- Any indeterminate sentence
- Category A during previous sentence
- Current/previous terrorist offences
- Been potential/provisional Category A whilst on remand

Or any two of the following:
- Previous sentence of 10 years or over
- Previous escape - not abscond
- Current or previous serious offence involving: violence, threat to life, firearms, sex, arson, drugs or robbery

If none of the above apply, but any of the following apply, you will be considered as **Category C**.
- Previous sentence of 12 months or more for violence, threat of violence, arson, sex offence, drug dealing or importation
- Current sentence of 12 months or more for violence, threat of violence, arson, sex offence, drug dealing or importation
- Abscond, failure to surrender, breach of bail, HDC or ROTL within past 3 years
- Outstanding confiscation order or further charges

If none of these apply, you will be considered suitable for **Category D**. This initial categorisation is then subject to a risk assessment to determine if a higher or lower category than indicated should be applied.

When will I be recategorised?
Categorisation reviews ensure that you are held in the lowest security conditions necessary to manage your risk.

A review of your security categorisation must take place whenever there is a material change in circumstances that impacts security risk. This may be either an increase or a reduction in risk. Such reviews can take place at any time.

The maximum time between categorisation reviews is based on the individual's current category and time left to serve to their earliest date of release (EDR).

The EDR for determinate sentences will generally be the Conditional Release Date but may be the Parole Eligibility Date for some Extended Determinate Sentence Prisoners.

The EDR for standard recalls may not be known until the Parole Board 28-day review is finalised. Where necessary, the timing of the next review should be amended once the outcome of the review is known.

Adult individuals serving a determinate sentence and held in closed conditions (Categories B and C) must be reviewed every 12 months until they have less than three years left to their EDR. At this point routine reviews must be 6 monthly.

Where the time left to serve at the point of initial categorisation is less than three years, 6 monthly reviews will commence immediately.

Categorisation - Female
The security categories of women prisoners differ from those of male prisoners. For women, the official definitions of security categories are:
Category A - Same as male.
Restricted Status - Any female whose escape would present a serious risk to the public.
Closed Conditions - Prisoners for whom the very highest conditions of security are not necessary.
Open conditions - Prisoners who present a low risk; can reasonably be trusted in open conditions.

What determines my initial security categorisation?
Prison Service Instruction 39/2011, **updated 13th May 2021**, sets out the principles that determine the categorisation and recategorisation of women prisoners, apart from the very few women prisoners, who are Category A or Restricted Status. These are categorised and reviewed by HMPPS Headquarters.

The purpose of categorisation is to assess the risks posed by a prisoner in terms of:
• Likelihood of escape or abscond;
• The risk of harm to the public in the event of an escape or abscond;
• Any control issues that impact on the security and good order of the prison and the safety of those within it

The prisoner is assigned to the lowest security category consistent with managing those risks.

Allocation often follows immediately after categorisation but is a separate process whose purpose is to assign the prisoner to a suitable establishment.

All prisoners, unless serving an indeterminate sentence, when initially categorised, must be regarded as suitable for open conditions unless:
• The current sentence is 3 years or more
• The prisoner has been treated as provisional category A whilst on remand
• The current or previous sentence is for terrorist (or terrorist related) offences
• There has been a previous escape from closed prison, police custody (except arrest or post-arrest) or escort
• There is a real history of serious offending
• There is a serious criminal association
• Further charges are outstanding (other than those of a minor nature)
• There has been a previous sentence of 7 years or more (from which the prisoner was released within the last 5 years)
• The prisoner is diagnosed with or is suspected of suffering from, serious mental health problems
• There is reasonable concern regarding risk of abscond
• There have been previous breaches/failures to surrender
• There are victim issues or issues of public

confidence that mean open conditions are inappropriate

The prisoner is subject to MAPPA level 2 or 3 management, prompting serious consideration of the individual circumstances
• An OASys risk of harm level which cannot be reasonably managed in open conditions
• The prisoner has been identified as a priority or a prolific offender (PPO)
• A Serious Crime Prevention Order has been imposed
• The prisoner is subject to a confiscation order - consideration must then be given as to whether amount and default sentence imposed, might increase risk of abscond
• A prisoner has more than 2 years left to serve

Two years is considered to be the maximum time a prisoner should spend in open conditions. However, assessment of a prisoner's individual needs and risks may support earlier categorisation to open conditions. Prisoners with a sentence of less than 12 months must be considered for categorisation to open conditions and allocation to open conditions as soon as possible after sentencing under a streamlined risk assessment process, subject to a requirement that they spend a minimum of seven days in closed conditions.

Life and IPP sentence prisoners can only be transferred to open conditions following a recommendation by the Parole Board and/or a decision by the Secretary of State to grant them open status.

When will I have a categorisation review?
Women serving indeterminate sentences will be subject to sentence planning and review meetings, which must be held every 12 months, at which a woman's security category should be reviewed.

Prisoners serving a determinate sentence of more than 12 months but less than 4 years, extended sentence prisoners serving a sentence of less than 4 years and prisoners in the last 24 months of their sentence, should have a review every 6 months.

Determinate sentence prisoners and those serving extended sentences with a sentence of 4 years or more should have a review every 12 months until they are in the last 2 years of their sentence, when they should then have 6 monthly reviews.

Prisoners may also have their security category reviewed whenever there has been a significant change in their circumstances or behaviour that impacts on the level of security required, whether negative or positive, eg. a key piece of offending behaviour work or a detoxification or opiate substitute maintenance regime is completed.

Who will decide on my recategorisation?
Recategorisation of all female prisoners is carried out by the OCA Unit. Decisions may be made by a board or by a single manager. Procedures must be completed by staff specially trained and able to competently fulfil the OCA role. Staff completing the form are responsible to a senior manager as designated by the Governor.

Can I appeal if I am not happy with the result after a review of my categorisation?
Yes. If, after a categorisation decision or review, you do not believe that you have been placed in the correct category, you should pursue your concerns via the internal complaints system. A fresh review of all the facts must then be done by a manager senior to the officer, who countersigned the original decision

In the case of Category A prisoners, you can still use the complaints procedure but your complaint form will be sent to Prison Service Headquarters for a response, rather than being answered in the prison.

If you feel your concerns have still not been addressed you can appeal to the Prisons and Probation Ombudsman (PO Box 70769, London, SE1P 4XY). It is possible on occasion to judicially review categorisation decisions, although this is increasingly difficult, especially since 2013 when legal aid funding for categorisation cases was cut.

The Prison Service has a duty to give reasons for decisions about categorisation, so in order to mount your appeal you should request a full explanation of the decision and relevant reports in writing.

CONFISCATION ORDERS

If you are believed to have made a financial gain from crime the court can impose a Confiscation Order - this sets out the amount of money you must repay and if you fail to make that payment you will have to serve longer in prisoner - what is known as a 'term in default'.

The Serious Crime Act 2015 makes a number of amendments to the Proceeds of Crime Act 2002 (POCA). Significant provisions include:
- A requirement to set out any known details of third party interests in confiscation proceedings;
- Strengthening prison sentences for failing to pay confiscation orders;
- Enabling assets to be frozen more quickly and earlier in investigations;
- Significantly reducing the time that the courts can give offenders to pay confiscation orders, and
- Extending the investigative powers in POCA so that they are available to trace assets once a confiscation order is made.

It replaces the existing scheme of 12 tiers with 4 tiers, where the maximum length of a default term is based on the amount of the confiscation order as follows:

Confiscation Order	Max Term
Up to £10,000	6 months
> £10,000 to £500,000	5 years
> £500,000 to £1,000,000	7 years
> More than £1,000,000	14 years

Prisoners can only be detained to serve a term in default at their sentence release date if the default term has been activated by a Magistrates' Court, and a warrant of commitment issued to the prison.

Confiscation order proceedings

While you have on-going confiscation proceedings you keep all your usual sentence entitlements. However, the fact that you may receive a further term of imprisonment can affect the prison's considerations of your suitability for ROTL and Cat D/open conditions.

The default term is a **'term of imprisonment'**, and not a **'sentence of imprisonment'**, as imposed for a criminal offence. This affects your eligibility for HDC and the Early Removal Scheme, both of which only apply to sentences of imprisonment.

If you are serving a default sentence you are **not** eligible for HDC and foreign national prisoners who have a default term to serve are **not** eligible for ERS, although very short default terms may be waived on application for those serving long sentences.

Where the default sentence is activated on or after 1st June 2015 and it is for more than £10m you will not be released until you have served the full sentence.

A term in default runs **consecutive** to the original sentence of imprisonment.

When you are imprisoned on a default term the Governor must usually take away any money you have in your prison account help pay the confiscation order, but only if this will advance the release date by reducing the term. You have a right of appeal against this and the Governor may decide not to appropriate the money if they are satisfied, for example, that the funds do not belong to you, or that undue hardship to you or your family would result.

Additional days **cannot** be awarded as a punishment to anyone serving a term in default activated on or after 4 April 2005.

Open Conditions

The fact that you are subject to a confiscation order does not mean you cannot go to an open prison, it all depends on the risk you represent in terms of abscond, the size of the outstanding debt, and whether you are believed to have assets abroad.

If you are already in open conditions when a confiscation order is imposed, this may trigger a categorisation review resulting in your return to closed conditions.

Release on Temporary Licence (ROTL)

The ROTL eligibility criteria for those with default terms to serve are based on their overall period of imprisonment (the criminal sentence plus the default term). This is the only purpose for which the two custodial periods are aggregated. Normal ROTL criteria apply.

All risk assessments must reflect your individual circumstances, a refusal to grant ROTL or Category D/Open status solely because you have an on-going confiscation order proceedings, for example, would not be lawful.

EDUCATION IN PRISON

On 1st April 2019 the **Prison Education & Library Services for adult prisons in England Policy Framework** was issued - you can obtain access to this via the Library.

Section 86 of the Apprenticeships, Skills, Children and Learning Act 2009 provides that the Secretary of State must secure the provision of such education and training facilities as he considers appropriate for education and training suitable to the requirements of persons who are subject to adult detention. Adult detention applies to persons subject to a detention order, aged 19 or over, or aged under 19 and detained in a prison or a YOI, or part of a YOI, used wholly or mainly for those aged over 18, for example persons sentenced to prison and those on remand in custody.

4.2 Under Rule 32 of the Prison Rules 1999 :
(1) Every prisoner able to profit from the education facilities provided at a prison shall be encouraged to do so.
(2) Educational classes shall be arranged at every prison and, subject to any directions of the Secretary of State, reasonable facilities shall be afforded to prisoners who wish to do so to improve their education by training by distance learning, private study and recreational classes, in their spare time.
(3) Special attention shall be paid to the education and training of prisoners with special educational needs, and if necessary they shall be taught within the hours normally allotted to work.
(4) In the case of a prisoner of compulsory school age as defined in section 8 of the Education Act 1996(8), arrangements shall be made for his participation in education or training courses for at least 15 hours a week within the normal working week.

Prison education is contracted out by the Ministry of Justice under the Offender Learning and Skills Service (OLASS) system. Courses and tutors are provided by regional education providers. Tutors are not employed directly by the Prison Service.

When prisoners arrive at their first prison part of the induction process will be an assessment of their skills level in literacy (reading and writing) and numeracy (maths). Some inmates can get upset at the idea of sitting the tests, particularly if they feel embarrassed or ashamed at problems they have over reading, writing or doing maths.

Since education is regarded as one of the key 'pathways' to reducing offending, a significant number of prisoners can find that they have been put down on the list for education. In many prisons not having the right certificates can prevent prisoners from getting paid jobs in prison.

If you have been identified as a potential 'learner' and given a 'personal learning plan' then there are few options. The best course of action will probably be to attend the classes and try to get the required Level 1 certificates in literacy and maths.

Thousands of prisoners have learned basic reading and writing in prison education classes and it can bring real benefits, such as being able to read books and forms, fill in apps by yourself and write to family and friends.

A second chance at education – even if you really don't like the idea of sitting back in a classroom – can offer you an opportunity to improve your life skills and may even get you work on release. These days the number of jobs that don't demand at least some basic level of literacy skills are pretty low.

Your other option is to refuse to attend education classes and risk getting IEP warnings or even get placed on a charge (a 'nicking').

Another is to show up at the classroom and then refuse to actually do anything or else play around. Either of these choices can also end up with IEP warnings or nickings. Depending on your sentence, these can really cause you trouble when it comes to getting and keeping your Enhanced level or even harm your parole prospects if you are a lifer or on an IPP sentence.

Which Courses to Do?
Assuming you do decide to cooperate and get stuck in as a learner, where you start is likely to depend on your literacy and numeracy skills. Those who have little or no reading skills are likely to work their way through the

Entry Level courses, followed by Level 1. Those with more skills could start on Level 1 and then progress onto Level 2 (equivalent to GSCEs). Generally speaking, prisons don't offer any courses above Level 2 unless the prisoner can fund it themselves or can get a grant or a student loan.

If your first language isn't English, then you might be enrolled on an English for Speakers of Other Languages (ESOL) course to help you improve your spoken and written English.

Once the basics are out of the way, there are other options to improve your existing skills, learn new ones or gain certificates that will prove what you are capable of doing. Every prison education department is different, but most will offer some Information Technology (IT) courses. Others might provide business and enterprise skills or citizenship courses. Some may also offer art classes.

In addition, it might be possible to gain some vocational qualifications, depending on what the specific prison offers. There are qualifications linked to some training needed to do prison jobs – such as food hygiene or catering in order to work in the kitchens or on the servery. Industrial cleaning courses may be required in order to do work such as deep cleansing of kitchens, offices and cells.

You may also be able to take certificate courses in health and safety, as well as first aid (eg Heartstart). Some of these qualifications can cost hundreds of pounds to get out in the community, so getting them free of charge in prison can be very worthwhile.

If a prison still has a farm or gardens department, it might be possible to gain vocational qualifications, as well as practical knowledge and skills. Prisons that have laundries may be able to offer specialist qualifications that would be helpful if you are considering working in this sector after release.

Some establishments also provide courses in bricklaying or painting and decorating. Even if you aren't planning for a future career in this work, the skills learned can still be handy when the other half wants the house redecorated!

It may also be possible to qualify for a Construction Skills Certificate Scheme (CSCS) card which is increasingly required for work on building sites. This course can cost money out in the community, so if you can qualify while you are still inside it can save you cash and time in the future.

The Prison Service is increasingly making use of peer mentors, such as Insiders or in education departments, to support other prisoners. Some prisoners can gain qualifications as peer advisors. These can be valuable if you think you might want to work with ex-offenders in the community after your own release.

Many prisons now offer gym qualifications aimed at gym orderlies and others who might be thinking about a future career in a gym, as a personal trainer or sports coach. If you are keen on physical activities and spend as much time as possible in the gym, then this could be a good option to consider.

Certain prisons offer specialist training as barbers and hairdressers. You can gain practical experience, as well as qualifications, by cutting hair for fellow inmates in classrooms that are fitted out as barber shops or hairdressing salons.

Prison workshops sometimes offer specific courses and certificates. It is often worth asking staff what qualifications it is possible to gain.

A few prisons offer other specialised vocational courses such as rail track maintenance. Recent figures state that around 67 per cent of prisoners who complete these courses and gain the qualifications do on go to find paid work on release in the railway maintenance sector.

How to Apply

If you are interested in specific education or vocational courses, ask your personal officer, a member of the education department staff or your wing education rep what courses you can sign up for. There may be a waiting list or some courses may only run a few times each year. Sometimes courses will be advertised on education notice boards.

Further and Higher Education
Some prisoners who are serving longer sentences may consider applying to study for more advanced level qualifications such as A-levels or degrees. Funding for almost all courses above Level 2 now has to be arranged by the individual prisoner either from their own resources, or via an education grant or a student loan. Ask for advice in your education department.

If you are an ex-armed services veteran, you may be eligible for support to fund educational courses that will contribute to your rehabilitation and resettlement. Ask your local SSAFA representative for guidance.

Remember that a governor's approval will be required for applications and you will need to be at least six years from your release date (if you have one) in order to commence degree courses.

The Open University (OU) specialises in offering both undergraduate and postgraduate levels for serving prisoners. Most OU course modules are accessible to those who are studying in custody as material can be made available in other formats in cases where there is no internet access.

Many prisoners who start studying for a first degree by distance learning (unless they already have A-levels or equivalent qualifications) are likely to begin with an access course before proceeding with their undergraduate degree. For most postgraduate courses, a first degree is likely to be required.

The Institute of Prison Law
This organisation, accredited by the Law Society, delivers the eight module distance learning course leading to the award of the Certificate of Competency in Prison Law – it is available to serving prisoners at half price.

The Certificate of Competency in Prison Law is the only comprehensive prison law course of its kind and has been devised and delivered by recognised experts in their field since 2007.

It consists of an eight module course, requiring around 150 hours of study with modular examinations - almost 800 prisoners have successfully passed the course. The course has recently been fully updated and was released again in September 2020. More information: www.prisonlaw.org.uk

The OU publishes a specific guide for learners who are in prison entitled Studying with the Open University. The OU also has a specialist registration team for Offender Learners and Students in Secure Units (OLSU).

Prisoners' Education Trust
The Prisoners' Education Trust (PET) has been providing access to learning opportunities for prisoners since 1989. A charity, PET works with 125 prisons in England and Wales and helps more than 2,000 prisoners each year. It offers access to distance learning, arts and hobby materials, as well as advice and guidance to prisoners. Through PET, prisoners have access to over 200 vocational and academic courses.

PET's Access to Learning programme offers a distance learning curriculum guide to over 200 courses.

A copy of this can be obtained by writing to:
FREEPOST PRISONERS' EDUCATION TRUST
The Foundry, 17 Oval Way,
London SE11 5RR

EQUALITY
You have the right not to be subject to any form of discrimination on the grounds of race, age, disability, sexual orientation, religious beliefs, gender or ethnicity.

If you are disabled you should not be discriminated against "in any aspect of prison life".

This means you are classed as disabled if you have a physical or mental impairment and the impairment has a substantial and long-term adverse affect on your ability to carry out normal day-to-day activities in prison.

By 'Long term' it means will or has lasted for a year, and 'substantial' means it is not minor. This definition of disability is very wide, and can include a range of conditions, which can be mental or physical, and lifelong or temporary. Examples of conditions which come under the scope of the Equality Act include:
• Diabetes;
• Physical impairments such as mobility problems;
• Learning difficulties such as dyslexia, and dyspraxia;
• Learning disabilities;
• Mental health conditions such as bi-polar disorder and Depression.
• Sensory impairments, such as difficulties hearing or seeing.
What does not constitute a disability?
• Addiction (e.g alcohol)
• Hayfever;
• Tendency to start fires;
• Tendency to steal;
• Tendency to physical or sexual abuse of other persons;
• Exhibitionism / Voyeurism.

Do I need certification to prove that I have a disability?
You do not need a certificate to prove you are disabled. You must simply be able to demonstrate that you have a physical or mental impairment and that the adverse effect is substantial and long term.
The Equality Act Guidance states that, in general to come under the definition of 'disabled' the person must:
• have a physical or mental n impairment;
• the impairment must have adverse effects which are substantial;
• the substantial adverse effects must be long-term;
• the long-term substantial adverse effects must be effects on normal day-to-day activities.

Have you been discriminated against?
There are three types of discrimination covered by the Act: direct, indirect, and discrimination arising from a disability.
Direct discrimination occurs when a person discriminates against someone because of his/her disability, and treats that person less favourably than a non-disabled person.

Indirect discrimination: A person or public body (e.g. a prison) discriminates against a disabled person if they apply a provision, criterion or practice which is discriminatory in relation to his/her disability.
Examples of indirect discrimination include:
• Not making 'reasonable adjustments' for a wheelchair user who wishes to attend Education by failing to provide either a lift or Education classes on the ground floor.
Prohibited acts under the Equality Act:
Harassment
Harassment of a disabled person because of their disability is prohibited under the Act. Harassment means that a person engages in unwanted conduct towards the disabled person, and the conduct is aimed at either:
• Violating the persons dignity;
• Creating an intimidating, hostile, degrading, humiliating or offensive environment.
Victimisation of disabled persons is prohibited. Victimisation occurs when a person subjects a disabled person to detriment because of his/her actual or perceived disability.
If you have a recognised disability under the Act, the prison has a legal obligation to make any necessary reasonable adjustments for you under section 20 of the Equality Act.
Generally, this applies where a criteria or physical feature puts a disabled person at a substantial disadvantage in comparison to a non-disabled person. Where this is the case, there is a legal obligation upon the prison to remove this obstacle.
This also applies where, without the provision of an auxiliary aid such as a wheel chair or zimmer frame, the disabled person is put at a disadvantage. If this is the case, the prison is under a duty to provide the aid free of charge.
Some examples of reasonable adjustments may include:
• A ramp to allow for wheelchair access;
• Providing a wheelchair or crutches;
• Modified offending behaviour courses for people with learning difficulties;
• Orthopaedic mattresses for people with back pain/spinal injuries.

STOP EXTREMISM

EXTREMISM

In late 2019 and early 2020 England saw two terrorist attacks in London by two individuals previously convicted of terrorism offences.

These offenders had been automatically released at the halfway point of their sentence, without any involvement of the Parole Board.

The first attack, the London Bridge Attack, occurred on November 30, 2019, and resulted in the offender killing two people before the police shot him dead.

The Streatham Attack occurred on 2 February 2020, and resulted in the offender injuring two people before the police shot and killed him.

As a result of the two incidents and the threat posed by the impending release of additional offenders, the government introduced the **Terrorist Offenders (Restriction of Early Release) Act**.

The Act stops those convicted of terrorist offences, or offences with a terrorist connection, serving a determinate sentence being automatically released prior to the end of their sentence - unusually it is retrospective so applies to terrorist offenders in prison before the Act became law. Such offenders continue to remain eligible for early release, but must apply to the Parole Board for conditional release 2/3 point of sentence.

The legislation was challenged by judicial review in July 2020 in the case of Khan v Secretary of State for the Justice [2020] EWHC 2084 but the case was thrown out - the court drew a clear distinction between the sentence passed by the judge and the administration of that sentence by the Government, saying such prisoners extend the threat of radicalisation beyond those arrested for terrorist offences. Other prisoners, which likely means you, both Muslim and non Muslim serving sentences for offences unrelated to terrorism are nevertheless vulnerable to radicalisation by Islamist Extremists - and you need to be aware of this. According to a recent review found the threat from IE can manifest itself in prison in various ways, including:

• Muslim gang culture and the consequent violence, drug trafficking and criminality inspired or directed by these groups;
• TACT (Terrorism **ACT**) offenders advocating support for Daesh and threats against staff and other prisoners;
• charismatic IE prisoners acting as self-styled 'emirs' and exerting a controlling and radicalising influence on the wider Muslim prison population;
• aggressive encouragement of conversions to Islam;
• unsupervised collective worship, sometimes at Friday Prayers including pressure on supervising staff to leave the prayer room;
• attempts by IE prisoners to engineer segregation by landing, by wing, or even by prison;
• attempts to prevent staff searches by claiming dress is religious;
• books and educational materials promoting extremist literature available in chaplaincy libraries or held by individual prisoners;
• intimidation of prison Imams;
• exploitation of staff fear of being labelled racist.

The threat from IE is usually most prevalent in the HSE - but by no means is it restricted to that part of the estate. It can exist all over the prison system and you need to be alert to recognise it. The safest way to avoid becoming entangled in it is to keep yourself to yourself, do not be drawn into religious discussions, religion is private, personal to you, and you should consider anyone who seeks to alter your own religious views as potentially dangerous. If you feel threatened by it you must take steps to protect yourself, speak to other prisoners who you trust, seek out the advice of inmates who are respected, Listeners are a good example. You should only go to staff as a last resort as this can create far more serious problems than it will ever solve.

FACILITIES LIST (PAGE 242)

The latest (July 2020) Facilities List sets out what you can have in prison, either what you can buy, and from where, what you can have sent in or handed in.

There are two types of Facilities List - a General List and Local list.

The General Facilities List shows all the items that prisoners *may* be allowed to have in possession in a prison.

The Local Facilities List - which for every prison is available on every prison entry on the www.prisonoracle.com- is the list of items each Governor selects from the *General List* and applies only to their particular prison and its application to each level of the IEP scheme.

Governors may select any item from the General List for their own Local Facilities List - but they are not allowed to add to it.

The General Facilities List is what you MAY be able to have, not what you're are entitled to - in fact you are entitled to very little, privileges have to be earned and paid for.

All your property will be listed on a Property Card, and it is divided into 'stored property' and 'property in possession' (often called i/p).

The maximum number of each item shown on the local facilities list (that which applies to the prison you are in), is the total number you are allowed to have on your *property card* as a whole.

For example - if you can have 15 upper garments in your possession this means you can have 10 in your possession and 5 in your stored property. You cannot have 15 upper garments in your possession and then additional upper garments in your stored property also.

If you have your maximum allowance you must first take other items off your property card, before you can have new items handed in or order them via the catalogue.

The catalogue system is separate to the hand in process you will use when you first arrive (and during your annual kit exchange). HMP generally have several catalogues available for you to order items from, ranging from clothes to games to electrical goods. Due to security restrictions on some of the items most prisons have a catalogue list similar to the facilities list, which lets you know exactly what you can and cannot order.

This stops you from thinking you can order something you can't and makes the whole process more efficient – so your order gets to you as quickly as possible. To place a catalogue order you must have the following:
• Enough money in your spends account to pay for the items. Remember when ordering from the catalogue that this may affect your canteen allowance for the week.
• Room on your property card for new items.
If you are already at your maximum allowance and wish to order more, you must first make space on your property card for them by contacting the property department and choosing from one of the options mentioned above. Your catalogue order will not be processed until this has been done.
• The correct IEP level you have to be on enhanced to have CD/DVD players.

FAMILY MATTERS
Your Family Outside and How To Help Them Through Your Sentence
Most people have families of some kind, although not everyone has good relations with their own relations. Prisoners often find that having family – including their own children – is what helps them get through their sentence, whether it is a long stretch or a short proverbial 'shit and a shave'.

Prisoners' families sometimes refer to themselves as serving 'the second sentence'. While their loved one is inside, they end up

Family Law

struggling to keep the family together and a roof over their heads. They have the additional worry about what is happening to the member of the family who is behind bars. Many families also end up sending in money on a regular basis in order to keep the prisoner afloat, especially in prisons where there is little or no work available.

Then there is the social stigma of having a prisoner in the family. In the worst case scenarios this can impact on housing, as well as on tenancies and insurance once a person who has a criminal record is released back into the community.

Despite the fact that HM Prison & Probation Service (HMPPS) recognises that strong family ties can play a key role in reducing reoffending – according to the Ministry of Justice's own research family support is identified as one of the key 'pathways' to living a law-abiding life after release and can reduce reoffending by 39% – it can seem as if little is done in practice to help strengthen those ties while an inmate is in custody. Prisoners can be transferred to prisons many miles from home and keeping in touch can be subject to long distance visiting and having access to wing phones during association periods that have often become rare in some of our overcrowded and understaffed jails.

Prison PIN phones cost money. Tariffs are much higher than on the outside, so those inmates with little or no cash are much less likely to be able to phone home regularly. Many prisoners – perhaps around half of all adults in custody – also struggle with reading and writing, so letters may not be the most effective way for many to keep in touch with their loved ones. So how can prisoners help their families through their sentences?

• Write home regularly if you can. Or ask a friend or Insider to help with writing a few lines each week. Every prisoner should be given a free letter and envelope weekly, so just making sure your loved ones receive something can be very important. Family members often get very worried about those inside, especially at a time when there are regular news stories about disorder and even major riots in British prisons. Getting a letter, however brief, can put minds at rest.

• If you have problems with reading and writing, prison can offer an opportunity to improve your skills, either through education or through the Shannon Trust's Reading Plan which is delivered to prisoners by trained prisoners acting as peer mentors.

• Greetings cards are often available to buy on the canteen sheet or they can be made in your cell. You don't need to write a lot to keep in touch.

• Help your family organise visits. Some prisons have modern phone or online booking systems, others still rely on Visiting Orders being applied for by the prisoner and sent out. Make sure you know what the rules are at your establishment and ensure things are done in time so your family can visit you regularly.

• When you have a visit from your family members don't put them under pressure to smuggle in contraband items for you or others. Visitors who are found to be bringing in illegal items, particularly mobile phones, SIM cards or drugs are very likely to face prosecution and a possible prison sentence of their own. It can also result in you as a prisoner being placed on 'closed visits' where you are separated from your visitors by a glass screen and no physical contact is permitted.

In addition to the well-known **emailaprisoner.com** there is a new system being made available in prisons called **Prison Voicemail**, its a very good system here is how it works.

Your family sign up with Prison Voicemail, (prisonvoicemail.com) paying a monthly fee for the amount of minutes they want to pay for - the Gold Package costs £10 a month for 100 minutes, but a fiver a month gives 25 minutes. Once signed up they call their Prison Voicemail number from their mobile at any time and leave a message. The message is instantly available at the other end.

You then simply dial the Prison Voicemail number from any phone in the prison, the call costs you the price of a normal landline call. After listening to the message left by your family, you can leave a reply - your family will receive a notification that you've left a message and they can pick it up, listen and leave another message.

• If your family is having financial problems over visiting you, make sure they are aware of the Assisted Prison Visits Scheme (APVS). The Ministry of Justice maintains a website online

> Research has shown **close ties between prisoners and key family members** can **significantly reduce the risk of reoffending** – which costs society **£15 billion every year.**
>
> Ministry of Justice

to help families in this situation: Get help with the cost of prison visits:
https://www.gov.uk/help-with-prison-visits
There is also a booklet that explains how the APVS system works available online at: www.gov.uk
Those eligible to apply for assistance with visits costs include:
a) A prisoner's husband, wife or civil partner who were living as a couple before the prisoner went into prison.
b) Parent or Grand-parent (includes step-parent or adoptive parent) Brother or Sister (includes half-sibling or step-sibling)
c) Son or Daughter (includes step or adoptive)
d) Next of Kin (as noted by the prisoner in prison records)
e) Sole Visitor (only social visitor in the four weeks before a visit claimed)
f) Escort to a qualifying adult or child

The criteria for applying for assistance via the APV Scheme include:
• Low income
• Income Support
• Income - based Job Seekers Allowance
• Employment and Support Allowance (Income related)
• Universal Credit*
• Working Tax Credits (with Disability or Child Tax)*
• Child Tax Credits*
• Pension Credit
• Hold HC2 or HC3 Certificate

For those who qualify under the APV Scheme the following help can be provided:
• The scheme provides help for one visit every two weeks.
• The maximum number of assisted visits is 26 in any 12 month period.
• A contribution is made towards travel costs, a light refreshment allowance for longer journeys and in limited cases a contribution towards overnight costs.
• Money is paid towards petrol costs or the cheapest method of public transport for the journey to the prison. If you choose to use a more expensive way of travelling to the prison, for example a peak time train, the extra costs will not be refunded.
• A light refreshment allowance is paid if you

NOTHING TAKES THE PAST AWAY LIKE THE FUTURE

are away from home for over 5 hours and expenditure incurred.

While you are in prison, your well-being matters to your family and close friends. Avoiding getting into situations involving drugs and debt. These can have a negative impact on both you and your family.

According to a July 2017 report by the Prisons and Probation Ombudsman since 2013 at least 79 prisoners have died in custody due to use of drugs such as spice and mamba. Running up prison debts that you know you can't pay can leave you at risk of bullying and serious violence.

Emergency Situations
If you are experiencing an emergency situation and you urgently need to contact a family member, you can apply via prison staff for emergency phone credit. You may also be able to ask a member of the chaplaincy team for advice or to facilitate a compassionate telephone call. In some cases, the prison may be able to arrange for a member of staff to contact your family to pass on a genuinely urgent message.

GETTING OUT: A PRE-RELEASE CHECKLIST
If you have a release date (either on licence from a fixed-term sentence or being released on parole licence) no doubt you have been counting down the days, maybe even marking them off on that calendar on your cell notice board. For any prisoner the opposite of being inside is being on the out.
How many sleeps do you have left?
Although the idea of release is great, it can also be quite scary for some people, especially if there won't be family or friends waiting outside the gate to meet you. And then, for most prisoners, there will be the matter of licence

conditions to consider. Getting out is likely to be less stressful and scary if you have done some forward planning before the big day.

Everyone's circumstances will be different so this checklist is just a reminder of some of the things you should be thinking about.

1. Licence Conditions

Most prisoners who are released these days will be on licence for either a fixed period or, in the case of lifers and those serving IPP sentences, possibly for the rest of their lives. Every licence includes what are called 'standard conditions' (to be of good behaviour etc), but some licences may also contain specific conditions relating to the offence(s). These may place restrictions on where you can live, what activities you must avoid doing or places you shouldn't go. Your licence conditions may also ban any contact with named people, including victims.

You will be given a copy of your licence to read and sign before you can be released. Make sure you know what your specific licence conditions are.

Breaking them can lead to a recall to prison and you could end up serving either another 28 days or a period of months or even years while your case is reconsidered by the Parole Board.

If you are on a fixed-term sentence you could find yourself serving the rest of your total time inside, rather than on licence.

2. Your Supervising Officer

If you are released on licence you will have a supervising officer (Offender Manager). Most ex-prisoners who are classed as low to medium risk will be supervised by a member of staff from their local Community Rehabilitation Company (CRC). People with higher risks are likely to be the responsibility of a probation officer from the National Probation Service. You should already know the name and contact details of your Offender Managerbefore you are released from prison.

You should be told when your first appointment with them will be and this is likely to be on the same day as you are being released. Make sure you attend this meeting on time or telephone if you are delayed due to transport problems. Don't get recalled on your first day out!

You will probably need to attend regular meetings at set intervals, possibly each week to start with. Not attending a scheduled meeting with your supervisor can be classed as a breach of your licence conditions.

3. Discharge Grant

If you are aged at least 18, have served a minimum of 14 days in custody (other than remands who are being released directly from court) and do not have savings of more than £16,000 then you should be eligible for a discharge grant of £46. This will be given to you in cash in reception during the release process.

Prisoners whose convictions have been quashed by the Court of Appeal or whose sentences have been reduced and who are being released from court may apply for a discharge grant as long as they have served as least 14 days in custody. Those awaiting deportation from the UK are not eligible for a discharge grant.

The discharge grant is supposed to cover you immediate needs following release from custody until you have either found paid work or made a benefit claim. In addition to the discharge grant a further £50 can be paid directly to a housing provider to cover your accommodation for the first night. This will need to have been arranged in advance.

If there is any money left in your prison accounts you should also be given this in cash at the same time as your discharge grant.

4. Rail Warrant

Unless you are living locally to the prison or someone is picking you up with transport at the gate you can apply for a rail warrant. This can be exchanged at the local train station for a single ticket to a destination closest to your discharge address.

5. Accommodation

Some prisoners who are categorised as high or very high risk are likely to be required to reside at approved premises (usually a hostel) for an initial period following their release from custody. This will be specified in licence conditions. This is likely to apply particularly to lifers and those serving an IPP sentence, although it can also be the case for other high risk prisoners. Local authorities no longer have to prioritise newly released prisoners on their housing lists, however, if you wish to apply to be placed on the list it is best to do so as soon as you have been released from prison. Some prisoners who are serving the final part of their sentences in open conditions (Cat-D) should apply for ROTL in order to register for accommodation as early as possible.

Many ex-prisoners who do not have their own accommodation are likely to spend some time living with family or friends while they claim benefits or search for work. If possible try to make firm arrangements in advance so that you won't have the stress of facing homelessness on your first night out. In some cases you may be able to arrange temporary accommodation in advance of your release through one of the charities that provides specific support to ex-prisoners, such as NACRO or the St Giles Trust. If you are concerned about homelessness when you are released, getting in touch with one or more of these organisations may mean that you will have a roof over your head after you walk through the gate. Another temporary option may be a bed at a local Salvation Army Hostel.

Prison staff may be able to get you the address of a local hostel before you are released. Otherwise you can try the local Citizens Advice Bureau.

6. Benefits

Most newly released prisoners will need to apply for benefits from the Department of Work and Pensions (DWP). This can be done at a JobcentrePlus. Most claims must now be made online, but there are computer terminals and staff who can help you if you are unfamiliar with computers or have literacy problems or other difficulties.

The main benefit available for newly released ex-prisoners will be Job Seekers Allowance (JSA) if you are available for work, but if you have a disability or need additional support from a carer you may be eligible to make a claim for Personal Independence Payment (PIP).

JSA payments are usually paid every two weeks into your bank or building society account and the maximum rates are (2017):
Aged 18-24: up to £57.90 per week
Aged 25+: up to £73.10 per week
Couple 18+: up to 114.85 per week

Payment of JSA is subject to an initial interview shortly after you have made a claim. For this you should bring evidence of your identity (passport if you have one, a driving licence, your prison discharge document and your National Insurance number). Some pilot areas are now rolling out a new system called Universal Credit. Your JobcentrePlus will advise you if this applies in your area. You will be assigned a work coach who will discuss your progress in looking for a job and be required to attend a JobcentrePlus office every two weeks to sign on. You may also have to carry out specific tasks such as completing an up to date CV. If you fail to keep evidence of your search for work or fail to sign on as required you may face sanctions, including the loss of some or all of your JSA for a set period.

If you will be paying rent for your accommodation (whether to an approved premises, private landlord, housing association or local authority) you may be eligible to claim Housing Benefit. You should do this at the same time as you apply for JSA. If you are going to be living with a partner after your release only one of you can claim Housing Benefit.

7. Pensions

Payment of pensions ceases if a person is sent

- 124 -

to prison. If you were eligible for the Basic State Pension when you were sent to prison, or you have now reached state pension age you will need to make a claim as soon as you are released from prison.

The age at which a person becomes eligible for a Basic State Pension varies depending on their date of birth. If your date of birth was on or before 5 April 1970, you should be eligible to claim a state pension at age 65. If you were born between 6 April 1970 and 5 April 1978 your eligibility will be from age 67 (although this is being reviewed). If you were born after 6 April 1978 your eligibility age will be 68.

You can claim your pension online, by telephone or by printing off a claim form which you will need to complete and send by post to your local pension office. The level of Basic State Pension is calculated by previous contributions you have paid through your National Insurance contributions.

8. Work

Contrary to what the tabloid newspapers would have us believe, most prisoners do want to find paid, legal work. Many ex-prisoners find jobs through family or friends. Others prefer to set up their own businesses and become self-employed. In some circumstances JobcentrePlus can give advice on self-employment and some short-term financial support may be available. If you don't already have some work lined up, while you are waiting for release it can help to make a list of your skills and qualifications, including those gained while inside. Most employers will require a curriculum vitae (CV) so it can be very helpful to get one put together while you are still in prison. Your prison may offer a business skills course or other resettlement assistance, so try to get your CV prepared.

Remember that while you are still on licence you should ensure that your supervising officer knows you are seeking work as any employment will need to be approved until you are off licence.

Quick Pre-Release Checklist:
 Yes No
1. Do I have a licence?
2. Do I understand my conditions?
3. Have I signed my licence?
4. Do I know the name of my Offender Manager?
5. Do I know the date, time & place of the 1st meeting?
6. Applied for my Subsistence Payment?
7. Have I any money in my prison accounts?
8. Do I need a rail warrant to get to my home area?
9. Do I know where I will be sleeping on my 1st night out?
10. Have I registered for local authority accommodation?
11. Will I need to apply for benefits at the JobcentrePlus?
12. Do I know when my JSA interview will be?
13. Do I know my signing on date and time?
14. Am I eligible for a Basic State Pension?
15. Have I claimed my pension?
16. What work would I want to do?
17. Have I got an up to date CV?

HEALTHCARE

Healthcare in prisons is a concern to many prisoners, particularly those who are injured or who have ongoing or chronic conditions. On 31st March 2020 there were 5,176 people aged over 60 in prison, and 8,588 aged 50–59 in prisons in England and Wales. The Prisons Inspectorate say 15 prisons have 30% who are aged 50 or over. In four of these, 10% of prisoners were aged 70 or over.

As our prison population is growing older, with more and more inmates now in their 80s or 90s pressures on healthcare providers has increased and is expected to continue to do so.

Public Health England is responsible for commissioning healthcare for prisoners - but in August 2020 it was announced this body is to be replaced. Some prison healthcare is now contracted out to the local NHS, while others are managed by private providers such as Care UK or Virgin Care.

In theory, prisoners are supposed to receive the same standard of healthcare as citizens using NHS services in the community.

However, the experience of many prisoners is that the care provided often falls short and this is often reflected in the number of complaints about poor care or inadequate treatment, as well as in reports issued by official watchdogs. In numerous Fatal Incident (death in custody) Reports the Prisons Ombudsman finds poor healthcare has contributed to inmate deaths with a lack of respect also criticised - these PPO criticisms are very largely ignored.

Healthcare and You

All prisoners coming into custody are supposed to be given an initial healthcare screening by medical personnel. These interviews aim at identifying each prisoner's individual medical history and include questions about physical health, including any pre-existing conditions, mental health and any issues with alcohol and/or substance misuse. Specific clinical needs, such as prescribed medication, should be noted and actioned.

While some prison healthcare departments do provide timely and appropriate medical care, recent concerns have included shortage of medical personnel, particularly GPs, as well as prison short-staffing that leads to cancellation of urgent appointments at hospitals because no escorts are available. Some prisons have no regular doctors, so cover is provided by locums (temporary doctors) and concern has also been expressed over the high turnover of medical and administrative personnel as this can lead to problems with follow-up appointments and the monitoring and treatment of prisoners' health conditions.

Healthcare staff in prisons can make a request for your medical records from your own GP. However, they must ensure that you give your consent before they can make such as request.

Prison healthcare departments should provide all prisoners with a full range of health advice and services such as smoking cessation, dietary and weight management support and sexual health screening. They should also provide, in confidence, condoms, dental dams and lube for prisoners who are sexually active in prison. Healthcare staff can make referrals for prisoners requesting support with drug or alcohol dependencies.

If You Have A Complaint about Prison Healthcare

If you feel that you have not received appropriate treatment from healthcare in your prison then you have a right to complain. It is important that your complaint is made in the right way to the correct organisations.

In the first instance you should complain to the specific healthcare provider in your prison. There should be posters in the healthcare waiting area with information about how to make a complaint. If not, you can ask at the reception desk in healthcare.

If you are not satisfied by the response from the healthcare provider, then you can take your complaint (if your prison is in England) to:
NHS England
Complaints Manager NHS England
PO Box 16738
Redditch, B97 9PJ
Tel: 0300 311 122 33

If your prison is in Wales, then you should write to your local Community Health Council. You can find out which one is local to you by contacting the Board of Community Health Councils in Wales:
Board of Community Health Councils in Wales
3rd Floor
33 - 35 Cathedral Road
Cardiff, CF11 9HB
Tel: 0845 644 7814 / 02920 235 558

If after making complaints to both the healthcare provider and NHS England or a Welsh Community Health Council you are still unsatisfied, you can make a complaint to

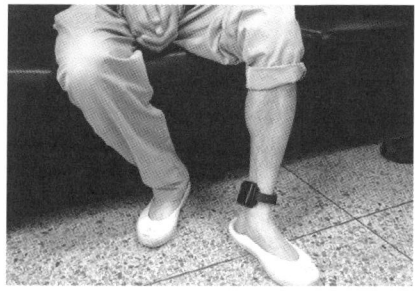

the Parliamentary and Health Service Ombudsman (PHSO):
The Parliamentary and Health Service Ombudsman
Millbank Tower
Millbank
London, SW1P 4QP
Tel: 0345 015 4033

Getting Help to Make a Complaint
NHS Complaints Advocacy, a registered charity, can assist you in making a complaint concerning prison healthcare. They offer a free, confidential service and can:
• Explain the NHS Complaints process.
• Help you write letters to the right people.
• Prepare you for meetings and come to them with you.
• Put you in touch with other organisations who can help you.
   You (or your family) can contact NHS Advocacy by telephone: 0300 330 5454 or you can write to them at:
NHS Complaints Advocacy
VoiceAbility
Mount Pleasant House
Huntingdon Road, Cambridge, CB3 0RN
email: nhscomplaints@voiceability.org.
   If you believe that you have suffered or are suffering as a result of medical negligence or serious mismanagement of your health needs or medical conditions by a prison healthcare provider, then you may be able to make a claim for personal injury. It is important that you try to keep a detailed recorded of your problems, including dates and what has happened (or not happened if treatment or hospital appointments have been cancelled).
   You should always seek professional legal advice from a firm of solicitors or direct access barristers specialising in prison personal injury claims. They should be able to advise you on your rights and how to pursue a claim.

HOME DETENTION CURFEW 2020
The HMPPS HDC Policy Framework was last **updated on 26th June 2021** to reflect abolition of CRCs and it cancels all previous regulations on HDC; you can access a copy via the library by making an application.
   HDC, more commonly known as 'tagging' is the means by which some prisoners may spend a proportion of their sentence confined to their home during a specified period of the day, usually for 12 night time hours. The person has to wear an electronic tag, normally around an ankle, for the duration of the HDC. The tag emits an electronic signal which is monitored by a private company contracted to the Prison Service to ensure the prisoner does not breach the curfew. The maximum period of HDC is 135 days (4. months), unless your sentence is shorter than 18 months, in which case the maximum HDC period will be equivalent to a quarter of the total sentence.

How do I know if I am eligible for HDC?
Prisoners serving sentences of 12 weeks or over but less than 4 years' imprisonment are eligible to be considered for HDC once they have served half their custodial sentence. However some groups of prisoners are ruled out are ineligible to apply.
   Others are 'presumed unsuitable' unless there are 'exceptional circumstances'. At the other end of the spectrum, some low-risk prisoners are presumed to be automatically suitable for HDC unless there are compelling reasons why it should not be granted.

Ineligible prisoners - banned by law
• Sentenced to 4 years or more for any offence.
• Sex offenders required to register.
• Offenders convicted of violent or sexual offences serving an extended sentence.
• ROTL failures to return.
• Sentenced for breach of the curfew requirement of a Community Order.
• FNPs recommended for deportation.
• Offenders with less than 14 days to serve.

- Offenders who have ever been recalled to prison for failing to comply with the HDC curfew conditions.
- Offenders who have ever been returned to custody by the court for committing an imprisonable offence during the at-risk period.
- Offenders currently serving a recall from early release on compassionate grounds.

Presumed unsuitable unless there are wholly 'exceptional circumstances'
- Homicide (including death by reckless, dangerous or careless driving, aggravated vehicle-taking resulting in death)
- Explosives related charges
- Terrorism
- Possession of offensive weapons
- Possession of firearms with intent
- Cruelty to Children
- Offences aggravated on the grounds of race, religion or sexual orientation

Presumptive HDC
This applies to short term prisoners (ie 3 months to under 12 months) with no history of violent, sexual, or drugs offending. There is a presumption that all eligible prisoners will be released on HDC unless there are exceptional and compelling reasons not to.

The following current or past offences exclude a prisoner from presumptive HDC:
- ABH or attempted ABH
- Administer poison
- Aggravated Burglary
- Arson
- Assault court/prison /police officer
- Assault w/i to cause GBH
- Assault w/i resist arrest
- Common Assault
- False Imprisonment
- Harassment
- GBH/wounding or attempted GBH
- Kidnap
- Riot, Violent disorder, Affray, Threatening /Disorderly Behaviour and other violent Public Order Act offence
- Robbery or assault w/i to rob
- Any other violent offence
- Any sexual offence

Current offence only
- Previous convictions for drug possession do not bar prisoners from presumptive HDC).

The presumption of unsuitability will only be displaced in very limited circumstances, and will be determined on a case-by-case basis. Such circumstances may arise where:
- The likelihood of re-offending on HDC is extremely small
- The prisoner has no previous convictions
- The prisoner is infirm by nature of disability or age

Foreign national prisoners (FNPs)
Foreign national prisoners are not eligible if:
- Liable to deportation under the Immigration Act 1971, s.3(5) or (6)
- They have been notified of a decision to refuse leave to enter Britain
- They are an illegal entrant
- Liable to removal under s.10(1) of the Immigration and Asylum Act 1999.

In exceptional circumstances (eg if deportation is not possible in the near future), FNPs will be risk assessed for release on HDC.
Risk assessment

Where possible, the HDC risk assessment must commence 10 weeks before the eligibility date. Unless they have requested not to be considered, prisoners must normally be released on HDC unless there are substantive reasons for retaining them in custody. These reasons must fall under one of these headings:
(i) unacceptable risk to others
(ii) a pattern of offending indicating likelihood of re- offending during the HDC period
(iii) likelihood of failure to comply with the conditions of the curfew
(iv) lack of suitable accommodation
(v) shortness of the potential curfew.

In the case of McCreaner v MOJ [2014] an ex-prisoner was entitled to damages for the six weeks he was detained after he should have been released on HDC where the prison had been negligent in failing to give his application the priority the policy demanded.

Default terms for confiscation orders
Prisoners with confiscation order default

terms are ineligible for HDC on the default term but can get HDC on their main sentence in some circumstances (see Confiscation Orders info sheet for more detail).

Revocation of HDC
HDC may be revoked and you will be recalled to prison if, whilst the curfew condition is in force it appears that you have failed to comply with any condition included in your licence, or your whereabouts can no longer be electronically monitored at the place for the time specified in the curfew condition included in the licence.

There is no specific appeals procedure; however appeals may be pursued via the complaints system, up to the Prisons and Probation Ombudsman.

INCENTIVES POLICY FRAMEWORK
With effect from 8th July 2020

The basic rule behind the IEP system is that the better you behave, the more you engage, the more you receive as a reward - but its snakes and ladders, like interest rates what goes up can come down - and quickly too.

The IEP system has been in prisons for 20 years, it was revised in 2013, amended again in 2015 and changed again in 2019. Like a lot of things in prison there is often a huge gap between the theory and the practice.

IEP Levels and Requirements
Under the IEP scheme, you are expected to demonstrate a commitment towards your rehabilitation, engage in purposeful activity for example, attend work and / or education, reduce your risk of reoffending, behave well and help other prisoners / staff. You cannot be penalised if your failure to demonstrate any of the above is through no fault of your own (e.g. where you're willing to engage but where no opportunities exist).

The new IEP scheme that was published in July 2019 operates now on just three levels - Entry Level has gone:

Basic, Standard and Enhanced.

The definitions of these levels and the specific requirements are set out below. In addition to those requirements you are required to

Behaviour Principles and Incentive Level Definitions — Annex A

The definition of each incentive level up to enhanced is set out below. Governors can add additional criteria for any levels they create above enhanced.

Basic level is for those prisoners who have not abided by the behaviour principles. To be considered suitable for progression from Basic, prisoners are expected to adequately abide by them.

Standard level is for those prisoners who adequately abide by the behaviour principles, demonstrating the types of behaviour required.

Enhanced level is for those prisoners who exceed Standard level by abiding by the behaviour principles and demonstrating the required types of behaviour to a consistently high standard, including good attendance and attitude at activities and education/work and interventions.

Behaviour Principles

Example behaviour principles are provided below which can be used by prisons or replaced with alternatives, allowing prisons to respond to local challenges and priorities. Beneath the principles are example behaviour expectations which staff, including key workers where they are in place can use to coach prisoners on the types of behaviour required to meet a principle. Governors can tailor the expectations to meet local circumstances or to set short term goals for individual prisoners, - e.g. to target any specific behaviours that they want to improve – or to meet alternative behaviour principles where these are in place.

1. Be respectful to staff and other prisoners

Behaviour expectations; prisoners can demonstrate the principle by:
- Behaving honestly and openly with staff, and prisoners, and avoiding threatening/abusive behaviour.
- Being aware and considerate of the impact of behaviour on others.
- Respecting others' possessions, rather than taking items from others.
- Acting with decency at all times remembering prisons/cells are not private dwellings (this includes not engaging in sexual activity).

2. Comply with rules and compacts

Behaviour expectations; prisoners can demonstrate the principle by:
- Following rules/compacts and staff instructions, and avoiding adjudications.
- No trafficking or other criminal behaviour. It's important to look beyond superficial compliance.
- Respecting prison property, taking care of living areas and maintaining cleanliness of the prison.
- Only having items that prisoners are allowed to have.

3. Make progress on personal goals and on your sentence plan

Behaviour expectations; prisoners can demonstrate the principle by:
- Taking an active part in the regime and sentence plan, including work, education or interventions
- Demonstrating behaviours to show progress in areas of:
  - **self-management**, such as managing emotions and solving problems.
  - **interpersonal skills**, such as communicating effectively with others and developing relationship skills
  - **personal care**, such as taking showers and looking after their cell and belongings.

4. Refrain from using drugs or alcohol

Behaviour expectation; prisoners can demonstrate the principle by:
- Giving urine/breath samples, when asked, to test for illegal drugs/alcohol/medicine not prescribed for them.
- Staying free of illegal drugs like heroin, cocaine and alcoholic liquids or medicines that were not prescribed for them by a healthcare professional
- Taking part in activities which help them not to take illegal drug/alcohol/medicines not prescribed for them

SNAKES AND LADDERS

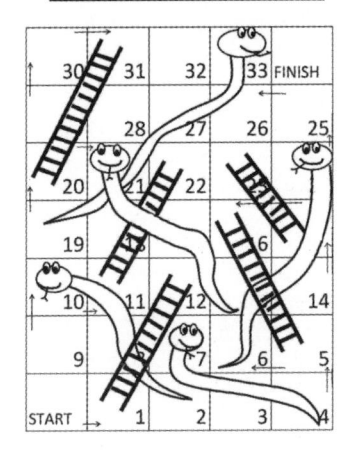

www.prisons.org.uk

comply with the 'Behavioural Expectations' section set out later.

In order to give you incentives to behave and progress there are benefits (and sanctions) attached to each IEP level. Where possible, the following 6 designated 'key earnable privileges' must be included in local IEP schemes at levels appropriate for Basic, Entry, Standard and Enhanced:
• Extra and improved visits;
• Eligibility to earn higher rates of pay;
• Access to in-cell television;
• Opportunity to wear own clothes;
• Access to more private cash;
• Greater time out of cell for association.
Governors can add more privileges to this list.

Basic Level
Basic level is for those prisoners who have demonstrated insufficient commitment to rehabilitation and purposeful activity, or behaved badly and/or who have not engaged sufficiently with the regime to earn privileges at a higher level.

While on Basic access to private cash - money you have in your account in the prison and are able to spend - is limited to £25 per week for unconvicted prisoners and £5 per week for convicted prisoners - this is in addition to any money you earn through working in the prison or if no work is available the amount you are paid at the unemployed or sick pay rate.

All prisoners on Basic level will continue to receive the entitlements laid down in Prison/YOI Rules and other instructions in relation to visits, letters, telephone calls, provision of food and clothing, and any other minimum activity provided locally for all prisoners, apart from those on punishment.

Prisoners on Basic will be considered suitable for progression to the next appropriate level if they:
• Where appropriate, complete the induction process;
• Where apt, attend offending behaviour courses or treatment programmes;
• Engage and co-operate with health, drug and alcohol assessments, drug testing and where identified recovery focused interventions/services;

• Engage and co-operate with the prison regime and any identified purposeful activity, for example, attend work or education;
• Where appropriate, engage with the early days in custody screening interview and demonstrate a willingness to address any identified issues. For example housing and drug and alcohol misuse;
• Wear prison issue clothing, unless permitted not to do so for reasons related to a protected characteristic, such as religious belief or disability. The requirement to wear prison issue clothing does not apply to unconvicted prisoners and prisoners in female prisons at any level of the IEP scheme.

Standard Level
'Standard' level of the IEP scheme is for all prisoners who have successfully completed the 'Entry' level requirements and those who are considered to be meeting rehabilitation expectations, participating in the regime and behaving well.

While on Standard access to private cash - money you have in your account in the prison and are able to spend - is limited to £55 per week for unconvicted prisoners and £18.00 per week for convicted prisoners - this is in addition to any money you earn through working in the prison or if no work is available the amount you are paid at the unemployed or sick pay rate.

Prisoners are expected to:
• Engage with the requirements of their sentence plans;
• Demonstrate a willingness to attend and engage in offending behaviour courses;
• Where appropriate, be willing to attend and engage in purposeful activity such as education / work and where appropriate seek to obtain qualifications;
• Engage and co-operate with drug and alcohol assessments, drug testing and identified recovery focused interventions;
• Actively seek to engage with treatment assessments/programmes;
• Engage and co-operate with the prison regime by attending activities as required, by following orders and instructions from staff and completing any other additional requirements imposed by the Governor.

Enhanced Level

The 'Enhanced' level of IEP scheme is reserved for those prisoners who have demonstrated, for a minimum period of 3 months, that they are fully committed to their rehabilitation, seeking to reduce their risk of reoffending and complying with the regime. While on Enhanced access to private cash - money you have in your account in the prison and are able to spend - is limited to £60.00 per week for unconvicted prisoners and £30.00 per week for convicted prisoners - this is in addition to any money you earn through working in the prison or if no work is available the amount you are paid at the unemployed or sick pay rate.

In addition, Enhanced level prisoners must demonstrate that they have helped other prisoners or staff, for example, acting as Listener, mentoring other prisoners. It is recognised that opportunities such as this may be limited and it is for the Governor to determine what activities enable prisoners to demonstrate that they have helped others or given something back for a sufficient period to be able to earn Enhanced status. A prisoner must not be elevated to Enhanced status without meeting this requirement. Governors must ensure all prisoners have an equal opportunity to demonstrate such behaviour and make reasonable adjustments for those who may find it more difficult for reasons such as disability.

To reach and remain on Enhanced level, prisoners must:

• Show a commitment to their rehabilitation;
• Demonstrate a proactive and self motivated level of engagement with the requirements of their sentence plans;
• Demonstrate a proactive and self motivated level of engagement in identified offending behaviour courses;
• Demonstrate an exemplary attendance and attitude towards purposeful activity such as education / work and where possible seek to obtain qualifications;
• Fully engage in recovery focused interventions/services and drug testing;
• Where appropriate, demonstrate a proactive and self motivated level of engagement with treatment assessments/programmes;
• Help other prisoners or prison staff (e.g. be involved in the Listener Scheme, Toe by Toe, Buddy Scheme, peer supporter/recovery champion, Wing Representative, assist prisoners with disabilities);
• Demonstrate an exemplary attitude towards staff;
• Engage and co-operate with the prison regime by attending activities as required, by following orders and instructions from staff and completing any other additional requirements imposed by the Governor.

Behavioural Expectations

Moving between one IEP level and another also requires what are called *behavioural expectations* - you are expected to behave in a certain way such as:

• Treating others in the prison with respect, avoiding violent, intimidating, threatening and abusive language and behaviour;
• Behaving in a way that respects the diversity of others in the prison;
• Acting with decency at all times remembering prisons/cells are not private dwellings (this includes not engaging in sexual activity);
• Maintaining awareness of the effect of noise on others and keeping noise to an acceptable level;
• Co-operating with staff in the performance of their duties including complying with orders and requests;
• Behaving honestly and openly with staff, other prisoners and visitors to the prison in a way that promotes trust and integrity.

- Complying with prison compacts, rules and regulations;
- Making sure you only have items to which you are allowed access;
- Following all the requirements of the prison's safer custody and violence reduction policies, avoiding trafficking or taking items from other prisoners;
- Co-operation with drug and alcohol testing policies;
- Avoid selling and trading items, taxing or gambling;
- Staying within designated boundaries;
- Having due regard for personal hygiene and health (including appearance, neatness and suitability of clothing);
- Maintaining the cleanliness of cell/prison/equipment;
- Respecting prison property and that belonging to others;
- Complying with fire safety procedures, including rules governing smoking;
- Demonstrating a willingness to build good relationships with other prisoners;

KEEPING YOUR HOME IN PRISON

Homelessness is often one of the most worrying aspects of being held in prison on remand or following a short sentence.

If you are a homeowner who is paying a mortgage, then you will need to consider your options in order to continue making your payments, especially if you have no income while you are inside. One option might be to sublet part or all of your home while you are in prison. You should notify your mortgage lender of this in advance and you may also need to tell your insurance provider of the change in circumstances.

You may want to consider getting a local estate agent to manage your property for a fee while you aren't able to do so. Some offer a rent guarantee scheme that can cover you if a tenant fails to keep up with their rental payments. It is always wise to seek professional advice before taking any action. If you are being held on remand and you are eligible for housing benefit you should be able to make a claim if you are likely to be in prison for less than 52 weeks. If you are already receiving housing benefit you must ensure that you notify your local Housing Executive of your circumstances. Make sure that you have all the relevant contact details and reference numbers, including your National Insurance number, in your address book.

If you have been convicted and will be in prison for 13 weeks or less, then you may still be eligible for housing benefit. However, it is important to note that the 13 weeks cut-off point includes any time spent on remand prior to conviction. If you are even one day over the 13 week total, you may not be eligible for housing benefit.

Although every case is likely to be different there might be other ways of keeping your rented accommodation while you are in prison. Some private landlords might be willing to agree to a sub-letting arrangement and someone else would then be able to pay rent while you are inside. However, this would need to be agreed with the landlord in advance.

It is also possible, in some cases, to reach an agreement with a local authority housing executive or housing association on having what is called a 'nominated person' to move into your accommodation and pay rent while you are in prison. This won't necessarily be possible in every case, but it is always worth making a request as this might be one way of keeping your tenancy.

If you are paying rent privately and are not receiving housing benefit then as long as your rent continues to be paid (eg by direct debit or standing order via your bank) then you should be able to keep your accommodation while you're in prison. However, if the property is going to be unoccupied, some landlords may require you to notify them of this change of circumstance for security and/or insurance purposes. Whatever you circumstances, as soon as you are released from prison you should immediately make a fresh claim for housing benefit if you are eligible. If you are going to be spending some time in approved premises (a hostel) as part of your licence conditions, you will probably require housing benefit in order to cover your accommodation costs.

There are various charities and advice services dealing with the issue of accommodation and homelessness. You may be able to get advice from Citizen's Advice Bureau (CAB) or from specialist charities such as Shelter or NACRO.

SPICE

Danger of death

LEGAL HIGHS - DANGER OF DEATH
New psychoactive substances (NPS), often known as 'legal highs', are substances designed to mimic the effects of drugs such as cannabis, cocaine and ecstasy - they are exceptionally dangerous.

Having been behind the door for 23 hours a day we know the temptation to seek a chemical 'escape' can be huge, but so too are the dangers because one of the difficulties around NPS is that we don't know for certain what's in it. The chemicals in it may not have even been used for human consumption before - what does that tell you?

Risks of NPS include reduced inhibitions, drowsiness, excited or paranoid states, psychosis, hallucinations, dizziness, sickness, overheating, coma and seizures. Many NPS are directly linked to emergency hospital admissions and, in over 100 prisoner cases....

DEATH
NPS can have very different effects on users and risks and side effects are increased if used with alcohol or other drugs. One type of substance can also be much stronger than another that's often its linked to.

Stimulant NPS can make you overconfident and disinhibited, and can induce feelings of anxiety, panic, confusion, paranoia and can even cause psychosis. They can put a strain on your heart and nervous system, they can effect your immune system so you might get more cold-sore infections. Its also likely to lead to increasing drug debts and the physical danger that in itself represents to you.

Psychedelic or hallucinogenic NPS can make you hallucinate. Some strong hallucinatory reactions ('bad trips') can lead to the person acting erratically, sometimes without regard to their safety. Some psychedelic drugs create strong dissociative effects, which make you feel like your mind and body are separated. Both of which can interfere with your judgement, which could put you at risk of acting carelessly, dangerously, or hurting yourself or others, particularly in an unsafe environment. In short don't go near them, find other ways to occupy your time in a positive way - it isn't worth your life.

MAINTAINING INNOCENCE
The prison system isn't designed to deal with the innocent who have been wrongly convicted, although some allowances are made for people who have been convicted by a jury but are pursuing appeals through the Court of Appeal, by and large the position of the Prison Service is that it has to respect the verdicts of the court. So until a higher court quashes a finding of guilt, the conviction must stand.

This makes maintaining innocence a test both of wills and stamina, especially after an appeal against conviction has been dismissed by three judges sitting in the Court of Appeal.

Since pursuing an appeal immediately after conviction can take a year or more, there is likely to be a 'truce' between the individual prisoners and the prison authorities, especially the Offender Management Unit (OMU). Any prisoner with an active appeal against conviction will be expected to produce an appeal case reference number (this should appear on any correspondence with the Court of Appeal). This number should be accepted as evidence that there is an appeal pending and it can reduce pressure to admit guilt or to undertake certain offending behaviour programmes and courses.

However, once the Court of Appeal has dismissed an appeal – the most common

www.prisons.org.uk

outcome – prisoners can find themselves at the mercy of a system that really has difficulty managing individuals who are 'in denial' of their offence. Although this tends to be more of a problem for those convicted of sexual offences, it can also impact on lifers who are maintaining innocence of murder and other serious crimes.

Convicted prisoners are presented with a sentence plan in the months after they have been convicted. This sets out the expectations and goals required if they are to progress through their sentence. The plan also includes offending behaviour courses that the individual is expected to complete.

For prisoners who are maintaining innocence but without a live appeal, the sentence plan can be a major obstacle. In theory no prisoner should be denied Enhanced level status within the IEP system merely because they are maintaining innocence.

The Incentives Policy Framework (7.25) says that prisoners who are appealing against conviction are eligible for Enhanced.

Those prisoners who refuse to accept their guilt and have either had an appeal refused or are not appealing then Governors can consider them for Enhanced status depending on their response to personal progression, progress on their sentence plan and constructive engagement in prison life generally.

However, in practice the experience of many inmates is very different and they can easily find themselves getting demoted to Standard level or even Basic because they are deemed not to be following their sentence plans.

The main problem is that most offending behaviour courses require an initial analysis of the offence in order to proceed. For a prisoner who is maintaining innocence – whether of murder, a sexual offence or other serious crime – this presents a serious dilemma. Admitting guilt becomes formalised and this can prove to be a barrier, both legal and psychological, for anyone who is maintaining innocence.

Ironically, the Prison Service itself does acknowledge that on occasions some prisoners maintain innocence because they are factually innocent and it is recognised that people can have their convictions quashed after many years due to new evidence emerging. However, in practice there is a disconnect between this acknowledgement and the way in which OMUs manage prisoners and their sentence plans.

Much is likely to depend on the relationship between the individual prisoner and the Offender Supervisor (inside probation). Developing a positive relationship with your OS can reduce the risk of losing your IEP status, as can showing willingness to participate in courses that are not offence-specific and do not require any admission of guilt, such as TSP.

In the end, the extent to which an individual is willing to maintain their position on their own innocence must be a personal decision. Wrongful convictions can and do happen, so remember that you are not alone and there are various support groups that are willing to offer advice and encouragement to people who are in prison and maintaining innocence.

OFFENDING BEHAVIOUR COURSES
Courses updated to 2021
Correctional Services Accreditation and Advice Panel (CSAAP)
In July 2021, in response to a written question from Tonia Antoniazzi MP about the availability of offending behaviour programmes, Prisons Minister Alex Chalk MP replied: "A strategic review of all HMPPS designed accredited programmes is underway." Early scoping work to review HMPPS Interventions Services designed accredited programmes commenced in 2019. This was paused to enable operational responses to the pandemic and resumed in late 2020 and therefore this work is still in an

early stage of development.
The review is being led by HMPPS Interventions Services. HMPPS are exploring a refined Accredited Programmes (AcPs) suite to increase their focus on quality in delivery, enable improved evaluation and, ultimately, seek to improve the impact on reduced reoffending rates. Ministers will be sighted on this work as it progresses but as of September 2021 no completion date has been anticipated.
Accredited Offending Behaviour (OB) courses and programmes are offered in prison with the objective of reducing reoffending. Some courses are only available in custody, others only in the community.

If you are being recommended for a specific OB course or programme while you are in prison, this should be discussed between you and your Prison Offender Manager (POM) and your Community Offender Manager (COM) when your sentence plan is being developed or reviewed.

Even though a course may appear on your sentence plan, you may still need to wait because of a shortage of places. In some cases you may also need to be transferred to another prison to participate in a course because your current establishment does not offer that particular course or programme.

The long wait for a place on specific OB courses may cause delays for prisoners who are serving life or IPP sentences as completion of certain courses may be key to demonstrating to members of the Parole Board that an individual has reduced their risk of reoffending. If you are preparing for a Parole Board hearing you must seek professional legal advice about these issues.

Many prisoners who are serving short sentences will not be referred for OB courses as there is often a long waiting list to participate. Unless you are serving a long enough sentence to complete a specific course, it is very likely that you will be able to participate in one while you are still in custody. Some may be expected to attend courses in their local area after they have been released.

Refusing to participate in a course that has been included in your sentence plan when it is available may result in a review of your IEP status as it may be decided that you are not 'following your sentence plan' and you could be demoted to Standard or even Basic. This may present a problem for prisoners who are maintaining innocence of certain offences, including murder and sexual offences.

There has been much debate over the effectiveness of certain OB courses and programmes, especially the Core Sex Offenders Treatment Programme (SOTP), due to a recent Ministry of Justice study that found participants had a higher reoffending rate than those who had not taken part in the course. As a result, both the Core and Extended SOTP programme were replaced in 2017 by two new OB courses: Horizon and Kaizen.

Some prisoners and ex-prisoners say that participation in OB courses that involve victim awareness, anger management and improved thinking skills have assisted them in avoiding reoffending. Others remain more sceptical and regard participation in courses as merely a means to 'tick a box' on their sentence plans.

CORRECTIONAL SERVICES ACCREDITATION AND ADVICE PANEL (CSAAP)
Currently Accredited Programmes 2021

ACCREDITED FOR DELIVERY IN THE COMMUNITY

Becoming New Me + (BNM+)
Provided by HMPPS Interventions Services
BNM+ is for high or very high-risk adult men who have learning disabilities or learning challenges and have been convicted of a sexual offence. It supports development of skills to strengthen pro-social identity and plan for an offence-free life.

Breaking Free: Health and Justice Package
Provided by Breaking Free Online Ltd
This comprises two accredited programmes: Breaking Free Online. An 8-session digital behaviour change programme which addresses the underlying psychological and lifestyle difficulties behind alcohol/drug use and offending behaviour. The programme targets 70 problem substances including illegal substances, New Psychoactive

Substances (NPS), and prescribed medications. Pillars of Recovery. A 12-session behaviour change programme that targets the underlying psychological and lifestyle difficulties behind alcohol/drug use and offending behaviour.

Building Better Relationships (BBR)
Provided by HMPPS Interventions Services
BBR is for adult men convicted of an Intimate Partner Violence (IPV) offence. BBR is a moderate-intensity cognitive-behavioural programme which recognises that IPV is a complex problem which is likely to have multiple causes. BBR responds to individual needs and provides opportunities to develop skills for managing thoughts, emotions, and behaviours

Building Skills for Recovery (BSR)
Provided by HMPPS Interventions Services
BSR) is a psychosocial programme for adult men and women who are dependent on substances or alcohol. The programme aims to reduce offending and problematic substance misuse with the ultimate goal of recovery.

Drink Impaired Drivers Programme (DIDP)
Provided by HMPPS Interventions Services
DIDP is a cognitive-behavioural and educational programme that targets non-dependent drink-drive individuals. DIDP teaches participants about alcohol and supports development of skills to avoid future drink driving situations through:
• greater self-awareness
• self-monitoring of drinking behaviour improved planning
• greater understanding of consequence decision making

Healthy Identity Intervention (HII)
Provided by HMPPS Interventions Services
HII is designed for those who have committed extremist offences. It supports desistance and disengagement from extremism. It encourages stronger positive and pro-social aspects of identity. It helps individuals develop resilience and supports them to identify ways of meeting their identity needs. For example, need for belonging, need for recognition, without involvement in extremism.

Horizon
Provided by HMPPS Interventions Services
Horizon is designed for medium and above risk adult men who have been convicted of a sexual offence. It supports participants to develop optimism, and skills to strengthen their pro-social identity and plan for a life free of offending.

iHorizon
Provided by HMPPS Interventions Services
iHorizon is a version of Horizon for men whose sexual offending is internet only. Offences involve possessing, downloading, and/or distributing indecent images.

Identity Matters (IM)
Provided by HMPPS Interventions Services
IM is a one to one programme for adult men whose offending and harmful behaviour is motivated by their identification with a gang. It supports desistance by encouraging participants to develop a stronger individual identity and develop resilience. It identifies ways of meeting their needs without group driven offending.

Mentalization-based Treatment (MBT)
Provided by HMPPS/NHS Offender Personality Disorder Team
MBT is a psychoeducation programme. It is for people with some traits of Antisocial or Borderline Personality Disorder. It teaches social functioning, and addresses violent and suicidal thoughts, and risky behaviours. There are weekly psychotherapy groups, and monthly one-to-one meetings for a year.

New Me Strengths (NMS)
Provided by HMPPS Interventions Services
NMS is designed for medium and above risk adult men who have learning disabilities or learning challenges (LDCs) and a conviction(s) for any offence. It supports development of skills to strengthen pro-social identity and plan for an offence-free life.

Living as New Me (LNM)
Provided by HMPPS Interventions Services
LNM is an accredited skills maintenance (booster) programme for those individuals

who have already completed NMS or BNM+ and may require further additional support.

Resolve
Provided by HMPPS Interventions Services
Resolve is designed for adult men with a medium to high risk of reoffending with convictions for violent offences. Resolve aims to support participants with histories of violence to reduce the use of aggression and/or violence by developing insight in to behaviours and skills to support achieving pro-social goals.

Thinking Skills Programme (TSP)
Provided by HMPPS Interventions Services
TSP is designed for adult men and women with a medium/high risk of reoffending. TSP supports participants to develop thinking (cognitive) skills to manage risk factors, develop protective factors, and achieve pro-social goals.

ACCREDITED FOR CUSTODY

Alcohol Dependence Treatment Programme (ADTP)
Provided by The Forward Trust
ADTP is a 6-week programme for men with a medium-high risk of reoffending, who are dependent on alcohol. Participants stop drinking and do Steps 1-3 of the Twelve Steps of Alcoholics Anonymous (AA). They can access group therapy, peer support, AA meetings, and individual support.

Becoming New Me + (BNM+)
Provided by HMPPS Interventions Services
BNM+ is for high or very high-risk adult men who have learning disabilities or challenges and have been convicted of a sexual, Intimate Partner Violence (IPV) or general violent offence. It supports participants to develop optimism and skills to strengthen their pro-social identity and plan for an offence-free life.

Breaking Free: Health and Justice Package (Custody)
Provided by Breaking Free Online Ltd
This comprises two accredited programmes: Breaking Free Online: an 8-session digital behaviour change programme which addresses the underlying psychological and lifestyle difficulties behind alcohol/drug use and offending behaviour. The programme targets 70 problem substances including illegal substances, New Psychoactive Substances (NPS), and prescribed medications of abuse; and
Pillars of Recovery: a 12-session behaviour change programme that targets the underlying psychological and lifestyle difficulties behind alcohol/drug use and offending behaviour.

Building Better Relationships (BBR)
Provided by HMPPS Interventions Services
BBR is for adult men convicted of an Intimate Partner Violence (IPV) offence. BBR is a moderate-intensity cognitive-behavioural programme which recognises that IPV is a complex problem which is likely to have multiple causes. BBR responds to individual needs and provides opportunities to develop skills for managing thoughts, emotions, and behaviours.

Building Skills for Recovery (BSR)
Provided by HMPPS Interventions Services
Building Skills for Recovery (BSR) is a psychosocial programme for adult men and women who are dependent on substances or alcohol. The programme aims to reduce offending and problematic substance misuse with the ultimate goal of recovery.

Challenge to Change (C2C)
Provided by Kainos Community
A six-month offending behaviour programme for men in prison. Participants live on a dedicated unit within a prison. Through cognitive behavioural therapy they learn to challenge and change their thinking, attitudes and behaviour. Participants become active members of the community, agreeing rules, meeting together, and providing peer support. Peer mentors play an important part.

Choices, Actions, Relationships, Emotions (CARE)
Provided by HMPPS Interventions Services
CARE is for women who are medium and

above risk, and have a history of violence and complex needs. CARE aims to assist women with understanding and therefore learn how to manage the risk they pose to themselves and others, and to live a more satisfying and pro-social life.

Control of Violence for Angry Impulsive Drinkers – Group Secure (COVAID-GS)
Provided by Delight Services
A cognitive-behavioural programme for men in secure settings who are violent under the influence of alcohol. Consisting of ten group sessions with supplementary individual support sessions, it encourages individuals to understand their behaviour and practise skills for change so that risk of violence is reduced.

Control of Violence for Angry Impulsive Drinkers – Group Secure Women (COVAID-GSW)
Provided by Delight Services
A cognitive-behavioural programme for women in secure settings who are violent under the influence of alcohol. This programme has been developed with and for women in prison.

Democratic Therapeutic Community Model (DTC)
Provided by HMPPS/NHS Offender Personality Disorder Team
DTCs are part of the Offender Personality Disorder Pathway. They are for people with complex psychological and emotional needs, likely to meet the criteria for a diagnosis of 'personality disorder'. They provide a 24/7 therapeutic environment. Most DTC residents have committed violent offences, some of which may be sexually motivated.

Therapeutic Communities Plus (TC+)
Provided by HMPPS/NHS Offender Personality Disorder Team
TC+ is part of the Offender Personality Disorder Pathway. These communities are for people who are eligible for but unable to participate in, mainstream DTC due to mild to moderate learning disability. TC+ services provide group and creative psychotherapies in a 24/7 living-learning environment. Most TC+ residents have committed violent offences, some of which may be sexually motivated.

Healthy Identity Intervention (HII)
Provided by HMPPS Interventions Services
HII is designed for those who have committed extremist offences. It supports desistance and disengagement from extremism. It encourages stronger positive and pro-social aspects of identity. It helps individuals develop resilience and supports them to identify ways of meeting their identity needs. For example, need for belonging, need for recognition, without involvement in extremism.

Healthy Sex Programme (HSP)
Provided by HMPPS Interventions Services
HSP is designed for adult men who have a conviction of a sexual offence or an offence with a sexual element. Regardless of level of risk of sexual reoffending, HPS is designed to respond to the needs of individuals with learning disabilities and challenges and is delivered one to one.

Horizon
Provided by HMPPS Interventions Services
Horizon is designed for medium and above risk adult men who have been convicted of a sexual offence. It supports development of skills to strengthen pro-social identity and plan for an offence-free life.

Identity Matters (IM)
Provided by HMPPS Interventions Services
IM is a one to one programme for adult men whose offending and harmful behaviour is motivated by their identification with a gang. It supports desistance by encouraging participants to develop a stronger individual identity and develop resilience. It identifies ways of meeting their needs without group driven offending.

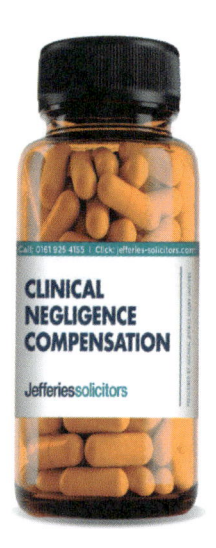

IT'S THE BEST CURE FOR MEDICAL NEGLIGENCE, AND WE'LL GET WHAT'S DUE TO YOU

Preventation is always better than cure however it seems even harder to apply the sentiment when you're in prison.

The reported cases of clinical and dental negligence during confinement is on the increase. Whether it is due to a lack of resources or inept practitioning there is no excuse if your health has suffered physically or mentally, as a result you could be due 1000's of pounds in compensation. Negligence may not just affect you now it could have painful or expensive repercussions far into the future which is why you need expert, experienced advice to secure the compensation which is due to YOU.

As one of the country's leading personal injury lawyers Jefferies Solicitors have been successfully representing prisoners in cases of clinical and dental negligence for many years. We have won compensation from 100's to 1000's of pounds all on a NO WIN NO FEE basis.

If you feel you've been badly treated, misdiagnosed or kept waiting for an unacceptable amount of time contact us now and we will get the compensation you deserve.

CLAIM WHAT IS DUE TO YOU

Jefferiessolicitors

Call: 0161 925 4155 | Click: jefferies-solicitors.com | email: info@jefferiessolicitors.com
write to us at: Jefferies Solicitors Limited | The Triangle | 8 Cross Street | Altrincham | Cheshire | WA14 1EQ

www.prisons.org.uk

Kaizen
Provided by HMPPS Interventions Services
The version of Kaizen accredited for custody is for high or very high risk adult men who have been convicted of a sexual, Intimate Partner Violence (IPV) or general violent offence. It supports participants develop the skills to strengthen their pro-social identity and plan for a life free of offending.

Living as New Me
Provided by HMPPS Interventions Services
LNM is an accredited skills maintenance (booster) programme for those individuals who have already completed NMS or BNM+ and may require further additional support.

New Me Strengths
Provided by HMPPS Interventions Services
NMS is designed for medium and above risk adult men who have learning disabilities or learning challenges (LDCs) and a conviction(s) for any offence. It supports participants to develop optimism, and skills to strengthen their pro-social identity and plan for a life free of offending.

Resolve
Provided by HMPPS Interventions Services
Resolve is designed for adult men with a medium to high risk of reoffending with convictions for violent offences. Resolve aims to support participants with histories of violence to reduce the use of aggression and/or violence by developing insight in to behaviours and skills to support achieving pro-social goals.

The Bridge Programme
Provided by The Forward Trust
The Bridge is a 6-week programme for men with a medium to high risk of reoffending and a history of substance dependence.
Participants give up drugs and do Steps 1-3 of the Twelve Steps of Narcotics Anonymous (NA). They can access group therapy, peer support, AA and NA meetings, and individual support.

Thinking Skills Programme (TSP)
Provided by HMPPS Interventions Services
TSP is designed for adult men and women with a medium/high risk of reoffending. TSP

supports participants to develop thinking (cognitive) skills to manage risk factors, develop protective factors, and achieve pro-social goals.

MARRIAGE - *getting married while in prison, including civil partnerships*

If you wish to marry or enter into a civil partnership while in a prison, you have the right to do so under Article 12 of the European Convention of Human Rights - the rules relating to it are fairly complicated and are set out in Prison Service Instruction 14/2016 updated **1st October 2021**; you should request to see a copy via the applications process.

If the ceremony is to take place in prison you must obtain a statement of authority from the prison governor which states that there is no objection to the prison being named as the place at which the marriage or civil partnership will take place.

To get the ball rolling you need to make an application to the Governor setting out that you wish to marry or enter a civil partnership, it will normally be granted as long as you have at least three months left to serve.

If you wish to marry or enter into a civil partnership you will need to confirm that you are:

Not already in a marriage/civil partnership;

16 years or older (parental/carer consent is required up to the age of 18);

Not a close relative of their intended partner;

In the case of a civil partnership, of the same sex as their intended partner.

Couples may be regarded as a same sex couple if one or both parties have changed their gender and acquired a full gender recognition certificate under the Gender Recognition Act 2004.

Category A and B prisoners will usually be required to have the ceremony in the prison, Category C may be allowed to hold it outside the prison and Category will normally be allowed to hold the ceremony outside of the prison.

If the ceremony is to be held inside the prison you should be allowed to have a small number of close family visitors, including two witnesses to attend the ceremony subject to the usual security checks and the searching of those who attend.

- 141 -

OPEN PRISONS

Everyday Life in a Cat-D: what is it really like to live and work in open conditions?

Because only a minority of prisoners actually make it to open conditions there is often confusion about what Cat-D is really like. Because making the transition between a closed prison and an open jail can be so difficult, this section aims to give you an insight into the realities of Cat-D life.

The first thing to state is that not every Cat-D prisoner will eventually get transferred to open conditions. Some who are categorised as suitable for open conditions may well find themselves released before transfer if they are serving short sentences. There can be a waiting list for open conditions, so long delays can also occur. It pays to be patient.

For many long-term prisoners – especially lifers and IPPs – a transfer to an open prison is an essential, but often unwelcome stage in their progression towards eventual parole. No-one is supposed to serve more than 24 months in open conditions, but it is what happens during that period that can make the difference between being recommended for parole by the Parole Board and getting a knock back.

Many lifers do become anxious once they have been approved as suitable for open conditions. Benefits of being a lifer – including single cells – can suddenly disappear, especially if their Cat-D prison is one of the old military bases or detention centres. Facilities can be very basic and in some a shared cell is likely to become a reality that, after years of having your own personal space, is a very unwelcome prospect.

Arriving at an open prison usually involves travelling in a standard sweatbox and your property may or may not arrive with you. In fact it might follow on weeks later.

The open prison experience starts when you get out of the sweatbox and there are no handcuffs. In fact, there is no perimeter wall (although some Cat-D establishments do have a boundary fence) or barred gates. Cells are called rooms and other than routine roll-checks you probably only have to be in your room between midnight and 7am.

The main rule is just not trying to abscond (you can't legally escape from an open nick, only abscond by breaking bounds). Many jobs involve working within the perimeter without much supervision and roll-checks apart you may find yourself working all day without seeing much in the way of staff unless you are an orderly.

Cat-Ds have tightened up various rules in the past few years. It was once upon a time possible to go shopping in the local town on Temporary Release (ROTL) and bring stuff back to the prison. This is now largely forbidden. Some prisoners even had digiboxes for their TVs and various other luxuries and perks that are now firmly banned thanks mainly to negative tabloid media coverage of 'holiday camp' open prisons.

The biggest difference between closed and open conditions is that you will be expected to sort out your own timetable, get yourself out of bed and turn up for work and meals. There are, generally speaking, no lockdowns and relatively few cell spins. Most inmates wear their own clothing when not in work gear and for those who want it there is a social life – of a kind. Some open prisons have a range of social activities, including rock bands. In others, there is access to at least cardio equipment (if not weights) throughout the day.

If you have spent years, maybe decades, in the confines of a closed jail, open conditions can take some getting used to. At one Cat-D we used to watch men who hadn't been outside of a prison wall by themselves for years wander slowly round and round the playing fields as if this vast space was just a big exercise yard.

There are hazards and pitfalls to avoid, especially if you are serving a long or indeterminate sentence. Cat-D is difficult to gain and easy to lose. Some open prisons don't bother with adjudications or IEP warnings. They just ship inmates straight back to Cat-B jails and ask questions afterwards. Any illicit drug use is a case in point and at times many open nicks have daily buses transferring those who have 'failed' in open conditions.

Generally speaking there are no prisoners on Basic regime in the open estate. Getting busted to Basic is usually a one-way ticket back to the local Cat-B. Similarly there is often no Block. Most prisoners serving long or indeterminate sentences arrive on Enhanced level, with only a small number of inmates serving very short stretches transferred in on Standard level.

Open conditions also mean the chance of Release on Temporary Licence (ROTL – see the section). Eligibility starts after your initial 'lay down' period (usually two months) during which you will be constantly monitored and assessed. Your first day ROTL to the local town is likely to be escorted by an officer in plain clothes and after that it can become a regular event – up to three times a month.

After that comes the chance of overnight leaves – up to four nights every 30 days – when prisoners either go home to stay with their family or to an approved premises in the area where they will eventually be released.

There are likely to be opportunities to volunteer for work with local charities and, for a minority, even paid work for approved employers.

And unlike prisoners in closed nicks, prisoners in most open prisons are encouraged to buy approved pre-paid mobile phones that are kept in lockers in the gatehouse and used when outside the establishment. Wallets with bank cards and cash can also be stored for use when on ROTL or work placements. Just don't bring cash or mobiles into the prison grounds or the sweatbox could be waiting to ship you out.

Preparing yourself mentally for Cat-D
• Cat-Ds accommodate a fair number of short sentenced prisoners, often in for non-violent offences. Some can behave like complete idiots and make life difficult for lifers and IPPs. Don't allow yourself to get provoked by Herbert's who are in for the proverbial 'shit and a shave' and have nothing to lose.
• If you have to share a room on arrival, try to cope with it. Otherwise you might find yourself sharing a locked cell with another complete stranger back in a Cat-B.
• Set yourself reasonable targets and manage your expectations. Be prepared for the two month 'lay down' period and discuss the timings of ROTLs with your OMU officer.

• Just because you have made it to Cat-D doesn't automatically mean you will get ROTLs anytime soon, especially if you have over a year before your next parole hearing. Remember, any ROTL is a privilege you are eligible to apply for, not a right.
• Do prepare yourself for disappointments and don't kick off if your ROTL application is turned down. Arguing with an OMU officer or kicking office doors is a guaranteed one-way ticket back to the local Cat-B.
• Going out to the local town can be a big deal if you have been away for years. Don't let temporary freedom go to your head. Getting back late or having consumed alcohol are common reasons for a ship-out back to closed conditions.

• Steer clear of drugs and alcohol, including NPS. Although many Cat-D prisons do have a significant drug and contraband culture getting caught is another sure fire way to blow any chance of parole.
• Think carefully about what type of voluntary or paid work you might eventually apply to do. Lots of local organisations, ranging from charity shops to animal sanctuaries, rely on prisoner volunteers. Setting up placements does take time, so discuss your ideas with your OMU officer well in advance.
• And if you are considering going on the run from an open nick, at least think about the longer-term consequences for you and your family. The local police will put your mug shot online and in the papers, while your family's home will be regularly raided and ripped apart.

PAD MATES: HOW TO SHARE A CELL WITH MINIMAL GRIEF & FRICTION

Sharing a cell can be one of the most stressful things about being banged-up in jail. It was bad enough sharing a bedroom at home with a brother or sister, so suddenly having to share your very limited personal space with a complete stranger – often one who snores, burps, farts and wants to watch crap on TV – is never going to be easy. However, establishing a view ground rules can prevent a drama becoming a crisis.

When our Victorian prisons were built, the general idea was that convicts should have their own cells. It was thought that the isolation would encourage prisoners to think about their crimes, read their Bibles and not pick up any handy tips on house-breaking or pick-pocketing from fellow cons. However, since our prison population has more than doubled since 1994 – at the time of printing there are more than 86,000 men and women in prison in England and Wales – sharing a cell has become the norm outside of the high security estate. In the worst case scenarios two or even three inmates can be crammed into a cell designed for single occupancy.

Being blessed by having a decent pad mate can make all the difference. Sharing similar interests and TV channels can help to avoid stand-offs over the evening's viewing. At the same time, being considerate of each others needs for privacy, silent time or personal space can make a real difference.

Tensions often arise when a new pad mate moves in. The existing resident is likely to want to establish boundaries and rules for 'his' or 'her' pad, while the newcomer is expected to respect the status quo.

These little power struggles can result in unspoken resentment, especially if the first prisoner has got the best bunk, most comfortable mattress and is hogging all the cupboard space, as well as the cell pin-board. The final straw is often the choice of TV programmes. 'He (or she) who holds the TV remote, controls the viewing.'

With more and more prisoners living with mental health problems and substance addictions, sharing a cell can be even more stressful. Try to develop coping strategies to maintain your own psychological and emotional well-being. Prison strips so much from each person that it can become a battle to hold on to what little you have. Being willing to share anything – even personal space – can be difficult, but if you find the right pad mate your cell can at least become a bit like a boys' night in and killing your bird can become that little bit easier. Who knows, you might even make a friend for life.

Here are a few tips from someone who had 14 pad mates during his time inside:
• Try to get to know your pad mate. If you really are totally incompatible, be honest and try to negotiate a cell swap as soon as you can. This works best if you already have a potential pad mate in mind. Avoid conflict where possible.
• Try to negotiate your TV viewing in advance. Find programmes you both want to watch and be tolerant of your pad mate's viewing choices. Don't just hog the remote.
• Don't play your music without earphones unless your pad mate is cool with it. Remember that listening to pumped out music is used by the US military as a form of torture.
• Never borrow or use your pad mate's stuff without permission. Respect their boundaries and expect yours to be respected too.
• Never, ever touch personal things like diaries, letters, photos.
• Keep yourself and your clothing as clean as you can. No-one ever made friends stinking like a rancid warthog. Don't sit on the top bunk dangling your smelly socks in your pad mate's space.
• Keep your trainers under control and try to air them out by the window.
• Unless it is absolutely unavoidable try not to take a crap in a shared cell WC. If you can regulate your bowels to time with unlock make use of the communal facilities whenever you can. Otherwise at least invest in a couple of air fresheners from the canteen.
• Don't bring trouble into a shared cell. If you have contraband (mobile phone, SIM card, drugs) and you get caught, at least don't try to put the blame on your innocent pad mate.
• Don't bring half the wing into a shared cell unless your pad mate is happy with your flatshare becoming a social club.
If in doubt ask first.

- 144 -

YOU DON'T HAVE TO STOMACH THESE JUST BECAUSE YOU'RE IN PRISON

DENTAL NEGLIGENCE

MEDICAL NEGLIGENCE

ACCIDENTS AT WORK

PERSONAL INJURY

www.prisons.org.uk

Being in prison is hard enough to swallow, being denied your basic rights is totally unacceptable. If you've suffered from any form of personal injury, negligence or an accident at work you have the right to compensation... just the same as those not in prison.

As one of the country's leading personal injury lawyers we have been representing prisoners for many years winning claims from hundreds to many thousands of pounds. All on a no win no fee basis.

IF YOU THINK YOU'VE BEEN A VICTIM OF NEGLIGENCE, PERSONAL INJURY OR AN ACCIDENT AT WORK CONTACT US NOW AND CLAIM THE COMPENSATION THAT'S DUE TO YOU!

CLAIM WHAT IS DUE TO YOU

Jefferies solicitors

NO WIN NO FEE

pila

O.K.

Call: 0161 925 4155 | Click: jefferies-solicitors.com | email: info@jefferiessolicitors.com
write to us at: Jefferies Solicitors Limited | The Triangle | 8 Cross Street | Altrincham | Cheshire | WA14 1EQ

• If you need some 'personal time' for some solo sexual relief, try to find opportunities when your pad mate is in the gym, in the library, out on exercise etc - don't do it when your pad mate is present; 'knocking one out' is hardly a spectator sport - and clean up after yourself.

PRISON DEBT: WHY TO AVOID IT

Prison debt is a massive underground problem that often goes unnoticed until something really nasty happens to a prisoner on a wing. The Prison Rules (1999) are very clear that any form of selling, trading, lending or borrowing between prisoners is strictly prohibited and a disciplinary offence that can end up in a 'nicking' (charge).

However, a significant number of inmates supplement their meagre prison pay by running illegal businesses on the side, including drug dealers and hooch (jail alcohol) brewers. There are also plenty dodgy loan sharks and tobacco barons who underpin the whole undercover prison economy – tobacco (and especially nicotine patches) has become even more of a currency now with the roll out of the nationwide Smoking Ban.

Prisoners who have absolutely no kind of financial support from family or friends outside face a pretty miserable existence, particularly in those establishments that seem to have stopped handing out basic toiletries and hygiene items, such as toothpaste or even toilet paper. Genuine hunger can also be a factor in an era of falling catering budgets.

That's why many prisoners who can afford to do so supplement their prison meals with canteen purchases: instant noodles, tinned fish, cereals, biscuits and confectionary. Anything to get a carb or protein hit and stave off the hunger pangs when you're banged up in a concrete box and can't pop down to the corner shop or phone up to order a pizza. Satisfying your craving for food also costs money and there are no special deals or multi-buys on offer on the canteen sheets. It's full price up front or nothing.

The situation can be even worse for inmates who are in prisons where there is significant overcrowding and little or no paid work available. Your average prisoner really does need to work in jail, even if the pay is often pitifully low – with an average range of around £8.00 to £10.00 per week. Occasionally a prison's Prisoner Monies department will mess up the weekly accounts and people won't get paid at all, thus fuelling the spiral of debt across the wings.

For most inmates in prisons where smoking in cells is still permitted (the no smoking ban at the time of writing (September 2017) applies to around 33% of prisons), the weekly tobacco purchase from the canteen sheet is the main expenditure. An estimated 80 percent of adult male inmates smoke, so 'burn' (rolling tobacco) is a must-have. If you run out midweek, then it can be several agonisingly slow days until the next canteen delivery, since most public sector prisons only have one weekly canteen day.

So what's the alternative? Well, that nice bloke 'Big Dave' up on the 3s is always willing to 'tick out a bit of burn'. Like any payday lender he's delighted to have a new customer. The key question is: what will his interest rate be?

Readers who have already been in prison, or those who are familiar with prison memoirs and diaries, will no doubt recognise the term 'bubble'. It means interest in prison slang. A borrower can be offered terms of 'bubble and a half' – meaning the return of the item loaned, plus 50 per cent – or 'double bubble' – which is, as the name suggests, the original loan plus the same again on top. Repayment is strictly scheduled to coincide with canteen delivery day.

So borrow half an ounce (12.5g) of baccy on 'double bubble' and come the next canteen delivery you'll be owing the original debt (£6.00 or so), plus another half ounce of burn, meaning the lender has just doubled his investment within a few days. It might not sound a lot, but believe me when your entire income is £8.00 per week, that's a massive hit to take.

So what happens when repayment is not forthcoming? Well, the usual pattern is that the debtor pays off the initial loan on the due date but asks for the interest to be deferred until next canteen day. Most loan sharks are, in fact, delighted with this turn of events because they already have their outlay covered. They've lost nothing in real terms, but needless to say the extended credit terms might be another 'half bubble' – so the debtor will need to find another quarter ounce in addition to the original interest payment. Sometimes it can be another 'double bubble' so they now owe double the amount of interest, and so it goes on.

Eventually, the debt can spiral out of control and the debtor is royally screwed. So what are the options? Well, Big Dave has a wide range of possible courses open to him. The first is to give the lad owing money a really good battering – a 'serving' as it is sometimes known in prison circles. Maybe the defaulting prisoner will have a heavy steel cell door slammed shut on his fingers, breaking his hand. This doesn't cancel the debt, but sends a clear message to all other debtors that they had better pay up on time.

Another option is to turn the debtor into a sort of slave: a 'joey'. Any dirty work the loan shark doesn't want to do himself, including dishing out good hidings or running errands can be delegated to his joey. This term can also mean a small package of illicit drugs and the enslaved 'joey' can also end up carrying several little 'joeys' in his anus or hiding them in his cell until his 'master' requires them. Joeys can also be forced to act as mules to smuggle incoming drugs during visits from their families or friends. It's a sad fact that debt in prisons can impact on whole families who may get dragged into couriering drugs to save their loved one from a beating or worse.

One 78 year old grandmother contacted prisons.org.uk recently out of her wits that she had been told to pay another £5000 to prevent her nephew (who prisoners wrongly believed to be wealthy) being battered.

Alternatively, the debtor will have to beg family or friends to help him get out from under the mountain of debt he has incurred. This happens particularly regularly when the supply of drugs is involved. Many debtors are still trying to service their habits, even when they are already on the prison's methadone programme.

The value of any drugs inside prisons is substantially higher than on the street outside. Very good money can be made by dealers whose connections can ensure a reliable supply of contraband narcotics or what are now known as New Psychoactive Substances (NPS) such as spice or mamba. Sometimes these transactions can be settled by cash payments outside that never come anywhere near the prison. It's just another demand-driven, highly profitable business.

When a debtor finally reaches the end of the road and his credit is exhausted, he can throw himself on the mercy of the prison staff and confess he is so deeply in debt that his safety is at risk. That can mean a temporary move to the Block (segregation unit) where he'll be held in solitary confinement until he can be transferred to another prison.

Alternatively he might be moved to another wing or possibly even to a Vulnerable Prisoner Unit (VPU - see below) which holds sex offenders ('nonces' or 'bacons'), grasses (prison informers), ex-police and prison officers and other washed-up debtors. This is

www.prisons.org.uk

called 'going on the Numbers' (taking its name from Prison Rule 45 – historically it was Rule 43 – Removal from Association). It's a move of last resort, but can be a serious debtor's only option if he is to avoid being on the receiving end of serious violence or being forced to work as an unpaid drugs mule.

Even after taking these extreme measures a debtor's reputation is likely to follow him and, prisons being prisons, he will eventually run into an associate of his creditor who will mete out the required punishment, perhaps the slashing of his face with razor blades that have been fixed into a plastic toothbrush or cutlery handle, known as a 'shank'. This is done deliberately to ensure the wounds are very difficult to stitch without leaving visible scars that will serve as a permanent 'brand' that other inmates will understand.

So when you next see criticism of predatory payday lenders in the media, spare a thought for those prisoners who are trapped in a vicious circle of prison debt. At least 'Donga' or 'Quick Buck' (not to be confused with existing lenders of last resort with similar names) won't come round to your cell and slash your face or make you shove a packet of drugs up where the sun doesn't shine.

PROPERTY INSIDE

Most prisoners have some personal property with them in prison, whether these items have been brought in from initial reception, sent in by family or friends or purchased while in prison from the canteen sheet or via one of the approved catalogues. Having some items 'in possession' can make your time inside that little bit more comfortable.

For some inmates, what they have with them in the cell might be pretty much their entire worldly goods (other than one set of clothing held by reception to be worn on discharge). Others may have jewellery, personal clothing, a duvet and bedding, books, a radio or stereo system, CDs, DVDs, games, a musical instrument... There can be a stark difference between the prison haves and have not's.

At the same time, no-one likes to lose their possessions, especially if it has taken months or longer to save some money each week to buy something. People in prison are no different. In fact, because most inmates have comparatively little personal property even a small loss can mean a lot.

The rules and regulations concerning prisoners' personal property can be found in PSO 1250 (amended by PSI 11/2010). Broadly speaking there are two types of personal property when you are in prison. The first is stored property (often referred to as 'stored prop'). This may be kept in a storage box in reception, especially for those people serving a short sentence, or sent to the national storage facility at Branson in the cases of prisoners who are serving longer terms.

Particularly valuable items (including passports, bank cards, expensive jewellery) should be stored as 'valuable prop' and listed on a separate card. These items should then be stored in a secure cabinet or safe.

Stored prop includes any item that prisoners cannot have in possession, or items that would exceed each prisoner's personal allowances (volumetric control). Some confiscated items (although not mobile phones or drugs) may also be placed in stored prop. Some property is also stored in the event of a prisoner's escape, absconding, release or death, although in 2010 a limit of 12 months was imposed on the length on time allowed for such storage (it had previously been three years).

In addition to stored prop, a prisoner may also have property that is held 'in possession'. This includes anything that has been issued to the prisoner and recorded on his or her property card ('prop card'). It also includes canteen purchases, although most of these items are not recorded on the

IF YOU HAVE BEEN A VICTIM OF MEDICAL NEGLIGENCE **SPEAK UP!** YOU COULD HAVE A **CLAIM FOR 1000S** OF POUNDS.

www.prisons.org.uk

NO WIN, NO FEE!

If you feel you have suffered as a result of substandard or negligent medical treatment you could be entitled to compensation.

Mental or physical discomfort and pain as a result of poor treatment is simply unacceptable in prison. As one of the country's leading personal injury lawyers we have been specialising in prisoner representation for many years, winning claims worth thousands of pounds.

If you think you have been a victim of medical or any other negligence or personal injury SPEAK UP, WE ARE LISTENING! and we will claim the compensation that's due to you!

pila

Make a claim
0800 808 9740   0333 323 1428
www.firstpersonalinjury.co.uk
The Triangle, 8 Cross Street, Altrincham, Cheshire, WA14 1EQ

First Personal Injury is a trading name of Jefferies Solicitors Ltd.

first personal injury

CODE CO02

IF YOU HAVE BEEN A VICTIM OF DENTAL NEGLIGENCE **SPEAK UP!** YOU COULD HAVE A **CLAIM FOR 1000S** OF POUNDS.

NO WIN, NO FEE!

Being in prison is hard enough, receiving fair and adequate dental treatment is a basic right... not a privilege.

If you've suffered from any form of personal injury, negligence or an accident at work you may have the right to compensation.

As one of the country's leading personal injury lawyers we have been specialising in prisoner representation for many years, winning claims worth thousands of pounds.

If you think you've been a victim of dental or any other negligence in prison SPEAK UP, WE ARE LISTENING! and we will claim the compensation that's due to you!

Make a claim
0800 808 9740 0333 323 1428
www.firstpersonalinjury.co.uk
The Triangle, 8 Cross Street, Altrincham, Cheshire, WA14 1EQ

First Personal Injury is a trading name of Jefferies Solicitors Ltd.

first personal injury

CODE C001

prop card. Due to volumetric control there are various limits on how much prop can be held in possession. Individual limits and restrictions can be found in the National Facilities List, but broadly speaking extends to two official storage boxes, plus a few specific outsize items such as a musical instrument and legal papers.

Prisoners are considered responsible for their own prop when in possession. Reception staff warn against having expensive items, particularly watches and jewellery, on the wings. Generally speaking, if items are stolen from a prisoner's cell, the prison will very rarely accept responsibility unless a member of staff has unlocked a cell and allowed access to a prisoner who doesn't live in that cell.

However, if prisoners have personal clothing in possession and this goes missing when it has been placed in bags to go to the prison laundry, then a claim for compensation may be made if items of clothing have disappeared or been damaged. In such cases, an app to the governor should be made listing all the lost or missing items of clothing and their approximate value.

According to the Prison Rules, prisoners are forbidden to lend, sell or gift any item to another inmate. It is a disciplinary offence to do so. Therefore, if you lend a mate a CD, DVD, a computer game, a book or some clothing and he or she trashes or loses it, then it's difficult to make a complaint without admitting to breaking the rules and risking an IEP warning or even a nicking.

There is also a risk in having other people's prop in your cell if staff carry out a cell search ('spin') and find items that are not on your prop card. This can land you in trouble as you are likely to be suspected of stealing other people's stuff or buying/selling items.

Unsurprisingly a significant amount of prisoners' property does get lost every year. Transfers between prisons are often a time when prop gets lost. Some private sector providers of prison transport ('sweat boxes') will not carry a prisoner with all their prop boxes and bags, so it often has to follow on and this is where a significant amount gets mislaid or lost in the system.

When stored property goes missing or has been stolen (not entirely unknown) as long as the item has been listed on the stored prop card a prisoner can make a claim for the value of the item by applying to the governor via the internal complaints system. In many cases, especially where the item is a relatively low value, compensation can be sometimes be agreed.

However, according to the Prisons and Probation Ombudsman (PPO) a significant amount of complaints made by prisoners concerns lost, damaged or confiscated property. For example, in 2014-2015 28 per cent of all complaints investigated by the PPO were about property. This suggests that prison managers are not particularly efficient when it comes to dealing with lost property complaints, especially since the PPO will only accept complaints that have already exhausted the usual prison internal complaints procedures.

On occasion, some prisoners who have hit a brick wall over their lost property have taken the governor to the County Court - claims in the County Court for less than £10,000 are known as Small Claims. The small claims court is intended to be for disputes where both sides do not employ lawyers but act for themselves - generally speaking if you instruct a solicitor, even if you win, you will not be able to claim their costs - but it also means that the prison service cannot claim his costs from your if he wins..

Generally you will have to show that the prison had been negligent, meaning you have to prove (that it was more likely than not on a 51% to 49% test) that the prison had 'control' of your property, either it was in stored property, marked on your property card, or that it was in your cell when you were removed from the wing (and say taken to the block) and that your cell door was left open so others could steal your property and the prison cannot now produce it.

You can get advice about from any Citizens Advice Bureau by writing or calling them.

Going to court means you usually have to pay a fee but as a serving prisoner you are entitled to ask the court to waive these fees - known as fee remission.

If you are currently serving a prison

sentence, on remand or in custody at one of Her Majesty's Prisons, Remand Centres or Young Offenders Institutes, you are eligible to apply for a fee remission. You are subject to the same disposable capital test as everyone else - the value of houses, cars, furniture etc you or your partner own is worth less than £3000). You are also subject to the gross monthly income test - you have to show that your monthly gross pay from the prison is less than £1,085.

If you have a partner you need to know that their disposable capital and gross monthly income are also counted - giving false information is a criminal offence so don't be tempted to 'wing it'. You must give the court or tribunal evidence to support your fee remission application - the court will tell you how to do this, or you can ask your family to download their booklet EX160 from HM Courts & Tribunals web site.

RECALL

Updated 1st October 2021 the **Recall, Review and re-release of recalled prisoners**, is the document you need to obtain to understand your rights if you're recalled - get a copy of it through your Library.

The Policy sets out what all HMPPS staff involved in the recall, review and re-release of recalled prisoners MUST do.

It includes requirements for:
- the recall of those offenders (including young offenders) released subject to licensed supervision for indeterminate, determinate and extended sentences
- the recall of those offenders released subject to home detention curfew
- unlawfully at large recalled offenders
- recalled prisoners upon return to custody
- executive release
- review & re-release of recalled prisoners

The Policy Framework contains the **'Recall Best Practice Guide: Working with Recalled Prisoners'** for use by all probation and prison staff involved in the recall process.

The Recall Policy Framework replaces all the previous Instructions & Orders on Recall - if you want to know about recall and your rights in relation to it, *this is the document that you should obtain and read.*

Don't take 'No' for an answer: under the *Library Services Policy Framework* all prison Libraries **MUST** make it available to you.

All determinate and indeterminate sentenced prisoners released into the community subject to licensed supervision are liable to be recalled to custody by the Secretary of State where they have breached the conditions of their licence. It is the responsibility of the Probation Service, Youth Offending Teams (YOT) or CRCs to start the recall process by applying for recall through the Public Protection Casework Section (PPCS) at the MOJ.

- **Recall of Indeterminate sentenced offenders.** Offender managers must demonstrate a **"causal link"** in behaviour on licence similar to that present at the time of your original offence - for example if you were sentenced as a result of drug or alcohol misuse, and then abuse drugs or alcohol on Licence, that is enough to show a causal link. It is also enough to show that on licence you are showing behaviour likely to give rise (or does give rise) to a sexual or violent offence, or are associated with the commission of a sexual or violent offence, or you are not in contact with your offender manager and the assumption can be made that sexual violent offences may arise. Offender managers must ensure there's proof of increased risk of harm to the public.

The decision to start the recall process must be made by the responsible offender manager, but it is the PPCS that responsible for deciding whether to authorise indeterminate recall requests. This decision must take place within two hours of receipt of the recall request and supporting paperwork.

- **Recall of Determinate sentenced offenders.**
1. The recall of **Extended Sentenced Offenders** and **Discretionary Conditional Release Offenders** are the same for Indeterminate sentenced offenders above.
2. **Recall of Determinate Sentenced offenders** can happen where an offender has breached the conditions of their licence, the offender's behaviour indicates that they present an increased or unmanageable RoSH to the public or there is an imminent risk of further offences being committed. Recall can also happen where contact with the offender has broken down.

Once a decision has been made to revoke your licence, there is legal power to arrest you and recall you to prison. You are considered to be 'unlawfully at large' for any period between licence revocation and return to prison. The Criminal Justice and Courts Act 2015 created a new offence of 'remaining unlawfully at large after recall', which carries a maximum penalty of a two year custodial sentence.

Types of recall
There are three types of recall: fixed term, standard and emergency.
The legal framework for them all is contained in the Criminal Justice and Immigration Act 2008, subsequently amended by the Legal Aid, Sentencing and Punishment of Offenders Act (LASPO) 2012. More details are contained in PSI 30/2012 and PSI 30/2014.

Fixed term recall (FTR)
Before the introduction of the Rehabilitation of Offenders Act 2014, this fixed period of recall was 28 days, as you could only be recalled if you were serving a sentence longer than 12 months. If you were sentenced before 1/2/2015, this still applies.

However, if you were sentenced after 1/2/2015, you can be recalled for a fixed period of 28 or 14 days, depending on whether your sentence was over or under 12 months.

Under the changes brought in by LASPO, all prisoners are eligible to be considered for FTR unless they are serving an extended sentence. However, whether a prisoner is considered suitable for FTR or standard recall is determined by the PPCS based on the level of risk in each case.

You will only be released at the end of the 14 or 28 day period if you are not considered to present an 'identifiable' risk of serious harm (either physical or psychological) based on a current OASys assessment. If assessed as high or very high risk, then you will not be considered suitable. It is also likely that greater scrutiny will be given to those groups of prisoners, who were previously ineligible for FTR, ie those who:
- Are serving a sentence imposed for a sexual or violent crime listed in Schedule 15 of the CJA 2003;
- Were recalled before their automatic release date after being released early on Home Detention Curfew or compassionate grounds;
- Had been recalled before on the same sentence.

Standard recall
A standard recall can result in you remaining in prison for the whole of your licence period and only being released at your sentence expiry date. However, either the SSJ or the Parole Board can release you earlier if they are satisfied that your imprisonment is no longer necessary for the protection of the public. Once you are recalled your case should be reviewed at least annually.

Emergency recall
This is identical to the standard recall except that you have been identified as being a risk of serious harm and/or that your risk of reoffending is unmanageable or imminent.

What happens next?
On return to custody all prisoners are entitled to know the reasons for their recall within 24 hours and to be advised of their right to make representations to the Parole Board. If you are on an FTR and make representations then your case must be referred to the Parole Board

'expeditiously' and, if the Board orders release, then the SSJ must release you. If you do not make representations then your case will not automatically be referred to the Parole Board. The SSJ through the Post Release Team can also exercise an executive power to re-release before a fixed recall period expires if an offender manager makes a request in writing. Additional licence conditions can be added to your original licence at the point of release.

If you are on a standard recall you will have your detention reviewed by the PPCS and/or Parole Board. The SSJ has the power to re- release at any time. However, all cases must be referred to the Parole Board for consideration once you have been in custody for 28 days.

The Parole Board can:
1. Order immediate release:
2. Fix a date for future release within one year;
3. Make no recommendation for release (in which case the SSJ must refer the case back to the Board within a year or sooner if the circumstances or risk assessment change);
4. Order release at sentence expiry (if there is less than a year left to serve).

The test for release
In order to direct release the Parole Board must be satisfied that it is no longer necessary for a prisoner to be detained in order to protect the public from serious harm to 'life and limb'. After the fixed term has been served, a prisoner becomes automatically eligible for re-release. However, you will only be released if the Parole Board is satisfied you pose no risk of serious harm to the public. Additionally, since the Criminal Justice and Courts Act 2015 has come into force, a prisoner will not be eligible for automatic release if it appears to the Secretary of State that they are highly likely to breach their licence conditions and so it would be inappropriate to release them.

The Parole Board is not required to balance risk of harm against the benefits to the public or prisoner of their release.

What if I was sentenced under the Criminal Justice Act 1991?
If you were sentenced under the CJA 1991 (you are serving a sentence for an offence committed before 4/4/05 and were convicted before 3/12/12) and you have been released on licence, then you are liable to recall up to your licence expiry date (LED). This is at the point of your total sentence. If you were recalled prior to 14/7/08 then you remain subject to the recall procedures in PSI 48/2007 and have to be released at your LED.

However if you were recalled on or after 14/7/08, you will be treated as if you were under the CJA 2003. This means that you can be held in custody until your SED unless you are released by the Parole Board or SSJ. If re-released, you'll be on licence until SED.

'RECONSIDERATION MECHANISM'
The reconsideration mechanism allows a Parole Board decision to be challenged by a prisoner or the Justice Secretary within 21 days of the Parole Board decision.
Reasons for reconsideration
The reconsideration mechanism will give people the right to ask for a parole decision to be looked at again by the Parole Board if they have reasons to show the decision is either:
Procedurally unfair - the correct process was not followed in the review of the offender for parole - for example, important evidence was not shared.
Irrational - the decision makes no sense based on the evidence of risk that was considered and that no other rational panel could come to the same conclusion.
Being unhappy with the decision is not grounds for reconsideration.
Types of prison sentence this applies to
The reconsideration mechanism applies to prisoners serving:
- Indeterminate sentences (Life or IPP),
- Extended sentences,
- Some determinate sentences where the initial release is at the discretion of the Parole Board (Discretionary Conditional Release (DCR) cases and Sentences for Offenders of Particular Concern (SOPC)).
- Recalled prisoners serving these sentences.

People who can apply for reconsideration
Only the Secretary of State or the prisoner can apply to the Parole Board for reconsideration as they are parties to the proceedings.

An application must be received within three weeks (**21 calendar days**) of the decision being issued to the parties in the case (the prisoner and the Secretary of State).

The initial decision will be made final if there have not been any applications during the 21 day window.

Any requests made after the three weeks will not be accepted by the Parole Board.

If there is serious concern with the decision once the 21 day window has closed, then people can still apply for 'Judicial Review' — through the Administrative Court.

How prisoners can apply

A prisoner can apply for a decision to be reconsidered themselves, or through their legal representation. This application will be sent directly to the Parole Board Reconsideration Team.

If possible, the form should be sent via email rather than post because the timeframe to challenge a decision is just 21 days.

RELEASE ON TEMPORARY LICENCE

ROTL means being allowed out for a specific purpose and set time. ROTL rules are now set out in the **ROTL Policy Framework was updated 17th August 2021** - you can get a copy in the Library.

There are two forms of ROTL - Standard and Restricted.

The following are Restricted ROTL

• *Indeterminate sentence prisoners (ISPs);*
• *Prisoners serving Extended Determinate Sentences, or other legacy extended sentences;*
• *Prisoners serving sentences imposed under section 236A of the Criminal Justice Act 2003 (offenders of particular concern);*
• *Any other offender who is currently assessed as high or very high risk of serious harm on OASys.*

Restricted ROTL includes:
• Men must be in open prison, women must be assessed as suitable for open conditions
• Decisions made by Governor or D/Gov;
• Board must be chaired by a senior manager
• Board must see an enhanced behaviour monitoring (EBM) assessment);
• Enhanced behaviour monitoring for those who require it.
• Mandatory consultation with offender manager and police
• Mandatory views of offender managers
• Higher level of monitoring whilst on release

All other offenders will be considered under the Standard ROTL regime.

Types of ROTL

ROTL comes in various forms, but essentially it means being given permission to go outside a prison for a specific purpose and for a set time. ROTL comes in four types of licence.
• **Resettlement Day Release (RDR)**
• **Resettlement Overnight Release (ROR)**
• **Childcare Resettlement Licence (CRL)**
• **Special Purpose Licence (SPL)**

Resettlement Day Release (RDR)

You may be released on RDR to undertake activities that are linked to objectives in your sentence plan - such as:
• Paid or unpaid work placements
• Work placement assessment
• Training or education
• Other activities linked to sentence plan or resettlement goals

Resettlement Overnight Release (ROR)

The main purpose of ROR is to allow offenders to spend time at their release address re-establishing links with family and the local community.

Childcare Resettlement Licence (CRL)

The onus will be on you to show you are a primary carer of a child under 18, for example providing documents from school, nursery, GP, social services, etc to support you claim; and the prison will have evidence about the claimed relationship based on contact during the current period of custody and information from probation in some cases.

Special Purpose Licence (SPL)

SPL may generally be issued in response to a specific event or set of circumstances that would not usually require release on a regular basis. The governor can allow a licence to cover overnight absences.

SPL can be granted for:
• Compassionate, such as visits to dying relatives, funerals or other tragic personal circumstances;
• Medical, to attend medical out-patient appointments, or inpatient requirements.

- Marriage or civil partnership of the offender
- Inter-prison transfers, for Standard ROTL offenders transferring from closed to open prisons, and Standard or Restricted ROTL offenders transferring from one open prison to another, may do so under licence.
- Court, tribunal or inquiry proceedings

This includes cases where the offender's presence is required, and those where it is in the offender's interests to attend proceedings such as tribunals, and family matters in a civil court.

- Conferences with legal advisers, Offenders must not be released or escorted to attend legal conferences outside the prison unless this is necessary. Legal Advisers should instead attend the prison for a legal visit.

SELF-HARM: COPING IN CUSTODY
Many people self-harm while they are in prisons. In the year to March 2021 there were 53,000 self-harm incidents.

Who Can Help?
There is a range of people who may be able to provide you with advice and support while you are in prison and self-harming:
- Safer Custody Team staff
- Mental Health staff
- Healthcare staff
- Members of the Chaplaincy Team
- Personal officer
- Other member of prison staff
- Listeners
- The Samaritans (by telephone)
- Insiders
- Other prisoners you trust
- Family members
- Friends outside prison

This brief guide aims to help you understand what self-harm is and how it can be managed while you are inside. It could also help you identify others at risk because of self-harm.

Self-harm can be defined as hurting yourself deliberately, for example by cutting, biting, scratching or burning. Self-harm may also involve the misuse of drugs and/or alcohol. Some people self-harm only in one particular way, others try different methods depending on how they are feeling or what they have around them in their cell. Self-harm is different to having suicidal feelings or thoughts.

There has always been self-harm in prisons. However in recent years the number of recorded cases has been rising. During 2016 there were 40,161 reported cases of self-harm in prisons in England and Wales, in the current year that rose to almost 58,000. Each person has their own reasons for self-harming. Many people who self-harm do it because they are finding it difficult to cope with their feelings or their moods. Some say that it helps them cope while they are in custody, others that it makes them feel a bit more in control of their own bodies and their emotions.

It is important to note that while acts of self-harm always mean that something is wrong, it is NOT always a sign that the person has a mental illness. Nor should self-harming ever be dismissed as 'attention seeking'. In some circumstances it is actually a distressed person's way of coping, while some are also asking for help, understanding and support.

All prisons in England and Wales have a duty of care to prisoners in their custody.

The Safer Custody framework is set out in **PSI 64/2011 updated July 2021**: Management of prisoners at risk of harm to self, to others and from others (Safer Custody).

Each prison must have a Safer Custody Team. Prisons also have mental health teams responsible for managing the care of inmates with mental health conditions.

The Prison Service has clear guidelines on how members of staff should treat people who are self-harming. This emphasises that those who self-harm should never be accused of 'attention seeking behaviour'.

Prisoners who self-harm should not be punished for harming themselves.

Prisoners who are identified as being at risk of self-harm or suicide are managed under the Assessment, Care in Custody, Teamwork (ACCT) system. This is sometimes referred to as being "on the ACCT" or "on the ACCT book". If you are on an open ACCT document you will be regularly monitored in your cell and will have regular discussions with a member of staff who is involved in your care.

You should be involved in the

ACCT management process. Your feelings and views should always be taken into account. The ACCT document will only be closed when the Safer Custody Team is satisfied that your risk of self-harm has been reduced.

Helping Yourself

If you self-harm, stopping should be a decision you make for yourself, not because others are pressuring you. It might help if you understand more about the reasons why you self-harm and there are people who you can speak to about this. When you do self-harm there may also be ways in which you can do this more safely. With the right support you might be able to self-harm less.

Reducing Self-Harm or Deciding to Stop

The first step to stopping or reducing your self-harming is to think about it for yourself. You may decide that now isn't the right time for you to stop, but thinking about your options is a good start.

- Some people find that making a list of reasons why you self-harm and then why you would like to stop can help.
- At first you might try reducing your amount of self-harming as a step in taking back your own control.
- If you feel like self-harming you could delay – say for 15 minutes – to see if the feelings pass.

Everyone is different so this may or may not help.

- If delaying self-harming does work for you, you could then try waiting for longer periods.
- Can doing other things help? Try to find things that work for you.
- Ask yourself: are there other ways I can cope without harming myself?
- Does talking with another person help you manage your feelings better?

SEX IN PRISON

There were 270 sexual assaults in prisons in 2020 – that sounds a lot but when seen against the 36,000 physical assaults it should help to quell fears that you are about to be raped every time you step into the shower.

Without doubt, a wide range of sexual activity does take place in prisons, both in the male or the female estate. While most of this is, broadly speaking, consensual there is a real concern over unequal and exploitative relationships, as well as the issues of rape and sexual assaults.

Faced with the issue of sexual activity behind bars, the prison authorities also struggle with serious inconsistencies in terms of official policy. For example, PSI 05/2018 makes it clear that consensual sex between prisoners is not a specific offence: "there is no Rule specifically prohibiting sexual acts between prisoners" (1.76). A potential disciplinary charge only arises if sexual acts are observed by a member of staff.

Different prisons seem to interpret these inconsistent rules in very different ways.

Some establishments take a hard line stance on any form of sexual activity by prisoners, including masturbation when observed by a member of staff. Other jails tend to turn a blind eye to sexual relationships that appear to be consensual.

What Does 'Prison Gay' Mean?

Male prisoners who identify as gay or bisexual, and who have stable relationships with partners outside prison, are much less likely to engage in same-sex activity while in custody, even if serving long sentences, including life or IPP.

In general most openly gay or bisexual men serving time in prison aren't notably promiscuous even when opportunities do present themselves. A minority of gay or bisexual men do develop sexually active relationships while in prison and, by and large, these are either ignored or tacitly tolerated by prisoners and staff.

A relatively small number of self-identified heterosexual males do 'experiment' with same-sex activity in prison or take advantage of opportunities for sexual acts when offered by other inmates. This type of sexual behaviour seems to be almost entirely opportunistic in character. It also tends to be very covert.

In terms of men who would normally consider themselves to be entirely heterosexual when not in custody, yet are willing to have some form of sex while they are in prison, the recurrent pattern seems to be that if an otherwise heterosexual prisoner (particularly, although not exclusively, serving a substantial sentence) finds himself sharing a cell with another male who he knows to be, or perceives to be, gay or bisexual he then might take advantage of this situation.

It's what is sometimes known inside as being 'prison gay'. Such prisoners usually self-identify very strongly as heterosexual and can be prone to react very violently if anyone dares to suggest otherwise.

For this reason, sexual activity in these situations also tends to be very secretive in nature, with activities taking place at night after the final evening head count has been done by wing staff.

The vital issue of consent

Keeping yourself safe in prison involves being aware of the risks, including sexual assaults. No one has the right to touch you sexually or make you engage in any form of sexual activity against your will. Sexual offences committed in prison are crimes inside jail just as they are out on the street. As a prisoner you are entitled to feel safe in custody.

• If you feel under pressure to engage in sexual activity speak to someone about your concerns. This could be a Listener, an Insider or a member of staff, for example your personal officer or a member of the chaplaincy team.

• No one has the right to force you to do anything sexual against your will. You always have the right to say no.

• Be aware that other prisoners who offer to lend you things or give you gifts may have an ulterior motive. Be careful not to get into any kind of debt to others.

• If you become the victim of a sexual assault in prison – whether from a fellow inmate or a member of staff – you should feel able to report what has happened. Don't blame yourself. Don't suffer in silence. Sexual assaults can have a devastating impact on people's mental and physical health. Seeking support and professional counselling can help.

There is still a culture of official denial in some prisons when it comes to sexual assaults and rape inside some of our prisons. There is also evidence that in some prisons the management prefers to avoid reporting such allegations to the local police and instead makes use of internal disciplinary processes. This can make prisoners reluctant to report incidents of sexual assaults.

Although recent official statistics reveal that reported incidents of sexual assault in prison have risen significantly – to 469 cases in the year to March 2019 – a tripling since 2012 – this is likely to only be the tip of a much larger iceberg of sexual abuse inside our prisons owing to chronic under-reporting of sexual assaults, especially by men. Fortunately, most people who are serving a custodial sentence will not experience rape or sexual assault while they are in prison. However being aware of the potential dangers and knowing your legal rights can play an important role in keeping yourself safe.

PRISON SLANG: A BRIEF GUIDE

Adjudication: prison disciplinary hearing
App: An official application to do something
Bacon: A sex offender
Bang-up: To lock up in a cell
Banged-up: To be locked up in a cell
Baron: One who lends tobacco etc
Basic: To be on Basic regime
Bend up: Held in restraint position
Bird: A prison sentence
Blagger: Armed robber
Block: Segregation Unit
Blood: Friend
Boss: Term of address for a prison officer
Box: Post box for applications or complaints
Brew: Prison-made alcohol
Bud: Cannabis
Burglars: Prison staff conducting a cell search
Burn: Tobacco (esp rolling tobacco)
Cell spin: Cell search by staff
Clown suit: Coloured overalls worn by high risk prisoners or those on the Escape List
Comp: A complaint form
Course: An offending behaviour course
Cucumbers: On the numbers (Rule 45 or vulnerable prisoner unit)
Deps: Depositions or Court paperwork
Diesel: Prison tea
E-List: Potential or former escapee
Fours: Fourth floor of a prison wing
Fraggle: Mentally ill prisoner
Fraggle Rock: Psychiatric unit
Gat: Firearm
Ghost: To be moved prison without notice
Grass: Informer
Hooch: Prison-made alcohol

- 158 -

IEP: Incentives and Earned Privileges
IPP: Indeterminate Sentence for Public Protection
In possession: An item that a prisoner has in his or her possession legally
Insider: A prisoner who provides advice to other inmates
Joey: A prisoner who does dirty jobs for stronger inmates
Jugged: To have hot water thrown in the face
Kanga: Prison officer (from kangaroo = screw)
Knock back: An official refusal, esp from the Parole Board
Lifer: A life sentenced prisoner
Line: A string used to transfer items via cell windows
Listener: A prisoner trained by the Samaritans who supports other inmates
Lockdown: To cancel normal activities and leave cells locked
Lump: A long prison sentence
Mamba: Psychoactive substances
MDT: Mandatory Drug Test
Meds: Medication
Nicking: Being placed on a charge
Nonce: A sex offender
Numbers: On Rule 45 (segregation or a Vulnerable Prisoner Unit)
Ones: The ground floor of a prison wing
Out: On the outside (ie free)
Pad: Cell
Pad mate: Cell mate
Pad thief: One who steals from other cells
Pat down: A basic body search over clothing
Piece: Firearm
Plastic screw: An Operational Support Grade (OSG) member of staff
Plugged: To be carrying contraband in the rectum
Plugging: To insert contraband into the rectum
Porridge: A prison sentence
Prop card: A document listing every item of a prisoner's possessions
Red band: A trusted prisoner (often an orderly)
Regime: Daily timetable
Riot squad: Tornado team (prison officers trained in riot control)
Rub down: A basic security search over clothing)
Safe: OK
Screw: Prison officer
Screw boy: A prisoner who is seen as being too close to prison staff
Seg: Segregation Unit

Serving: Punishment beating
Shank: Weapon
Ship out: To be transferred to another prison
Skinny burn: Thin roll-up cigarette
Skins: Cigarette papers
Snout: Tobacco (dated)
Spice: Psychoactive substances
Strap: Firearm
Stretch: Prison sentence
Striped: To be slashed with a razor
Strip search: Full body search involving removal of clothing
Sweat box: Secure transport vehicle
Tech - mobile phone
Threes: Third floor of a prison wing
Two'd up: Sharing a cell
Twos: Second floor of a prison wing
VPs: Vulnerable prisoners
Wrap up: To be restrained by staff
Yard: Exercise yard

TRANSFERS - *how do I get transferred?*
Bottom line: you can't demand a transfer.
Under English law you can be held in any prison and transferred from one prison to another at the sole discretion of the Secretary of State (Prison Act 1952, section 12).
How do I apply for a transfer?
Transfer decisions are made by the governor of the holding prison, although the prison you are being moved to will also have a say in whether to accept you or not.
How long does it take?
If an answer to an application has not been received within seven days it would be reasonable to submit a further application.
What factors might influence the decision about my transfer application?
Factors which may give an application priority include:
• If the main visitor has medical problems which make normal visiting impossible. A doctor's letter confirming this would be necessary.
• Sentence planning may require that a prisoner complete a course that is unavailable in the holding prison. For prisoners whose release is determined by the Parole Board, completion of certain courses can play a highly significant role in this process.
• Problems such as bullying or assaults. Once staff have been informed about such

problems, there is a legal obligation to take reasonable steps to keep individual prisoners safe. A transfer may be a solution in such a situation though it is not the only option open to the prison in terms of keeping the individual safe.

• A prisoner should not normally be held at a prison where he or she is involved in legal proceedings (either criminal or civil claims for compensation) concerning staff at that prison.

How do I appeal if I am unhappy with the governor's decision?

If the decision is clearly unreasonable then it may be appropriate to pursue a compliant via form COMP1. If the issue is still unresolved to your satisfaction once the two stages of the complaints procedure have been exhausted the next and final stage is to complain to the Prisons and Probation Ombudsman.

VETERANS IN CUSTODY

Support for armed services veterans in prison can be provided via special groups such as Veterans in Custody Support (VICS) which are as partnership between the Ministry of Justice and the Ministry of Defence. These groups are often organised by ex-servicemen and woman who are now serving on the prison staff. In many prisons VICS has representatives on each wing who are tasked with providing support and advice to fellow veterans.

Regular meetings may take place during which veterans can talk frankly about their experiences and any special needs that they may be facing. Support can also be provided by outside organisations such as the Royal British Legion and the armed forces charity SSAFA. There is more information available from SSAFA (address: 4 St Dunstan's Hill, London EC3R 8AD, tel: 020 7403 8783).

SSAFA states that it can provide advice and support to veterans who are currently in custody, as well as those who are being released. In addition, the families of prisoners who are armed service veterans can also seek help and support. The basic qualification to apply for SSAFA support is that you are either still serving in the armed forces or have received one day's pay for service in the Royal Navy, the Army, the Royal Marines or the royal Air Force, including the Volunteer Reserve Forces and military nursing services. Families and dependants of veterans who are in prison are also eligible to receive support from SAAFA. For veterans who are still in prison (including on remand), SSAFA operates a prison in-reach team and are able to provide advice and assistance with housing and resettlement for those who are eligible. Some local branches of SSAFA and the Royal British Legion organise meetings for veterans in prisons, including advice sessions focused on resettlement issues.

If you are an armed services veteran and your prison does not currently have a VICS group or you would like to meet in person with the local SSAFA representative to discuss support and advice you may need, put in an app requesting a meeting.

One Prisoner's Personal Experience

When I went into prison for the first time it was pretty bewildering. However, I was asked in reception whether I had served in the military and I said I had. The officer took my basic service details and the same day I was met by two lads who are also ex-army. They really helped me settle in and gave me real support.

I joined the prison's VICS group which was really well organised. We had regular monthly meetings organised by a gym officer who was also a veteran and he was really approachable about anything. He suggested I could do the training to become a gym orderly, which I did.

We also had regular visits on the wing from the local SSAFA rep. He was really helpful and explained all the ways SSAFA could support me and my family outside. He helped one of my mates from VICS supported accommodation for his release and this lad also had specialist PTSD counselling to help with his psychological problems – all sorted out with help from SSAFA. Another ex-army lad who had no family to support him was given help to buy a small music system for his pad.

VPU'S: WHAT ARE THEY AND WHO CAN APPLY TO GO *'ON THE NUMBERS'* ?

Many wrongly believe Vulnerable Prisoners' Units (VPUs) only accommodate prisoners who have been convicted of sexual offences, or are former police or prison officers.

While it is true many of those on VPUs fall into these categories, it is not true of everyone - but the attitudes of prisoners from mains wings or normal location to those who go 'on the numbers' (a reference to Prison Rule 45 (formerly 43a) will assume that this is what you are.

You can apply for Rule 45 - but the Governor does not have to grant it. They may decide that you can be safely located in another part of the prison or, in more extreme cases, transferred to another prison although this is becoming more difficult as all prisons become overcrowded.

However, almost all prisons now have some form of VPU and these units (or landings) often house a very diverse group of people.

Although many prisoners living on VPUs have been convicted of sexual offences, or are on remand awaiting trial, a fair proportion of residents have opted to go on these wings for their own safety. Some may have been convicted of particularly violent – although non-sexual – offences against children or the elderly, while others might include former police or prison officers, as well as ex-magistrates or judges. The average VPU will also accommodate a few debtors who can't settle their debts, pad thieves who have been caught or suspected 'grasses' (informers) all of who fear retribution from fellow inmates.

Most prisoners who are placed on a VPU will be assigned there from first reception based on their offences. The Prison Service has a duty of care to take reasonable measures to protect inmates, so anyone who is considered vulnerable is likely to be sent to a VPU. However, you can insist on being placed on a main wing. but the staff will probably require you to sign a waiver accepting the risks to their own safety. For most prisoners the decision to go on a VPU will impact on the rest of their time inside.

It is rare for an inmate who has spent time on a VPU to move back onto the mains, even if they transfer to another prison.

Prisoners assigned to a VPU may find that the range of prison jobs open to them is very limited, sometimes to roles such as wing cleaners or servery workers. Prison staff must ensure that VPs do not come into contact with mains prisoners, so movement within a prison is tightly controlled and inmates are likely to be escorted at all times.

Daily life on a VPU

In general VPUs tend to be much quieter than mains wings. The average age of prisoners is often much higher, with some men in their 70s or 80s (a reflection of the increased number of prosecutions for so-called 'historical' sexual offences). Fewer residents are likely to be involved with the drugs culture and riots are almost unheard of. Overall, the levels of violence are also much lower.

Some prison staff will admit privately to preferring to work on a VPU because prisoners tend to be much less volatile and demanding, although others may find it difficult to remain objective when working with inmates who may have committed serious sexual offences.

VPUs are odd communities. There is often a higher proportion of well educated former professionals (such as teachers and doctors), but there is still likely to be a hierarchy of offences.

Child killers tend to be at the bottom of the pile, while ex-prison officers often get a particularly hard time from former colleagues. Debtors who transfer in from mains wings may refuse to interact with inmates convicted of sexual offences.

The shortage of work for prisoners is likely to be much more acute on a VPU because many roles are barred due to the need to mix with inmates from mains wings. On the other hand, since many more residents are classed as retired, there may be more time out of cell on a VPU with prisoners playing board games or cards.

Finally remember this: things are never as bad as they first appear, going on the numbers is a big step that you should not take unless you are absolutely sure that its necessary for your personal safety.

Prisoners will make assumptions about you and you will rarely be able to escape from it during the rest of your sentence.

Speak to staff about personal safety concerns you have - you are sent to prison as punishment not for punishment and you should do what you can to try and avoid Rule 45 protection for as long as possible.

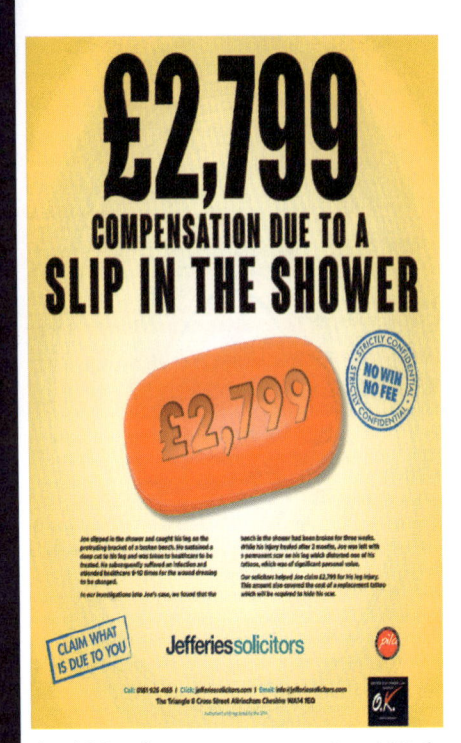

WORK AND PAY - *What are the rules on work?*
The Prison Rules state that work is compulsory for convicted adult prisoners. Relevant PSOs and PSIs include:
• PSO 4460 on Prisoners' Pay
• PSI 01/2012 Manage Prisoner Finance
• PSI 06/2012 Employment, Training & Skills

The rules require that 'Useful work' must be undertaken for a maximum of 10 hours per day. Arrangements can be made for prisoners to work outside the cells and in association with one another, where possible.

Unconvicted prisoners can choose to work as if they were convicted and at the same rates of pay. Work is graded by the type of labour, with No 1 being heavy, No 2 being medium and No 3 being light.

No prisoner should be required to do work of a heavier type than their labour grade.

It is a disciplinary offence for convicted prisoners to refuse to work or to not work properly. Article 4 of the ECHR, which outlaws forced labour is specifically excluded from applying in prison.

All new prisoners should be given access to the National Careers Service (NCS) upon induction. The prisoner is offered assessment after which an Individual Learning Plan may be set out to help him with his progress whilst in prison, based on his career aspirations and goals.

Are there any exceptions?
Prisoners who are ill may be completely excused from work by the medical officer or written off work for a stated period.

The Prison Rules state that arrangements are to be made to not require Christian prisoners to do any unnecessary work on a Sunday and for prisoners of other religions to not do any unnecessary work on their days of religious observance.

Prisoners are also not expected to work with items that are opposed to their religious faith.
What are the rates of pay?
The minimum weekly rates of pay are as follows:
• Unemployed – £2.50
• Employed - £4.00
• Short-term sick (sick for up to 4 weeks) -£2.50
• Long-term sick (sick for more than 4 weeks) - £3.25
• Retired/maternity leave/ full-time child care - £3.25
• Outside hospital allowance - £4.35 (60p a day)

Higher rates of pay are available under the Incentives and Earned Privileges Schemes (IEPS).

Prisoners earning over the threshold for Income Tax and National Insurance are not exempt from payments. Prisoners will only receive unemployment pay if they are willing to work but no work can be found for them.

£29,950
COMPENSATION BECAUSE OF A PRISON SLIP

NO WIN NO FEE — STRICTLY CONFIDENTIAL

Adam was playing pool when he slipped on a wet floor, badly injuring his back. Our solicitors secured him nearly £30,000 in compensation.

Adam was playing pool when he slipped on rainwater on the floor and fell onto his buttocks, injuring his lower back. The rainwater had come in through broken windows and the prison staff hadn't put up any signs to warn inmates about the wet floor. Adam visited healthcare and an MRI scan showed that he was suffering from degenerative disc disease in his lower spine.

2 years after the accident, Adam still experienced stiffness in his back. He struggled to stand for long periods and the back pain disturbed his sleep. Our solicitors arranged for him to see an orthopaedic expert who stated that Adam's symptoms were unlikely to improve and that, unfortunately, he would probably experience long-term back pain.

We secured Adam £29,950 to compensate him for his pain and suffering.

Jefferies solicitors

CLAIM WHAT IS DUE TO YOU

pila

INSTITUTE OF PRISON LAW Qualified
O.K. Jefferies Solicitors

Call: 0161 925 4155 | Click: jefferiessolicitors.com | Email: info@jefferiessolicitors.com
The Triangle 8 Cross Street Altrincham Cheshire WA14 1EQ

Authorised and regulated by the SRA

www.prisons.org.uk

SECTION THREE.
Personal Injury in Prison

Michael Jefferies, Solicitor.

Senior Partner Jefferies Personal Injuries Solicitors.

Chairman: Prison Injury Lawyers Association

Basics.

HM Prison and Probation Service (HMPPS) has a legal duty to keep you safe.

Article 2 of the Human Rights Act protects your right to life.

It requires the Government to take steps to safeguard the lives of everyone within the UK's jurisdiction and as a government department, this extends to HM Prison Service.

Prisons have a duty of care towards all prisoners, that means you, and they must take reasonable measures to keep them safe during their sentence. The Prison has a responsibility to ensure the safety of prisoners, which includes protecting vulnerable inmates from being assaulted.

If the Prison fails in its duties to guard you against potential risks and you become injured as a result, you are entitled to take legal action. While you lose many of your rights when you enter prison, you maintain your entitlement to compensation for an injury if it wasn't your fault.

Prisons are violent places and never more so than at the present time - in the year to March 2017 there were almost 20,000 assaults by prisoners on prisoners, almost 8,000 assaults by prisoners on staff - these are the highest recorded levels ever. In prison, there are a variety of incidents in which you may sustain an injury including:
- an assault
- a slip, trip or fall
- an accident in your cell
- an accident at work in the prison, or
- as a result of medical negligence (including dental negligence)

It can sometimes be difficult to prove that negligence has taken place in prison because it is tricky to produce reliable independent witnesses and to gather evidence within the prison setting.

However, it is entirely possible to successfully claim against the Prison Service.

To make sure that you receive the maximum amount of injury compensation you are entitled to, it is important that you have an expert legal team behind you.

Limitation

Strict time limits apply to personal injury claims; you have a fixed period of time during which a formal claim can be made. Usually, claims must be brought within 3 years of an accident taking place or within 3 years of when you first became aware of your injury.

Types of prison claims

Assaults

Prisons are dangerous places. Compared to 2010, there are now about 7,000 fewer prison officers, supervising offers and custodial managers working in England and Wales. This has resulted in a higher risk of injury for both officers and prisoners and, which has been illustrated by a growing number of assaults.

If you are assaulted whilst in prison it is not always possible to bring legal action; sometimes violent incidents are unexpected and unavoidable. However, in some instances, assaults can be prevented. The prison is legally required to protect vulnerable prisoners from potential attacks and to implement violence reduction strategies to deal with violent inmates.

Some prisoners are at particular risk of assault, because of their offence or background. In these cases, the prison must take extra measures to protect these individuals. In the most serious cases, vulnerable prisoners may be segregated under Rule 45 for their own safety.

The prison is required to make a proper risk assessment on inmates and assign them to cells according to their profile. If they fail to do this or make a grave error in the process which leads to an assault or other violent incident taking place, they may be liable.

When a prison officer receives intelligence that an assault is going to happen, e.g. from an inmate complaining that they have received threats, they must work to protect this prisoner from assault. There are a number of documents they should complete, including intelligence reports and the risk to you should be assessed. If the prison fails to take steps to stop an assault taking place, legally, this is negligence.

If you have been a victim of assault and it can be proven that steps could have been taken to prevent the incident, you may be able to take legal action.

It doesn't matter if you were assaulted by a fellow inmate, prison officer or another member of staff, if the prison could have protected you from injury, but has failed to do so, you are legally entitled to make a claim for compensation.

How much could you receive?
The amount you can claim for assault will depend on the type of injury you have sustained. Past claims have resulted in compensation awards ranging from £1,000 to £250,000.

Slips and trips
Slips and trips in prison commonly occur on wet or badly maintained floor surfaces. They can also be caused by obstructions, poor lighting or prisoners wearing inappropriate footwear.

Areas should be well-lit and properly maintained. In addition, the prison should have cleaning systems in place to promptly deal with spillages or wet surfaces which cause a hazard.

If prison staff have been negligent in their duty to adhere to health and safety procedures, and this leads to you slipping and becoming injured, you can hold them to account and claim for your injuries.

It can sometimes be difficult to prove that negligence has taken place because it is tricky to produce reliable independent witnesses and to gather sufficient evidence. Nevertheless, it is possible to successfully make a claim against the Prison Service for an accident of this kind.

How much could you receive?
Because slips and trips can result in a wide range of different injuries, it is tricky to give an indication of how much compensation you might receive. To find out the value of your claim, contact a personal injury solicitor who will be able to assess your circumstances.

An injury in your cell
The prison is required to provide all prisoners with a reasonable and safe standard of living.

This includes ensuring that the furniture within your cell and communal areas is not faulty and does not create a hazard.

If there are any broken or hazardous furniture or fittings in your cell or bathroom that have the potential to harm you or others, you should report it to a prison officer immediately. The prison should then take steps to address the problem and replace or repair the faulty item.

How much could you receive?
Like slips and trips, there are a variety of different injuries that may be sustained as a result of faulty furniture or fittings. An experienced personal injury solicitor will be able to give you an idea of how much you could claim once they have learnt more about the incident.

Case study
Joe slipped in the shower and caught his leg on a broken bench. He sustained a deep cut on his leg which became infected. Because of the infection, he had to attend healthcare 10 times for the wound dressing to be changed.

His injury healed but Joe was left with a permanent scar on his leg which distorted one of his tattoos. When he made a claim, Joe's solicitor discovered that the bench had been broken for three weeks and the prison had not tried to fix it. The Prison was sued for negligence and Joe received £2,799 in compensation.

Bunk bed falls

Your bunk bed in prison should be in a safe condition and should be equipped with sufficient safety precautions such as a guard rail on the top bunk. If the prison has provided you with a bed that is unsafe and you become injured as a result, you can claim

If you have a serious medical condition that increases your risk of injury this should be catered for by the Prison. In respect of your sleeping arrangements, you should be allocated the bottom bunk bed or supplied with

www.prisons.org.uk

a safety guard if you sleep on the top bunk. In the event that the Prison fails to do this and you sustain an injury as a result, you are legally entitled to hold the prison liable for negligence.

Case study

Liam fell from the top bunk of his bed after experiencing a night terror. There was no safety rail attached to the bed, even though he had asked repeatedly for one to be fitted along his bunk.

When he fell, Liam hit his head on a pipe, badly cutting his head and suffering whiplash to his neck and lower back. The bleeding from the cut triggered his Post Traumatic Stress Disorder (PTSD) which he had suffered after serving in the army for 10 years.

After contacting a personal injury solicitor, Liam claimed for both his physical injuries and his psychological symptoms and he received £6,000 in compensation.

Accidents at work

Prisoners are also owed a duty of care to ensure that their place of work is safe. The prison should carry out sufficient risk assessments in order to provide a safe working environment. Adequate training must be given and suitable Personal Protective Equipment (PPE) such as gloves, boots or googles must be provided.

If you are injured while working in prison, in the workshop, kitchen, laundry room or other location, because prison staff have failed in the above duties, you might be able to claim.

Case study

Sean slipped on some loose plastic while breaking up window frames in the prison workshop. He landed on his left arm, breaking his left wrist.

At the time of the accident, Sean was not wearing any Personal Protection Equipment and the trainers he was wearing were unsuitable for the area and the job he was doing. He had also not been given any training or guidance from the prison staff about keeping the floor clear in the area he was working in.

His wrist injury caused Sean pain and discomfort for almost three years. He sought the help of a leading prison injury solicitor and claimed £5,000 in compensation for his injuries.

Medical negligence

Even though you are incarcerated, you are still entitled to receive healthcare and treatment when necessary. However, inmates are in the hands of the prison service when it comes to medical treatment.

Sometimes, prisons do not deliver treatment or refer prisoners for care when they should do and this can cause an injury or illness to become worse. This is a form of medical negligence.

In addition, healthcare should supply you with any medication you require for an existing medical condition while you are incarcerated. If you have been denied prescription medication for an extensive period of time and this has led to your condition worsening, you are legally permitted to claim for this.

If you have experienced substandard care or been denied treatment or medication in prison and this has led to hospitalisation or a delayed recovery, you may be able to claim medical negligence compensation.

Dental negligence

Prisoners are also legally entitled to receive a good standard of dental treatment. Unfortunately, because of a shortage of dentists in prison and the large numbers of inmates requiring treatment, many prisoners experience long delays in dental treatment and some receive poor care. Consequently, many it is not uncommon for prisoners to suffer from toothache and continuing problems with their teeth.

However, there is no excuse for substandard or delayed treatment and if your teeth suffer as a result, you may be entitled to take legal action and claim dental negligence compensation.

How much could you receive?

Medical and dental negligence claims are often very complex. Until your circumstances are properly assessed, it is impossible to say how much your claim might be worth. If you have suffered negligence at the hands of a doctor, dentist or other medical professional while in prison, it is essential that you seek expert legal advice as soon as possible.

Case study

On entering prison, Steve immediately requested dental treatment as he knew some of his teeth were in bad condition. It took 5 months for him to be seen by a dentist. By this time, one of his teeth was badly decayed and needed to be removed. However, it was not removed for more than a year.

Because of the delay in treatment, Steve experienced prolonged pain and suffering. What's more, because the prison dentist had failed to properly assess the condition of his teeth, he required further dental treatment that he may not have needed had he been seen by a dentist sooner.

After he pursued a claim for dental negligence, Steve received £2,500 in compensation.

What to do if you sustain a personal injury

If you are unfortunate enough to be injured in prison, there are a number of steps you should take. You must:

• Report your injury by informing a member of staff. Request that they complete a Report of Injury to Prisoner form with details of the time, date and place of the incident. If they refuse to do this, put in a COMP1 form detailing the accident and make it clear that the Officers do not want to record it.

• Make a note of the specific prison officer you spoke to.

• If anyone else witnessed the incident, make a note of their names too.

• Report to healthcare for assessment and treatment. Write down the names of the healthcare staff you dealt with.

• Request that photos of your injury are taken. Do this immediately both verbally and in writing using a COMP1 form.

• Request that CCTV of the area is retained. Prisons usually get rid of CCTV footage every 3 months so it's important that you do this as soon as possible. Make a request in writing via the complaints system.

• Contact an experienced personal injury solicitor to claim compensation.

Remember that you have 3 years from the date of your injury to make a claim.

What you can claim for

In legal terms, the compensation awarded in personal injury claims both in and out of prison is known as damages. There are two types of damages: general damages and special damages.

General damages

General damages are the portion of your compensation that covers the physical aspects of your injury. The amount you receive will depend on:

• the type of injury you have sustained,

• the level of pain you have endured, the length of time you have suffered

• how long you are likely to continue to suffer in the future if you have not yet fully recovered

• any long-term loss of function, permanent scarring or other negative physical factors you've experienced

• any mental stress and psychological trauma you've suffered

Special damages

The special damages part of your claim will take into account how your injury has impacted you financially and includes:

• any loss of earnings you have experienced (or will experience)

• any out-of-pocket expenses you've incurred e.g. the cost of postage or telephone calls

• the cost of any ongoing care or future surgery you may require

It is important to remember that you could continue to experience the effects of your injury after you have been released from prison. When calculating the special damages part of your claim, depending on the length of your sentence, your solicitor may take into consideration how your injury might impact your life on the outside, including your future ability to work and earning capacity.

The claims process with Jefferies

When you first contact the team at Jefferies Solicitors, we will assess your circumstances and if you have a valid claim, we will send you some paperwork to fill in. These forms will ask for further details about the incident, your injuries and who you reported it to.

We will then write to the Prison (or

relevant Hospital Trust in the case of medical negligence) by sending a Claims Notification Form or a Letter of Claim. They will then have 3 months to respond and give their stance on liability (whether they believe they are responsible for your injury). If liability is admitted, we will then seek medical evidence to help value your claim before looking to settle your case.

If liability is denied by the Prison or Hospital Trust, we will work to gather further evidence, such as additional witness statements or medical reports, to support your claim and persuade the third party to reconsider their decision. If the Prison continues to deny liability, we might look to issue court proceedings. This does not necessarily mean that your claim will reach the court stage; it could be settled out-of-court before the hearing date.

Frequently asked questions
Why should I claim?
The personal injury compensation system was set up to help people who are injured because of someone else's negligence. Making a claim can help to bring about a sense of justice and hold the person responsible to account.

If you are injured in an accident that wasn't your fault, you are legally entitled to claim compensation for your suffering and to recover any losses you may have experienced as a result of your injury.

If a prison or hospital trust has been negligent in its duties and this has resulted in you becoming injured, you can hold them liable. You have 3 years from the date of your accident or injury in which to make a personal injury claim.
How much could I claim?
The amount of compensation you could receive will depend on a number of factors. These include:
• the level of injury you have suffered
• the severity of your condition
• the length of time you have been suffering for
• any complications you have experienced

After taking on your claim, your solicitor fully assess your circumstances in order to value your claim. Throughout the legal process, they will update you on the progress of your claim and will ensure that they work hard to recover as much compensation as we can for you.
How long will my claim take?
It can be difficult to predict how long a claim will take at the outset. If the prison deny liability for your injury, we may need to issue court proceedings which may prolong the length of your claim.
What information will I need to provide?
You will need to provide your solicitor with full details of the accident or assault, the injuries you have suffered and who you reported the incident to. Any other information such as photographs of your injury or CCTV of the incident can also be really helpful.
Will I have to pay anything?
Most personal injury lawyers, including Jefferies, usually handle claims on a no win, no fee basis. Under a no win, no fee agreement (sometimes known as a Conditional Fee Agreement).

If we don't win your case, you won't owe us a penny. If we do win your case, the amount you pay is capped at a fixed amount of your compensation (usually 25%).
Can a family member speak to you on my behalf?
Many prisoners prefer to have a partner or loved one on the outside communicate with their solicitor on their behalf. If this is something you would like, you will need to give written permission by signing a form of authority and returning it to your solicitor.
Will I have to go to court?
Most claims are settled before they reach the court stage. If your claim does go that far, your solicitor will make sure that you are fully aware of what is expected of you and will be on hand to answer your questions and queries.

Jefferies Solicitors, The Triangle, 8 Cross Street, Altrincham WA14 1EQ. 0161 925 4155

£5,000 COMPENSATION FOR DELAYED DENTAL TREATMENT

After delays in his dental treatment, Stuart experienced 2 years of horrendous toothache, and ultimately needed to have all of his teeth removed. The dental negligence team at Prison Injury Lawyers secured him £5,000 in compensation.

Stuart visited the dentist in prison with toothache in August 2013. He was told that he needed 5 teeth extracting and several fillings but a follow-up appointment was not scheduled until 10 months later. Unfortunately, Stuart was moved to another prison the day before the appointment and missed it.

Following various delays and appointments cancelled by healthcare, Stuart was finally seen by a dentist 2 years later, who told him that it would be necessary to remove all of his teeth. We looked into his case and found that if he hadn't had to wait for so long before being treated, he would have experienced significantly less pain and suffering. Stuart's claim in March 2019 for £5,000.

"WE UNDERSTAND PRISONERS AND PRISON INJURY CLAIMS. WE ARE THE UK'S LEADING PRISON INJURY LAWYERS AND WILL FIGHT FOR WHAT YOU DESERVE."

At Prison Injury Lawyers, we can help you claim for:

- Dental negligence
- Medical negligence
- Slips, trips and falls
- Workplace accidents
- Burns
- Assaults
- Bunk bed falls
- Transport accidents
- Accidents in the gym

STRICTLY CONFIDENTIAL · NO WIN NO FEE · STRICTLY CONFIDENTIAL

PRISON INJURY LAWYERS

0800 808 9577 | prisoninjurylawyers.co.uk
info@prisoninjurylawyers.co.uk

The Triangle 8 Cross Street Altrincham
Cheshire WA14 1EQ

Prison Injury Lawyers is a trading name of Jefferies Solicitors Limited

www.prisons.org.uk

SECTION FOUR.
Helpful Organisations

Government
PARLIAMENT
House of Commons, London SW1A 0AA (House of Lords, London SW1A 0PW) The Palace of Westminster Switchboard 020 7219 3000 Web www.parliament.uk Email hcinfo@parliament.uk If you don't know who your MP is, call the House of Commons Information Office on 020 7219 4272. Please note that a prisoner's parliamentary constituency is the one in which he or she lived prior to going to prison.

QUALITY CARE COMMISSION
National Customer Service Centre Citygate Gallowgate Newcastle upon Tyne NE1 4PA Telephone: 03000 616161.

We're the independent regulator of health and social care in England. We make sure health and social care services provide people with safe, effective, compassionate, high-quality care and we encourage care services to improve. We monitor, inspect and regulate services to make sure they meet fundamental standards of quality and safety and we publish what we find, including performance ratings to help people choose care. We work in the following ways. Making sure services meet fundamental standards that people have a right to expect whenever they receive care. Registering care services that meet our standards. Monitoring, inspecting and regulating care services to make sure that they continue to meet the standards. Protecting the rights of vulnerable people, including those whose rights are restricted under the Mental Health Act. Listening to and acting on your experiences. Involving the public and people who receive care in our work and working in partnership with other organisations and local groups. Challenging all providers, with the worst performers getting the most attention. Making fair and authoritative judgements, supported by the best information and evidence. Taking appropriate action if care services are failing to meet fundamental standards of quality and safety. Carrying out in-depth investigations to look at care across the system.

Reporting on the quality of care services, publishing clear and comprehensive information, including performance ratings to help people choose care.

CRIMINAL CASES REVIEW COMMISSION
5 St Philip's Place Birmingham B3 2P
Web www.ccrc.gov.uk
Email info@ccrc.gov.uk
The Criminal Cases Review Commission is the independent public body that was set up to investigate possible miscarriages of justice in England, Wales and Northern Ireland. The Commission assesses whether convictions or sentences should be referred to a court of appeal.

CROWN PROSECUTION SERVICE
Head: Max Hill QC;
CPS Public Enquiries
102 Petty France
London
SW1H 9EA Tel: 020 3357 0899
Web www.cps.gov.uk
Email enquiries@cps.gov.uk
The Crown Prosecution Service is responsible for prosecuting criminal cases investigated by the police in England and Wales.

DISCLOSURE AND BARRING DBS
Customer services PO Box 3961 Royal Wootton Bassett SN4 4HFE
customerservices@dbs.gsi.gov.uk
DBS helpline 03000 200 190
Web www.crb.gov.uk
Email info@crb.org.uk
This service REPLACED THE CRB and enables organisations in the public, private and voluntary sectors to make safer recruitment decisions by identifying candidates who may be unsuitable for certain work, especially that involve children and vulnerable adults.

HOME OFFICE
Head: The Rt Hon Priti Patel MP, Home Secretary
Direct Communications Unit, 2 Marsham Street, London SW1 P4DF Tel: 0207 035 4848
Web www.homeoffice.gov.uk
public.enquiries@homeoffice.gov.uk
The Home Office is the lead government department for immigration and passports, drugs policy, counterterrorism and police.

HM INSPECTORATE OF PRISONS
Chief Inspector Of Prisons: Peter Clarke. HM Inspectorate of Prisons, 3rd floor, 10 South Colonnade, Canary Wharf, London. E14 4PU.
Tel: 020 7340 0500
www.justiceinspectorates.gov.uk/hmiprisons
The Inspectorate conducts unannounced inspections of all prisons, YOI's and immigration

holding centres in England and Wales. The inspectorate provides independent scrutiny of the conditions for and treatment of prisoners and other detainees, promoting the concept of 'healthy prisons' in which staff work effectively to support prisoners and detainees to reduce reoffending or achieve other agreed outcomes.

MINISTRY OF JUSTICE
Head: Rt.Hon Robert Buckland QC MP. 102 Petty France London SW1H 9AJ
Email general.queries@justice.gsi.gov.uk
Telephone 020 3334 3555
Core components of the MoJ are:
• HM Prison & Probation Service (HMPPS): administration of correctional services in England and Wales through Her Majesty's Prison Service and the Probation Service, under the umbrella of HMPPS
• Youth Justice and sponsorship of the Youth Justice Board
• Sponsorship of the Parole Board, Her Majesty's Inspectorates of Prison and Probation, Independent Monitoring Boards and the Prison and Probation Ombudsmen
• Criminal, civil, family and administrative law: criminal law and sentencing policy, including sponsorship of the Sentencing Guidelines Council and the Sentencing Advisory Panel and the Law Commission.
• The Office for Criminal Justice Reform: hosted by the Ministry of Justice but working trilaterally with the three CJS departments, the Ministry of Justice, Home Office, Attorney General's Office
• HM Courts Service: administration of the civil, family and criminal courts in England and Wales
• The Tribunals Service: administration of tribunals across the UK
• Legal Aid and the wider Community Legal Service through the Legal Services Commission
• Support for the Judiciary: judicial appointments via the newly created Judicial Appointments Commission, the Judicial Office and Judicial Communications Office
• The Privy Council Secretariat and Office of the Judicial Committee of the Privy Council
• Constitutional affairs: electoral reform and democratic engagement, civil and human rights, freedom of information, management of the UK's constitutional arrangements and relationships including with the devolved administrations and the Crown Dependencies
• Ministry of Justice corporate centre: focused corporate centre to shape overall strategy and drive performance and delivery.

HM PRISON & PROBATION SERVICE (HMPPS).
Head: Dr. Jo Farrar, Chief Executive, Clive House 70 Petty France London SW1H 9EXE
public.enquiries@noms.gsi.gov.uk
Main switchboard 0300 047 6325 HMPPS, which is the name for the fused Prison & Probation Services, was created in 2017, it was formerly known as NOMS but it became HMPPS in April 2017 when it lost its powers to commission services and decide on policy – both of which were transferred to the MOJ.

PAROLE BOARD
Head: Caroline Corby, Chief Executive Claire Bassett The Parole Board for England and Wales 52 Queen Anne's Gate London SW1H 9AG,
info@paroleboard.gsi.gov.uk
Telephone 020 3334 4402
The Parole Board was created in 1968 under the Criminal Justice Act 1967. It became an independent Public Body on 1st July 1996 under the Criminal Justice and Public Order Act 1994. In January 2008 the Court of Appeal ruled in the case of Brooke v The Parole Board that the Board lacked sufficient legal independence and it is expected that the composition of the Parole Board will be completely changed.

PRISONS/PROBATION OMBUDSMAN
Head: Sue McAllister
Prisons & Probation Ombudsman Prisons and Probation Ombudsman, 3rd floor, 10 South Colonnade, Canary Wharf, London. E14 4PU. Tel: 020 7633 4100
Web www.ppo.gov.uk
Email mail@ppo.gsi.gov.uk
The Prisons and Probation Ombudsman is appointed by the Home Secretary and investigates complaints from prisoners and those subject to probation supervision, or those upon whom reports have been written. The Ombudsman is completely independent of both the Prison Service and the National Probation Service (NPS). The current Ombudsman post is vacant following the retirement in August 2017 of Nigel Newcomen. The PPO is assisted by a team of deputies, assistants, investigators and other staff. The Ombudsman is also responsible for investigating all deaths of prisoners and residents of probation hostels and immigration detention accommodation.

YOUTH JUSTICE BOARD
Youth Justice Board for England and Wales 102 Petty France London SW1H 9AJ Tel: 020 3334 5300 Fax: 020 3334 2250
Email: enquiries@yjb.gsi.gov.uk
The Youth Justice Board for England and Wales (YJB) is an executive non-departmental public body. Twelve board members are appointed by the Secretary of State for Justice. The YJB oversees the youth justice system in England and Wales. YJB work to prevent offending and reoffending by children and young people under the age of 18, and to ensure that custody for them is safe, secure and addresses the causes of their offending behaviour.

Prison Help Groups
ACTION FOR PRISONER'S FAMILIES
15-17 The Broadway, Hatfield, Hertfordshire, AL9 5HZ
Web www.familylives.org.uk
Tel Helpline 0808 800 2222
Office 020 7553 3080
Email press@familylives.org.uk
Action for Prisoners' and Offenders' Families merged with Family Lives in 2014 and supports those families who are or who have been affected by imprisonment. You can find information on our web site for families and professionals, and also our Hidden Sentence training for professionals working with families. We also have a number of leaflets for families, as well as resources for professionals working with prisoners' and offenders' families. What we believe families should not be judged or discriminated against because of having someone in prison. All families, parents and children affected by imprisonment or offending should have access to information, resources and services as soon as someone is sent to prison or receives a community sentence.

ADFAM
Vivienne Evans OBE, Chief Executive
Adfam, 120 Cromer Street London WC1H 8BS
Web www.adfam.org.uk
Email admin@adfam.org.uk
Adfam was founded in 1984 and the charity has been working with and for the families of drug and alcohol users. Adfam has helped many thousands of families over the years: initially through services such as their helpline and now through direct support work in prison visitors centres.

AFFECT
58 Haylands, PORTLAND, Dorset, DT5 2LA
T: 03003653651
W: www.affect.org.uk
E: affect01@hotmail.com
Affect is an organisation for families and friends facing possible 'life' long prison sentences. Members of Affect have experience of a close relative or friend sent to prison. Affect provide a range of support services in the West Sussex and Hampshire area.

ALTERNATIVES TO VIOLENCE PROJECT
Greyston Centre, 28 Charles Square,
London N1 6HT
Web www.avpbritain.org.uk
Tel: 0207 324 4755
The Alternatives to Violence Project-Britain, is a national network of volunteers running workshops for anyone who wants to find ways of resolving conflict without resorting to violence. AVP currently works in the community and prisons throughout Britain.

AMBER
Chief Executive Paul Rosam
Amber Foundation, Ashley Court, Chawleigh, Devon EX18 7EX. Tel: 01769 581011
Web www.amber-web.org
Email info@amberweb.org
Amber's centres, Ashley Court, Bythesea Lodge and Farm Place become a young person's temporary home where they can work towards achieving a better future. Almost all who come to us are unemployed and homeless, many have a history of addiction or have been involved in crime or have been in prison.

ANGULIMALA
The Forest Hermitage, Lower Fulbrook, Warks CV35 8AS Tel: 01926 624385
Web www.angulimala.org.uk
enquiries@angulimala.org.uk
To make available facilities for the teaching and practice of Buddhism in Her Majesty's Prisons and other places of lawful detention or custody. It seeks to recruit and advise a team of Buddhist visiting chaplains to be available as soon as there is a call for their services; to act in an advisory capacity, and to liaise with the Home Office chaplaincy officials, with individual chaplains within HM Prisons, and with any other relevant bodies or officials; to provide an aftercare and advisory service for prisoners after release.

APEX TRUST
1st Floor, Century House
Hardshaw Street, St. Helens, Merseyside
WA10 1QU
Tel: 01744 612 898
Email: sthelens@apextrust.com
Web: www.apextrust.com
Apex Charitable Trust seeks to help people with criminal records to obtain appropriate jobs or self-employment by providing them with the skills they need in the labour market and by working with employers to break down the barriers to their employment. Apex Trust was founded in 1965 by Neville Vincent.

ASSISTED PRISON VISITS UNIT
PO Box 2152, Birmingham,
West Midlands B15 1SD
assisted.prison.visits@noms.gsi.gov.uk
Telephone: 0300 063 2100
Web www..gov.uk/help-with-prison-visits
The APVU is part of the Prison Service and administers the Assisted Prison Visits scheme, enabling families on benefits to receiving financial assistance with travel costs. They also administer the Prisoner Location Service.

BIRTH COMPANIONS
Dalton House 60 Windsor Avenue London SW19 2RR. Phone: 07786 136 363
www.birthcompanions.org.uk
helen@birthcompanions.org.uk
Media: naomi@birthcompanions.org.uk
Birth Companions is a small charity providing practical and emotional support to women who face giving birth whilst in detention. Birth Companions provides trained and experienced birth supporters who support pregnant women in detention, during labour and after the birth of their babies. We started work mainly in London but now expanding to provide support in the community to pregnant asylum seekers/refugees who have been released from detention.

BOOKS TO PRISONERS
27 Old Gloucester Street, London. WC1N 3XX
www.havendistribution.org.uk
info2019@havendistribution.org.uk
A registered charity providing free educational publications to prisoners. For further information, send a stamp with your name and address to the above address.

CENTRE: CRIME AND JUSTI
Director Richard Garside Kings Co
26-29 Drury Lane, London WC2B 5RL
Tel: 0207 840 6110
www.crimeandjustice.org.uk
Email info@crimeandjustice.org.uk
The Centre for Crime and Justice Studies, (CCJS) is a charity which aims to inform and educate about all aspects of crime and the criminal justice system from an objective standpoint, and in accordance with the values of the centre. CCJS hope to encourage and facilitate healthy debate and understanding of the complex nature of issues concerning crime.

CLEAN SHEET
PO Box 306, Plaistow Street, Lingfield RH7 9BA
info@cleansheet.org.uk
0300 123 3045
We want to help you to find work. If you want to work after prison, then contact us either before you leave or ASAP after release. Our Employers will actively consider you for vacancies, despite your conviction. As a Clean Sheet Member (it's free) you'll get full access to our Employers National Directory. Once you get a job, you can come back to us when you want to progress to a new role. So, get in touch with us (or ask your Offender Manager) and we'll help you to get going on the pathway to work

CLINKS
CEO: Anne Fox Head Office, Tavis House, 1-6 Tavistock Square, London WC1H 9NA
Tel: 020 7383 0966
Web www.clinks.org
Email info@clinks.org
Clinks is a membership body that supports and develops the work that voluntary organisations (NGOs) undertake with the Criminal Justice system in England and Wales. Clinks believe that a strong voluntary sector is crucial to reducing reoffending and building safer communities.

CONVERSE
PO Box 679 Bury. lancs, BL8 9RU
Tel: 0845 474 0013   www.prisons.org.uk
Email converse@prisons.org.uk
Converse is the largest distribution national monthly newspaper for prisons in England and Wales. It is distributed free of charge throughout the prison estate and to an extensive mailing list of individuals and organisations involved in penal affairs.

...s PO Box 200, East ...H19 3GG

...ık
...uk
...dom provides crime ...ntation programmes to It also delivers drug ...grammes to offenders. It is a registered charity and the programmes are available to anyone regardless of race, religion, sex, age, disability or offence committed. Criminon organisations worldwide provide the programme using courses that address some of the key factors that are known to cause criminality; such as lack of self respect, illiteracy and a lack of moral values.

FINE CELL WORK
Executive Director Dr. Katy Emck
Fine Cell Work, 38 Buckingham Palace Road, London SW1W 0RE
Tel: 020 7931 9998
Web www.finecellwork.co.uk
Email enquiries@finecellwork.co.uk
Fine Cell Work teaches needlework to prison inmates and sells their products. The prisoners do their work when they are locked in their cells, and the earnings give them hope, skills and independence. Savings reduce the likelihood of offenders returning to crime. Prisoners often send the money they earn from Fine Cell Work to their children or families, or use it to pay for accommodation upon release.

HOWARD LEAGUE FOR PENAL REFORM
Contact: Administrator 1 Ardleigh Road, London N1 4HS Tel 020 7249 7373 Fax 020 7249 7788
Web www.howardleague.org
Email info@howardleague.org
The Howard League was founded in the 1860s as the Howard Association, in the name of the 18th century prison reformer John Howard. Today they lead campaigns on children in prison, community penalties, women in prison, suicide and self-harm, and youth justice. The League also run the Youth Justice Law Project, providing free legal advice and assistance to young prisoners. Publish Howard League Magazine and The Howard Journal of Criminal Justice.

INQUEST
89-93 Fonthill Road, London N4 3JH
Tel: 020 7263 1111

Web www.inquest.org.uk
Email inquest@inquest.org.uk
Inquest was launched in the early 1980s to campaign against deaths in custody and for changes in the Coroner's Court system. Provide information and assistance to bereaved families.

INSTITUTE OF PRISON LAW
Director: Mark Leech FRSA
PO Box 679 Bury BL8 9RU
Tel: 0845 474 0013
www.prisonlaw.org.uk
customer.services@prisons.org.uk
Founded in 1998 the Institute of Prison Law is a legal training body authorised by the Solicitors Regulation Authority and accredited by the Bar Standards Board, IPL delivers the acclaimed Certificate of Competency in Prison Law course.

JOHN SANDY TRUST HMP FEATHERSTONE SUPPORT
Executive John Perry MBE
Head Office: 9 St James Crescent, Acton Trussell, Stafford ST17 0RP
Tel: 01785 713241
Email lizperry30@yahoo.com
Provides facilities, advice and information for visitors to prisoners in HMP Featherstone.

JUSTICE
Director: Andrea Coomber 59 Carter Lane, London EC4V 5AQ
Tel: 020 7329 5100 Fax: 020 7329 5055
Web www.justice.org.uk
Email admin@justice.org.uk
JUSTICE researches, publishes and lobbies on human rights legislation. Their excellent research reports cover such ground as the life sentence and child homicide.

KOESTLER TRUST
Koestler Arts Centre, 168a Du Cane Road, London W12 OTX
Tel: 020 8740 0333 Fax: 020 8742 9274
Web www.koestlertrust.org.uk
Email info@koestlertrust.org.uk
Prison Art and The Koestler Trust are the UK's best-known prison arts charity. The Koestler Trust award, exhibit and sell artworks by offenders, detainees and high security patients.

LIBERTY
Liberty House, 26-30 Strutton Ground, London, SW1P 2HR
Tel: 020 7403 3888

Web www.liberty-human-rights.org.uk
Liberty is one of the UK's leading human rights and civil liberties organisations founded in 1934 as the National Council for Civil Liberties. Liberty campaigns to protect basic rights and freedoms through the courts, in Parliament and in the wider community. They do this through a combination of public campaigning, test case litigation, parliamentary work, policy analysis and the provision of free advice and information. We believe in a society based on the democratic participation of all its members and the principles of justice, openness, the right to dissent and respect for diversity. We aim to secure the equal rights of everyone that do not infringe on the rights of others.

MUSIC IN PRISONS
Projects Director Sara Lee
The Irene Taylor Trust, 7-14 Great Dover Street London SE1 4YR
Telephone: 020 3096 7862
Web irenetaylortrust.com
Email sara@irenetaylortrust.com
Music in Prisons specialises in the delivery of weeklong intensive creative music projects within prisons, working with men and women aged 15 upwards. The projects are delivered by their core team of professional musicians who are all highly experienced in delivering music projects in secure settings.

NACRO
46 Loman Street London SE1 0EH
Tel: 0300 123 1889
Email helpline@nacro.org.uk
Nacro can help you when leaving prison, finding accommodation or employment. Since 1966 we've worked to give ex-offenders, disadvantaged people and deprived communities the help they need to build a better future.
Nacro has over 200 projects across England and Wales. 60,000 people benefit directly from our work each year, while many more benefit from the work we carry out with national, regional and local agencies.

NATIONAL ASSOCIATION FOR YOUTH JUSTICE
Contact: Dr Rachel Morris
Mayo House, Llangammarch Wells, LD4 4EF
Tel: 01904 321226
Web www.thenayj.org.uk
Email info@thewnayj.org.uk
The NAYJ was established in Britain in 1994, its purpose is to promote the rights of, and justice for, children in trouble.
The NAYJ campaigns for the development and implementation of policies and practice that are consistent with this purpose by promoting responses to children within the criminal justice system, which encourage them to take responsibility for their actions while remaining in the community.

OUTSIDE CHANCE
Chair: Ian Ross
First Floor Suite 7 Feltham Business Complex Browells Lane Feltham TW13 7LW
Phone 020 8890 4941
Web www.outsidechance.org
Email: ianoutsidechance@aol.com
Helping young people to help themselves running various young offender institution projects.

PARTNERS OF PRISONERS SUPPORT GROUP (POPS)
Contact: Diane Curry OBE; Director Valentine House, 1079 Rochdale Road, Manchester M9 8AJ
Tel/Fax 0161 702 1000.
www.partnersofprisoners.co.uk
Email mail@partnersofprisoners.co.uk P
Partners of Prisoners and Families Support Group (POPS) aims to provide a variety of services to support anyone who has a link with someone in prison, prisoners and other agencies. POPS provides assistance to these groups for the purpose of enabling families to cope with the stress of arrest, imprisonment and release.

PRISON ADVICE & CARE TRUST (PACT)
Director Andy Keen-Downs 29 Peckham Road, London SE5 8UA
Freephone: 0808 808 3444
Web www.prisonadvice.org.uk
Email info@prisonadvice.org.uk
The Prison Advice & Care Trust (pact) is an independent national charity working with prisoners and with prisoners' families at prisons and in communities across Greater London, in Devon & Cornwall and in Milton Keynes (HMP Woodhill), with projects in development in Gloucestershire, Wales and other areas. Our current services and projects include pact centres, which are child-friendly centres run by pact staff and volunteers outside prisons. These provide services and support for visiting children & families of prisoners, and are open to friends, agencies and legal visitors.

PRISON FELLOWSHIP
Contact: Peter Holloway
CEO PO Box 68226, London, SW1P 9WR
Tel: 0207 799 2500
Web www.prisonfellowship.org.uk
enquiries@prisonfellowship.org.uk
Prison Fellowship England and Wales is one of 112 independent Prison Fellowship organisations chartered to Prison Fellowship International (PFI). Each national organisation pays an annual charter fee to PFI (6% of general income excluding restricted funds). This helps to provide leadership training, programme research and design, and relief and development projects, especially for new and financially disadvantaged ministries.

PRISON ME NO-WAY!
No-Way Trust, The Deep Business Centre, Tower Street, Hull HU1 4BG Tel: 01482 224382
Email: info@pmnw.co.uk
Web www.pmnw.co.uk
The trust is an independent charity that has been in existence since 1995. The co founders realised there was a lack of informative support missing in the lives of our young. It is therefore important that they receive accurate information that enables them to adopt positive lifestyles.

PRISON PHOENIX TRUST
Contact: Sam Settle; Director
PO Box 328, Oxford OX2 7HF
Tel: 01865 512521
Web www.prisonphoenixtrust.org
The Prison Phoenix Trust encourages prisoners in the development of their spiritual welfare, through the practices of meditation and yoga, working with silence and the breath. We offer personal support to prisoners around the UK and Eire through teaching, workshops, correspondence, books and newsletters - and to prison staff too. We work with people of any faith, or of none, and honour all religions. We are a registered UK charity.

PRISON RADIO ASSOCIATION
Director: Andrew Wilkie
The Prison Radio Association HMP Brixton London SW2 5XF
www.prisonradioassociation.org
The PRA is an award winning education charity that provides support, guidance and expertise to existing prison radio stations and advises prisons interested in setting up radio stations and radio training facilities. The PRA was established in response to a growing demand from prisons to engage in prison radio. The PRA is working on the development of a National Prison Radio Service, with the potential to reach every prisoner in England and Wales.

PRISONERS' ADVICE SERVICE
Contact: Deborah Russo. Managing Solicitors
PO Box 46199, London EC1M 4XA.
Tel: 0207 253 3323
Helpline open Mon Wed, Fri 0930-1300/1400-1730
advice@prisonersadvice.org.uk
www.prisonersadvice.org.uk
The Prisoners' Advice Service is a charitable organisation providing free and confidential legal advice to prisoners. We believe that everybody has an equal right to fair and reliable legal representation regardless of means, circumstances or background. We aim to ensure that all prisoners are treated both within the law and in accordance with the principles of human rights.

PRISONERS' EDUCATION TRUST
The Foundry, 17 Oval Way, London, SE11 5RR
Tel: 020 3752 5676
www.prisonerseducation.org.uk
info@prisonerseducation.org.uk
The Trust was the brainchild of David Burton, a former education officer at HMP Wandsworth, and barrister Vernon Cocking. Recognising that the narrow range of classes on offer could not meet prisoners' needs, David, Vernon and a group of others considered how more education and training could be provided. They decided that offering prisoners the opportunity to study by distance learning (correspondence courses) would tackle the problem. The Trust was established in 1989.

PRISONERS PACT.
CEO: Andy Keen-Downes
29 Peckham Road, London SE5 8UA
Free Tel: 0808 808 3444
www.prisonadvice.org.uk
info@prisoneradvice.org.uk
Prisoners' Families and Friends Service - now known as PACT - is an independent voluntary agency which has been helping prisoners' families for nearly 40 years. The main aims of the service are to provide the families and friends of anyone sentenced to imprisonment or remanded in custody with: Advice and information; Support and assistance at court; Support and friendship. Prisoners' Families and Friends Service aims to provide a high quality service for partners, close relatives or friends of prisoners by

promoting their interests and offering friendship, support, advice and information which is free, confidential and appropriate to their needs.

PRISON REFORM TRUST
Head. Peter Dawson, Director
15 Northburgh Street, London EC1V 0JR.
Tel: 020 7251 5070
Web www.prisonreformtrust.org.uk
Email prt@prisonreformtrust.org.uk
PRT have covered many areas in their twenty years, including young fathers in prison, prison population, prison regimes, and HIV/AIDS in prison. Publish Prison Report.

REHABILITATION OF ADDICTED PRISONERS TRUST (RAPt)
The Foundry, 2nd Floor, 17 Oval Way London. SE11 5RR
Telephone: 020 3752 5560
Web www.rapt.org.uk
Email info@rapt.org.uk
The RAPt believes that a high standard of drug treatment should be made available to all members of the community. Offenders with a history of substance abuse can, with help from specialist services, take steps to move away from an addictive pattern of behaviour, and lead positive and rewarding lives. RAPt provides services to offenders with chemical dependencies. We aim to reduce crime by helping them to turn their lives around. We do this by providing a variety of treatment models that include advice, counselling group work and intensive 12 step programmes.

REPRIEVE
Contact Ken MacDonald QC
REPRIEVE, PO Box 72054, London. EC3P 3BZ
Tel: 0207 553 8140
Web www.reprieve.org.uk
Email info@reprieve.org.uk
Reprieve is a committed human rights group. Founded in 1999 by British human rights lawyer Clive Stafford Smith, they provide free legal and investigative support to some of the world's most vulnerable people: British, European and other nationals facing execution.

THOMAS WALL TRUST
Skinners' Hall, London, EC4R 2SP
Email: information@thomaswalltrust.org.uk
Web: http://www.thomaswalltrust.org.uk
One-off small grants to assist people with the cost of training courses that improve their chances of employment. Assistance is offered to help people overcome barriers to work and study. The barriers must be more than just the financial implication of studying.

Who is eligible?
Grants to help people living in the UK with the cost of training courses that improve their chances of employment needs are more than just financial.

For example, recent grants have gone to individuals who are qualifying to work after a period in prison, those experiencing poverty as a result of family breakdown and people recovering from illness or addiction. Please note: If your ability to pay for your training is your only barrier, the Thomas Wall Trust cannot help you.

How to apply? Applications are made online at the Trust's website. The Trust is open to applications all year around or until funds runs out. Please note: Only successful applicants will be notified by the Trust. All information on the Trust is available on its website.

Other information. Grants are also given to charitable organisations in the field of education and social welfare, especially those that are small or of a pioneering nature.

> *Be Stong enough to stand alone, Smart enough to know when you need help, and be Brave enough to ask for it!*

TURN2US
Head Office, 200 Shepherds Bush Road, Hammersmith, W6 7NL
Turn2us helps people in financial need gain access to welfare benefits, charitable grants and other financial help – online, by phone and face to face through our partner organisations.. They have teams covering the following areas:
Commercial Partnerships
Communications (press and media)
Digital Services (technical / website content)
Finance
Fundraising
Grants (Turn2us Elizabeth Finn Fund, Turn2us Response Fund, Edinburgh Trust, Edinburgh Trust Community Programme)
Human Resources
Face-to-Face Team (working with intermediaries who are working with people in financial need)
Workshops and presentations
Volunteering

CHARITABLE GRANTS FOR OFFENDERS AND EX-OFFENDERS
PRISONERS EDUCATION TRUST
Grants are available for prisoners aged 18 and above who are in custody in England and Wales and still have at least six months of their sentence to serve, towards further education..
Only prisoners serving in one of 60 specific prisons are eligible (this number is increased as funds allow).
Who is eligible?
Prisoners aged 18 and above who are in custody in England and Wales and still have at least six months of their sentence to serve.
How to apply?
Applications should be submitted on a form available from the trust or through a prison education department, for consideration monthly. Initial telephone enquiries are welcome. Endorsement by a prison education manager is essential.
Contact use the freepost address: FREEPOST PRISONERS' EDUCATION TRUST.
Other information
The organisation also provides advice about distance learning courses and how they relate to employment paths and possibilities. They support learners in prisons and in some prisons and regions they train people to act as peer learning mentors. Funding arrangements for prisoner's education changes dramatically in 2012 with funding from the government for distance learning courses being withdrawn, and prisoners also now having to apply for student loans to cover the costs. The impact of this on the trust and on the wider landscape of prisoners learning has yet to be seen.
Prisoners' Education Trust
The Foundry, 17 Oval Way,
London SE11 5RR
Email: info@prisonseducation.org.uk
Web: http://www.prisonseducation.org.uk

THE LONGFORD TRUST
Financial grants for ex-prisoners undertaking higher education courses to degree level (Eligibility remains open for up to five years after release.) Applicants must be at a UK university or equivalent UK institute.
Who is eligible?
Ex-offenders or those awaiting release in the near future whose sentence was or is still being served in a UK prison. Applicants must have identified a specific course they want to study at degree level offered by an institute of higher education and have obtained a provisional offer of a place

(Eligibility remains open for up to five years after release).

How to apply?
Application forms can be downloaded from the Longford Trust website or are available by contacting the trust in writing. Applications for courses beginning in the September of any year must be made by 1 June in that year.

Other information
Recipients of scholarships are also assigned a mentor who can offer practical and emotional advice.
The trust also administers the Patrick Pakenham Educational Awards, for ex-prisoners wishing to study law to degree level.

Contact details
PO Box 64302
London NW6 9JP
Email: info@longfordtrust.org
Web: http://www.longfordtrust.org

MICHAEL & SHIRLEY HUNT CHARITABLE TRUST

Financial grants for relatives and dependants of prisoners, such as their spouses and children.

Who is eligible?
Prisoners and their relatives and dependants, such as their spouses and children.

How to apply?
In writing to the charity contact address. Applications can be made directly by the individual or through a third party such as Citizens Advice, probation service or a social worker.

Contact details
Michael and Shirley Hunt Charitable Trust
Ansty House
Henfield Road, Small Dole, Henfield
West Sussex
BN5 9XH
Telephone: 01903 817116

SACRO TRUST – FOR SCOTTISH OFFENDERS

Grants are available for residents of Scotland in need:
* who are subject to a license/court order, or
* who have been released from prison in the last two years, or
* young people who have been involved with criminal activity but who have not been dealt with by way of a custodial sentence.

Applications have to be made by a local authority worker, voluntary sector worker, health visitor or similar person working with the person in need. A grant is usually for a maximum of £300, although applications for larger sums may be considered. Applications will be considered for grants for home furnishings including electrical goods, for clothing, and for support for education and training.

Who is eligible?
Grants are only available to eligible people who are living in Scotland.
Applications will be considered:
* from workers who are supporting people who are subject to a licence/court order, or who have been released from prison or other custodial setting in the two years preceding the application and
* from workers who are supporting young people who have been involved with criminal activity but who have not been dealt with by way of a custodial sentence.

Please note: Applicant workers are required to have exhausted all other avenues of funding before applying to the Trust for financial assistance.

A person who has previously received a grant from the Sacro Trust cannot have another.

Grants will not be made for driving lessons.

How to apply?
Applying for a grant
Applications must be made on the standard form that is available from the Sacro Trust administrator, with additional supporting evidence appended as considered appropriate by the applicant worker.

Applications will only be accepted if they are made through a local authority worker, voluntary sector worker, health visitor or similar person.

Applications for grants of £300 or less will be considered by the Trust's assessors once every two months.

Applications for larger sums will only be considered twice a year, and will require considerably more supporting evidence than that which may be sought for a standard application.

Payment
Payment will only be made to a bank account of the organisation employing the worker making the application.

To ensure that a grant is spent appropriately, and that receipts are submitted to the Sacro Trust for auditing purposes, it is a requirement that an applicant worker supervises the spending of any grant that is made.

Contact details
Fund Administrator, The Sacro Trust
29 Albany Street
Edinburgh
EH1 3QN
Telephone: 0131 624 7270
Email: info@sacro.org.uk
Web: http://www.sacro.org.uk

NIACRO EDUCATIONAL TRUST – FOR NORTHERN IRELAND OFFENDERS

Grants available for ex-prisoners, ex-offenders and their immediate relatives from Ireland who are seeking access to education and/or training and for whom no other sources of funding are available.

Who is eligible?
Ex-prisoners, ex-offenders and their immediate relatives from Ireland who are seeking access to education and/or training and for whom no other sources of funding are available.

How to apply?
On a form available from the charity contact address. They are considered every four to six weeks.

Other information
The foundation's main activities are supporting ex-offenders and their relatives.

Contact details
c/o NIACRO
4 Amelia Street
Belfast BT2 7GS
Northern Ireland
BT2 7GS
Telephone: 028 9032 0157
Web: http://www.niacro.co.uk

BAN THE BOX CAMPAIGN
EMPLOYMENT AFTER RELEASE - WHY BAN THE BOX IS CRUCIAL - AND WORKING!

Over 11 million people in the UK have a criminal record, yet three quarters of employers admit to discriminating against applications with a criminal conviction.

Mainstream recruitment practices often exclude people with convictions from employment opportunities - sometimes deliberately, often inadvertently.

The criminal record tick box is used on many application forms as a filtering mechanism during recruitment and can discourage people from applying. 'Ban the Box' is a campaign to remove the tick-box asking you to disclose criminal convictions from early stages in the recruitment process. It calls on UK employers to give ex-offenders a fair chance to compete for jobs by removing the tick box from application forms and asking about criminal convictions later in the recruitment process.

So far over 80 firms have done so, relating to over 715,000 jobs.

Here is a list of those employers who have signed up to the Ban The Box campaign - starting with a piece by Michaela Booth from her blog about why Ban The Box is so important.

michaelamovement.blog

Why do I think Ban the Box is a good idea?

Lets say in 2009, you made a huge, one off...life changing mistake. A mistake that lets you see the inside of a prison cell, one that causes many people a great deal of trauma, tears and costs them a fortune financially and emotionally. A mistake that was never previously considered, was not premeditated and could have easily happened to anyone who enjoys a few drinks out with the girls at a weekend.

Imagine this happened when you were a teenager and haunts you for the rest of you life on an application form while applying for a job, or at least, for the next 13 years, until now when your conviction is finally spent. Is it really relevant for me to disclose on a job application form, as a 26 year old woman, that I have a conviction from my teenage years, for a single, silly mistake.

In my current and ongoing search for employment I have always been honest about my past, my past has, of course, made me the woman I am today. Strong, ambitious, driven and passionate about securing a career. My past has ensured I have a strong work ethic and a need to succeed. My past, however, is why I sit in front of my laptop on this Sunday evening, typing this blog about my present struggles. Why is my past stopping my future progression, holding me back from reaching my full potential and killing my self confidence on a daily basis?

The reason or at least part of the reason is because of the box I tick on an application form to say I have an unspent criminal conviction. Which then follows with "please give details of the offence or custodial sentence" so here I am supposed to write "GBH – 4 years". This box for 'details' is hardly a place for me to be writing I was convicted as a teenager for a drunken offence and go into detail of the time passed, the progress I have made and the ins and outs of my court case and prison sentence. While on the subject of the 'detail' box, it may be worth me adding that on most forms it does say something along the lines of "please note, ticking this box will not automatically mean you will not be considered for the position".

In my experience, that is exactly what happens, unless of course, the recruitment agency are late to disclose your conviction to an employer who has already offered you a job, then retracts it based on your late disclosure. So, that time I was lucky, I actually got an interview, got the job then the job got taken off me. For ticking the box, being honest and trying to move on with my life.

Another recruitment agency who I was working closely with in my quest to find a new job, had assumed that the two year gap on my C.V was a career break to have a baby. This lady was putting me forward for various roles and interviews and contacting me regularly via email with new job vacancies until one day she called me regarding an interview, where she mentioned my two year career break to have a baby, when I informed her that gap in my C.V was not to have a baby it was because I was in prison, I never heard from her again. Her voice changed in an instant and I knew that was the end of that particular agency helping me any further.

I applied for an admin role in an office via a third recruitment agency and a few days after my application was received I had a call from a lady who wanted to set up an interview for me, she briefly asked me questions about my current situation and a few things about my C.V. Needless to say, she asked what I had been doing in the two year gap and again I informed her of my past conviction and she actually said to me "well, I wont inform the company because although they can't discriminate they probably still will". I mean, what hope have I got, if recruitment agencies are telling me this? And again, needless to say, the job in question, I didn't get an interview for and I didn't ever hear from that woman again.

In my current situation I cannot progress at all if recruitment agencies are unwilling to work with me and companies take job offers away from me after finding out about my past, which I don't ever try and hide. For me, ticking this box either means I wont even get an interview at all or I will get an interview and once the conviction is disclosed I wont be successful, with no explanation as to why.

There are laws in place to stop discrimination, I have committed a crime and been punished for that. These companies and recruitment agencies who discriminate against me because of my conviction, are in essence breaking the law but of course, they have their employment lawyers in place and loopholes which allow them to carry on doing this. Its a shame and so ironic that the people who are unwilling to help me and give me a chance based on my past behaviour are showing unethical and immoral practice at fair employment, so in actual fact isn't their current behaviour verging on being just as bad as mine was?

With so many people in prison or serving community sentences, how will they survive if they are treated this way, when they want to break the cycle of reoffending and ending up back in prison but due to being unemployed they revert back to crime, because for them it pays the bills. If people with convictions can not find a job, can not pay their own way and support their self or their family they have two options, sit on benefits or commit crime.

Many people in the criminal justice system, are not criminally minded, they have simply made a mistake, and even the ones who once were hardened criminals can change and want to live a life as a law abiding citizen. Prison changes people, life changes people and a job for a person with a criminal conviction or who is being released from prison can be the biggest and most important factor in them not reoffending.

For companies and recruitment agencies that are unwilling to assist in the employment of people with a conviction, they are missing out on hard working, loyal and ambitious employees. We face so many barriers and are held back from so many things that when we are finally given a chance, we don't bite the hand that feeds us.

ACCENTURE
Sector: Accountants and Management Consultants Ban the Box Employer since: October 2014

ADNAMS
Sector: Food and drink
Ban the Box Employer since: January 2015
How and when do they ask? Adnams has banned the box for all roles including those regulated by the Financial Conduct Authority. Where required, and in particular for regulated roles, Adnams would ask candidates about their criminal convictions once an offer of employment has been made.
"At Adnams we believe in giving all applicants a fair chance and simply want to employ the best person to do the job. We embrace diversity within our business and accept that any of us can make poor choices at some point in life. The effects of doing so shouldn't stay with you forever. If an applicant has the skills and experience, or the ability and the aptitude to learn them then why wouldn't we want them working in our business."
Sadie Lofthouse,
Head of Human Resources

ALDERMANS
Sector: Industrials and Engineering
Ban the Box Employer since: June 2015
How and when do they ask? Aldermans does not ask about convictions until candidates have been shortlisted. They offer the opportunity for disclosure at the final interview stage.
"We believe that all candidates should be treated fairly and be given every opportunity to succeed and impress. Our experiences have shown that employee engagement and commitment are key to driving success and candidates from all walks of life should be given this chance." Karen Friendship, Managing Director

ALLEN & OVERY
Sector: Legal
Ban the Box Employer since: June 2015
How and when do they ask? Job applicants are only asked about criminal convictions at the point at which they are offered a job. Some roles are regulated by the Solicitors Regulation Authority of England and Wales, and will have had a criminal record check prior to applying for a role at Allen & Overy.

"The principles of Ban the Box are very much aligned with our existing approach to recruitment and it is a campaign that we are proud to support. We recognise that people are different – it doesn't matter where people have come from or what their background is: we look for their skills, experience and potential. In return we aim to provide an environment where they can achieve their full potential and make a valuable contribution." Sasha Hardman, HR.

AMEY
Sector: Support services
Ban the Box Employer since: May 2015
How and when do they ask? Amey does not ask about criminal convictions at any stage in their recruitment process for the majority of roles.
Amey conduct criminal record checks for regulated roles where there is a legal requirement to do so, and they also may undertake basic disclosure checks on employees when it is stipulated as part of a new contract.

"As a responsible business, we have a duty to ensure that we're employing the best people to deliver our services across the UK. For us, that means operating a fair recruitment process that offers equal opportunities to all as well as providing the right training and development for people to succeed." Ian Deninson, Group HR & Communications Director

BACK ON TRACK
Sector: Not for Profit
Ban the Box employer since: February 2016
How and when do they ask? Back on Track only ask about criminal convictions if an applicant is shortlisted for interview. They are asked to bring a sealed letter of disclosure if they have an unspent criminal conviction, which is only opened if Back on Track decide to offer the candidate the job.
Any criminal convictions are reviewed at this point, and Back on Track will speak to the candidate's Offender Manager or Police Liaison Office to ascertain suitability for the role.

"The aim of our work is to enable ex-offenders and others to move on from the past to a better future. We understand all too well that people can feel the system is stacked against them. Back on Track is committed to Ban the Box because we want to attract the best candidates to work or volunteer with us and be sure that recruitment is fair and inclusive, putting the focus on current skills and abilities not past mistakes. We want to inspire other employers to do the same and remove the barriers that stop people succeeding in life." Siobhan Pollitt, Chief Executive

BAIN & COMPANY
Sector: Management consultancy
Ban the Box Employer since: May 2014
How and when do they ask? Bain & Company discuss relevant information with candidates and, before employment contracts are signed, undertake criminal convictions checks alongside other background screening such as credit checks.

"It is critical for a premier professional services business to attract and retain the best talent. Whilst we expect our employees to disclose all relevant information during our interview process, we believe that this can be best considered during these discussions rather than missing out on a talented individual due to a box on an application form." Julian Critchlow, Director, Bain & Company

BARCLAYS
Sector: Financial Services
Ban the Box Employer since: January 2015
How and when do they ask? Barclays does not ask candidates about their criminal convictions at application stage for any roles within the Personal and Corporate Banking division. Checks are conducted within the candidate screening process, when applicants are asked to disclose unspent criminal convictions. The Bank also recruits for regulated roles, for which further checks would be conducted and information about both spent and unspent convictions is requested.

"Ban the Box is a common sense way to ensure that businesses don't make assumptions about prospective employees before learning the facts, whist still ensuring that appropriate questions are asked through the process. We wouldn't have found some of our best apprentices if we hadn't made this change ourselves. That is why Barclays is backing this important programme in partnership with Business in the Community." Matt Hammerstein, Head of Client and Customer Experience

BOOTS UK
Sector: Food and drugs
Ban the Box Employer since: October 2013
How and when do they ask? Boots UK was the first company to sign up to support Ban the Box as part of the BITC campaign and positioned themselves right behind the campaign, talking with the press and encouraging their supply chain to Ban the Box. They now do not ask about criminal convictions at any stage in the recruitment process. Boots UK convened a Taskforce of supply chain companies in early 2012 to level the playing field for ex-offenders to get into work.
"This is not a simple issue. People end up offending for a variety of complex reasons and as employers the most powerful thing we can do is to help create a second chance for offenders so that it is possible for people with criminal convictions to enter employment and get back on track." Marco Pagni, Group Legal Counsel and Chief Administrative Officer Walgreen Boots Alliance

BUSINESS IN THE COMMUNITY
Sector: Third sector
Ban the Box employer since: October 2013
How and when do they ask? Business in the Community does not ask about criminal convictions during the recruitment process unless it is for a regulated role. In this instance, BITC only asks about criminal convictions and conducts criminal records checks once an offer has been made.
"Screening based on a tick box is not a way of excluding inappropriate applicants - we can't assume that everybody with a criminal conviction poses a risk. A successful organisation needs to take a long-term view, looking for the potential offered by candidates from a variety of walks of life, rather than recruiting in your own image." Francoise Seacroft, HR Director

CAMBRIDGE UNIVERSITY PRESS
Sector: Media, Marketing and PR
Ban the Box employer since: February 2016
How and when do they ask?
Cambridge University Press do not ask about criminal convictions until interview stage, when applicants are given form to disclose any convictions.
"Our purpose at Cambridge University Press is to unlock people's potential with the best learning and research solutions. We have a diverse workforce of 2,400 people working in 50 countries.
We are committed to promoting equality of opportunity in an inclusive environment. We recognise colleagues whose work demonstrates our values of innovation, collaboration, teamwork, customer service and delivery.
We want to attract the best talent to help us deliver our mission, by giving all applicants a fair chance and by employing the best person to do the job."
Cathy Armor, Director for People

CARBON 60
Sector: Recruitment
Ban the Box employer since: September 2019
How and when do they ask?
Carbon 60 asks for a declaration of criminal convictions after an offer of employment has been made.
They make it clear to applicants and clients that this will be requested at a later stage of the recruitment process.
"In our continued ambition to be the most trusted provider, partner and developer of people in technical recruitment, we continually work to be a responsible business that meets the highest standards of ethics and professionalism.
We are therefore committed to Ban the Box and the fair treatment of our staff and candidates, regardless of offending background.
We also recognise the contribution the employment of ex-offenders can make to tackle the UK's skills shortages in our markets."
Alex Downard, Operations Director

CENSUS DATA
Sector: Support Services
Ban the Box employer since: November 2014
How and when do they ask? Census Data includes questions about criminal convictions as part of the interview process.
"At Census Data, some of our very best people are currently employed whilst serving the remaining term of their prison sentence. We've taken the decision to ban the box as we want to build a pipeline of talented colleagues from diverse backgrounds. We believe we can access a broader talent pool by being open minded about people's pasts and giving them an opportunity to become a valued member of our team. We also want to give back to the communities in which we work and have a positive impact on local people." Lyn Rutherford, HR Director

CHOICE SUPPORT
Sector: Not for Profit
Ban the Box employer since: June 2017

How and when do they ask? Choice Support ask after interview.

CHWARAE TEG
Sector: Not for Profit
Ban the Box employer since: October 2015
How and when do they ask? Chwarae Teg do not ask about criminal convictions at any stage of the recruitment process.
"We're very proud to support this campaign and help re-build lives - employment reduces offending by up to 50%, so it's in every community's interest to reduce the barriers to work for people with criminal convictions!" Gemma Hughes, HR Partner

CITY AND GUILDS
Sector: Public
Ban the Box employer since: February 2016
How and when do they ask? The City & Guilds Group do not ask about criminal convictions at any stage in the recruitment process.
"The City & Guilds Group is a leader in global skills development, it works with education providers, employers and governments in over 100 countries across the world, to help people and organisations develop their skills for personal and economic growth."
Chris Jones, CEO

CIVIL SERVICE
Sector: Public
Ban the Box employer since: February 2016
How and when do they ask? On 8 February 2016 David Cameron announced his support for Ban the Box, stating that the Civil Service would be banning the box across all departments. Business in the Community is working with the Civil Service to help to implement this change.
"They've done it in America – it's called 'ban the box'- and I want to work with businesses, including the many who've already signed up to the Business in the Community campaign, to see if we can do this here. And because I believe in leading by example, I can announce today that every part of the Civil Service will be 'banning the box' in these initial recruitment stages." The Rt Hon David Cameron MP, former Prime Minister

CLINKS
Sector: Third sector
Ban the Box employer since: May 2017
How and when do they ask? Clinks does not ask about convictions at any stage of the recruitment process.
At Clinks we support voluntary organisations across England and Wales, but we also lead by example. Ban the box is a great way to show you believe that people who have been in the criminal justice system deserve to live their lives free from discrimination and prejudice. Everybody deserves the chance to change, a job is a vital step on that ladder and we won't allow people to be disadvantaged because of their past." Anne Fox, CEO

CONCEPT DESIGN
Sector: Public
Ban the Box employer since: June 2016
How and when do they ask? Concept Design Solutions only ask about criminal convictions where there is a contractual requirement to do so, and will only ask after the initial sift has taken place.
"I have a record and have found problems with employment." Paul Slater, Director

CRI
Sector: Third Sector
Ban the Box employer since: April 2014
How and when do they ask? CRI only ask about convictions if they consider it to be relevant to the role. If this is considered to be the case, candidates will be informed that any job offer will be conditional to a disclosure. In some cases CRI consider it necessary to ask at interview stage, however candidates will be informed if this is the case and will be given ample time and opportunity to discuss convictions in a confidential manner.
Are there any roles that are exempt from these processes? Many of CRI's roles involve working with children or vulnerable adults. These roles require DBS checks; however CRI treats every conviction individually and assesses risk through a defensible decision process.
"CRI is pleased to publicly state our position on the recruitment of individuals who have previously committed offences. We believe passionately in people's ability to change and that individuals should therefore be judged upon their abilities, merits and strengths rather than on mistakes made or offences committed in their past. Employment is a key factor in people's social connectivity and ability to live independent and purposeful lives. We believe that our organisation is stronger for the breadth of talent we have within our ranks – drawn from a range of professional disciplines as well as those who are experts through their personal experiences of recovery and rehabilitation." Mike Pattinson, Executive Director

CURRIE & BROWN
Sector: Construction
Ban the Box employer since: March 2016
How and when do they ask? Currie & Brown only asks about criminal convictions after a job offer has been made. For regulated roles in sites such as schools Currie & Brown are required to conduct criminal record checks; however these are only performed after an employee has joined the business.
"We are proud to sign up to Ban the Box. This demonstrates our commitment to giving people a fair shot at employment without discrimination. For individuals with a criminal record, this move provides them with the opportunity to account for historic offences in a frank and open discussion. As a business, this prevents us from deselecting otherwise credible candidates, and gives us the opportunity to have a two-way discussion around any criminal record.
James Grinnell, Group People Director

CUBIQUITY
Sector: Media, Marketing and PR
Ban the Box employer since: March 2016
How and when do they ask? Cubiquity asks about criminal convictions on a form sent to applicants after a job offer has been made. The conviction is then taken into account along with satisfactory references.
"Our commitment to positive recruitment activity is underpinned by our company's Equality Policy and we encourage all applicants who can be assured of an open, transparent and positive experience with applying for roles with our business."
Alison Deymond, HR Director

DESTRIA PARTNERS
Sector: Management Consultants
Ban the Box employer since: April 2014
How and when do they ask? Destria Partners does not ask about criminal convictions in the first stage of their application process. At the point of making an offer of employment, the company will ask the applicant to disclose unspent criminal convictions.
"Destria Partners activates ideas for good; and a good idea is not to have any unnecessary barriers to recruiting talent and for ex-offenders trying to re-enter the workforce. Our team has been and always will be recruited on abilities and fitness for the role, and any conversations about convictions will be had much later in the recruitment process."
John O'Brien, Co-Founder

EVERSHEDS
Sector: Legal
Ban the Box employer since: October 2014
How and when do they ask? Eversheds will only request information about unspent convictions once a job offer has been made.
"Eversheds believes innovation comes from diversity and people – the two go hand in hand. A fair, equal recruitment process is bigger than just the application stage, but barriers must be removed to ensure talented people have access to the opportunities available. Only by removing barriers like the tick box will organisations progress on the journey of becoming diverse and inclusive employers. We're proud this is a step we've taken and we have great people working with us because initiatives like this have made it possible."
Moira Slape, HR Director

FAIR TRAIN
Sector: Not for Profit
Ban the Box employer since: March 2016
How and when do they ask? Fair train asks about criminal convictions at interview stage, giving the opportunity for explanation.
"Fair Train has recently started working with prisons to improve the quality of their work experience provision, through the national Work Experience Quality Standard accreditation. Providing prisoners with high quality training and work experience helps them to access employment opportunities on release, improve their life chances and reduce re-offending. Central to this process is employers seeing the potential in ex-offenders and giving them a second chance. That's why Fair Train is leading from the front and supporting Ban the Box."
Beth Gardner, CEO

FARRELLY BUILDING
Sector: Construction
Ban the Box employer since: April 2016
How and when do they ask? Farrelly Building Services does not ask about criminal convictions at any stage in their recruitment process. They signed up to the campaign after hearing about it from Interserve.
"We believe in equal opportunities for all persons and respect the right of individuals to have equal rights of access to work. If a person has the skills required for the job their past is irrelevant.." Paul Farrelly, Director

FRESHFIELDS
Sector: Legal
Ban the Box employer since: January 2014
How and when do they ask? Freshfields only request information about unspent convictions once a job offer has been made, and convictions that are later disclosed will be assessed on a case-by-case basis. They have implemented a robust policy and process to consider the risk and relevance of any disclosed convictions to the firm. This process is handled by the HR team at the same time as pre-employment checks, and is the same for their regulated and unregulated roles.
"The success of working with ex-offenders that was demonstrated through the Ready for Work programme gained support at senior level for the Ban the Box campaign, allowing us to integrate our commitment to corporate responsibility with our mainstream recruitment practises. By banning the box, we are ensuring that the same candidates that accessed support and opportunities via the Ready for Work programme are now able to compete on a level playing field through the firm's mainstream recruitment processes."
Philip Richards, Partner

GENIUS
Sector: Education, Employment and Training
Ban the Box employer since: July 2016
How and when do they ask? Genius Within CIC do not ask about criminal convictions until interview stage.
"Here at Genius Within we are committed to celebrating individual strengths and promoting social inclusion. We strongly believe in rehabilitation and individual's capacity for change. Whilst we already employ several ex-offenders and actively work with offenders through NOMS CFO round 3 projects, we are always looking to continuously improve our recruitment processes to ensure equality of opportunity, so "Banning the Box" was a no-brainer in terms of value matching."
Kate Gilbert, Head of Business Development

GENTOO
Sector: Housing and Homelessness
Ban the Box employer since: October 2015
How and when do they ask? Gentoo do not ask about criminal convictions until a job offer has been made.
"At Gentoo we truly believe that our staff are the biggest factor in our business success. We are interested in the talent and passion of our employees and want each applicant to feel confident knowing their job success will be based on their ability. Joining the Ban the Box campaign means that all of our future employees will have access to a non-discriminatory application process that reflects our inclusive work ethic. Lifting barriers such as these will hopefully encourage more people to fulfil their career aspirations therefore improving their Art of Living and helping to tackle employment issues.."
John Craggs, Acting Chief Executive

GENUINE SOLUTIONS
Sector: Technology / Environmental
Ban the Box employer since: November 2015
How and when do they ask? Genuine Solutions does not ask about criminal convictions at application stage, but asks candidates to discuss any gaps in their CV at a later stage in the recruitment process.
"At Genuine Solutions, we believe very much in second chances and that people should not be judged on their past mistakes providing they are genuine in wanting to turn their lives around. We realise that people may go down the wrong path for reasons open to them at the time and are keen to open up the choices to prove that there is a different way of achieving success for themselves. Very much like our business where we give technology waste a new lease of life, we believe we can do the same with people. If the applicant is keen to learn from past mistakes, has the ability and desire to change ,there is no reason why they should not be part of our team."
Paul Crossman, UK Managing Director

GLEEDS
Sector: Surveyors
Ban the Box employer since: July 2016
How and when do they ask? Gleeds only asks about criminal convictions if there is a contractual requirement to do so. In this case they will ask about criminal convictions at interview stage, or after an offer is made.
"As an equal opportunities employer, Gleeds believes that all applicants should be treated fairly regardless of their background and history. All candidates should be assessed on the merits of their application and aptitude for the role, not by their past. Whilst we would expect potential employees to disclose relevant information during our interview process, we do not believe that a box on an application form should limit a candidate's progress in applying for a job with Gleeds."
Richard Steer, Chairman of Gleeds Worldwide

HIGH PEAK FOOD
Sector: Third sector
Ban the Box employer since: July 2016
How and when do they ask? High Peak Food Bank advertise for people with broad life experiences so a criminal record is not usually a problem. Applicants are free to tell us about this in a way that suits them – discussion, on paper etc. separately to the application process.
"We want employees with wide life experiences, for some people this might include previous criminal activity. We acknowledge that most often, having a job prevents criminality and that many people who have a conviction are keen to make a new start. It is important that employers recognise this and the fact that employees with a record are likely to be more loyal and want to demonstrate their capabilities because, against the odds, they've been given a chance."
Paul Bohan, Area Coordinator

HORTECH
Sector: Facilities Management
Ban the Box employer since: February 2016
How and when do they ask? Hortech do not ask about criminal convictions at the first stage of recruitment, but instead ask at interview stage, when candidates are advised that they may need to undergo a DBS check.
"The business case is that we accept that individuals may have made mistakes, however they should be entitled to a period of rehabilitation and should not be discriminated against because of this. We also acknowledge that we could be missing out on good qualified and experienced individuals who could do well within our business."
Duncan Jones, Director

INDERFLAME
Sector: Facilities
Ban the Box employer since: May 2016
How and when do they ask? Inderflame have never have a box, and only as about criminal convictions once applicants have been shortlisted. We are a forward thinking organisation, we have never had a 'box' and take each candidate on their own merit. We believe in personal and professional change.."
Rachel Mackenzie, Director

INTERSERVE
Sector: Facilities Management
Ban the Box employer since: December 2013
How and when do they ask? Interserve does not ask about criminal convictions in the first stage of their application process for any roles. Only where it is a legal or contractual requirement do they ask at a later stage. They announced their support for BITC's Ban the Box campaign via a company-wide 'Good News Friday' newsletter on Friday 31st January and their Business Support Services Newsletter for February. This reaches a wide and diverse audience. encouraging their peers and employees to find out about the Ban the Box campaign.
"Interserve is proud of our equality and diversity credentials with people joining us from many diverse backgrounds. Ban the Box supports this culture and allows people to be assessed on their skills and abilities rather than pre-judged on their criminal convictions."
Scott Hill, HR Director, Interserve Support Services

INTUITIVE THINKING
Sector: Medical and Health
Ban the Box employer since: May 2016
How and when do they ask? Intuitive Thinking Skills supports people to move on from substance misuse and the criminal justice system, and all employees have a background of this sort.
Intuitive Thinking Skills do not ask at the first stage of recruitment, however their roles are DBS checked.
"As an employer who actively employs ex-offenders I find that generally they bring huge assets that are often not found in other areas of the workforce."
Peter Bentley, Director

ISS UK
Sector: Facilities Services
Ban the Box employer since: March 2014
How and when do they ask? ISS UK Ltd does not ask about criminal convictions in the first stage of their application process for any roles. In certain circumstances, or if it is required by a client, ISS UK Ltd will conduct checks of unspent criminal convictions once an offer of employment has been made.
"Removing barriers which discriminate against talent of any type or background is good for the individual and good for business. Ban the Box is a great initiative that demonstrates business has a real role to play in reducing re-offending rates by judging people first on their skills and potential. Ban the Box helps promotes a positive personal spiral based on improving self-esteem and a solid job. I would encourage all businesses to grasp the challenge and Ban the Box."
Richard Sykes, Chief Executive Officer

J.M. SCULLY LTD
Sector: Construction
Ban the Box employer since: March 2014
How and when do they ask? J.M. Scully Ltd will not ask about criminal convictions through their application forms or formal recruitment process.
"J.M. Scully is an Equal Opportunities Employer and it is our policy that all persons have equal opportunity for employment and advancement on the basis of their ability, qualifications and suitability to do a job. The aim of the policy is to ensure that no job applicant or employee receives less favourable treatment. We believe that by banning the box this will allow us to recruit from a wider pool and all applicants will be judged on a level playing field."
Shirley Scully, Managing Director, J.M. Scully

J.P. CONCRETE
Sector: Construction
Ban the Box employer since: August 2015
How and when do they ask? J P Concrete will not ask about criminal convictions through their application forms or formal recruitment process.
"JP Concrete are proud to be associated with ban the box. As a company we have an ongoing relationship with HMP Onley assisting with the rehabilitation and training of prisoners. We believe ex-prisoners should be given a fair chance when re-entering society and ban the box is an important step towards this."
Philip White, Director, J P Concrete

KINNERTON
Sector: Food and Beverage
Ban the Box employer since: November 2014
How and when do they ask? Kinnerton Confectionery asks about criminal convictions once an offer of employment has been made. A form to declare unspent criminal convictions is sent out to new starters with the offer letter and contract of employment.
"At Kinnerton we believe in employing people based on their skills and experience and that everyone deserves a chance. We understand that people may have made mistakes, therefore should a conviction be declared by a candidate after the offer of employment, we can be confident that the conviction is considered without prejudicing the interview/job offer."
Lisa Martin, HR Operations Manager

LANCASHIRE GROUP
Sector: Insurance
Ban the Box employer since: December 2014
How and when do they ask? Lancashire Group does not ask about criminal convictions in the first stage of their application process. After an offer of employment has been made, Lancashire Group carries out a criminal record check as part of general background screening. Senior positions within the company are regulated by the FCA and the same process for recruitment applies in these instances.
"Recruiting the right people for Lancashire is a high priority for the business and we promote the value of having a diverse workforce. We base all recruitment decisions on the ability of our prospective employees to do the job, without consideration to race, age, gender, sexual orientation, disability, beliefs, or background. Ban the Box aligns with our commitment to being an equal opportunities employer. The campaign further aligns with our corporate social responsibility efforts, in particular, our partnership with St Giles Trust, a charity which supports ex-offenders and prepares them for training and employment opportunities."
Charles Mathias, Group Chief Risk Office

LAND SECURITIES
Sector: Real Estate
Ban the Box employer since: December 2013
How and when do they ask about criminal convictions? Land Securities does not ask about criminal convictions at the first stage of their recruitment process. The majority of Land Securities' employment is through their supply chain and supporting disadvantaged groups who are furthest from the job market is a key priority in Land Securities' CSR strategy, particularly in London through the company's London Employment Strategy.
"Land Securities seeks the most talented people as team members, who are representative of the communities in which we work. As such we seek to recruit from as diverse a pool as possible. Ruling anyone out from the beginning would not give us the wide range of applicants we are looking for."
Diana Breeze, Group HR Director

LEO BURNETT
Sector: Communications.
Ban the Box employer since: October 2014
How and when do they ask? Leo Burnett does not ask about criminal convictions at any stage of their application process, and worked with Business in the Community to create an awareness campaign called 'second chance'.

"Leo Burnett have always supported attracting and nurturing the very best talent wherever it comes from. We very much value our employees as it is their creativity and ideas that help make our creative product great and make our agency culture unique. As a result of this we want to ensure we don't cut off any potential talent sources, and we therefore fully support Ban the Box and do not include or ask about criminal convictions on our application forms. We believe everyone should be judged on merit and their potential, rather than what may have happened in their past. Everyone deserves a second chance."
Rob Varcoe, Group HR Director and Sarah Bowmann, Group Talent Strategy Director

LINKLATERS
Sector: Legal
Ban the Box employer since: September 2015
How and when do they ask? Linklaters have banned the box from all application forms, and no not ask about criminal convictions at any stage in the recruitment process. Checks for regulated roles are carried out by the Solicitors Licensing Authority before applicants apply for a role.
"Our goal is to foster a working environment in which individual differences are respected and valued, and everyone has the opportunity to excel. An important dimension of this approach is our support for Ban the Box, ensuring that every candidate is seen for what they offer now and not for moments in their past. We are working hard to overcome barriers to employment, whether they are absolute or perceived and Ban the Box is a visible and clear statement that we are delighted to endorse and employ."
Felix Hebblethwaite, Global Head of Recruitment and Resourcing

LIVERPOOL VISION
Sector: Government Administration
Ban the Box employer since: September 2014
How and when do they ask? Liverpool Vision does not ask about criminal convictions in the first stage of their application process. At the point of making an offer of employment, the company will ask the applicant to disclose unspent criminal convictions.

MACS PLASTERBOARD
Sector: Construction
Ban the Box employer since: October 2014
Macs Plasterboard Systems will not ask about criminal convictions through their application forms or formal recruitment process.

"Our business believes that every person deserves a second chance in life. We have living proof this can happen and assist candidates into a better life."
Tom McLoughlin, CEO

MATRIX APA
Sector: Product Design and Procurement
Ban the Box employer since: April 2014
How and when do they ask? Matrix APA Ltd does not ask about criminal convictions at any stage of their application process.
"After a 'Seeing is Believing' visit to HMP Brixton, it was clearly evident that getting offenders back into work was a top priority if we want to see national crime rates fall. Banning the box is the first step in creating opportunities for ex-offenders and will make the critical difference to the employment prospects for many thousands of people leaving prison.
Our own culture focuses heavily on fairness and the opportunity for a second chance; we all make mistakes in life, some bigger than others, but we believe those who fall hardest need the greatest amount of help. Being part of Ban the Box helps in a big way to achieve this."
Charlie Bradshaw, Managing Director

MVF
Sector: Technology
Ban the Box employer since: October 15
How and when do they ask? MVF does not ask about criminal convictions at any stage of their application process.
"MVF has never included a box for convictions on our application form, but we are now taking the positive step of joining the ban the box movement and making this part of our company policy.
We believe candidates should be considered for roles based on their talent and skills alone and everyone should have the opportunity to apply. We feel it is the responsibility of business to lead by example and be a force for good in the community, and this movement is something we are proud to be part of."
Titus Sharpe, CEO

NACRO
Sector: Third Sector
Ban the Box employer since: February 2014
How and when do they ask? Nacro does not ask about criminal convictions in the first stage of their application process. At the interview stage, once a shortlist of candidates has been created

Nacro asks them to fill out a criminal record declaration form. This contains sufficient room for applicants to provide a written disclosure statement, which they can take along to the interview and hand to the panel.
"Nacro believes that this campaign will help employers to consider applicants first and foremost on their merits; this should enable people who have put their criminal past behind them to get into work so they can become productive, financially independent members of society."
Lucy Anderson, Director of HR and Organisation Development

NBC BIRD
Sector: Support Services
Ban the Box employer since: December 2013
How and when do they ask? NBC Bird and Pest Solutions does not ask about criminal convictions at the first stage of their application process. At the point of interview, the company will ask the applicant to disclose any unspent criminal convictions.
"NBC decided to ban the box for several reasons, we didn't feel the question was relevant to our decision making process when looking for a new team member. We assess them on many criteria with a focus on their ability now and so long as we felt that there was nothing that would prevent them from meeting our expectations as an employer now their past had little or no relevance."
John Dickson, Managing Director

ONLY CONNECT
Sector: Not for Profit
Ban the Box employer since: May 2015
How and then do they ask? Only Connect have removed the tick box on all online and paper applications forms. Instead, they ask candidates to disclosure unspent criminal convictions at interview stage, where they explore a candidate's knowledge of the criminal justice system.
"Steady employment after prison makes a significant difference to reoffending rates. In today's day and age there is no room for discrimination. Some of our most valuable employees have been through the criminal justice system, and companies that discriminate are missing out on some of the most diverse talent out there."
Beth Murray, Public Engagement Director

COMMUNITY INTEREST COMPANY
Sector: Education
Ban the Box employer since: April 2015
How and when do they ask? Community Interest Company On Course South West does not use application forms but instead accept video applications. In most cases they do not ask about convictions, but where a DBS check is required this is clearly advertised and only sought following an offer of employment.
"Adult learning is about working in partnership with individuals to maximise opportunities and look forwards to the future. We recognise that every person brings a different dimension to the organisation and that to exclude individual talents on the basis of past actions will stop our organisation from fully representing our community. In order to reflect society and engage those who feel marginalised, individuals who can provide authentic representation of the transformative power of learning are a powerful resource. Safeguarding our learners is of course essential, however our recruitment process ensures that attitude and commitment have a chance to shine and that potential is not lost due to arbitrary judgements."
Heather Morris, Curriculum Manger & HR Director

PRISON REFORM TRUST
Sector: Not for profit
Ban the Box employer since: May 2016
How and when do they ask? In line with their objectives as a charity, the Prison Reform Trust takes a proactive approach to recruiting people with criminal convictions. They do not ask about convictions at the first stage, but may ask at interview stage where relevant.
"The Prison Reform Trust's aim is to create a just, humane and effective penal system. We work to improve prison regimes and conditions, address the needs of prisoners' families and promote alternatives to custody. We have a strong track record of changing justice policy and practice. We believe work is an important rehabilitative step, and do not discriminate on the basis of criminal record. We have a long record of employing former offenders and providing voluntary opportunities."
Sam O'Sullivan, Head of Finance & Human Resources

PEER POWER YOUTH
Sector: Not-for-profit
Ban the Box employer since: February 2017
How and when do they ask? Peer Power Youth only asks about criminal convictions after shortlisting candidates.

PRO-DRIVER
Sector: Logistics
Ban the Box employer since: October 2013
How and when do they ask? PRO-Driver does not ask about criminal convictions at any stage of their application process.
"Peer Power Youth are committed to the recruitment of a diverse team, that reflects the diversity of our beneficiaries.."
Anne-Marie Douglas CEO

PROJECTSIMPLY
Sector: PR and Communications
Ban the Box employer since: October 2014
How and when do they ask about criminal convictions? ProjectSimply will not ask about criminal convictions at any stage of their application process.

QUESERA
Sector: Utilities
Ban the Box employer since: February 2017
How and when do they ask? Quesera does not ask about criminal convictions at any stage, and actively seeks to employ ex-offenders.
"We believe that people should have an opportunity based on desire, skill and a good fit with a current position, not on historical blemishes. Inclusion and rehabilitation is an ongoing process brought about by acceptance, purpose and pride."
Christian Hill, CEO
"Because we are Sole Ex-offender Employer we don't even ask about previous convictions! Every ex-offender should be given a 2nd chance"
Kenneth Ford Wyatt, Managing Partner

RECORD UK
Sector: Utilities
Ban the Box employer since: June 2016
How and when do they ask? Record UK does not ask about criminal convictions until the final interview stage, as DBS checks are required to fulfil some of their contracts.

RIOCH UK
Sector: IT
Ban the Box employer since: October 2014
How and when do they ask? Rioch UK does not ask about criminal convictions in the first stage of their application process. At the point of making an offer of employment, the company will ask the applicant to disclose unspent criminal convictions. Are there any roles that are exempt from these processes? For regulated roles such as in field service operations, Ricoh UK will require spent and unspent convictions to be disclosed and request the appropriate DBS check prior to employment.
"Ricoh UK pride themselves on being an employer of choice and have robust policies ensuring fairness and equality around employment: when we were asked to support the 'Ban the Box' campaign we put in place actions to remove the box from our recruitment process, Every time I support a ban the box event I feel inspired at the drive and desire of the individuals involved to take any second chance offered and prove they can move on and be successful. By removing the declaration of convictions box from applications, Ricoh UK are able to judge individuals on their skills and abilities and not their past."
Phil Keoghan, CEO, Ricoh UK

ROAST RESTAURANTS
Sector: Hospitality
Ban the Box employer since: August 2014
How and when do they ask about criminal convictions? Roast Restaurants Ltd does not ask about criminal convictions at any stage of their application process.
"We see no need to highlight people's pasts and have a long-established commitment to working with ex-offenders. We have successfully recruited people with criminal convictions over many years and look to what role their future plays in ours."
Iqbal Wahhab, Founder, Roast Restaurants Ltd

SAFETY ACCESS
Sector: Utilities
Ban the Box employer since: November 2015
How and when do they ask? Safety Access Solutions do not ask about criminal convictions, recognising that most of their employees have gone through the necessary checks to work on a prison site.

2ND CHANCE
Sector: Charity / Third Sector
Ban the Box employer since: July 2014
How and when do they ask? 2nd Chance Project does not ask about criminal convictions in the first stage of their application process, and only asks at a later stage for regulated roles. For regulated roles where applicants will be working directly with children and vulnerable adults, 2nd Chance Project will ask candidates about their criminal convictions and carry out enhanced DBS checks before an employment offer is finalised.

"We are passionate about inspiring change and achievement. In order to do so we are proud to promote an end-to-end solution. This means the clients we engage have the potential to progress through 2nd Chance and potentially volunteer or work for our organisation as we believe they can be the most effective solution and help us to become a market leader."

James Mapstone, Managing Director

SERENITY SERVICES
Sector: Third Sector
Ban the Box employer since: September 2014
How and when do they ask? Serenity Services does not ask about criminal convictions in the first stage of their application process. At the point of making an offer of employment, the organisation will ask the applicant to disclose unspent criminal convictions.
For regulated roles, where applicants will be working directly with children and vulnerable adults, Serenity Services will ask candidates about their criminal convictions and carry out enhanced DBS checks before an employment offer is finalised. If an applicant's conviction means they are unsuitable for the particular role applied, Serenity Services will retain their details for any future suitable positions.
"The act of discrimination from a perspective employer will break the confidence, a high probability of ex-offender re-offending. Our aim is not only to improve an ex-offender's reading, writing, spelling and employability skills but to employ some ex-offenders for suitable positions within the organisation."

Andrius Remeikis, Trustee and Director

SHEKINAH MISSION
Sector: Third Sector
Ban the Box employer since: October 2014
How and when do they ask? Shekinah Mission does not ask about criminal convictions in the first stage of their application process. At the point of interview, the organisation will ask the applicant to disclose unspent criminal convictions. This information will only be shared with the organisation's HR team and not the recruitment panel.
For regulated roles, Shekinah Mission will follow the same process but at the point of interview will ask about spent and unspent criminal convictions, requesting the appropriate DBS check.
"We want to recruit staff who can make a real difference to people's lives. People with 'lived experiences' can make a significant contribution to that but are often put off by barriers. Disclosure of convictions should be part of the conversation, but not the starting point."

John Hamblin, CEO

SITEVIALITY
Sector: Digital Marketing
Ban the Box employer since: May 2014
How and when do they ask? SiteVisibility Marketing Ltd does not ask about criminal convictions in the first stage of their application process. At the point of final interview, the company will ask the applicant to disclose any unspent criminal convictions.
"To give people a second chance."

Jason Woodford, Chief Executive Officer

SOCIETY
Sector: Recruitment
Ban the Box employer since: May 2015
How and when do they ask? Society does not ask about criminal convictions at any stage of their recruitment process.
"We're strongly supportive of Business in the Community's Ban the Box campaign. Far too many people are being effectively excluded from the workforce by antiquated recruitment practices that screen them out before there's been a chance for the Hiring Manager to get to know them as a human being, to understand their journey, or to put their past into its full context. A small tweak to the way organisations select people for interview can remove this enormous yet invisible barrier, and will benefit both companies, employees and society at large."

Simon Lucas, Managing Director, Society

SODEXO
Sector: Support services
Ban the Box employer since: May 2015
How and when do they ask? Sodexo do not ask about criminal convictions at any stage in the recruitment process, with the exception of their Ministry of Justice roles which require that they ask at application stage, and their regulated rolls where a DBS check is carried out only if the candidate is successful.
"Sodexo is proud to Ban the Box. As a services company working to improve quality of life across a variety of industries our most valuable asset is our people. We want to attract the best people and recognize that the tick box may have been keeping us from a very valuable pool of talent. In addition, as a company responsible for both prison and probation contracts, we understand

how important employment is to rehabilitation. Ban the Box gives ex-offenders the opportunity to compete on a level playing field for employment."
Angela Williams, HR Director, UK and Ireland

SOUTHBANK CENTRE
Sector: Arts
Ban the Box employer since: June 2014
How and when do they ask? At the point of making an offer of employment, the company will ask the applicant to disclose unspent criminal convictions. Southbank Centre hire for some roles working with children or vulnerable adults. These roles require DBS checks; however Southbank Centre will not ask about convictions or initiate DBS checks until after an offer is made, aligning with their commitment to assess applicants' skills first.
"Southbank Centre changes people's lives every day through encounters with art and culture. We are determined to make these encounters available to all regardless of background. By offering a fair employment opportunity to ex-offenders, we will increase the vibrancy and diversity of Southbank Centre. This will help us welcome the world to our much-loved site. We are proud to support Ban the Box."
Richard Buxton, Human Resources Dire

SOVA
Sector: Third Sector
Ban the Box employer since: April 2015
How and when do they ask about criminal convictions? Sova highlights that it welcomes applications from ex-offenders, and explains that the regulated nature of many of its roles means a criminal record check may be necessary. Sova therefore discreetly offers applicants the opportunity to confidentially discuss convictions before applying.
"Sova believes that everyone has the capacity to change their life for the better. We also believe that to make those changes you often need someone on your side – someone who understands you and what you are going through."
Sophie Wilson, COO

STYLES & WOOD
Sector: Architects
Ban the Box employer since: February 2015
How and when do they ask? Styles & Wood has removed the question about criminal conviction from job application stage and potential employees are only required to disclose convictions at a later stage where it is deemed a requirement by the client.

"Finding stable employment is widely recognised as a contributing factor to the successful rehabilitation of ex-offenders, so industry must step up and accept their role in the process. Around 42% of construction companies struggle to recruit employees with the right skills and with a well-publicised skills gap, we can't simply exclude 17% of the UK population from the recruitment process on the basis that they have a criminal record. The box is much more than a tick on a page; it's a permanent reminder and for many, a challenging hurdle to overcome. We need to ban the box then employers can focus on an individual's skills and experience as opposed to a tick on page."
Karen Morley, HR Director

ST LEGER HOMES
Sector: Housing
Ban the Box employer since: June 2016
How and when do they ask? St Leger Homes only ask about criminal convictions if an applicant reaches application stage.
"We actively promote equality of opportunity for all with the right mix of talent, skills and potential and welcome applications from a wide range of candidates, including those with criminal records. We only ask job candidates to tell us about 'unspent' convictions as defined in the Rehabilitation of Offenders Act 1974. We only take into account unspent convictions, when making recruitment decisions, where the 'unspent' convictions are relevant to the post. We select all candidates for interview based on their skills, qualifications and experience."
Linda Keeling, Head of Human Resources and Health and Safety

THAMES TIDEWAY TUNNEL
Sector: Utilities
Ban the Box employer since: August 2016 Tide
"Working in Partnership with Ban the Box to achieve the Thames Tideway Tunnel objective, we believe in providing opportunities to those from all backgrounds"
Julie Thornton, Head of HR

TRAFFORD HOUSING
Sector: Housing
Ban the Box employer since: August 2015
How and when do they ask? Trafford Housing Trust was the first housing association to sign up to the campaign. They do not ask about criminal convictions at the first stage of the recruitment

process. Candidates will be asked to disclose criminal record information at the point at which they are shortlisted.

"People will have a fair chance to get to an interview based on their competency for a vacancy, rather than being excluded automatically because of a conviction unrelated to their ability to perform the role in question."
Matthew Gardiner, Chief Executive

TRUE STORY

Sector: Media, Marketing and PR
Ban the Box employer since: October 2013
How and when do they ask about criminal convictions? True Story does not ask about convictions at application stage, but does ask gaps in employment history at interview and have in place a full induction process and probation period. They feel that this is more relevant to manage the inherent risk of the recruitment process.

"We don't believe there is any merit in having a 'tick box' to screen out ex-offenders because we want to put the emphasis on skills, abilities and best fit for our company. We invest time in the recruitment, induction and probation process to give us the best chance of making this work. We're a relatively small company with around 80 employees but businesses like ours have a big role to play in ensuring people have the opportunity to compete."
Jayne Mayled, CEO

UNLOCK

Sector: Third Sector
Ban the Box employer since: February 2014
How and when do they ask? Unlock only asks about convictions once a job offer has been made. At this stage, they ask applicants to complete a self-disclosure form. They may then arrange a discussion with the candidate. The rationale for this process is to ensure that the organisation only considers the convictions of the person they want to offer a position to. It also means that applicants who do not reach the final stage of the process do not have to disclose sensitive personal information unnecessarily. They have a clear policy on their website which sets out this process, so that applicants can have confidence in knowing how the recruitment process works. "We believe that, by banning the box, employers are better able to consider convictions at a more appropriate stage in the recruitment process, and at the same time are able to give people with convictions a better opportunity to compete for jobs."
Christopher Stacey, Director (Services)

VIRGIN TRAINS

Sector: Utilities
Ban the Box employer since: February 2016
How and when do they ask? Virgin Trains does not ask about criminal convictions until an initial job offer has been made.

"We already work with people with convictions so banning the box seemed a logical step to take given our current work. We do not want to put people off applying for roles with us and would like to make our decisions based on where the candidate is now and what they can add to our business."
Kathryn Wildman, Lead Recruiter

VIRIDOR

Sector: Utilities
Ban the Box employer since: November 2015
How and when do they ask about criminal convictions? Viridor does not ask about convictions at any stage in their recruitment process, to reflect a desire to build on strengths and not weaknesses.

"Viridor's objective is to be the UK's leader in renewable energy and resource management, with the customer and the heart of everything we do. We can only achieve this by having a first-class, talented, motivated and skilled workforce. We are not so interested in what you've done in the past but what you can achieve in the future. By building on your positive attributes and experiences, not those you regret. We have the opportunity to help each other to do things right, not do things wrong."
Simon Catford, HR & Regulatory Director

WALKING WITH THE WOUNDED

Sector: Third Sector
Ban the Box employer since: September 2014
How and when do they ask? At the point of interview, Walking with the Wounded will ask the applicant to disclose unspent criminal convictions. Where it is a legal requirement, Walking With The Wounded will inform the applicant at interview that they will be undertaking a DBS check.

"Walking With The Wounded supports the Ban the Box campaign because it is absolutely right. A past criminal conviction has no bearing on an individual's ability to do a good job today. It will reduce reoffending, give individuals a second chance and increase our access to the talent pool in the wider community. We as a collective workforce are proud to wholeheartedly adopt this policy."
Fergus Williams, Director of Operations PR

SECTION FIVE. Legal Section

THE PRISON RULES 1999
Updated to November 2021

PART I.
ARRANGEMENT INTERPRETATION
1. Citation and commencement
2. Interpretation
2A Coronavirus period – transition period

PART II. PRISONERS GENERAL
3. Purpose of prison training and treatment
4. Outside contacts
5. After care
6. Maintenance of order and discipline
7. Classification of prisoners
8. Privileges
9. Temporary release
9A. Covid Temporary Release **(Note automatically cancelled on 25/3/2022)**
10. Information to prisoners
11. Requests and complaints

WOMEN PRISONERS
12. Women prisoners

RELIGION
13. Religious denomination
14. Special duties of chaplains and prison ministers
15. Regular visits by ministers of religion
16. Religious services
17. Substitute for chaplain or prison minister
18. Sunday work
19. Religious books

MEDICAL ATTENTION
20. Health services
21. Special illnesses and conditions
22. Notification of illness or death

PHYSICAL WELFARE AND WORK
23. Clothing
24. Food
25. Alcohol and tobacco
26. Sleeping accommodation
27. Beds and bedding
28. Hygiene
29. Physical education
30. Time in the open air
31. Work

EDUCATION AND LIBRARY
32. Education
33. Library

COMMUNICATIONS
34. Communications generally
35. Personal letters and visits
35A. Interception of communication
35B. Permanent log of communication
35C. Disclosure of material
35D. Retention of material
36. Police interviews
37. Securing release
38. Visits from legal advisers
39. Delivery and receipt of legally privileged material

REMOVAL, SEARCH, RECORD AND PROPERTY
40. Custody outside prison
41. Search
42. Record and photograph
43. Prisoners' property
44. Money and articles received by post

CONTROL, SUPERVISION, RESTRAINT AND DRUG TESTING
45. Removal from association
46. Close supervision centres
47. Use of force
48. Temporary confinement
49. Restraints
50. Compulsory testing for controlled drugs
50A. Observation of prisoners by means of an overt closed circuit television system
50B. Compulsory testing for alcohol

OFFENCES AGAINST DISCIPLINE
51. Offences against discipline
51A. Interpretation of rule 51
52. Defences to rule 51(9)
52A. Defences to rule 51(10) and rule 51(11)
53. Disciplinary charges
53A. Determination of mode of enquiry
53B Determination of mode of inquiry in a coronavirus period
54. Rights of prisoners charged
55. Governor's punishments
55A. Adjudicator's punishments
55B. Review of adjudicator's punishment
56. Forfeiture of remission to be treated as an

award of additional days
57. Offences committed by young persons
58. Cellular confinement
59. Prospective award of additional days
59A. Removal from a cell or living unit
60. Suspended punishments
61. Remission and mitigation of punishments and quashing of findings of guilt

PART III
OFFICERS OF PRISONS
62. General duty of officers
63. Gratuities forbidden
64. Search of officers
65. Transactions with prisoners
66. Contact with former prisoners
67. Communications to the press
68. Code of discipline
69. Emergencies

PART IV
PERSONS HAVING ACCESS TO A PRISON
70. Prohibited articles
70A. List C Articles
71. Control of persons and vehicles
72. Viewing of prisons
73. Visitors

PART V
INDEPENDENT MONITORING BOARD
74. Disqualification for membership
75. Independent monitoring board
76. Proceedings of boards
77. General duties of boards
78. Particular duties
79. Members visiting prisons
80. Annual report

PART VI
SUPPLEMENTAL
81. Delegation by governor
82. Contracted out prisons
83. Contracted out parts of prisons
84. Contracted out functions at directly managed prisons
85. Revocations and savings

Interpretation
2. (1) In these Rules, where the context so admits, the expression -

"controlled drug or specified drugs" means any product or substance containing one or more of the chemical compounds listed in Schedule 2 to these Rules;

"convicted prisoner" means, subject to the provisions of rule 7(3), a prisoner who has been convicted or found guilty of an offence or committed or attached for contempt of court or for failing to do or abstain from doing anything required to be done or left undone, and the expression "unconvicted prisoner" shall be construed accordingly;

"coronavirus" has the meaning given by section 1 of the 2020 Act (meaning of "coronavirus" and related terminology);

"coronavirus period" means the period of time inclusive of a transmission control period and the transition period which follows it;

"electronic cigarette" means a product that can be used for the consumption of nicotine-containing vapour via a mouth piece, or any component of that product, including a cartridge, a tank, and the device without cartridge or tank (regardless of whether the product is disposable or refillable by means of a refill cartridge and a tank, or rechargeable with single use cartridges).

"governor" includes an officer for the time being in charge of a prison;

"legal adviser" means, in relation to a prisoner, his counsel or solicitor, and includes a clerk noting on behalf of his solicitor;

"officer" means an officer of a prison and, for the purposes of rule 40(2), includes a prisoner custody officer who is authorised to perform escort functions in accordance with section 89 of the Criminal Justice Act 1991[3];

"prison minister" means, in relation to a prison, a minister appointed to that prison under section 10 of the Prison Act 1952;

"short-term prisoner" and "long-term prisoner" have the meanings assigned to them by section 33(5) of the Criminal Justice Act 1991, as extended by sections 43(1) and 45(1) of that Act.

"the 2020 Act" means the Coronavirus Act 2020(7);

"transition period" means the period provided for by rule 2A;

"transmission control period" has the meaning given by paragraph 5 of Schedule 21 to the 2020 Act.".

(2) In these Rules -

(a) a reference to an award of additional days means additional days awarded under these Rules by virtue of section 42 of the Criminal Justice Act 1991;

(b) a reference to the Church of England includes a reference to the Church in Wales; and

(c) a reference to a numbered rule is, unless otherwise stated, a reference to the rule of that number in these Rules and a reference in a rule to a numbered paragraph is, unless otherwise stated, a reference to the paragraph of that number in that rule.

Coronavirus period – transition period

2A.—(1) Subject to paragraphs (2) to (5), a transition period is the period of 3 months starting on the date on which a transmission control period ends.

(2) The Secretary of State may declare that a transition period is extended by such period of up to 1 month as is specified in the declaration, if the Secretary of State considers that the declaration is necessary as a result of the effects, existing or new, of coronavirus on or in relation to prisoners or prisons.

(3) The Secretary of State—

(a) may declare that a transition period which has already been extended is further extended by such period of up to 1 month as is specified in the declaration; and

(b) subject to paragraph (4), may make further such declarations.

(4) The total period of the transition period must not exceed 6 months.

(5) The Secretary of State may at any time declare that a transition period has ended, or is to end, on such date, earlier than the transition period would otherwise end as is specified in the declaration.

(6) Any declaration under paragraph (2), (3) or (5) must be published in such a manner as the Secretary of State considers appropriate.

PART II. PRISONERS: GENERAL

3. Purpose of prison training and treatment

The purpose of the training and treatment of convicted prisoners shall be to encourage and assist them to lead a good and useful life.

4. – Outside contacts

(1) Special attention shall be paid to the maintenance of such relationships between a prisoner and his family as are desirable in the best interests of both.

(2) A prisoner shall be encouraged and assisted to establish and maintain such relations with persons and agencies outside prison as may, in the opinion of the governor, best promote the interests of his family and his own social rehabilitation.

5. After care

From the beginning of a prisoner's sentence, consideration shall be given, in consultation with the appropriate after-care organisation, to the prisoner's future and the assistance to be given him on and after his release.

6. – Maintenance of order and discipline

(1) Order and discipline shall be maintained with firmness, but with no more restriction than is required for safe custody and well ordered community life.

(2) In the control of prisoners, officers shall seek to influence them through their own example and leadership, and to enlist their willing co-operation.

(3) At all times the treatment of prisoners shall be such as to encourage their self-respect and a sense of personal responsibility, but a prisoner shall not be employed in any disciplinary capacity.

7. – Classification of prisoners

(1) Subject to paragraphs (1A) to (1D), prisoners shall be classified, in accordance with any directions of the Secretary of State, having regard to their age, temperament and record and with a view to maintaining good order and facilitating training and, in the case of convicted prisoners, of furthering the purpose of their training and treatment as provided by rule 3.

(1A) Except where paragraph (1D) applies, a prisoner who has the relevant deportation status must not be classified as suitable for open conditions.

(1B) If, immediately before the relevant time—

(a) a prisoner has been classified as suitable for open conditions; and

(b) the prison has received notice that the prisoner has the relevant deportation status, the prisoner's classification must be reconsidered in accordance with this rule as soon as practicable after the relevant time.

(1C) If—

(a) a prisoner has been classified as suitable for open conditions (whether before or after the relevant time); and

(b) the prison receives notice after the relevant time that the prisoner has the relevant deportation status, the prisoner's classification must be reconsidered in accordance with this rule as soon as practicable after the prison receives that notice.

(1D) This paragraph applies if a prisoner has been classified as suitable for open conditions and is located in open conditions immediately before the prisoner's classification is reconsidered, whether under paragraph (1B) or (1C) or otherwise.

(1E) For the purposes of this rule, a prisoner has the relevant deportation status if—

(a) there is a deportation order against the prisoner under section 5(1) of the Immigration Act 1971(3); and

(b) no appeal under section 82(1) of the Nationality, Immigration and Asylum Act 2002(4) ("the 2002 Act") that may be brought or continued from within the United Kingdom in relation to the decision to make the deportation order—

(i) could be brought (ignoring any possibility of an appeal out of time with permission), or

(ii) is pending (within the meaning of section 104 of the 2002 Act(5)).

(1F) In paragraph (1E), the reference to the decision to make the deportation order includes a decision that section 32(5) of the UK Borders Act 2007(6) applies in respect of the prisoner.

(1G) In this rule, "the relevant time" means 5.00 p.m on 13th August 2014

(2) Unconvicted prisoners –

(a) shall be kept out of contact with convicted prisoners as far as the governor considers it can reasonably be done, unless and to the extent that they have consented to share residential accommodation or participate in any activity with convicted prisoners; and

(b) shall under no circumstances be required to share a cell with a convicted prisoner.

(3) Prisoners committed or attached for contempt of court, or for failing to do or abstain from doing anything required to be done or left undone:

(a) shall be treated as a separate class for the purposes of this rule;

(b) notwithstanding anything in this rule, may be permitted to associate with any other class of prisoners if they are willing to do so; and

(c) shall have the same privileges as an unconvicted prisoner under rules 20(5), 23(1) and 35(1).

(4) Nothing in this rule shall require a prisoner to be deprived unduly of the society of other persons.

8. – Privileges

(1) There shall be established at every prison systems of privileges appropriate to the classes of prisoners there, which shall include arrangements under which money earned by prisoners in prison may be spent by them within the prison.

(2) Systems of privileges established under paragraph (1) may include arrangements under which prisoners may be allowed time outside their cells and in association with one another, in excess of the minimum time which, subject to the other provisions of these Rules apart from this rule, is otherwise allowed to prisoners at the prison for this purpose.

(3) Systems of privileges established under paragraph (1) may include arrangements under which privileges may be granted to prisoners only in so far as they have met, and for so long as they continue to meet, specified standards in their behaviour and their performance in work or other activities.

(4) Systems of privileges which include arrangements of the kind referred to in paragraph (3) shall include procedures to be followed in determining whether or not any of the privileges concerned shall be granted, or shall continue to be granted, to a prisoner; such procedures shall include a requirement that the prisoner be given reasons for any decision adverse to him together with a statement of the means by which he may appeal against it.

(5) Nothing in this rule shall be taken to confer

on a prisoner any entitlement to any privilege or to affect any provision in these Rules other than this rule as a result of which any privilege may be forfeited or otherwise lost or a prisoner deprived of association with other prisoners.

9. – Temporary release

(1) Subject to paragraph (1A), the Secretary of State may, in accordance with the other provisions of this rule, release temporarily a prisoner to whom this rule applies.
(1A) A prisoner who has the relevant deportation status must not be released under this rule unless the prisoner is located in open conditions immediately before the time of release.
(2) A prisoner may be released under this rule for any period or periods and subject to any conditions.
(3) A prisoner may only be released under this rule:
(a) on compassionate grounds or for the purpose of receiving medical treatment;
(b) to engage in employment or voluntary work;
(c) to receive instruction or training which cannot reasonably be provided in the prison;
(d) to enable him to participate in any proceedings before any court, tribunal or inquiry;
(e) to enable him to consult with his legal adviser in circumstances where it is not reasonably practicable for the consultation to take place in the prison;
(f) to assist any police officer in any enquiries;
(g) to facilitate the prisoner's transfer between prisons;
(h) to assist him in maintaining family ties or in his transition from prison life to freedom.
(4) A prisoner shall not be released under this rule unless the Secretary of State is satisfied that there would not be an unacceptable risk of his committing offences whilst released or otherwise failing to comply with any condition upon which he is released.
(5) The Secretary of State shall not release under this rule a prisoner serving a sentence of imprisonment if, having regard to:
(a) the period or proportion of his sentence which the prisoner has served or, in a case where paragraph (10) does not apply to require all the sentences he is serving to be treated as a single term, the period or proportion of any such sentence he has served; and
(b) the frequency with which the prisoner has been granted temporary release under this rule, the Secretary of State is of the opinion that the release of the prisoner would be likely to undermine public confidence in the administration of justice.
(6) If a prisoner has been temporarily released under this rule during the relevant period and has been sentenced to imprisonment for a criminal offence committed whilst at large following that release, he shall not be released under this rule unless his release, having regard to the circumstances of this conviction, would not, in the opinion of the Secretary of State, be likely to undermine public confidence in the administration of justice.
(7) For the purposes of paragraph (6), "the relevant period":
(a) in the case of a prisoner serving a determinate sentence of imprisonment, is the period he has served in respect of that sentence, unless, notwithstanding paragraph (10), the sentences he is serving do not fall to be treated as a single term, in which case it is the period since he was last released in relation to one of those sentences under Part II of the Criminal Justice Act 1991 ("the 1991 Act") or Chapter 6 of Part 12 of the 2003 Act;
(b) in the case of a prisoner serving an indeterminate sentence of imprisonment, is, if the prisoner has previously been released on licence under Part II of the Crime (Sentences) Act 1997 or Part II of the 1991 Act or Chapter 6 of Part 12 of the 2003 Act, the period since the date of his last recall to prison in respect of that sentence or, where the prisoner has not been so released, the period he has served in respect of that sentence; or
(c) in the case of a prisoner detained in prison for any other reason, is the period for which the prisoner has been detained for that reason; save that where a prisoner falls within two or more of sub-paragraphs (a) to (c), the "relevant period", in the case of that prisoner, shall be determined by whichever of the applicable sub-paragraphs produces the longer period.
(8) A prisoner released under this rule may be recalled to prison at any time whether the conditions of his release have been broken or not.

(8A) If, immediately before the relevant time, a prisoner has been released under this rule and the prison has received notice that the prisoner has the relevant deportation status, the prisoner must be recalled unless—
(a) the period for which the prisoner has been released is due to expire on 13th August 2014; or
(b) the prisoner was released from open conditions.
(8B) If a prisoner has been released under this rule (whether before or after the relevant time) and the prison receives notice after the relevant time that the prisoner has the relevant deportation status, the prisoner must be recalled unless—
(a) the period for which the prisoner has been released is due to expire on the day on which the prison receives that notice; or
(b) the prisoner was released from open conditions.
(9) This rule applies to prisoners other than persons committed in custody for trial or to be sentenced or otherwise dealt with before or by any Crown Court or remanded in custody by any court.
(10) For the purposes of any reference in this rule to an inmate's sentence, consecutive terms and terms which are wholly or partly concurrent shall be treated as a single term.
(11) In this rule:
(a) any reference to a sentence of imprisonment shall be construed as including any sentence to detention or custody; and
(b) any reference to release on licence or otherwise under Part II of the 1991 Act includes any release on licence under any legislation providing for early release on licence.
(c) any reference to a prisoner who has the relevant deportation status is to be read in accordance with rule 7(1E) and (1F); and
(d) any reference to the relevant time is to be read in accordance with rule 7(1G)

Rule 9A is automatically cancelled With Effect From 25th March 2022

9A.—Coronavirus Restricted Temporary Release
(1) During a transmission control period, the Secretary of State may, in accordance with the other provisions of this rule, temporarily release a prisoner falling within a description specified in a direction made under this rule.
(2) A prisoner may only be released under this rule (subject to paragraph (3)) if—
(a) a transmission control period is in effect; and
(b) the prisoner is—
  (i) a fixed term prisoner subject to release pursuant to section 244(a) of the 2003 Act; or
  (ii) a fine defaulter or contemnor subject to release pursuant to section 258(b) of the 2003 Act; and
(c) the Secretary of State is satisfied that the temporary release is—
  (i) for the purpose of preventing, protecting against, delaying or otherwise controlling the incidence or transmission of coronavirus; or
  (ii) for the facilitation of the most appropriate deployment of personnel and resources in, or in connection with, prisons in England and Wales.
(3) A prisoner must not be released under this rule if—
(a) the prisoner would not be eligible for release on temporary licence under the following restrictions on rule 9 of these Rules (temporary release)—
  (i) rule 9(1A) (prisoners with a relevant deportation status);
  (ii) rule 9(6) (prisoners who have committed offences whilst at large following temporary release);
  (iii) rule 9(9) (prisoners committed or remanded).
(b) the prisoner is subject to the notification requirements of Part 2 of the Sexual Offences Act 2003(c);
(c) the Secretary of State has classified the prisoner as Category A or restricted status in accordance with a direction under rule 7 (classification of prisoners).
(4) A description specified in a direction under this rule may be framed by reference to whatever matters the Secretary of State considers appropriate.
(5) A prisoner may be released under this rule for any period or periods and subject to any conditions.
(6) In particular, the Secretary of State may impose a condition which requires the prisoner to—
(a) report to a specified person at a specified place at a specified time;

(b) return to a prison at a specified time;
(c) comply with directions issued by the Secretary of State or another person.
(7) A prisoner released under this rule may be recalled at any time whether the conditions of his release have been broken or not.
(8) In this rule –
"coronavirus" has the meaning given by section 1 of the 2020 Act (meaning of "coronavirus" and related terminology);
"the 2020 Act" means the Coronavirus Act 2020(d);
"transmission control period" has the meaning given by paragraph 5 of Schedule 21 to the 2020 Act.

10. – Information to prisoners
(1) Every prisoner shall be provided, as soon as possible after his reception into prison, and in any case within 24 hours, with information in writing about those provisions of these Rules and other matters which it is necessary that he should know, including earnings and privileges, and the proper means of making requests and complaints.
(2) In the case of a prisoner aged less than 18, or a prisoner aged 18 or over who cannot read or appears to have difficulty in understanding the information so provided, the governor, or an officer deputed by him, shall so explain it to him that he can understand his rights and obligations.
(3) A copy of these Rules shall be made available to any prisoner who requests it.

11. – Requests and complaints
(1) A prisoner may make a request or complaint to the governor or independent monitoring board relating to the prisoner's imprisonment.
(2) The governor shall consider as soon as possible any requests and complaints that are made to him under paragraph (1).
(3) A written request or complaint under paragraph (1) may be made in confidence.

WOMEN PRISONERS
12. – Women prisoners
(1) Women prisoners shall normally be kept separate from male prisoners.
(2) The Secretary of State may, subject to any conditions he thinks fit, permit a woman prisoner to have her baby with her in prison, and everything necessary for the baby's maintenance and care may be provided there.

RELIGION
13. Religious denomination
A prisoner shall be treated as being of the religious denomination stated in the record made in pursuance of section 10(5) of the Prison Act 1952 but the governor may, in a proper case and after due enquiry, direct that record to be amended.

14. – Special duties of chaplains and prison ministers
(1) The chaplain or a prison minister of a prison shall (or during a coronavirus period shall so far as reasonably practicable) –
(a) interview every prisoner of his denomination individually soon after the prisoner's reception into that prison and shortly before his release; and
(b) if no other arrangements are made, read the burial service at the funeral of any prisoner of his denomination who dies in that prison.
(2) The chaplain shall (or during a coronavirus period shall so far as reasonably practicable) visit daily all prisoners belonging to the Church of England who are sick, under restraint or undergoing cellular confinement; and a prison minister shall do the same, as far as he reasonably can, for prisoners of his denomination.
(3) The chaplain shall (or during a coronavirus period shall so far as reasonably practicable) visit any prisoner not of the Church of England who is sick, under restraint or undergoing cellular confinement, and is not regularly visited by a minister of his denomination, if the prisoner is willing.

15. – Regular visits by ministers of religion
(1) The chaplain shall visit the prisoners belonging to the Church of England.
(2) A prison minister shall visit the prisoners of his denomination as regularly as he reasonably can.
(3) Where a prisoner belongs to a denomination for which no prison minister has been appointed, the governor shall do what he reasonably can, if so requested by the

prisoner, to arrange for him to be visited regularly by a minister of that denomination.

16. – Religious services
(1) The chaplain shall (or during a coronavirus period shall so far as reasonably practicable) conduct Divine Service for prisoners belonging to the Church of England at least once every Sunday, Christmas Day and Good Friday, and such celebrations of Holy Communion and weekday services as may be arranged.
(2) Prison ministers shall conduct Divine Service for prisoners of their denominations at such times as may be arranged.

17. – Substitute for chaplain or prison minister
(1) A person approved by the Secretary of State may act for the chaplain in his absence.
(2) A prison minister may, with the leave of the Secretary of State, appoint a substitute to act for him in his absence.

18. Sunday work
Arrangements shall be made so as not to require prisoners of the Christian religion to do any unnecessary work on Sunday, Christmas Day or Good Friday, or prisoners of other religions to do any such work on their recognised days of religious observance.

19. Religious books
There shall, so far as reasonably practicable, be available for the personal use of every prisoner such religious books recognised by his denomination as are approved by the Secretary of State for use in prisons.

MEDICAL ATTENTION
20. – Health services
(1) The governor must work in partnership with local health care providers to secure the provision to prisoners of access to the same quality and range of services as the general public receives from the National Health Service.
(2) Every request by a prisoner to see a health care professional shall be recorded by the officer to whom it was made and promptly communicated to a health care professional.
(3) If an unconvicted prisoner desires the attendance of a named registered medical practitioner or dentist other than one already working in the prison, and will pay any expense incurred, the governor must, if satisfied that there are reasonable grounds for the request and unless the Secretary of State otherwise directs, allow the prisoner to be visited and treated by that practitioner or dentist, in consultation with a registered medical practitioner who works in the prison.
(4) Subject to any directions given in the particular case by the Secretary of State, a registered medical practitioner selected by or on behalf of a prisoner who is a party to any legal proceedings must be afforded reasonable facilities for examining the prisoner in connection with the proceedings, and may do so out of hearing but in the sight of an officer
(5) A prisoner may correspond, in accordance with arrangements made by the Secretary of State for the confidential handling of correspondence, with a registered medical practitioner who has treated the prisoner for a life threatening condition, and such correspondence may not be opened, read or stopped unless the governor has reasonable cause to believe its contents do not relate to the treatment of that condition.

21. – Special illnesses and conditions
(1) A registered medical practitioner working within the prison shall report to the governor on the case of any prisoner whose health is likely to be injuriously affected by continued imprisonment or any conditions of imprisonment. The governor shall send the report to the Secretary of State without delay, together with his own recommendations.

22. – Notification of illness or death
(1) If a prisoner dies, becomes seriously ill, sustains any severe injury or is removed to hospital on account of mental disorder, the governor shall, if he knows his or her address, at once inform the prisoner's spouse or next of kin, and also any person who the prisoner may reasonably have asked to be informed.
(2) If a prisoner dies, the governor shall give notice immediately to the coroner having jurisdiction, to the independent monitoring board and to the Secretary of State.

PHYSICAL WELFARE AND WORK

23. – Clothing

(1) An unconvicted prisoner may wear clothing of his own if and in so far as it is suitable, tidy and clean, and shall be permitted to arrange for the supply to him from outside prison of sufficient clean clothing:
Provided that, subject to rule 40(3):
(a) he may be required, if and for so long as there are reasonable grounds to believe that there is a serious risk of his attempting to escape, to wear items of clothing which are distinctive by virtue of being specially marked or coloured or both; and
(b) he may be required, if and for so long as the Secretary of State is of the opinion that he would, if he escaped, be highly dangerous to the public or the police or the security of the State, to wear clothing provided under this rule.
(2) Subject to paragraph (1) above, the provisions of this rule shall apply to an unconvicted prisoner as to a convicted prisoner.
(3) A convicted prisoner shall be provided with clothing adequate for warmth and health in accordance with a scale approved by the Secretary of State.
(4) The clothing provided under this rule shall include suitable protective clothing for use at work, where this is needed.
(5) Subject to rule 40(3), a convicted prisoner shall wear clothing provided under this rule and no other, except on the directions of the Secretary of State or as a privilege under rule 8.
(6) A prisoner may be provided, where necessary, with suitable and adequate clothing on his release.

24. – Food

(1) Subject to any directions of the Secretary of State, no prisoner shall be allowed, except as authorised by a health care professional to have any food other than that ordinarily provided.
(2) The food provided shall be wholesome, nutritious, well prepared and served, reasonably varied and sufficient in quantity.
(3) Any person deemed by the governor to be competent, shall from time to time inspect the food both before and after it is cooked and shall report any deficiency or defect to the governor.
(4) In this rule "food" includes drink.

25. – Alcohol and tobacco

(1) No prisoner shall be allowed to have any intoxicating liquor.
(2) No prisoner shall be allowed to smoke or to have any tobacco, except in accordance with any directions of the Secretary of State.

26. – Sleeping accommodation

(1) No room or cell shall be used as sleeping accommodation for a prisoner unless it has been certified in the manner required by section 14 of the Prison Act 1952 in the case of a cell used for the confinement of a prisoner.
(2) A certificate given under that section or this rule shall specify the maximum number of prisoners who may sleep or be confined at one time in the room or cell to which it relates, and the number so specified shall not be exceeded without the leave of the Secretary of State.

27. Beds and bedding

Each prisoner shall be provided with a separate bed and with separate bedding adequate for warmth and health.

28. – Hygiene

(1) Every prisoner shall be provided with toilet articles necessary for his health and cleanliness, which shall be replaced as necessary.
(2) Every prisoner shall be required to wash at proper times, have a hot bath or shower on reception and thereafter at least once a week.
(3) A prisoner's hair shall not be cut without his consent.

29. – Physical education

(1) If circumstances reasonably permit, a prisoner aged 21 years or over shall be given the opportunity to participate in physical education for at least one hour a week.
(2) The following provisions shall apply to the extent circumstances reasonably permit to a prisoner who is under 21 years of age –
(a) provision shall be made for the physical education of such a prisoner within the normal working week, as well as evening and weekend physical recreation; the physical education activities will be such as foster personal responsibility and the prisoner's interests and skills and encourage him to

make good use of his leisure on release; and (b) arrangements shall be made for each such prisoner who is a convicted prisoner to participate in physical education for two hours a week on average.
(3) In the case of a prisoner with a need for remedial physical activity, appropriate facilities will be provided.

30. Time in the open air
If the weather permits and subject to the need to maintain good order and discipline, a prisoner shall be given the opportunity to spend time in the open air at least once every day, for such period as may be reasonable in the circumstances.

31. – Work
(1) A convicted prisoner shall be required to do useful work for not more than 10 hours a day, and arrangements shall be made to allow prisoners to work, where possible, outside the cells and in association with one another.
(2) A registered medical practitioner or registered nurse working within the prison may excuse a prisoner from work on medical grounds.
(3) No prisoner shall be set to do work of a kind not authorised by the Secretary of State.
(4) No prisoner shall work in the service of another prisoner or an officer, or for the private benefit of any person, without the authority of the Secretary of State.
(5) An unconvicted prisoner shall be permitted, if he wishes, to work as if he were a convicted prisoner.
(6) Prisoners may be paid for their work at rates approved by the Secretary of State, either generally or in relation to particular cases.

31A. - Prescription of certain matters in respect of prisoners' earnings
(1) The amount prescribed for the purpose of section 1(1)(b) of the Prisoners' Earnings Act 1996 ("the 1996 Act") is £20.
(2) The percentage prescribed for the purpose of section 1(2) of the 1996 Act is 40%.
(3) All amounts deducted or levied under section 1 of the 1996 Act shall be applied for the purpose referred to in section 2(1)(a) of the 1996 Act.

(4) Victim Support is prescribed as a voluntary organisation to which payments may be made under section 2(1)(a) of the 1996 Act.".

EDUCATION AND LIBRARY
32. – Education
(1) Every prisoner able to profit from the education facilities provided at a prison shall be encouraged to do so.
(2) Educational classes shall (or during a coronavirus period shall so far as reasonably practicable) be arranged at every prison and, subject to any directions of the Secretary of State, reasonable facilities shall be afforded to prisoners who wish to do so to improve their education by training by distance learning, private study and recreational classes, in their spare time.
(3) Special attention shall be paid to the education and training of prisoners with special educational needs, and if necessary they shall be taught within the hours normally allotted to work.
(4) In the case of a prisoner of compulsory school age as defined in section 8 of the Education Act 1996, arrangements shall (or during a coronavirus period shall so far as reasonably practicable) be made for his participation in education or training courses for at least 15 hours a week within the normal working week.

33. Library
A library shall be provided in every prison and, subject to any directions of the Secretary of State, every prisoner shall be allowed to have library books and to exchange them.

COMMUNICATIONS
34. – Communications generally
(1) Without prejudice to sections 6 and 19 of the Prison Act 1952 and except as provided by these Rules, a prisoner shall not be permitted to communicate with any person outside the prison, or such person with him, except with the leave of the Secretary of State or as a privilege under rule 8.
(2) Notwithstanding paragraph (1) above, and except as otherwise provided in these Rules, the Secretary of State may impose any restriction or condition, either generally or in

a particular case, upon the communications to be permitted between a prisoner and other persons if he considers that the restriction or condition to be imposed –
(a) does not interfere with the convention rights of any person; or
(b)(i) is necessary on grounds specified in paragraph (3) below;
(ii) reliance on the grounds is compatible with the convention right to be interfered with; and
(iii) the restriction or condition is proportionate to what is sought to be achieved.
(3) The grounds referred to in paragraph (2) above are –
(a) the interests of national security;
(b) the prevention, detection, investigation or prosecution of crime;
(c) the interests of public safety;
(d) securing or maintaining prison security or good order and discipline in prison;
(e) the protection of health or morals;
(f) the protection of the reputation of others;
(g) maintaining the authority and impartiality of the judiciary; or
(h) the protection of the rights and freedoms of any person.
(4) Subject to paragraph (2) above, the Secretary of State may require that any visit, or class of visits, shall be held in facilities which include special features restricting or preventing physical contact between a prisoner and a visitor.
(5) Every visit to a prisoner shall take place within the sight of an officer or employee of the prison authorised for the purposes of this rule by the governor (in this rule referred to as an "authorised employee"), unless the Secretary of State otherwise directs, and for the purposes of this paragraph a visit to a prisoner shall be taken to take place within the sight of an officer or authorised employee if it can be seen by an officer or authorised employee by means of an overt closed circuit television system.
(6) Subject to rule 38, every visit to a prisoner shall take place within the hearing of an officer or authorised employee, unless the Secretary of State otherwise directs.
(7) The Secretary of State may give directions, either generally or in relation to any visit or class of visits, concerning the day and times when prisoners may be visited.
(8) In this rule –
(a) references to communications include references to communications during visits;
(b) references to restrictions and conditions upon communications include references to restrictions and conditions in relation to the length, duration and frequency of communications; and
(c) references to convention rights are to the convention rights within the meaning of the Human Rights Act 1998.

35. – Personal letters and visits
(1) Subject to paragraph (8), an unconvicted prisoner may send and receive as many letters and may receive as many visits as he wishes within such limits and subject to such conditions as the Secretary of State may direct, either generally or in a particular case.
(2) Subject to paragraphs (2A) and (8), a convicted prisoner shall be entitled –
(a) to send and to receive a letter on his reception into a prison and thereafter once a week; and
(b) to receive a visit twice in every period of four weeks, but only once in every such period if the Secretary of State so directs.
(2A) A prisoner serving a sentence of imprisonment to which an intermittent custody order relates shall be entitled to receive a visit only where the governor considers that desirable having regard to the extent to which he has been unable to meet with his friends and family in the periods during which he has been temporarily released on licence.
(2B) During a coronavirus period, the Secretary of State may, either generally or in a particular case, and for such periods of time as the Secretary of State considers necessary, suspend any entitlement to a visit under paragraph (1), (2)(b) and (2A), if the Secretary of State considers that such a suspension is necessary as a result of the effects, or likely effects, of coronavirus on or in relation to prisoners or the prison and proportionate to what is sought to be achieved.
(3) The governor may allow a prisoner an additional letter or visit as a privilege under rule 8 or where necessary for his welfare or

that of his family.
(4) The governor may allow a prisoner entitled to a visit to send and to receive a letter instead.
(5) The governor may defer the right of a prisoner to a visit until the expiration of any period of cellular confinement.
(6) The independent monitoring board may allow a prisoner an additional letter or visit in special circumstances, and may direct that a visit may extend beyond the normal duration.
(7) The Secretary of State may allow additional letters and visits in relation to any prisoner or class of prisoners.
(8) A prisoner shall not be entitled under this rule to receive a visit from:
(a) any person, whether or not a relative or friend, during any period of time that person is the subject of a prohibition imposed under rule 73; or
(b) any other person, other than a relative or friend, except with the leave of the Secretary of State.
(9) Any letter or visit under the succeeding provisions of these Rules shall not be counted as a letter or visit for the purposes of this rule.

35A. – Interception of communications
(1) The Secretary of State may give directions to any governor concerning the interception in a prison of any communication by any prisoner or class of prisoners if the Secretary of State considers that the directions are –
(a) necessary on grounds specified in paragraph (4) below; and
(b) proportionate to what is sought to be achieved.
(2) Subject to any directions given by the Secretary of State, the governor may make arrangements for any communication by a prisoner or class of prisoners to be intercepted in a prison by an officer or an employee of the prison authorised by the governor for the purposes of this rule (referred to in this rule as an "authorised employee") if he considers that the arrangements are –
(a) necessary on grounds specified in paragraph (4) below; and
(b) proportionate to what is sought to be achieved.
(2A) The governor may not make arrangements for interception of any communication between a prisoner and

(a) the prisoner's legal adviser; or
(b) any body or organisation with which the Secretary of State has made arrangements for the confidential handling of correspondence, unless the governor has reasonable cause to believe that the communication is being made with the intention of furthering a criminal purpose and unless authorised by any one of the following: the chief executive officer of the National Offender Management Service; the director responsible for national operational services of that service; or the duty director of that service.
(3) Any communication by a prisoner may, during the course of its transmission in a prison, be terminated by an officer or an authorised employee if he considers that to terminate the communication is –
(a) necessary on grounds specified in paragraph (4) below; and
(b) proportionate to what is sought to be achieved by the termination.
(4) The grounds referred to in paragraphs (1)(a), (2)(a) and (3)(a) above are -
(a) the interests of national security;
(b) the prevention, detection, investigation or prosecution of crime;
(c) the interests of public safety;
(d) securing or maintaining prison security or good order and discipline in prison;
(e) the protection of health or morals; or
(f) the protection of the rights and freedoms of any person.
(5) Any reference to the grounds specified in paragraph (4) above in relation to the interception of a communication by means of a telecommunications system in a prison, or the disclosure or retention of intercepted material from such a communication, shall be taken to be a reference to those grounds with the omission of sub-paragraph (f).
(6) For the purposes of this rule "interception"
(a) in relation to a communication by means of a telecommunications system, means any action taken in relation to the system or its operation so as to make some or all of the contents of the communications available, while being transmitted, to a person other than the sender or intended recipient of the communication; and the contents of a communication are to be taken to be made

available to a person while being transmitted where the contents of the communication, while being transmitted, are diverted or recorded so as to be available to a person subsequently; and

(b) in relation to any written or drawn communication, includes opening, reading, examining and copying the communication.

35B. – Permanent log of communications

(1) The governor may arrange for a permanent log to be kept of all communications by or to a prisoner.

(2) The log referred to in paragraph (1) above may include, in relation to a communication by means of a telecommunications system in a prison, a record of the destination, duration and cost of the communication and, in relation to any written or drawn communication, a record of the sender and addressee of the communication.

35C. – Disclosure of material

The governor may not disclose to any person who is not an officer of a prison or of the Secretary of State or an employee of the prison authorised by the governor for the purposes of this rule any intercepted material, information retained pursuant to rule 35B or material obtained by means of an overt closed circuit television system used during a visit unless –

(a) he considers that such disclosure is -

(i) necessary on grounds specified in rule 35A(4); and

(ii) proportionate to what is sought to be achieved by the disclosure; or

(b) (i) in the case of intercepted material or material obtained by means of an overt closed circuit television system used during a visit, all parties to the communication or visit consent to the disclosure; or

(ii) in the case of information retained pursuant to rule 35B, the prisoner to whose communication the information relates, consents to the disclosure.

35D. – Retention of material

(1) The governor shall not retain any intercepted material or material obtained by means of an overt closed circuit television system used during a visit for a period longer than 3 months beginning with the day on which the material was intercepted or obtained unless he is satisfied that continued retention of it is –

(a) necessary on grounds specified in rule 35A(4); and

(b) proportionate to what is sought to be achieved by the continued retention.

(2) Where such material is retained for longer than 3 months pursuant to paragraph (1) above the governor shall review its continued retention at periodic intervals until such time as it is no longer held by the governor.

(3) The first review referred to in paragraph (2) above shall take place not more than 3 months after the decision to retain the material taken pursuant to paragraph (1) above, and subsequent reviews shall take place not more than 3 months apart thereafter.

(4) If the governor, on a review conducted pursuant to paragraph (2) above or at any other time, is not satisfied that the continued retention of the material satisfies the requirements set out in paragraph (1) above, he shall arrange for the material to be destroyed.

36. Police interviews

A police officer may, on production of an order issued by or on behalf of a chief officer of police, interview any prisoner willing to see him.

37. Securing release

A person detained in prison in default of finding a surety, or of payment of a sum of money, may communicate with and be visited at any reasonable time on a weekday by any relative or friend to arrange for a surety or payment in order to secure his release from prison.

38. – Visits from legal advisers

(1) Where the legal adviser of a prisoner in any legal proceedings, civil or criminal, to which the prisoner is a party visits the prisoner, the legal adviser shall be afforded reasonable facilities for interviewing him in connection with those proceedings, and may do so out of hearing but in the sight of an officer.

(2) On such a visit, a prisoner's legal adviser may, subject to any directions given by the Secretary of State, interview the prisoner in

connection with any other legal business out of hearing but in the sight of an officer.

39. – Delivery and receipt of legally privileged material
(1) A prisoner may deliver to, or receive from, the prisoner's legal adviser and any court, either by post or during a legal visit under rule 38, any legally privileged material and such material may only be opened, read or stopped by the governor in accordance with the provisions of this rule.
(2) Material to which this rule applies may be opened if the governor has reasonable cause to believe that it contains an illicit enclosure and any such enclosures shall be dealt with in accordance with the other provision of these Rules.
(3) Material to which this rule applies may be opened, read and stopped if the governor has reasonable cause to believe its contents endanger prison security or the safety of others or are otherwise of a criminal nature.
(4) A prisoner shall be given the opportunity to be present when any material to which this rule applies is opened and shall be informed if it or any enclosure is to be read or stopped.
(5) A prisoner shall on request be provided with any writing materials necessary for the purposes of paragraph (1).
(6) In this rule, "court" includes the European Commission of Human Rights, the European Court of Human Rights and the European Court of Justice; and "illicit enclosure" includes any article possession of which has not been authorised in accordance with the other provisions of these Rules and any material to or from a person other than the prisoner concerned, his legal adviser or a court.

REMOVAL, SEARCH, RECORD AND PROPERTY
40. – Custody outside prison
(1) A person being taken to or from a prison in custody shall be exposed as little as possible to public observation, and proper care shall be taken to protect him from curiosity and insult.
(2) A prisoner required to be taken in custody anywhere outside a prison shall be kept in the custody of an officer appointed or a police officer.
(3) A prisoner required to be taken in custody to any court shall, when he appears before the court, wear his own clothing or ordinary civilian clothing provided by the governor.

41. – Search
(1) Every prisoner shall be searched when taken into custody by an officer, on his reception into a prison and subsequently as the governor thinks necessary or as the Secretary of State may direct.
(2) A prisoner shall be searched in as seemly a manner as is consistent with discovering anything concealed.
(3) No prisoner shall be stripped and searched in the sight of another prisoner, or in the sight of a person of the opposite sex.

42. – Record and photograph
(1) A personal record of each prisoner shall be prepared and maintained in such manner as the Secretary of State may direct.
(2) Every prisoner may be photographed on reception and subsequently, but no copy of the photograph or any other personal record shall be given to any person not authorised to receive it.
(2A) In this rule "personal record" may include personal information and biometric records (such as fingerprints or other physical measurements).

43. – Prisoners' property
(1) Subject to any directions of the Secretary of State, an unconvicted prisoner may have supplied to him at his expense and retain for his own use books, newspapers, writing materials and other means of occupation, except any that appears objectionable to the independent monitoring board or, pending consideration by them, to the governor.
(2) Anything, other than cash, which a prisoner has at a prison and which he is not allowed to retain for his own use shall be taken into the governor's custody. An inventory of a prisoner's property shall be kept, and he shall be required to sign it, after having a proper opportunity to see that it is correct.
(2A) Where a prisoner is serving a sentence of imprisonment to which an intermittent custody order relates, an inventory as referred to in paragraph (2) shall only be kept where

the value of that property is estimated by the governor to be in excess of £100.
(3) Any cash which a prisoner has at a prison shall be paid into an account under the control of the governor and the prisoner shall be credited with the amount in the books of the prison.
(4) Any article belonging to a prisoner which remains unclaimed for a period of more than one year after he leaves prison, or dies, may be sold or otherwise disposed of; and the net proceeds of any sale shall be paid to the National Association for the Care and Resettlement of Offenders, for its general purposes.
(5) The governor may confiscate any unauthorised article found in the possession of a prisoner after his reception into prison, or concealed or deposited anywhere within a prison.

44. – Money and articles received by post
(1) Any money or other article (other than a letter or other communication) sent to a convicted prisoner through the post shall be dealt with in accordance with the provisions of this rule, and the prisoner shall be informed of the manner in which it is dealt with.
(2) Any cash shall, at the discretion of the governor, be –
(a) dealt with in accordance with rule 43(3);
(b) returned to the sender; or
(c) in a case where the sender's name and address are not known, paid to the National Association for the Care and Resettlement of Offenders, for its general purposes:
Provided that in relation to a prisoner committed to prison in default of payment of any sum of money, the prisoner shall be informed of the receipt of the cash and, unless he objects to its being so applied, it shall be applied in or towards the satisfaction of the amount due from him.
(3) Any security for money shall, at the discretion of the governor, be –
(a) delivered to the prisoner or placed with his property at the prison;
(b) returned to the sender; or
(c) encashed and the cash dealt with in accordance with paragraph (2).
(4) Any other article to which this rule applies shall, at the discretion of the governor, be –
(a) delivered to the prisoner or placed with his property at the prison;
(b) returned to the sender; or
(c) in a case where the sender's name and address are not known or the article is of such a nature that it would be unreasonable to return it, sold or otherwise disposed of, and the net proceeds of any sale applied in accordance with paragraph (2).

SPECIAL CONTROL, SUPERVISION AND RESTRAINT AND DRUG TESTING

45. – Removal from association
(1) Where it appears desirable, for the maintenance of good order or discipline or in his own interests, that a prisoner should not associate with other prisoners, either generally or for particular purposes, the governor may arrange for the prisoner's removal from association for up to 72 hours.
(2) Removal for more than 72 hours may be authorised by the governor in writing who may authorise a further period of up to 14 days.
(2A) Such authority may be renewed for subsequent periods of up to 14 days.
(2B) But the governor must obtain leave from the Secretary of State in writing to authorise removal under paragraph (2A) where the period in total amounts to more than 42 days starting with the date the prisoner was removed under paragraph (1).
(2C) The Secretary of State may only grant leave for a maximum period of 42 days, but such leave may be renewed for subsequent periods of up to 42 days by the Secretary of State.
(3) The governor may arrange at his discretion for a prisoner removed under this rule to resume association with other prisoners at any time.
(3A) In giving authority under paragraphs (2) and (2A) and in exercising the discretion under paragraph (3), the governor must fully consider any recommendation that the prisoner resumes association on medical grounds made by a registered medical practitioner or registered nurse working within the prison.
(4) This rule shall not apply to a prisoner the subject of a direction given under rule 46(1).

46. – Close supervision centres
(1) Where it appears desirable, for the maintenance of good order or discipline or to

ensure the safety of officers, prisoners or any other person, that a prisoner should not associate with other prisoners, either generally or for particular purposes, the Secretary of State may direct the prisoner's removal from association accordingly and his placement in a close supervision centre of a prison.

(2) A direction given under paragraph (1) shall be for a period not exceeding one month, or, during a coronavirus period, three months, but may be renewed from time to time for a like period, and shall continue to apply notwithstanding any transfer of a prisoner from one prison to another.

(3) The Secretary of State may direct that such a prisoner as aforesaid shall resume association with other prisoners, either within a close supervision centre or elsewhere.

(4) In exercising any discretion under this rule, the Secretary of State shall take account of any relevant medical considerations which are known to him.

(5) A close supervision centre is any cell or other part of a prison designated by the Secretary of State for holding prisoners who are subject to a direction given under paragraph (1).

46A. Separation centres

(1) Where it appears desirable, on one or more of the grounds specified in paragraph (2), the Secretary of State may direct that a prisoner be placed in a separation centre within a prison.

(2) The grounds referred to in paragraph (1) are—
(a) the interests of national security;
(b) to prevent the commission, preparation or instigation of an act of terrorism, a terrorism offence, or an offence with a terrorist connection, whether in a prison or otherwise;
(c) to prevent the dissemination of views or beliefs that might encourage or induce others to commit any such act or offence, whether in a prison or otherwise, or to protect or safeguard others from such views or beliefs, or
(d) to prevent any political, religious, racial or other views or beliefs being used to undermine good order and discipline in a prison.

(3) A direction given under paragraph (1) must be reviewed every three months.

(4) The Secretary of State may, at any time, revoke a direction given under paragraph (1) and direct that the prisoner be removed from the separation centre.

(5) In exercising any discretion under this rule, the Secretary of State must take account of any known relevant medical considerations.

(6) In this rule—
"act of terrorism" includes anything constituting an action taken for the purposes of terrorism within the meaning of section 1 of the Terrorism Act 2000(3);
"offence with a terrorist connection" means an offence listed in Schedule 2 of the Counter-Terrorism Act 2008(4), which also satisfies the definition in section 93 of that Act;
"separation centre" means any part of a prison for the time being used for holding prisoners who are subject to a direction under paragraph (1);
"terrorism offence" means an offence listed in section 41(1) of the Counter-Terrorism Act 2008.

47. – Use of force

(1) An officer in dealing with a prisoner shall not use force unnecessarily and, when the application of force to a prisoner is necessary, no more force than is necessary shall be used.

(2) No officer shall act deliberately in a manner calculated to provoke a prisoner.

48. – Temporary confinement

(1) The governor may order a refractory or violent prisoner to be confined temporarily in a special cell, but a prisoner shall not be so confined as a punishment, or after he has ceased to be refractory or violent.

(2) A prisoner shall not be confined in a special cell for longer than 24 hours without a direction in writing given by an officer of the Secretary of State. Such a direction shall state the grounds for the confinement and the time during which it may continue.

49. – Restraints

(1) The governor may order a prisoner to be put under restraint where this is necessary to prevent the prisoner from injuring himself or others, damaging property or creating a disturbance.

(2) Notice of such an order shall be given without delay to a member of the independent

monitoring board, and to a registered medical practitioner or to a registered nurse working within the prison.

(3) On receipt of the notice, the registered medical practitioner or registered nurse referred to in paragraph (2), shall inform the governor whether there are any medical reasons why the prisoner should not be put under restraint. The governor shall give effect to any recommendation which may be made under this paragraph.

(4) A prisoner shall not be kept under restraint longer than necessary, nor shall he be so kept for longer than 24 hours without a direction in writing given by an officer of the Secretary of State (not being an officer of a prison). Such a direction shall state the grounds for the restraint and the time during which it may continue.

(5) Particulars of every case of restraint under the foregoing provisions of this rule shall be forthwith recorded.

(6) Except as provided by this rule no prisoner shall be put under restraint otherwise than for safe custody during removal, or on medical grounds by direction of a registered medical practitioner or of a registered nurse working within the prison. No prisoner shall be put under restraint as a punishment.

(7) Any means of restraint shall be of a pattern authorised by the Secretary of State, and shall be used in such manner and under such conditions as the Secretary of State may direct.

50. – Compulsory testing for controlled drugs or specified drugs.

(1) This rule applies where an officer, acting under the powers conferred by section 16A of the Prison Act 1952 (power to test prisoners for drugs), requires a prisoner to provide a sample for the purpose of ascertaining whether he has any controlled drug in his body.

(2) In this rule "sample" means a sample of urine or any other description of sample specified in the authorisation by the governor for the purposes of section 16A of the Prison Act 1952.

(3) When requiring a prisoner to provide a sample, an officer shall, so far as is reasonably practicable, inform the prisoner:

(a) that he is being required to provide a sample in accordance with section 16A of the Prison Act 1952; and

(b) that a refusal to provide a sample may lead to disciplinary proceedings being brought against him.

(4) An officer shall require a prisoner to provide a fresh sample, free from any adulteration.

(5) An officer requiring a sample shall make such arrangements and give the prisoner such instructions for its provision as may be reasonably necessary in order to prevent or detect its adulteration or falsification.

(6) A prisoner who is required to provide a sample may be kept apart from other prisoners for a period not exceeding one hour to enable arrangements to be made for the provision of the sample.

(7) A prisoner who is unable to provide a sample of urine when required to do so may be kept apart from other prisoners until he has provided the required sample, save that a prisoner may not be kept apart under this paragraph for a period of more than 5 hours.

(8) A prisoner required to provide a sample of urine shall be afforded such degree of privacy for the purposes of providing the sample as may be compatible with the need to prevent or detect any adulteration or falsification of the sample; in particular a prisoner shall not be required to provide such a sample in the sight of a person of the opposite sex.

50A. – Observation of prisoners by means of an overt closed circuit television system

(1) Without prejudice to his other powers to supervise the prison, prisoners and other persons in the prison, whether by use of an overt closed circuit television system or otherwise, the governor may make arrangements for any prisoner to be placed under constant observation by means of an overt closed circuit television system while the prisoner is in a cell or other place in the prison if he considers that -

(a) such supervision is necessary for –

(i) the health and safety of the prisoner or any other person;

(ii) the prevention, detection, investigation or prosecution of crime; or

(iii) securing or maintaining prison security or good order and discipline in the prison; and

(b) it is proportionate to what is sought to

be achieved.
(2) If an overt cctv system is used for the purposes of this rule, the provisions of rules 35C and 35D shall apply to any material obtained.

50B. – Compulsory testing for alcohol
(1) This rule applies where an officer, acting under an authorisation in force under section 16B of the Prison Act 1952 (power to test for alcohol), requires a prisoner to provide a sample for the purpose of ascertaining whether he has alcohol in his body.
(2) When requiring a prisoner to provide a sample an officer shall, so far as is reasonably practicable, inform the prisoner –
  (a) that he is being required to provide a sample in accordance with section 16B of the Prison Act 1952; and
  (b) that a refusal to provide a sample may lead to disciplinary proceedings being brought against him.
(3) An officer requiring a sample shall make such arrangements and give the prisoner such instructions for its provision as may be reasonably necessary in order to prevent or detect its adulteration or falsification.
(4) Subject to paragraph (5) a prisoner who is required to provide a sample may be kept apart from other prisoners for a period not exceeding one hour to enable arrangements to be made for the provision of the sample.
(5) A prisoner who is unable to provide a sample of urine when required to do so may be kept apart from other prisoners until he has provided the required sample, except that a prisoner may not be kept apart under this paragraph for a period of more than 5 hours.
(6) A prisoner required to provide a sample of urine shall be afforded such degree of privacy for the purposes of providing the sample as may be compatible with the need to prevent or detect any adulteration or falsification of the sample; in particular a prisoner shall not be required to provide such a sample in the sight of a person of the opposite sex.

OFFENCES AGAINST DISCIPLINE
51. Offences against discipline
A prisoner is guilty of an offence against discipline if he –

(1) commits any assault;
(1A) commits any racially aggravated assault;
(2) detains any person against his will;
(3) denies access to any part of the prison to any officer or any person (other than a prisoner) who is at the prison for the purpose of working there;
(4) fights with any person;
(5) intentionally endangers the health or personal safety of others or, by his conduct, is reckless whether such health or personal safety is endangered;
(6) intentionally obstructs an officer in the execution of his duty, or any person (other than a prisoner) who is at the prison for the purpose of working there, in the performance of his work;
(7) escapes or absconds from prison or from legal custody;
(8) fails to comply with any condition upon which he is temporarily released under rule 9 *or rule 9A*;
(9) is found with any substance in his urine which demonstrates that a controlled drug has, whether in prison or while on temporary release under rule 9 *or rule 9A*, been administered to him by himself or by another person (but subject to rule 52);
(10) is intoxicated as a consequence of consuming any alcoholic beverage (but subject to rule 52A);
(11) consumes any alcoholic beverage whether or not provided to him by another person (but subject to rule 52A);
(12) has in his possession –
  (a) any unauthorised article, or
  (b) a greater quantity of any article than he is authorised to have;
(13) sells or delivers to any person any unauthorised article;
(14) sells or, without permission, delivers to any person any article which he is allowed to have only for his own use;
(15) takes improperly any article belonging to another person or to a prison;
(16) intentionally or recklessly sets fire to any part of a prison or any other property, whether or not his own;
(17) destroys or damages any part of a prison or any other property, other than his own;
(17A) causes racially aggravated damage to,

or destruction of, any part of a prison or any other property, other than his own;

(18) absents himself from any place he is required to be or is present at any place where he is not authorised to be;

(19) is disrespectful to any officer, or any person (other than a prisoner) who is at the prison for the purpose of working there, or any person visiting a prison;

(20) uses threatening, abusive or insulting words or behaviour;

(20A) uses threatening, abusive or insulting racist words or behaviour;

(21) intentionally fails to work properly or, being required to work, refuses to do so;

(22) disobeys any lawful order;

(23) disobeys or fails to comply with any rule or regulation applying to him;

(24) receives any controlled drug or specified drugs or, without the consent of an officer, any other article, during the course of a visit (not being an interview such as is mentioned in rule 38);

(24A) displays, attaches or draws on any part of a prison, or on any other property, threatening, abusive or insulting racist words, drawings, symbols or other material;

(25)

(a) attempts to commit,

(b) incites another prisoner to commit, or

(c) assists another prisoner to commit or to attempt to commit, any of the foregoing offences.

51A. Interpretation of rule 51

(2) For the purposes of rule 51 words, behaviour or material are racist if they demonstrate, or are motivated (wholly or partly) by, hostility to members of a racial group (whether identifiable or not) based on their membership (or presumed membership) of a racial group, and "membership", "presumed", "racial group" and "racially aggravated" shall have the meanings assigned to them by section 28 of the Crime and Disorder Act 1998(a).

52. Defences to rule 51(9)

It shall be a defence for a prisoner charged with an offence under rule 51(9) to show that:

(a) the controlled drug or specified drugs had been, prior to its administration, lawfully in his possession for his use or was administered to him in the course of a lawful supply of the drug to him by another person;

(b) the controlled drug or specified drugs was administered by or to him in circumstances in which he did not know and had no reason to suspect that such a drug was being administered; or

(c) the controlled drug was administered by or to him under duress or to him without his consent in circumstances where it was not reasonable for him to have resisted.

52A. Defences to rule 51(10) and rule 51(11)

It shall be a defence for a prisoner charged with an offence under rule 51(10) or (11) to show that –

(a) the alcohol was consumed by him in circumstances in which he did not know and had no reason to suspect that he was consuming alcohol;

(b) the alcohol was consumed by him without his consent in circumstances where it was not reasonable for him to have resisted;

53. – Disciplinary charges

(1) Where a prisoner is to be charged with an offence against discipline, the charge shall be laid as soon as possible and, save in exceptional circumstances, within 48 hours of the discovery of the offence.

(2) Every charge shall be inquired into by the governor or, as the case may be, the adjudicator.

(3) Every charge shall be first inquired into not later, save in exceptional circumstances or in accordance with rule 55A(5), or 53B(3) than:

(a) where it is inquired into by the governor, the next day, not being a Sunday or public holiday, after it is laid;

(b) where it is referred to the adjudicator under rule 53A(2) or 60(3)(b), 28 days after it is so referred.

(4) A prisoner who is to be charged with an offence against discipline may be kept apart from other prisoners pending the governor's first inquiry or determination under rule 53A.

53A. – Determination of mode of inquiry

(1) Before inquiring into a charge the governor shall determine (i) whether the charge is so serious that additional days should be awarded for the offence if the

prisoner is found guilty, or (ii) whether it is necessary or expedient for some other reason for the charge to be inquired into by the adjudicator

(2) Where the governor determines:

(a) that it is so serious or that it is necessary or expedient for some other reason for the charge to be inquired into by the adjudicator, he shall:

(i) refer the charge to the adjudicator forthwith for him to inquire into it;

(ii) refer any other charge arising out of the same incident to the adjudicator forthwith for him to inquire into it; and

(iii) inform the prisoner who has been charged that he has done so;

(b) that it is not so serious or that it is not necessary or expedient for some other reason for the charge to be inquired into by the adjudicator, he shall proceed to inquire into the charge.

(3) If:

(a) at any time during an inquiry into a charge by the governor, including an inquiry by the governor under rule 53B(2) or

(b) following such an inquiry, after the governor has found the prisoner guilty of an offence but before he has imposed a punishment for that offence, it appears to the governor either that the charge is so serious that additional days should be awarded for the offence if (where sub-paragraph (a)) the prisoner is found guilty or that it is necessary or expedient for some other reason for the charge to be inquired into by the adjudicator, the governor shall act in accordance with paragraph (2)(a)(i) to (iii) and the adjudicator shall first inquire into any charge referred to him under this paragraph not later than, save in exceptional circumstances, 28 days after the charge was referred.

Determination of mode of inquiry in a coronavirus period

53B.—(1) This rule applies during a coronavirus period.

(2) Where a charge has been referred to an adjudicator under rule 53A or rule 60(3) (b) and the Senior District Judge (Chief Magistrate) considers that because of the effects of coronavirus it is not reasonably practicable for the charge to be—

(a) first inquired into by an adjudicator in accordance with rule 53(3)(b) or rule 53A(3); or

(b) continued to be inquired into by an adjudicator, the Senior District Judge (Chief Magistrate) may refer the charge back to the governor as soon as possible for the governor to inquire into it.

(3) A charge referred back to the governor under paragraph (2) shall be first inquired into by the governor not later, save in exceptional circumstances, than 14 days after the Senior District Judge (Chief Magistrate) referred the charge back.

(4) A charge inquired into by the governor under paragraph (2) is not to be treated as one being inquired into by an adjudicator, and accordingly the governor cannot impose a punishment under rule 55A (adjudicator's punishments).

(5) This rule applies to a prisoner who has been charged with having committed an offence against discipline and referred to an adjudicator under rule 53A or 60(3)(b) before the date on which the rule came into force in the same way as it applies to a prisoner who has been charged with having committed an offence against discipline on or after that date.

54. – Rights of prisoners charged

(1) Where a prisoner is charged with an offence against discipline, he shall be informed of the charge as soon as possible and, in any case, before the time when it is inquired into by the governor or, as the case may be, the adjudicator.

(2) At an inquiry into a charge against a prisoner he shall be given a full opportunity of hearing what is alleged against him and of presenting his own case.

(3) At an inquiry into a charge which has been referred to the adjudicator, the prisoner who has been charged shall be given the opportunity to be legally represented.

55. – Governor's punishments

(1) If he finds a prisoner guilty of an offence against discipline the governor may, subject to paragraph (2) and to rule 57, impose one or more of the following punishments:

(a) caution;

(b) forfeiture for a period not exceeding 42

days of any of the privileges under rule 8;
(c) exclusion from associated work for a period not exceeding 21 days;
(d) stoppage of or deduction from earnings for a period not exceeding 84 days;
(e) cellular confinement for a period not exceeding 21 days;
(f) [...] Revoked (August 15, 2002)
(g) in the case of a prisoner otherwise entitled to them, forfeiture for any period of the right, under rule 43(1), to have the articles there mentioned.
(h) removal from his wing or living unit for a period of 28 days.
(2) A caution shall not be combined with any other punishment for the same charge.
(3) If a prisoner is found guilty of more than one charge arising out of an incident, punishments under this rule may be ordered to run consecutively but, in the case of a punishment of cellular confinement, the total period shall not exceed 21 days.
(4) In imposing a punishment under this rule, the governor shall take into account any guidelines that the Secretary of State may from time to time issue as to the level of punishment that should normally be imposed for a particular offence against discipline.

55A. – Adjudicator's punishments
(1) If he finds a prisoner guilty of an offence against discipline the adjudicator may, subject to paragraph (2) and to rule 57, impose one or more of the following punishments:
(a) any of the punishments mentioned in rule 55(1);
(b) in the case of a fixed-term prisoner, an award of additional days not exceeding 42 days.

Requirement to pay for damage to prison property
55AB.—(1) This rule applies where a prisoner is found guilty of an offence under rule 51(17) or 51(17A) in respect of destroying or damaging any part of a prison or any other property belonging to a prison ("the relevant disciplinary offence").
(2) The governor or, as the case may be, the adjudicator must require the prisoner to pay for the cost of making good the damage from, or replacing any property destroyed as a result of, the commission of the relevant disciplinary offence.
(3) A requirement imposed under paragraph (2) is referred to in this rule and in rules 55B, 61 and 61A as a "compensation requirement".
(4) The amount required to be paid under a compensation requirement must not exceed the cost of making good the damage from, or replacing any property destroyed as a result of, the commission of the relevant disciplinary offence and, in any event, must not exceed £2,000.
(5) A compensation requirement may be imposed instead of or in addition to any punishment imposed under rule 55 or 55A.
(6) A compensation requirement ceases to have effect after two years from the date on which it was imposed regardless of whether or not the full amount has been paid.
(2) A caution shall not be combined with any other punishment for the same charge.
(3) If a prisoner is found guilty of more than one charge arising out of an incident, punishments under this rule may be ordered to run consecutively but, in the case of an award of additional days, the total period added shall not exceed 42 days and, in the case of a punishment of cellular confinement, the total period shall not exceed 21 days.
(4) This rule applies to a prisoner who has been charged with having committed an offence against discipline before the date on which the rule came into force, in the same way as it applies to a prisoner who has been charged with having committed an offence against discipline on or after that date, provided the charge is referred to the adjudicator no later than 60 days after that date.
(5) Rule 53(3) shall not apply to a charge where, by virtue of paragraph (4), this rule applies to the prisoner who has been charged..

55B. – Review of adjudicator's punishment
(1) A reviewer means a Senior District Judge (Chief Magistrate) approved by the Lord Chancellor for the purposes of conducting a review under this rule or any deputy of such a judge as nominated by that judge.
(2) Where an adjudicator imposes a punishment under rule 55A(1), a

compensation requirement under rule 55AB(2) or both, a prisoner may, within 14 days of receipt of the punishment, or the imposition of the compensation requirement, whichever is late, request in writing that a reviewer conducts a review.
(3) The review must be commenced within 14 days of receipt of the request and must be conducted on the papers alone.
(4) The review may be of the punishment, the compensation requirement or both (whether or not the prisoner requested a review of both) but must not be a review of the finding of guilt under rule 55A.
(5) On completion of the review, if it appears to the reviewer that the imposition of the punishment, the compensation requirement or both was manifestly unreasonable he may do such of the following as he considers appropriate –
(a) reduce the number of any additional days awarded;
(b) for whatever punishment has been imposed by the adjudicator, substitute another punishment which is, in his opinion, less severe;
(c) quash the punishment entirely.
(d) reduce the amount of the compensation requirement.
(6) A prisoner requesting a review shall serve any additional days awarded under rule 55A(1)(b) unless and until they are reduced.

56. – Forfeiture of remission to be treated as an award of additional days
(1) In this rule, "existing prisoner" and "existing licensee" have the meanings assigned to them by paragraph 8(1) of Schedule 12 to the Criminal Justice Act 1991.
(2) In relation to any existing prisoner or existing licensee who has forfeited any remission of his sentence, the provisions of Part II of the Criminal Justice Act 1991 shall apply as if he had been awarded such number of additional days as equals the numbers of days of remission which he has forfeited.

57. –Offences committed by young persons
(1) In the case of an offence against discipline committed by an inmate who was under the age of 21 when the offence was committed (other than an offender in relation to whom the Secretary of State has given a direction under section 13(1) of the Criminal Justice Act 1982 that he shall be treated as if he had been sentenced to imprisonment) rule 55 or, as the case may be, rule 55A shall have effect, but –
(a) the maximum period of forfeiture of privileges under rule 8 shall be 21 days;
(b) the maximum period of stoppage of or deduction from earnings shall be 42 days;
(c) the maximum period of cellular confinement shall be ten days
(d) the maximum period of removal from his cell or living unit shall be 21 days.
(2) In the case of an inmate who has been sentenced to a term of youth custody or detention in a young offender institution, and by virtue of a direction of the Secretary of State under section 99 of the Powers of Criminal Courts (Sentencing) Act 2000, is treated as if he had been sentenced to imprisonment for that term, any punishment imposed on him for an offence against discipline before the said direction was given shall, if it has not been exhausted or remitted, continue to have effect:
(a) if imposed by a governor, as it made pursuant to rule 55;
(b) if imposed by an adjudicator, as if made pursuant to rule 55A.

58. Cellular confinement
Before deciding whether to impose a punishment of cellular confinement the governor, adjudicator or reviewer shall first enquire of a registered medical practitioner or registered nurse working within the prison, as to whether there are any medical reasons why the punishment is unsuitable and shall take this advice into account when making his decision.

59. – Prospective award of additional days
(1) Subject to paragraph (2), where an offence against discipline is committed by a prisoner who is detained only on remand, additional days may be awarded by the adjudicator notwithstanding that the prisoner has not (or had not at the time of the offence) been sentenced.
(2) An award of additional days under paragraph (1) shall have effect only if the prisoner in question subsequently becomes a

fixed-term prisoner whose sentence is reduced, under section 67 of the Criminal Justice Act 1967 or section 240 of the 2003 Act, by a period which includes the time when the offence against discipline was committed.

59A. Removal from a cell or living unit
Following the imposition of a punishment of removal from his cell or living unit, a prisoner shall be accommodated in a separate part of the prison under such restrictions of earnings and activities as the Secretary of State may direct.

60. – Suspended punishments
(1) Subject to any directions given by the Secretary of State, the power to impose a disciplinary punishment (other than a caution) shall include power to direct that the punishment is not to take effect unless, during a period specified in the direction (not being more than six months from the date of the direction), the prisoner commits another offence against discipline and a direction is given under paragraph (2).
(2) Where a prisoner commits an offence against discipline during the period specified in a direction given under paragraph (1) the person dealing with that offence may –
(a) direct that the suspended punishment shall take effect;
(b) reduce the period or amount of the suspended punishment and direct that it shall take effect as so reduced;
(c) vary the original direction by substituting for the period specified a period expiring not later than six months from the date of variation; or
(d) give no direction with respect to the suspended punishment.
(3) Where an award of additional days has been suspended under paragraph (1) and a prisoner is charged with committing an offence against discipline during the period specified in a direction given under that paragraph, the governor shall either:
(a) inquire into the charge and give no direction with respect to the suspended award; or
(b) refer the charge to the adjudicator for him to inquire into it

61. – Remission and mitigation of punishments, variation of compensation requirements and quashing of findings of guilt
(1) Except in the case of a finding of guilt made, or a punishment imposed, by an adjudicator under rule 55A(1), the Secretary of State may quash any finding of guilt and may remit any punishment or mitigate it either by reducing it or by substituting another award which is, in his opinion, less severe.
(1A) Where a compensation requirement has been imposed by a governor under rule 55AB(2), the Secretary of State may reduce the amount of the requirement
(2) Subject to any directions given by the Secretary of State, the governor may, on the grounds of good behaviour, remit or mitigate any punishment already imposed by an adjudicator or governor.

61A.—(1) Where a compensation requirement has been imposed under rule 55AB(2), the governor may debit any amount of money with which the prisoner has been credited in the books of the prison under rule 43(3) in order to recover the whole or part of the amount required to be paid under the compensation requirement.
(2) The amount debited under paragraph (1) on any occasion must not be such as to reduce below £5 the amount with which the prisoner is credited in the books of the prison under rule 43(3).
(3) Where—
(a) a compensation requirement has been imposed under rule 60AB(2) of the Young Offender Rules 2000(1), and
(b) the person against whom the compensation requirement was imposed is detained in a prison,
the compensation order may be enforced under paragraph (1) as if it was a compensation requirement imposed under rule 55AB(2).

PART III: OFFICERS OF PRISONS
62. – General duty of officers
(1) It shall be the duty of every officer to conform to these Rules and the rules and regulations of the prison, to assist and support the governor in their maintenance and to obey

his lawful instructions.
(2) An officer shall inform the governor promptly of any abuse or impropriety which comes to his knowledge.

63. Gratuities forbidden
No officer shall receive any unauthorised fee, gratuity or other consideration in connection with his office.

64. Search of officers
An officer shall submit himself to be searched in the prison if the governor so directs.
Any such search shall be conducted in as seemly a manner as is consistent with discovering anything concealed.

65. – Transactions with prisoners
(1) No officer shall take part in any business or pecuniary transaction with or on behalf of a prisoner without the leave of the Secretary of State.
(2) No officer shall without authority bring in or take out, or attempt to bring in or take out, or knowingly allow to be brought in or taken out, to or for a prisoner, or deposit in any place with intent that it shall come into the possession of a prisoner, any article whatsoever.

66. Contact with former prisoners
No officer shall, without the knowledge of the governor, communicate with any person whom he knows to be a former prisoner or a relative or friend of a prisoner or former prisoner.

67. – Communications to the press
(1) No officer shall make, directly or indirectly, any unauthorised communication to a representative of the press or any other person concerning matters which have become known to him in the course of his duty.
(2) No officer shall, without authority, publish any matter or make any public pronouncement relating to the administration of any institution to which the Prison Act 1952 applies or to any of its inmates.

68. Code of discipline
The Secretary of State may approve a code of discipline to have effect in relation to officers, or such classes of officers as it may specify, setting out the offences against discipline, the awards which may be made in respect of them and the procedure for dealing with charges.

69. Emergencies
Where any constable or member of the armed forces of the Crown is employed by reason of any emergency to assist the governor of a prison by performing duties ordinarily performed by an officer of a prison, any reference in Part II of these Rules to such an officer (other than a governor) shall be construed as including a reference to a constable or a member of the armed forces of the Crown so employed.

PART IV: PERSONS HAVING ACCESS TO A PRISON

70. Prohibited articles
No person shall, without authority, convey into or throw into or deposit in a prison, or convey or throw out of a prison, or convey to a prisoner, or deposit in any place with intent that it shall come into the possession of a prisoner, any article whatever. Anything so conveyed, thrown or deposited may be confiscated by the governor.

70A. List C Articles: A List C article is any article or substance in the following list— (a) tobacco; (b) money; (c) clothing; (d) food; (e) drink; (f) letters; (g) paper; (h) books; (i) tools; (j) information technology equipment; "(k)electronic cigarettes; (l)matches; (m)lighters.

71. – Control of persons and vehicles
(1) Any person or vehicle entering or leaving a prison may be stopped, examined and searched and in addition any such person may be photographed, fingerprinted or required to submit to other physical measurement.
(1A) Any such search of a person shall be carried out in as seemly a manner as is consistent with discovering anything concealed about the person or their belongings.
(2) The governor may direct the removal from a prison of any person who does not leave on being required to do so.

72. – Viewing of prisons
(1) No outside person shall be permitted to view a prison unless authorised by statute or the Secretary of State.

(2) No person viewing the prison shall be permitted to take a photograph, make a sketch or communicate with a prisoner unless authorised by statute or the Secretary of State.

73. – Visitors

(1) Without prejudice to any other powers to prohibit or restrict entry to prisons, or his powers under rules 34 and 35, the Secretary of State may prohibit visits by a person to a prison or to a prisoner in a prison for such periods of time as he considers necessary if the Secretary of State considers that such a prohibition is –
(a) necessary on grounds specified in rule 35A(4); and
(b) is proportionate to what is sought to be achieved by the prohibition.
(1A) During a coronavirus period, the Secretary of State may prohibit visits by all persons or classes of persons to a prison or to a prisoner in a prison for such periods of time as the Secretary of State considers necessary, if the Secretary of State considers that such prohibition is necessary as a result of the effects, or likely effects, of coronavirus on or in relation to prisoners or the prison.
(2) Paragraphs (1) and (1A) shall not apply in relation to any visit to a prison or prisoner by a member of the independent monitoring board of the prison, or justice of the peace, or to prevent any visit by a legal adviser for the purposes of an interview under rule 38 or visit allowed by the board of visitors under rule 35(6).

PART V: INDEPENDENT MONITORING BOARD

74. – Disqualification for membership

Any person, directly or indirectly interested in any contract for the supply of goods or services to a prison, shall not be a member of the independent monitoring board for that prison and any member who becomes so interested in such a contract shall vacate office as a member.

75. – Independent monitoring board

(1) A member of the board of visitors for a prison appointed by the Secretary of State under section 6(2) of the Prison Act 1952 shall subject to paragraphs (3) and (4) hold office for three years, or such lesser period as the Secretary of State may appoint.
(2) A member – (a) appointed for the first time to the independent monitoring board for a particular prison; or
(b) reappointed to the board following a gap of a year or more in his membership of it,
shall, during the period of 12 months following the date on which he is so appointed or (as the case may be) reappointed, undertake such training as may reasonably be required by the Secretary of State.
(3) The Secretary of State may terminate the appointment of a member if he is satisfied that
(a) he has failed satisfactorily to perform his duties;
(b) he has failed to undertake training he has been required to undertake under paragraph (2), by the end of the period specified in that paragraph;
(c) he is by reason of physical or mental illness, or for any other reason, incapable of carrying out his duties;
(d) he has been convicted of such a criminal offence, or his conduct has been such, that it is not in the Secretary of State's opinion fitting that he should remain a member; or
(e) there is, or appears to be or could appear to be, any conflict of interest between the member performing his duties as a member and any interest of that member, whether personal, financial or otherwise.
(4) Where the Secretary of State:
(a) has reason to suspect that a member of the independent monitoring board for a prison may have so conducted himself that his appointment may be liable to be terminated under paragraph (3)(a) or (d); and
(b) is of the opinion that the suspected conduct is of such a serious nature that the member cannot be permitted to continue to perform his functions as a member of the board pending the completion of the Secretary of State's investigations into the matter and any decision as to whether the member's appointment should be terminated, he may suspend the member from office for such period or periods as he may reasonably require in order to complete his investigations and determine whether or not the

appointment of the member should be so terminated; and a member so suspended shall not, during the period of his suspension, be regarded as being a member of the board, other than for the purposes of this paragraph and paragraphs (1) and (3).
(5) A board shall have a chairman and a vice chairman who shall be members of the board.
(6) The Secretary of State shall –
(a) upon the constitution of a board for the first time, appoint a chairman and a vice chairman to hold office for a period not exceeding twelve months;
(b) thereafter appoint, before the date of the first meeting of the board in any year of office of the board, a chairman and vice chairman for that year, having first consulted the board; and
(c) promptly fill, after first having consulted the board, any casual vacancy in the office of chairman or vice chairman.
(7) The Secretary of State may terminate the appointment of a member as chairman or vice chairman if he is satisfied that the member has
(a) failed satisfactorily to perform his functions as chairman (or as the case may be) vice chairman;
(b) has grossly misconducted himself while performing those functions.

76. – Proceedings of boards
(1) The independent monitoring board for a prison shall meet at the prison once a month or, if they resolve for reasons specified in the resolution that less frequent meetings are sufficient, not fewer than eight times in twelve months.
(2) The board may fix a quorum of not fewer than three members for proceedings.
(3) The board shall keep minutes of their proceedings.
(4) The proceedings of the board shall not be invalidated by any vacancy in the membership or any defect in the appointment of a member.

77. – General duties of boards
(1) The independent monitoring board for a prison shall satisfy themselves as to the state of the prison premises, the administration of the prison and the treatment of the prisoners.

(2) The board shall inquire into and report upon any matter into which the Secretary of State asks them to inquire.
(3) The board shall direct the attention of the governor to any matter which calls for his attention, and shall report to the Secretary of State any matter which they consider it expedient to report.
(4) The board shall inform the Secretary of State immediately of any abuse which comes to their knowledge.
(5) Before exercising any power under these Rules the board and any member of the board shall consult the governor in relation to any matter which may affect discipline.

78. – Particular duties
(1) The independent monitoring board for a prison and any member of the board shall hear any complaint or request which a prisoner wishes to make to them or him.
(2) The board shall arrange for the food of the prisoners to be inspected by a member of the board at frequent intervals.
(3) The board shall inquire into any report made to them, whether or not by a member of the board, that a prisoner's health, mental or physical, is likely to be injuriously affected by any conditions of his imprisonment.

79. – Members visiting prisons
(1) The members of the independent monitoring board for a prison shall visit the prison frequently, and the board shall arrange a rota whereby at least one of its members visits the prison between meetings of the board.
(2) A member of the board shall have access at any time to every part of the prison and to every prisoner, and he may interview any prisoner out of the sight and hearing of officers.
(3) A member of the board shall have access to the records of the prison, except that members of the board shall not have access to any records held for the purposes of or relating to conduct authorised in accordance with Part 2 of the Regulation of Investigatory Powers Act 2000.

80. –Annual report
(1) The independent monitoring board for a prison shall, in accordance with paragraphs (2) and (3) below, from time to time make a

report to the Secretary of State concerning the state of the prison and its administration, including in it any advice and suggestions they consider appropriate.

(2) The board shall comply with any directions given to them from time to time by the Secretary of State as to the following matters:
(a) the period to be covered by a report under paragraph (1);
(b) the frequency with which such a report is to be made; and
(c) the length of time from the end of the period covered by such a report within which it is to be made; either in respect of a particular report or generally; providing that no directions may be issued under this paragraph if they would have the effect of requiring a board to make or deliver a report less frequently than once in every 12 months.

(3) Subject to any directions given to them under paragraph (2), the board shall, under paragraph (1), make an annual report to the Secretary of State as soon as reasonably possible after 31st December each year, which shall cover the period of 12 months ending on that date or, in the case of a board constituted for the first time during that period, such part of that period during which the board has been in existence.

PART VI: SUPPLEMENTAL

81. Delegation by governor

The governor of a prison may, with the leave of the Secretary of State, delegate any of his powers and duties under these Rules to another officer of that prison.

82. – Contracted out prisons

(1) Where the Secretary of State has entered into a contract for the running of a prison under section 84 of the Criminal Justice Act 1991 ("the 1991 Act") these Rules shall have effect in relation to that prison with the following modifications –
(a) references to an officer in the Rules shall include references to a prisoner custody officer certified as such under section 89(1) of the 1991 Act and performing custodial duties;
(b) references to a governor in the Rules shall include references to a director approved by the Secretary of State for the purposes of section 85(1)(a) of the 1991 Act except –
(i) in rule 81 the reference to a governor shall include a reference to a controller appointed by the Secretary of State under section 85(1)(b) of the 1991 Act; and
(ii) in rules 62(1), 66 and 77 where references to a governor shall include references to the director and the controller;
(iii) in rules 45, 48, 49, 53, 53A, 53B, 54, 55, 55AB, 57, 60, 61 and 61A where references to a governor shall include a reference to the director or the controller;
(c) rule 68 shall not apply in relation to a prisoner custody officer certified under section 89(1) of the 1991 Act and performing custodial duties.

(1A) The director of a prison may, with the leave of the Secretary of State, delegate any of his powers and duties under rules 45, 48, 49, 53, 53A, 53B, 55, 57, 60 and 61 to another officer of that prison.

83. Contracted out parts of prisons

Where the SoS has entered into a contract for the running of part of a prison under section 84(1) of the Criminal Justice Act 1991, that part and the remaining part shall each be treated for the purposes of Parts II to IV and Part VI of these Rules as if they were separate prisons.

84. – Contracted out functions at directly managed prisons

(1) Where the Secretary of State has entered into a contract under section 88A(1) of the Criminal Justice Act 1991 ("the 1991 Act") for any functions at a directly managed prison to be performed by prisoner custody officers who are authorised to perform custodial duties under section 89(1) of the 1991 Act, references to an officer in these
Rules shall, subject to paragraph (2), include references to a prisoner custody officer who is so authorised and who is performing contracted out functions for the purposes of, or for purposes connected with, the prison.

(2) Paragraph (1) shall not apply to references to an officer in rule 68.

(3) In this rule, "directly managed prison" has the meaning assigned to it by section 88A(5) of the 1991 Act.

85. – Revocations and savings

(1) Subject to paragraphs (2) and (3) below, the Rules specified in Schedule 1 to these Rules are hereby revoked.

(2) Without prejudice to the Interpretation Act 1978, where a prisoner committed an offence against discipline contrary to rule 47 of the Prison Rules 1964 prior to the coming into force of these Rules, those rules shall continue to have effect to permit the prisoner to be charged with such an offence, disciplinary proceedings in relation to such an offence to be continued, and the governor to impose punishment for such an offence.

(3) Without prejudice to the Interpretation Act 1978, any award of additional days or other punishment or suspended punishment for an offence against discipline awarded or imposed under any provision of the rules revoked by this rule, or those rules as saved by paragraph (2), or treated by any such provision as having been awarded or imposed under the rules revoked by this rule, shall have effect as if awarded or imposed under the corresponding provision of these Rules.

Rehabilitation has never been the Primary Purpose of Prison - and Rightly so too.
By Sir Martin Narey
Fmr Director General HM Prison Service

As Dominic Raab arrived in the Ministry of Justice in September 2021, he will have been besieged by people telling him that prisons are failing because they don't rehabilitate.
But that supposes that rehabilitation is imprisonment's only purpose - when that has never been the case.

We also send people to prison for public safety, for deterrence and, importantly, for retribution. Those three purposes, the last in particular, are too often forgotten.

We seem almost to be ashamed of speaking about retribution. But retribution against offenders is what holds our society back from a vigilantism which could all to easily descend into barbarism. Taking away offenders' liberty, as a mark of society's intolerance of their criminality is, in reality, the primary role of a prison service. But all over the world, it is rehabilitation which is claimed to be the main or even the only purpose of imprisonment. And that despite a plethora of evidence which suggests that rehabilitation in a penal setting is not simply unlikely but, on any sort of sustained scale, pretty much impossible.

The overwhelming majority of those we incarcerate have led disadvantaged lives. Typically, they have had difficult childhoods, characterised by neglect and abuse. We now know that the trauma of such damaging childhoods can play out for decades. As adults, children who've experienced neglectful and sometimes physically abusive childhoods, often being cared for by different people as they're moved in and out of the care system, will have attachment difficulties. They'll find it difficult to develop relationships, to trust or to accept help or advice. And their lives will often be chaotic and characterised by severe disadvantage and an absence of hope. Against all the evidence, we have to stop thinking that a prison sentence can correct such embedded disadvantage. We have to stop believing that somehow, even in a few weeks or months, we can cure people.

My contention might be seen, by some, as defeatist, or perhaps even morally bankrupt. And some will recall – entirely accurately – that when I led the Prison Service for seven years, I invested hugely in offending behaviour courses which - as I assured Ministers - would make a significant dent in the reoffending rate. They didn't. And they couldn't. And the sooner we are honest about that the better. Because if Ministers were to be realistic about incarceration's limited capacity to rehabilitate, they might then put greater effort into making prisons more humane places; more decent places; more moral places. Places where if someone we loved were to be convicted of a serious crime, we could countenance them being held without it terrifying us (and them).

The real challenge, and it's a moral challenge is to run prisons which treat prisoners with decency and dignity. Winston Churchill, might have re-packaged a quote from Dostoyevsky and passed it off as his own, but he was right to say that

The mood and temper of the public in regard to the treatment of crime and criminals is one of the most unfailing tests of the civilization of any country.

Treating those we incarcerate with dignity and respect, allowing them a reasonable life within the confines imposed by a loss of liberty is a noble cause. But it's not an easy one. Making our prisons consistently moral and decent places would be to achieve something remarkable.

A decent prison is one which takes seriously the cleanliness of the cells in which prisoners live and the lavatories they use. It's about privacy when dealing with bodily functions. It's about the ability to be visited by loved ones in welcoming conditions. It's about access to books, television and cultural activities. Most of all it's about the way prisoners are addressed by staff and the respect present in staff prisoner relationships. It's about making a reality of the much-quoted observation that we send people to prison as a punishment, not for punishment.

I know that in politically charged administrations, decency can all too easily be caricatured as being soft on crime and providing no public purpose. One Government Minister would occasionally chastise me about decency, telling me that it wasn't enough if reoffending wasn't simultaneously reduced. It seemed to me it was a moral challenge in its own right. But, at the same time, I believed that rather than seeking to put prisoners through courses which promised to reduce their criminality, decency might provide the platform for some offenders to change their own lives. Research bears that out.

Decent prisons, in which prisoners are respected, seem to provide a foundation for prisoner self-growth. Indecent, unsafe prisons allow no such growth and further damage those who have to survive there. As the respected UK criminologist Alison Liebling has said:

It is important, whatever our overall attitude towards imprisonment, to understand the differences between prisons and penal systems that damage, and prisons or penal systems that support or repair.

Only once a prison has accomplished respect, humanity, safety, good staff-prisoner relationships, professionalism, and organization and clarity, does it become a place in which personal development – or engagement with the self – can take place.

This is echoed by a retired UK governor who managed the most challenging prison I've visited: The Maze. Some years ago, and prompted by a speech I made to an international Penal Conference, Duncan McLoughlin, a retired Northern Ireland governor of some distinction, wrote to me and said this:

Only prisoners can rehabilitate themselves. The task of the prison is to present opportunities to them to make that possible. But… if a prison is to be a positive influence on a prisoner then that can only be achieved if we treat prisoners with respect, that we provide decent living conditions, that we make the prison a place where there is dignity, an absence of fear, and where there is a sense of self-worth and self-respect.

And its worth listening to the thoughts of a good friend of mine, Mark Leech, the founder and editor of the splendid Prisons Handbook which has made the lives of thousands of prisoners and their families just a little bit easier - and of this book and others besides.

Mark wasn't always a friend. For many years he was considered to be one of the most dangerous and difficult prisoners in the UK, spending 14 years inside, largely in solitary confinement. Since his release, and alongside becoming a successful businessman, he's thrown himself into prison reform. He was a primary source of candid advice to me when I ran the Prison Service as he has been to my successors.

Here's his take:

Expecting our prisons to reform those who we throw into them from high-crime inner city housing estates, with their school exclusions, unemployment, poor opportunities, poor parenting and where gang, gun, drug, alcohol, violence and crime are embedded in its DNA is an impossible ask when the living experience in so many jails is one of disrespect and often abuse, violence and filth.

So, my advice to Dominic Raab is not to be as keen as some of his predecessors to find things to do to prisoners which might cure them. He should resist the siren calls of those who will insist that they have a six-week or six-month course which can undo the damage of a lifetime. When someone tells him that they have an intervention which can transform lives (transform is the word of which he should be particularly suspicious) he should politely suggest they read the research. Instead, he should accept that Prison can rarely make things better for those we incarcerate. The challenge then is to make them decent places, which can pass the Churchillian test and where individuals and their loved ones are treated with dignity. And he should resist the popular notion that poor physical conditions, inadequate architecture, or overcrowding make decency and respect impossible. They might make the challenge harder, but prisoners are consistent in telling researchers that relationships between staff and prisoners are more important than material conditions.

Decent prisons are less likely further to damage – and make more dangerous - the disadvantaged, often wretched, and sometimes despised individuals we lock up. Occasionally, life in an institution in which they are treated respectfully, might allow some individuals to grow, perhaps to take advantage of the educational opportunities available, to think about the employment programme that a prison might be offering and to make the first tentative steps to rehabilitating themselves. When that happens it's wonderful. But it's exceptional. Mostly, prison is something which is necessary for retribution, deterrence and public safety but which cannot rehabilitate. Pretending otherwise is simply a diversion from the moral challenge which is at the centre of depriving people of their liberty.

Sir Martin James Narey DL is an advisor to the British Government, and a former civil servant and charity executive. He served as director general of the Prison Service of England and Wales between 1998 and 2003, and chief executive of the National Offender Management Service from 2004 to 2005.

Prison Officers: Pay & Pensions
By Steve Gillan
General Secretary
Prison Officers' Association

Prisoners often suffer when prison staff take industrial action, ranging from the closure of education, workshops, and visits, to the complete lockdown of an establishment.
We invited Steve Gillan, General Secretary of the POA to explain the industrial grievances the POA have with the Government.

Pay

In 1994 a pernicious piece of legislation was passed through the House of Commons namely the Criminal Justice Public Order Act 1994, Section 127 which effectively made it illegal for any Prison Officer to induce or indeed to take any form of industrial action.
Many commentators over the years do not believe that Prison Officers should have the right to strike because of the role they carry out on behalf of society.

I can see both sides of the coin.

On one side and as a trade unionist I believe it is a basic fundamental human right to withdraw your labour in an industrial dispute, after all no employer or government gives you anything as every term and condition is fought for whether that is pay, pension age, holiday pay, holiday entitlement, working week and the list goes on.

On the flip side of the coin it is argued often because of the nature of the task that Prison Officers fulfil then that role is an essential service and therefore under no circumstances should they be allowed to take industrial action in pursuit of a cause. That argument has merit but if and when a Government rely on such a restriction then there must be adequate compensatory measures that are binding as described by the International Labour Organisation and that both parties have confidence in.

Over the years Prison Officer pay has been eroded with no mechanism in place to resolve the issue. In 2001 a Pay Review Body was introduced as a compensatory mechanism where Government via Employer put their submission and POA submitted their claim. But this is not and never has been a negotiation it is merely a submission and the review body who are selected and paid for by Government make their recommendations.

I have always argued individuals appointed onto the review bodies are not going to rock the boat and bite the hand that pays and appoints them and successive Governments have just hidden behind the review body recommendations and thus Prison Officers pay has been eroded but more so since austerity kicked in from 2010 onwards.

Fast forward to the last couple of years the Conservative Government haven't even adhered to the recommendations; the last one being a recommendation that the lowest paid Prison Officers should get a £3000 pay rise.

The POA challenged this decision by Judicial Review and in September 2021 the court refused our application that we've appealed.

Now I know the courts are slow but the old saying justice delayed is justice denied is very true in this case. The same courts and Ministers are not so slow when they believed the POA are allegedly breaching section 127; they seem to get an injunction the same day. It does make you wonder if there is political interference on this issue with the courts as I have never ever heard of delays such as this in the Judicial Review process.

The Government officials are quick to praise Prison Officers but I am afraid that doesn't pay the bills and people are simply voting with their feet and leaving the job.

Not just new staff but experienced staff as well which is causing a crisis with retention of staff in the Prison Service which has a massive knock on effect with regimes. I have been around the criminal justice system for over 30 years and I have never seen such an exit of staff. It was unheard of years ago when the leaving rate nationally was below 2 per cent, now it is just seen as a stepping-stone for some because the pay is poor and the retirement age is now linked to the state pension age. Sadly, Ministers appear not to recognise that the leaving rate nationally is over 10 per cent and they are effectively recruiting to keep pace with the leavers.

If you break that down to different areas the leaving rate can be as high as 30 per cent.

The Pay Review body recently said that the pay model was broken but Government do not seem to want to fix it. Perhaps they are content with the model they have of under paying Prison Officers and having this continued cycle of recruiting which is costly along with the training and people leaving. It just doesn't make sense and no other industry would do that so why treat Prison Officers as second-class citizens and the poor relations compared to other public servants?

What is the point of having a Pay Review Body make recommendations? If they can see the retention issue is due to low pay, then you have to pose the question why Government Officials and HM Treasury cannot see it and to save a few pounds in the short term is going to create a cost for the tax payer in the long run because eventually they are going to have to arrest this problem of being able to retain and attract good quality people to run the Prison Service?

This isn't Steve Gillan General Secretary having a moan about pay.

By paying Prison Officers poorly hardly enhances the image of attracting people to a career. This is important because if we as a nation are serious about rehabilitation and reform of our Prisons then it is vital that the Service attract good quality Officers that see the job once more as a professional career and that they want to stay to create a Prison Service that everyone can be proud of. But if pay continues to be eroded like it has been over the years then good quality dedicated people are simply going to walk away.

For me justice will be served if the current Secretary of State Robert Buckland recognises what I have continually stated and stands up to Treasury Officials rather than rubbishing the Pay Review Body reports as, after all, it was Government that selected them and who pay them, and they recognise that Prison Officer pay is not standing up.

Pensions

In 2012 the Coalition Government altered public sector pensions after the financial crash around the world to make the pension age the same as the state pension age, which effectively means that Prison staff will ultimately retire at state pension age rather than 60 years of age and they expected to do. This in reality means that Prison Officers will need to work on the wings and landings until the age of 66, 67 or 68 years of age which is dictated by the link to their respective retirement to state pension age.

Lord Hutton who reviewed pensions effectively pulled up the ladder on workers going forward. A case of "I'm alright jack I have my retirement age secure but the rest of you will have to pay for the financial crash."

It has been long argued by Hutton, and some members of the right-wing media, that public servants such as Prison Staff in the Civil Service have "a gold-plated" pension scheme compared to individuals in the private sector; what the failed to mention of course was the pension scheme was actually deferred pay.

Instead they introduced something that was effectively a race to the bottom and now Prison Officers have the unenviable task of working to the age ultimately of 68 years and perhaps beyond if the link of retirement age is kept in relation to the state pension age.

I am not suggesting the role of a Prison Officer is more stressful or difficult to that of any other occupation, other occupations clearly have their own pressures, but there is no doubt that the job of Prison Officer is different and, as you get older, the fitness levels generally are not the same for a 68 year old when compared to a 21 year old.

Everyone I speak to, of all political persuasions, agree with me that the retirement age of a Prison Officer should not be 68 years of age, yet no one is prepared to raise their head above the parapet and grasp the nettle and admit that Hutton got it wrong.

I have requested a meeting with Lord Hutton on three occasions since 2012 and my letters have gone unanswered.

I merely wanted to understand the rationale of his belief that it was ok for a Prison Officer to be treated differently to a fire-fighter, Police Officer or member of the Armed Forces who retain retirement at the age of 60

I cannot understand the rationale or reasoning by which he left out Prison Staff in his recommendations. Perhaps he simply did not understand Prisons, which is surprising given the time he spent in the Blair Government.

I have always known there are no votes in Prisons and prisoners and staff are not top of the agenda of any political party until something goes wrong, but we now have a ticking time bomb and unless someone is brave enough in Government to resolve this pension issue they will no longer be able to attract individuals into the Prison Service or indeed retain such people long term because of the retirement age and pay in general.

If Britain wants a Prison Service to be proud of, that doesn't just lock people up but wants to rehabilitate individuals and keep people out of prison, then I am afraid there needs to be urgent attention given to recruiting and retaining prison staff and making the job professional and for professionals everyone accepts them to be. You wouldn't ask a group of workers in the car industry to build a Rolls Royce with a hammer and a chisel, the same applies to Prison staff.

If the public want a professional service that attracts the very best then I am afraid the fundamental terms and conditions such as pay and pensions, needs to be very quickly addressed by negotiation with the Prison Officers' Association before long term damage becomes irreversible. Thank you.

DO YOU KNOW HOW TO SPOT AN EXIT? Looking back to the day of your offence you'll probably find many 'exits' existed that day which, had you taken them, would have meant you didn't end up in prison.

You had chances to change course by resisting peer pressure, stop drinking, go home, and avoid the crime altogether. Later there were exists to limit the damage by mitigating the consequences of exits either seen and ignored, or missed altogether.

Let give you one example of what I mean. Thirty-four year old Fiona Onasanya had been the MP for Peterborough for just seven weeks when in July 2017, her thoughts elsewhere, the MP and practising solicitor failed to notice the speedometer on her car slip past 40 in the 30 limit – and she missed the road-side speed camera too until its flash caught her in its trap.

Three weeks later when the forms arrived in the post, requiring her to name the driver, a clearly marked 'Exit' presented itself – all she had to do was take it and admit she was driving. Doing 41mph in a 30 limit would have ended with a slapped wrist, three points, minor fine perhaps and a few finger-wagging tweets on social media from those who would have insisted that as an MP she should have known better – but she didn't.

Instead, when she signed the forms insisting a friend was driving, not her, and popped those forms in the post, she flew straight past the 'Exit' and continued on her journey to disaster – but there was another Exit ahead – would she take that perhaps? No.

A month later, when interviewed by police, instead of taking the Exit by claiming confusion: *"I'm so sorry, I've now checked my diary, I had the dates wrong, it was me driving after all, ha ha ha, I'm a new MP, life has been so chaotic, I am so, so, sorry, blah blah blah."*

As a solicitor she knew how to mitigate, right? But again she ignored the Exit.

There were other Exits too on the road ahead: her first court appearance, entering of a plea and right the way up to the start of her trial, her path was littered with Exit signs – but defiant to the end she ignored them all, went to trial – and lost.

The friend she said was driving wasn't even in the UK at the time, a fact not even she could explain away. Her blindness to exits resulted in a three month prison sentence, the loss of her Parliamentary seat and its £79,468 a year salary, her reputation was trashed and finally, she was struck off the Solicitors Roll – and, I have to ask you, all for what? 11 mph.

In group therapy at Grendon prison I learnt to recognise these dangers, it was part of 'cognitive thinking', a process of learning to recognise dangerous situations, come up with options, and avoid the danger by taking one. Recognising Exits is crucial.

During my time in prison I met numerous people doing life for murder mostly because they failed to recognise Exits that day. Exits that had presented themselves many times on the day they took someone's life.

Exits presenting numerous opportunities that day to turn off, change course, resist peer pressure, seek help, turn left, not right.

Exits that, had they been taken, would have saved a life, spared their future and avoided the devastation murder victims families suffer all because Exits were ignored.

It's never too late to take the exit before disaster occurs – but to do so you first have to recognise they exist.

Which is why prisons like Grendon Underwood, and all the other Therapeutic Communities in prisons, are so vital.

They equip people with exit recognition skills and the ability, no matter what the pressure is to continue on a course that is destined to end in disaster, to take the Exit before it's too far too late - before it ruins your life and that of your victims and their loved ones too.

Do you know how to spot an exit?
Mark Leech FRSA

- 228 -

IN PRISON YOU HAVE RIGHTS UNDER THE FREEDOM OF INFORMATION ACT

Everyone has a right to know – and that includes you. All public bodies, from government departments to local councils, hospitals, schools and the prison service have to follow a law called the Freedom of Information Act. In the pages of Converse, the national monthly prisons newspaper - and the only one edited and published by successful reformed offenders - you will have read articles which mention the Freedom of Information Act and it is a very valuable tool for journalists, researchers and for prisoners too.

But Freedom of Information (or FOI) isn't just for journalists and campaign groups. It's meant to help anybody to get information that is helpful to them, to help them to understand decisions that are made. In particular, if you're in prison, your life is under the control of public bodies more than most. You should be able to find out about the decisions they make that affect you. Often you will find it more difficult than others to get access to information that affects you. So here are some tips on how you can use your right to know – whatever side of the cell door you may be on.

1. It's really easy
You don't need any specialist knowledge to make an FOI request. All you need is a question that you want answering. You might want to know how many complaints are made about a prison. Or want access to a policy or procedure used in prisons. It doesn't matter, all you need to do is ask.

2. Put your request in writing
Most FOI requests are made via email, but they don't have to be. Old-fashioned pen and paper is fine. You don't need to use any technical jargon, just set out what you want.

3. Send it to a public body
Only public bodies such as the Ministry of Justice, HMPPS, IMB's, hospitals, police forces and councils are covered. Private companies don't have to answer FOI requests, but if they act on behalf of public bodies, for example running prisons for them, you can still ask the public body that controls the contract (which would be the Ministry of Justice for private prison contractors). Some addresses for public bodies involved in prison and probation provision are provided below. The public body must respond to your request within 20 working days (four weeks).

4. It's free!
Public bodies can charge for things like photocopying and postage – in theory, but they rarely do. That said, someone is paying for it – the public. So make FOI requests responsibly – don't request information for the sake of it, just if there is genuinely something you want to know.

Public bodies can refuse your request if it will take too long to find the information you want. You are most likely to get what you want if you focus your request. So ask for a specific document or for a couple of facts. If necessary, you can always make another request if you want to know more.

5. Explain about your circumstances
It shouldn't matter who is asking for information or why. Public bodies are supposed to treat everyone the same when they receive requests. However, one of the reasons that they might turn down your request is if the information is already published (Prison Service Orders or Prison Service Instructions and Policy Frameworks would be examples of this). **But if there is a reason why you can't access information that has been published – for example, because you have no access to the internet – they have to take that into account. So being up-front about your circumstances could help you get what you want.**

6. Don't get personal
You are very unlikely to get information about other people such as other prisoners or prison officers. Data protection laws protect their information. However, data protection laws do allow you to make a 'subject access

www.cellcompanion.uk

request' to any organisation to access information about yourself. Just like making FOI requests, there is no special technique needed to do this – just write to the organisation concerned. You will usually have to provide proof of your identity, but otherwise all you have to do is ask.

7. Be polite
The people answering your request are just doing their job (it used to be my job). Many try their hardest to help, and being polite will increase the chances that they will go the extra mile to help you.

8. Public bodies are supposed to help you
Here's a thing. Public bodies have a duty to help you. If you're not sure what information they might have, you could write and ask them and (in theory at least) they have to give you advice. If you make a request and the person who receives it can't understand it, then they are supposed to help you to make your request clearer. If they think it will take too long to answer, they should tell you what changes you need to make so that they can do it. If you get an unhelpful response, consider making a complaint.

9. You won't always get what you want
There are reasons why you might not get what you ask for. If that's the case, the public body concerned has to explain why they can't provide the information. Read their response, and if you're not convinced it is really easy to get a review of the decision. Just send them a letter asking for the decision to be reviewed. If there are reasons why you think the information should be released to you, tell them.

10. What can I ask for?
Lots of things! For example ask **the MOJ:**
How many complaints about lost property have there been in your prison - or any prison - between certain dates?;
How many IPP prisoners are there?;
How many IPP prisoners are (a) 3 years, (b) 5 years, (3) 10 or more years over tariff?;
Can I please have a copy of the following Prison Service Instruction, Prison Service Order, or Ministry of Justice Policy Framework on... (see pages 237-245)
Can I please have a copy of the latest HMPPS Annual Reports & Accounts...

How to ask the MOJ under the Freedom of Information Act for information?
In order to ask these questions all you have to do is submit a normal COMP1 form and make absolutely clear that 'this is a request under the Freedom of Information Act....' The prison will then email your request to the Data Access Unit at the Ministry of Justice.

You can ask the **Independent Monitoring Board** in your prison - or in any prison - for example for:
A copy of the Minutes of your latest monthly Board meeting (and you can ask for minutes of any month not just the current one);
How does the IMB in HMP (name of Prison) make known to prisoners that it is subject to the Freedom of Information Act and how prisoners can apply?;
How many visits has the IMB made to this prison in the last 12 months?;
How many visits have the IMB made to this prison between 9pm and 6am in the last 12 months?;
Can I please have a copy of your latest annual report?

How to ask the IMB under the Freedom of Information Act for information?
In order to ask the IMB questions you can simply submit an IMB application form in the normal way - again it is really important that you make clear your request is made 'under the Freedom of Information Act'.

You can ask the **Prisons Inspectorate** for a copy of any of their reports), or a list of reports so you can select one and then ask for it, by writing or telephoning them as follows:
HM Inspectorate of Prisons, 3rd floor, 10 South Colonnade, Canary Wharf, London, E14 4PU. Tel: 020 7340 0500

You can ask the **Prisons & Probation Ombudsman** questions about deaths in custody, the number of complaints they have received and dealt with or for a list of their Reports so you can select a report and ask for it, you can ask by writing to them or telephoning them as follows:

Prisons & Probation Ombudsman, 3rd floor, 10 South Colonnade, Canary Wharf, London, E14 4PU. Tel: 020 7633 4149

11. There is a higher power
Sometimes you might find that a public body is being unhelpful. Or maybe you've asked for a review and you are still dissatisfied with the answer. When that happens you can ask the Information Commissioner to intervene.

The Information Commissioner has the power to force public bodies to release information if they disagree with their reasons for refusing requests.

Again, you don't need any special knowledge to launch an appeal to the Commissioner – just write to them, enclosing the correspondence that you have had with the public body.

They might not think that you have a valid complaint, but if they do, you could end up getting the information you want.

If you go down this route, just bear in mind that it can take time to get a decision – you will need to be patient. Sometimes though a bit of persistence will pay off in the end.

So if you want to know what rules prison officers have to follow, how complaints are dealt with in your prison, or why a decision was made that has affected you – there is a way to find out.

And it's not just you that has this right – your family and friends are also able to make FOI requests.

Give it a go – it's your right!

To make a complaint to the Information Commissioner just write to them at

Information Commissioner's Office
Wycliffe House
Water Lane
Wilmslow
SK9 5AF

Paul Gibbons, MSc, LLM, BCS is a consultant and trainer in information rights and information management. He was Parliamentary Records Manager in the Houses of Parliament and the Freedom of Information and Records Manager for the Greater London Authority, tasked with preparing the Mayor of London's headquarters for FOI coming into force. His last job before going freelance was in the higher education sector, as Information Compliance Manager for SOAS, University of London.

LIST OF CURRENT PRISON SERVICE INSTRUCTIONS, ORDERS AND POLICY FRAMEWORKS: 1st November 2021.

Via the library you have the right of access to the following documents, except the very few not available for security reasons.

PRISON SERVICE INSTRUCTIONS

05/2018	Prison adjudications policy
04/2018	Records management policy
02/2018	Post-incident care
07/2017	Regime management planning
05/2017	Separating prisoners
04/2017	Use of body cameras
20/2016	Equality analysis
18/2016	Public protection manual
16/2016	Information sharing agreements
15/2016	Parole Board Information
14/2016	Marriage or Civil Partnerships
11/2016	Health and safety
10/2016	Health, safety and fire issues
09/2016	Searching cells, areas and vehicles
08/2016	Dealing with evidence
07/2016	Procedures for searching people
06/2016	Information risk management
05/2016	Faith and pastoral care
04/2016	Prisoner communications
03/2016	Adult social care
02/2016	Accidents and injuries in prison
38/2015	Monitoring health and safety
37/2015	Health and safety risk assessment
36/2015	Workplace inspection
33/2015	Taking prisoners outside prison
31/2015	Managing litigation claims
30/2015	Use of force policy
29/2015	First aid
27/2015	Open source research
26/2015	Security of prisoners at court
21/2015	Unauthorised possession of knives
20/2015	Cell sharing risk assessments
19/2015	Control of radon exposure
18/2015	Safety of X-ray equipment
17/2015	Prisoners assisting other prisoners
16/2015	Keeping adult prisoners safe
14/2015	Disposing of property
11/2015	Fire safety in prisons
10/2015	Managing Escape Risk prisoners
09/2015	Identifying high security prisoners
07/2015	Early days in custody
06/2015	Managing health and safety

www.prisons.org.uk

05/2015	Vetting decisions by exception		63/2011	Managing the local security
04/2015	Prisoner rehabilitation services		62/2011	Transferring children/YPs MHA
03/2015	Determinate sentence prisoners		58/2011	Physical education for prisoners
02/2015	Prison service library		57/2011	Managing tools and equipment
01/2015	Prisoners who may be deported		55/2011	Prison keys and locks
46/2014	Crown copyright and licences		52/2011	Repatriation and removal of FNPs
42/2014	Exclusion of staff for misconduct		49/2011	Prisoner communications policy
41/2014	Probation cases for risk review		05/2018	Prison adjudications (B4 Feb 2019)
40/2014	Violent and sex offender register		46/2011	Witness intimidation by remands
39/2014	Offenders as mentors		44/2011	Prisoners ID for bank applications
37/2014	Open prison and ROTL for FNPs		39/2011	Categorising women prisoners
34/2014	Offender risk information		36/2011	Psychologist report format (SPR E)
32/2014	Drug appointments and licence		32/2011	Ensuring equality
29/2014	Release on licence of FNPs		30/2011	Handling mobile phones and SIMs
28/2014	Performance hub data quality		24/2011	Management Night Security
27/2014	Risk criteria for ex-offenders		23/2011	Playing films, television and music
23/2014	Prison-NOMIS		22/2011	Prison bedding fire standards
22/2014	Research applications		19/2011	Searching stored property
21/2014	Data gateway service		16/2011	Managing prison visits
19/2014	Sentence planning		15/2011	Visits security
15/2014	Serious self-harm or assault		14/2011	Managing prison gates
14/2014	Case allocation		13/2011	Communications and security
07/2014	Security vetting		12/2011	Managing prisoner property
06/2014	Use of force: young people's estate		58/2010	Prisons Probation Ombudsman
06/2014	Use of force form part 1 (MS Excel)		50/2010	Covert testing
06/2014	Use of force form part 2		44/2010	Prisoner meals
05/2014	Barred status of prisoners		38/2010	Activities in prison
23/2013	Prisoner retail		37/2010	Prisoners' access to the media
08/2013	High Security Categorisation		29/2010	Indeterminate sentence manual
04/2013	Early removal of FNPs		28/2010	Custody compacts
03/2013	Emergency response codes		16/2010	Confiscation orders
44/2012	Prison security passes		14/2010	Managing risk in prison industries
42/2012	Close supervision centre (CSC)		31/2009	Compact based drugs testing
32/2012	Open University higher education		19/2009	Restricting access to prison PABX
29/2012	The instruction system		07/2009	Housing benefit continuance
17/2012	Prisoner accommodation		25/2008	Removable media
14/2012	"Manage the sentence":		06/2008	Introduction of Brent equipment
10/2012	Controlling banned items		50/2007	Transferring prisoners MHA
09/2012	Bail services		39/2007	Radiation equipment
08/2012	Caring for YPs in custody		34/2007	Disinfecting tablets
07/2012	Accredited programmes		25/2007	Travel restriction orders
06/2012	Work and learning opportunities		09/2006	Rationalisation of doctors' duties
05/2012	Workshops and laundries		47/2005	Resettlement
04/2012	Enablers of services in prisons		46/2005	Drug treatment and self harm
03/2012	Allocating prisoners to activities		14/2005	Prison healthcare complaints
01/2012	Managing prisoners' money		04/2005	Prisoner information systems
76/2011	Deducting money from prisoners		10/2004	Healthcare Model induction
75/2011	Residential services		47/2003	Rationalisation of doctors' duties
72/2011	Prison discharge policy		46/2003	Medical treatment of prison staff
69/2011	Prison radio equipment		28/2003	Pharmacy services for prisoners
64/2011	Managing prisoner safety		16/2003	Modernising dental services

38/2002	Consent to medical treatment
25/2002	Protection health information
24/2002	Strategy for promoting health
44/2001	Guidance on nicotine therapy
40/2001	Night workers health assessment
48/2000	The bail system
29/1998	Food Safety Act
44/1997	Contractors Health and safety

PRISON SERVICE ORDERS: 1 Nov 2021

0160 Magistrates Training Visits To Prisons
0905 Police National Computer
1025 The Person Escort Record
1300 Investigations
1310 Anti Fraud Strategy
1600 Use Of Force
1700 Segregation
2400 Democratic Therapeutic Communities
2600 Legal Issues Relating To Prisoners
3050 Continuity Of Healthcare For Prisoners
3100 Clinical Governance
3200 Health Promotion
3550 Clinical Services
3601 Mandatory Drugs Testing
3625 Testing Of External Drug Workers
3800 Food Safety Act 1990
3802 Management Of Asbestos
3805 Zoonotic Infections
4350 Effective Regime Interventions
4455 Prisoners Name Change
4460 Prisoners Pay
4480 Prisoners Representative Associations
4600 Unconvicted Unsentenced And Civil
4625 Productions In Civil Proceedings
4700 Indeterminate Sentence Manual
4960 Detention Under Section
5400 Transport Manual
5901 Maintenance Of Prison Service Buildings
6000 Parole Release And Recall
6100 The Bail System
6300 Release On Temporary License (ROTL)
8525 POA Local Dispute Resolution
8805 Identification Of Prison Staff
9030 Requests For It
9050 Functional Mailboxes

MINISTRY OF JUSTICE
POLICY FRAMEWORKS 1 November 2021

- Pregnancy, MBUs and maternal separation in women's prisons Policy Framework 20 September 2021
- Probation service management of MAPPA level 1 cases Policy Framework 16 August 2021
- Information Requests Policy Framework 2 August 2021
- Licence conditions Policy Framework 8 September 2021
- Travel and transfer on licence and PSS outside of England and Wales Policy Framework 26 July 2021
- Prison dogs Policy Framework 23 July 2021
- Case Transfer Policy Framework 28 June 2021
- Polygraph examination licence condition policy framework 25 June 2021
- Enforcement of Community Orders, Suspended Sentence Orders and Post-sentence supervision Policy Framework 26 June 2021
- HMPPS Investigatory Powers Policy Framework 1 June 2021
- Information Sharing Policy Framework 28 May 2021
- Women's Estate Case Advice and Support Panel Policy Framework 17 May 2021
- Person Escort Record Policy Framework 24 May 2021
- Use of Narcotics Trace Detection Equipment on Correspondence Policy Framework 16 August 2021
- Homelessness Reduction Act: Duty to refer policy framework 9 April 2021
- Management of security at visits Policy Framework: Open estate 8 April 2021
- Management of security at visits Policy Framework: Closed estate 8 April 2021
- Secure Social Video Calling (Interim) Policy Framework 26 February 2021
- Implementation and use of OASys Sexual reoffending Predictor (OSP) Policy Framework 28 May 2021
- Restrictions on prisoner voting policy framework 11 August 2020
- Use of X-ray body scanners (adult male

prisons) Policy Framework 19 May 2020
- Post Sentence Supervision Requirements Policy Framework 26 March 2020
- Health and safety arrangements: management of workplace transport 16 March 2020
- Domestic abuse policy framework 2 April 2020
- Security categorisation policy framework 17 August 2021
- Information Security Policy Framework 26 June 2021
- Generic Parole Process Policy Framework 30 September 2021
- Recall, review and re-release of recalled prisoners 30 September 2021
- Parole Board oral hearing administration and attendance policy framework 4 November 2019
- HMPPS Finance Manual Policy Framework 12 November 2020
- Managing parole eligible offenders on licence policy framework 11 November 2020
- Serious and organised crime policy framework 3 October 2019
- The care and management of individuals who are transgender 27 January 2020
- Incentives Policy Framework 8 July 2020
- Prisoner complaints policy framework 20 September 2021
- HMPPS business continuity policy framework 3 July 2019
- Enhanced behaviour monitoring policy framework 28 May 2019
- Release on temporary licence 17 August 2021
- Counter corruption and reporting wrongdoing 26 June 2021
- Multi Agency Life Risk Assessment Panel 4 April 2019
- Progression regimes 13 May 2021
- Prison education and library services for adult prisons in England 2 April 2019
- Home detention curfew 26 June 2021
- Sustainable operations 18 May 2021
- Intelligence collection, management and dissemination in prisons and probation 31 October 2019
- Building Bridges: A Positive Behaviour Framework for the Children and Young

People Secure Estate 7 February 2019
- Strengthening Prisoners Family Ties Policy Framework 4 September 2019
- Smoke Free Policy Framework 18 May 2021
- Women's Policy Framework 26 June 2021
- Bail Accommodation and Support Service (BASS) 21 December 2018
- Access to Digital Evidence (A2DE) 21 December 2018
- Manage the custodial sentence 12 September 2018

LIST OF PRISON GROUPS &
PRISON GROUP DIRECTORS
November 2021.
ENGLAND AND WALES

Group - Cumbria & Lancashire Group
PGD - John Illingsworth
HMP Preston
HMP Lancaster Farms
HMP Wymott
HMP Havering
HMP Kirkham

Group - Greater Manchester, Merseyside & Cheshire
PGD - Tim Allen
HMP Liverpool
HMP Hindley
HMP Thorn Cross
HMP Buckley Hall
HMP Risley

Group - West Midlands
PGD - Teresa Clarke
HMP/YOI Brinsford
HMP Featherstone
HMP Hewell
HMP Stafford
HMP/YOI Stoke Heath
HMP/YOI Swinfen Hall

Group - Tees and Wear Reform
PGD - Alan Tallentire
HMP/YOI Durham
HMYOI Deerbolt
HMP/YOI Holme House
HMP Kirklevington Grange

Director Women's Estate HMPPS - Pia Sinha
HMP/YOI Downview
HMP/YOI East Sutton Park
HMP/YOI Drake Hall
HMP/YOI Eastwood Park
HMP/YOI Foston Hall

HMP/YOI Low Newton
HMP/YOI New Hall
HMP/YOI Askham Grange
HMP/YOI Send
HMP/YOI Styal

Group - Kent Surrey & Sussex
PGD - Susan Howard
HMP Coldingley
HMP Ford
HMP Elmley
HMP Lewes
HMP Standford Hill

Group - Yorkshire
PGD - Helen Judge
HMP/YOI Hatfield
HMP/YOI Hull
HMP Humber
HMP Leeds
HMP Lindholme
HMP/YOI Moorland
HMP Wealstun

Group - East Midlands
PGD - Paul Cawkwell
HMP Leicester
HMP Lincoln
HMP Onley
HMP Whatton
HMP North Sea Camp

Group - North Midlands
PGD - Alison Clarke
HMP Nottingham
HMP Ranby
HMP Stocken
HMP Sudbury

Group - Long Term High Security
PGD's - Gavin O'Malley (North)
       - Will Styles (South)
HMP Belmarsh (S)
HMP Swaleside (S)
HMP Frankland (N)
HMP Long Lartin (S)
HMP Gartree (N)
HMP Whitemoor (S)
HMP Wakefield (N)
HMP Manchester (N)
HMP Woodhill (S)
HMP Isle of Wight (S)
HMP Full Sutton (N)
HMP Garth (N)
HMP Aylesbury (S)

Group - Kent Surrey & Sussex
PGD - Susan Howard
HMP Coldingley

HMP Ford
HMP Elmley
HMP Lewes
HMP Standford Hill

Group - Hertfordshire, Essex & Suffolk
PGD - Simon Cartwright
HMP Chelmsford
HMP Warren Hill
HMP Hollesley Bay
HMP Highpoint
HMP The Mount

Group - Avon & South Dorset
PGD: Paul Woods
HMP Bristol
HMP Leyhill
HMP Portland
HMP The Verne

Group - South Central Group
PGD - Andy Lattimore
HMP Bullingdon
HMP Erlestoke
HMP & YOI Winchester
HMP Grendon/Spring Hill

Group - Devon & North Dorset
PGD - Jeannine Hendrick
HMP Channings Wood
HMP Dartmoor
HMP & YOI Exeter
HMP Guys Marsh

Group - Bedfordshire, Cambridgeshire & Norfolk Group
PGD - Gary Monaghan
HMP Bedford
HMP Bure
HMP Littlehey
HMP Norwich
HMP Wayland

Group - London
PGD - Ian Bickers
HMP Brixton
HMP Isis
HMP Pentonville
HMP Wandsworth
HMP Wormwood Scrubs
HMP High Down

Group - Youth Custody
Executive Director - Helga Swidenbank
Director Custody - Heather Whitehead
HMYOI Cookham Wood
HMYOI Feltham
Medway STC

HMYOI Werrington
HMYOI Wetherby

Group - Wales
PGD - Kenny Brown
HMP Cardiff
HMP Swansea
HMP Usk/Prescoed
HMP Parc
HMP Berwyn

Contracts Group
Neil Richards (Head of Custodial Contracts)
HMP Altcourse
HMP Ashfield
HMP Birmingham
HMP Bronzefield
HMP Doncaster

HMP Dovegate
HMP Five Wells (opens 2022)
HMP Forest Bank
HMP Lowdham Grange
HMP Northumberland
HMP Oakwood
HMP Peterborough
HMP Rye Hill
HMP Thameside

NOTES

Calendar 2022 UK

January		February		March	
1 Sa New Year's Day		1 Tu		1 Tu	
2 Su		2 We		2 We	
3 Mo Substitute day	1	3 Th		3 Th	
4 Tu		4 Fr		4 Fr	
5 We		5 Sa		5 Sa	
6 Th		6 Su		6 Su	
7 Fr		7 Mo	6	7 Mo	10
8 Sa		8 Tu		8 Tu	
9 Su		9 We		9 We	
10 Mo	2	10 Th		10 Th	
11 Tu		11 Fr		11 Fr	
12 We		12 Sa		12 Sa	
13 Th		13 Su		13 Su	
14 Fr		14 Mo	7	14 Mo	11
15 Sa		15 Tu		15 Tu	
16 Su		16 We		16 We	
17 Mo	3	17 Th		17 Th	
18 Tu		18 Fr		18 Fr	
19 We		19 Sa		19 Sa	
20 Th		20 Su		20 Su	
21 Fr		21 Mo	8	21 Mo	12
22 Sa		22 Tu		22 Tu	
23 Su		23 We		23 We	
24 Mo	4	24 Th		24 Th	
25 Tu		25 Fr		25 Fr	
26 We		26 Sa		26 Sa	
27 Th		27 Su		27 Su	
28 Fr		28 Mo	9	28 Mo	13
29 Sa				29 Tu	
30 Su				30 We	
31 Mo	5			31 Th	

www.prisons.org.uk

Calendar 2022 UK

April	May	June
1 Fr	1 Su	1 We
2 Sa	2 Mo Early May Bank Holiday 18	2 Th Spring Bank Holiday
3 Su	3 Tu	3 Fr Platinum Jubilee
4 Mo 14	4 We	4 Sa
5 Tu	5 Th	5 Su
6 We	6 Fr	6 Mo 23
7 Th	7 Sa	7 Tu
8 Fr	8 Su	8 We
9 Sa	9 Mo 19	9 Th
10 Su	10 Tu	10 Fr
11 Mo 15	11 We	11 Sa
12 Tu	12 Th	12 Su
13 We	13 Fr	13 Mo 24
14 Th	14 Sa	14 Tu
15 Fr Good Friday	15 Su	15 We
16 Sa	16 Mo 20	16 Th
17 Su	17 Tu	17 Fr
18 Mo Easter Monday 16	18 We	18 Sa
19 Tu	19 Th	19 Su
20 We	20 Fr	20 Mo 25
21 Th	21 Sa	21 Tu
22 Fr	22 Su	22 We
23 Sa	23 Mo 21	23 Th
24 Su	24 Tu	24 Fr
25 Mo 17	25 We	25 Sa
26 Tu	26 Th	26 Su
27 We	27 Fr	27 Mo 26
28 Th	28 Sa	28 Tu
29 Fr	29 Su	29 We
30 Sa	30 Mo 22	30 Th
	31 Tu	

Calendar 2022 UK

July		August		September	
1 Fr		1 Mo	31	1 Th	
2 Sa		2 Tu		2 Fr	
3 Su		3 We		3 Sa	
4 Mo	27	4 Th		4 Su	
5 Tu		5 Fr		5 Mo	36
6 We		6 Sa		6 Tu	
7 Th		7 Su		7 We	
8 Fr		8 Mo	32	8 Th	
9 Sa		9 Tu		9 Fr	
10 Su		10 We		10 Sa	
11 Mo	28	11 Th		11 Su	
12 Tu		12 Fr		12 Mo	37
13 We		13 Sa		13 Tu	
14 Th		14 Su		14 We	
15 Fr		15 Mo	33	15 Th	
16 Sa		16 Tu		16 Fr	
17 Su		17 We		17 Sa	
18 Mo	29	18 Th		18 Su	
19 Tu		19 Fr		19 Mo	38
20 We		20 Sa		20 Tu	
21 Th		21 Su		21 We	
22 Fr		22 Mo	34	22 Th	
23 Sa		23 Tu		23 Fr	
24 Su		24 We		24 Sa	
25 Mo	30	25 Th		25 Su	
26 Tu		26 Fr		26 Mo	39
27 We		27 Sa		27 Tu	
28 Th		28 Su		28 We	
29 Fr		29 Mo August Bank Holiday	35	29 Th	
30 Sa		30 Tu		30 Fr	
31 Su		31 We			

www.prisons.org.uk

Calendar 2022 UK

October		November		December	
1 Sa		1 Tu		1 Th	
2 Su		2 We		2 Fr	
3 Mo	40	3 Th		3 Sa	
4 Tu		4 Fr		4 Su	
5 We		5 Sa		5 Mo	49
6 Th		6 Su		6 Tu	
7 Fr		7 Mo	45	7 We	
8 Sa		8 Tu		8 Th	
9 Su		9 We		9 Fr	
10 Mo	41	10 Th		10 Sa	
11 Tu		11 Fr		11 Su	
12 We		12 Sa		12 Mo	50
13 Th		13 Su		13 Tu	
14 Fr		14 Mo	46	14 We	
15 Sa		15 Tu		15 Th	
16 Su		16 We		16 Fr	
17 Mo	42	17 Th		17 Sa	
18 Tu		18 Fr		18 Su	
19 We		19 Sa		19 Mo	51
20 Th		20 Su		20 Tu	
21 Fr		21 Mo	47	21 We	
22 Sa		22 Tu		22 Th	
23 Su		23 We		23 Fr	
24 Mo	43	24 Th		24 Sa	
25 Tu		25 Fr		25 Su Christmas Day	
26 We		26 Sa		26 Mo Boxing Day	52
27 Th		27 Su		27 Tu Substitute day	
28 Fr		28 Mo	48	28 We	
29 Sa		29 Tu		29 Th	
30 Su		30 We		30 Fr	
31 Mo	44			31 Sa	

Calendar 2023 UK

January		February		March	
1 Su New Year's Day		1 We		1 We	
2 Mo Substitute day	1	2 Th		2 Th	
3 Tu		3 Fr		3 Fr	
4 We		4 Sa		4 Sa	
5 Th		5 Su		5 Su	
6 Fr		6 Mo	6	6 Mo	10
7 Sa		7 Tu		7 Tu	
8 Su		8 We		8 We	
9 Mo	2	9 Th		9 Th	
10 Tu		10 Fr		10 Fr	
11 We		11 Sa		11 Sa	
12 Th		12 Su		12 Su	
13 Fr		13 Mo	7	13 Mo	11
14 Sa		14 Tu		14 Tu	
15 Su		15 We		15 We	
16 Mo	3	16 Th		16 Th	
17 Tu		17 Fr		17 Fr	
18 We		18 Sa		18 Sa	
19 Th		19 Su		19 Su	
20 Fr		20 Mo	8	20 Mo	12
21 Sa		21 Tu		21 Tu	
22 Su		22 We		22 We	
23 Mo	4	23 Th		23 Th	
24 Tu		24 Fr		24 Fr	
25 We		25 Sa		25 Sa	
26 Th		26 Su		26 Su	
27 Fr		27 Mo	9	27 Mo	13
28 Sa		28 Tu		28 Tu	
29 Su				29 We	
30 Mo	5			30 Th	
31 Tu				31 Fr	

www.prisons.org.uk

> Tip! On 26th July 2021 HMPPS issued an updated 'National Product List' for canteen items and prices; your family can download it from https://prisonoracle.com

Annex C

National Facilities List

Introduction

The National Facilities List (NFL) identifies the items that Governors need to consider when developing and operating their local incentive schemes. The items below are provided to offer a level of consistency and ensure that it provides Governors opportunities to tailor schemes for their local prison population.
The list is divided into two parts

- Part 1 – the Minimum list of items that Governors must allow each prisoner, where requested, irrespective of incentive level. Prisoners on Basic level must be restricted to items on part 1 of the list and

- Part 2 – Governors can choose additional items from part 2 of the list to add to their local facilities list for Standard and Enhanced levels or levels above Enhanced. It is for Governors locally to determine what incentive level prisoners must be on to have access to these items.

When allowing items Governors should consider whether the items chosen are suitable for in-cell use, and meet all relevant risk considerations, including fire, health and safety, and security. The NFL does not override PGI 03/2011 Management of the Local Security Strategy or any other relevant safety consideration. Furthermore, local infrastructure, including electrics, fire precautions, and health and safety considerations may impact whether certain items on the NFL can be accessed within individual prisons. There are no set numerical limits on the numbers of each item prisoners can have in possession, including consumables, but prisoners must not exceed the overall volumetric control limits as set out in national policy PSI 12/2011 Prisoners' Property.
In addition, the following items are not constrained by volumetric control:

- One birdcage (in prisons where birds are permitted) is exempt from volumetric control. However, if allowed, prisoners should be made aware at the outset that birds are not allowed in every prison establishment and if transferred they may not be able to take their bird with them;
- one musical instrument (e.g. a guitar);
- legal papers;
- bedding up to the standard cell scale issue;
- one set of clothing (whether prisoner's own clothing or prison issue), including that worn when the volume of property is monitored;
- posters etc. which are appropriate to be attached to cell walls; posters must not be attached to external walls;
- items held in possession for the care of babies in mother and baby units; Governors must be satisfied that such items are held for this purpose, and that the quantity held does not impede effective searching;
- Reasonable amounts of items that support Transgender prisoners to live in the gender they identify with. Governors must be satisfied that the quantity held does not impede effective searching
- religious texts and artefacts, essential for the practice of the prisoner's religion.

Incentives Policy Framework   Re-issued: 8 July 2020

Part 1 – Minimum list

Item	
Clothing	• Prison issued in line with local allowances.
Footwear	• Training Shoes/Shoes. No hook and eyes, no steel toe caps unless authorised by the prison for work in custody or outside, no stiletto heels • Flip flops / Sandals/ Sliders • Slippers
Jewellery	• Ring. No raised patterns/stones. • Earring/Stud/small sleeper for ears and body piercing if worn on initial reception. May be replaced if damaged. • Chain. No medallions but religious symbols are accepted. • Rheumatism band. • Wristwatch/Pocket Watch. Can include alarm and digital display but must not include data storage, recording, Bluetooth or WiFi capability, digital, TV, or mobile phone facility. No smart watches.
Personal hygiene and grooming items	• Towel. No sports teams/countries/ offensive slogans/designs. • Flannel / Sponge. • Comb / Hair brush. • Toothbrush. • Nail clippers. Possession of those with files to be determined locally by individual risk assessment. • Shaving brush. No metal allowed. • Nail brush. • Hair accessories e.g. scrunchies/ties, clips, extensions. Additional items to be determined locally by individual risk assessment. • Hair dryer. • Tweezers. • Shower cap. • Toilet/make-up bag. Not padded. • Small fans. • Make-up.
Stereo/radio and associated items	Radio and/or sound system i.e. compact disc player/cassette/ combined system. No MP3, MP4 or iPods, for example. If the system has a built-in MP3 / IPOD docking station it must be disabled /blocked with tamper proof seals. Items powered solely via a USB port will not be allowed. Radios / sound systems powered by other means but with USB ports as well must have the USB ports blocked using tamper-evident seals or permanently blocked or the setting reconfigured using USB control software to prevent its use. Radio/sound systems with proprietary Bluetooth are permitted. The authorisation and guidance for proprietary Bluetooth, HMPPS Bluetooth Guide and Regulations can be found at Annex I. • All audio systems are for in cell use. Governors need to be satisfied that the item does not present a security risk. Governors need to conduct a risk assessment when handling a request from a prisoner to be permitted to have a short-wave radio in-possession. • In line with Section 2 paragraph e) of Segregation (PSO 1700) Governors can, upon the recommendation of a Review Board,

		decide to remove a radio from a prisoner in segregation if the prisoner has not been willing to meet the targets set for them by the Board. However, "a decision to remove a radio should be given careful consideration and is one that should not be taken lightly. Further consideration should be given to the period of time the radio is removed and any changes in the behaviour/mental health the removal may have on the prisoner".
Cassette tapes		• Standard size with transparent casing only. Can be removed from prisoners in segregation as per Section 2e of PSO 1700 mentioned above.
Compact Discs		• Can be removed from prisoners in segregation as per Section 2e of PSO 1700 mentioned above. • CD Storage Case. Not padded. Can be removed from prisoners in segregation as per Section 2e of PSO 1700 mentioned above.
Earpiece/Headphones		• No wireless or Bluetooth headphone allowed. Can be removed from prisoners in segregation as per Section 2e of PSO 1700 mentioned above.
Alarm clock		• Battery operated only. No wall mounted types. Can have digital display.
Calculator		• Not programmable printout type.
Batteries		• No Rechargeable batteries.
2– Way adapter		• Only in establishments with the supporting electrical supply.
Miscellaneous		• Posters and Drawing Pins for use on cell poster boards only. No posters containing indecency, drugs or racially offensive material. • Tins and Tin Opener. Butterfly type only. Tins and Tin openers subject to individual risk assessment. Disposal of lids to follow the local safe system of work. • Storage Containers. Small plastic containers only. • Flask (unless kettles are provided).
		Where appropriate: • Bespoke Disability Equipment. • Prescription glasses, non-tinted unless there is a medical need for tinted lenses. • Hearing Aid. • Walking Sticks / Crutches. • Contact Lenses must be clear and not coloured unless there is a medical need. • Contact lenses solution.
Smoking Requisites (for possession in open prisons where the Governor permits smoking and only for use in designated outside areas, and applies only to 18 and over designated	Weekly purchase allowance of 125g for loose tobacco or 180 cigarettes / cigars. A maximum of double the weekly allowance can be retained in possession. Governors may wish to impose a limit on the quantity of these items that prisoners can hold in possession including: • Pipe, roller, lighter (disposable lighters only). • Loose Tobacco. • Cigarettes / Cigars.	

Incentives Policy Framework   Re-issued: 8 July 2020   25

establishments. Under 18 designated establishments operate a non-smoking policy).	
Nicotine Replacement Requisites Applies only to 18 and over designated establishments. Under 18 designated establishments operate a non-smoking policy.	• Electronic Vaping Device (Vapes) with vape charger and plug. Only 1 Vape Device, plug and charger in possession per prisoner • Vape Cartridges. A maximum of 6 packets of vaping cartridges are allowed in possession per prisoner • Electronic Cigarettes (disposable) • Nicotine Replacement Patches • Nicotine Replacement Lozenges
Writing and reading materials	• Books including for example dictionary, puzzle books, Sudoku or colouring books. Contents may be subject to restriction and placed in Stored Property if considered inappropriate. • Calendar. • Diary/Address Book. Not padded or electronic. • Writing Pad/Envelopes/ Stamped Addressed Envelopes - Subject to Security checks. • Greeting cards. • Writing utensils. • Photograph Album, Photograph Frames & Photos. Not padded, must be plastic / Perspex-fronted. No indecent photographs. • Magazines, Periodicals, newspapers. Contents may be subject to restriction and placed in Stored Property if considered inappropriate. • Playing cards. • Stamps. • Religious Artefacts (see PSI 05/2016 for further information).
Distraction packs	• Where provided by the prison.

Part 2 – Additional list of items for Governors to consider

Bedding – all must be fire retardant	• Duvet. • Pillows. • Single sheet. • Duvet cover & Pillow Cases. • Curtains (at local discretion if fittings allow). • Rug. • Floor Mat / Bathroom Set. • Table Cover
Clothing	• Coats • No black items permitted, with the exception of leggings. • No hoods. • No offensive slogans/designs, sports teams, countries etc. • Nothing padded or quilted. • Hats must not: o Cover the face

		○ Be of officer uniform type ○ Peak cap ○ Have side flaps that cover any part of the head. ○ Be lined, padded or quilted
Food utensils		• Basic cooking utensils including saucepans / baking trays – the utensil material to be determined locally subject to individual assessment Tea Towels.
Gaming and DVD players		• Games station. Consoles that do not have internet connectivity in their factory state may generally be considered suitable. USB ports must be blocked using tamper-evident seals or permanently blocked or the setting reconfigured using USB control software to prevent their use. The USB power supply for the Nintendo SNES Classic is permitted. Annex D provides further advice. • Consoles Game Discs – No 18 rated games. • Gaming memory cards. • DVD Player + DVDs. – No DVD players with hard drives, no 18 rated DVDs or blank/home recorded DVDs. • Blu-Ray players + discs – No Blu-Ray players with hard drives, no 18 rated discs or blank/home recorded discs
Grooming and hygiene		• Electric Hair Clippers. Any scissors /sharps will be removed and disposed/stored. • Beard trimmer. . • Nasal Hair Trimmer. • Electric Shaver • Hair straighteners. not gas powered. • Pin adapter
Miscellaneous		• Typewriter. USB ports must be blocked using tamper-evident seals or permanently blocked or the setting reconfigured using USB control software to prevent its use. • One bird and birdcage. • Ring folder. • Coat Hangers. Plastic or wood only, no metal. • Table lamp
Hobby activities		• Painting Brushes. Pencil type bristles only. • Hobby glue/adhesives as follows Pritt Stick, Bostick - 4600, PVA, No 8, Stick 'n' Fix, Copydex - Copydex, Childsplay, Woodfix. Dunlop - Wood Worker, Universal, A1585. Evostick - Nonflam, Safe 80, Resin W Wood, Watertite. Hermetite - Contact adhesive, wood glue, quick stick. • Hobby paints as follows Kera Colour - 29101 Paintbox (all colours) Paint - Maximum 12 tubes up to 25ml size. Acrylic Varnish - Maximum 2 paints up to 25ml size. No oil based paints. No thinners allowed. • Modelling Matches. Kits with metal hinges are permitted. No scissors. • Match Cutter. • Sandpaper. • Knitting needles - availability, size and material to be determined locally subject to risk assessment /sewing/embroidery kits. No scissors. • Musical instruments and accessories. • Word finder/spell check. No data facility.

	• Table board games e.g. chess/draughts. No data facility. • Jigsaws. • Painting Canvas
Sports equipment	• Yoga mat. • Heart rate monitor and strap. No data storage facility. • Protein Powders. No yeast extract allowed. Vitamin supplements permitted. • Table tennis bat, ball & cover. • Rugby / Football boots – Rubber studs only. • Weight training Belt / Gloves. • Shin Guards – plastic type. • Short tennis racket.

Annex D

Games Consoles and G ames

Governors are permitted to provide prisoners with access only to devices that do not provide internet connectivity in their factory state. 18 rated games are not permitted.

All prisons have previously been made aware that "new generation" games consoles which, in their factory state, have built in wireless access to the internet, are not permitted in possession. HMPPS' Information Security (InfoSec) & Services Team has constructed the following list of the types of consoles that are considered to present a low threat to security as they do not, on their own, provide internet connectivity:

- Original Microsoft Xbox - the version launched in 2002 (without network adaptor & associate cabling)
- Modified Microsoft Xbox One (purchased only through Gema Records. This modified console has been made safe for use in prisons. It is without internet and Bluetooth fuctionality, the hard drive is inaccessible, the USB and external storage ports are disabled and sealed with polymer rendering
- Nintendo GameCube (without modem or broadband adaptor & cabling)
- Nintendo GameBoy
- Nintendo GameBoy Colour (without infrared port)
- Nintendo GameBoy Advance
- Nintendo GameBoy Advance SP
- Nintendo GameBoy Micro
- Sony PlayStation
- Sony PlayStation 1
- Sony PlayStation 2 (without network adaptor & cabling)
- Nintendo SNES Classic (The USB power supply is permitted for this console)

N.B The Microsoft Xbox 360 is not permitted in posse ssion except in the limited circumstances de scribed below .

At the discretion of the Governor, and if the risk is deemed manageable, prisoners may retain consoles with disabled internet connectivity that were held in possession or which had been ordered prior to September 2014. The simple rule is that, otherwise, no games consoles, with Wi-Fi capability (whether or not that connectivity has subsequently been disabled) are to be allowed in possession. SOCT Group can provide further advice on threats to prison security presented by games consoles.

Annex F

SENDING AND HANDING IN OF BOOKS TO PRISONERS

Ordering books via approved retailers

Since 31 January 2015, friends and families of prisoners have been allowed to order books from approved retailers, which source and send the books on to prisoners. The current approved retailers are:

- Blackwell's
- Foyles
- Mr B's Emporium of Reading Delights (added 1 September 2015)
- Waterstones
- WH Smith
- Wordery (added 1 September 2015)

Three additional approved retailers have been added from 4 November 2019.

- Housmans
- Incentive Plus
- Prisons Org UK

Should a prisoner decide not to accept a book that has been sent in via an approved retailer (or is not permitted to have it in possession) and wishes to return it so that the sender can be refunded, the package should be returned to the person who ordered it. This will be at the prisoner's expense. If the prisoner does not wish to pay for the book to be returned, they should be asked whether they want the book to be sent out (at their own expense) or kept in their stored property. If the book is suitable, prisoners should have the option to offer the book to the prison library as a donation. PSI 12/2011, Prisoners' Property, (and, in particular, paragraph 2.41) sets out further information on how to handle property and the options available to Governors when excess property is received.

Sending and handing in of books directly by families and friends

From 1 September 2015, families and friends will also be allowed to send or hand in books to prisoners irrespective of whether or not there are exceptional circumstances. Visitors will not be allowed to hand books directly to prisoners; they will need to be left with staff to process.

Amount of books permitted in -cell

From 1 September 2015, there will no longer be a numerical limit on the number of books which prisoners can have in their cells. The number of books permitted will be subject only to the overarching volumetric control limits on property.

Further important points

- All books received must be searched before being passed to prisoners.
- Prisoners will continue to be allowed to order books through existing arrangements in place in prisons.
- The sending or handing in of audio books, whether via an approved retailer or (from 1 September 2015) directly from families and friends, is permitted in cassette or CD format.
- Audio books will form part of the overall general limits on the number of books that can be held in-cell. For the purposes of the standardised facilities list, such items are categorised as books, rather than CDs or cassettes.

Prison Establishment Map 2022

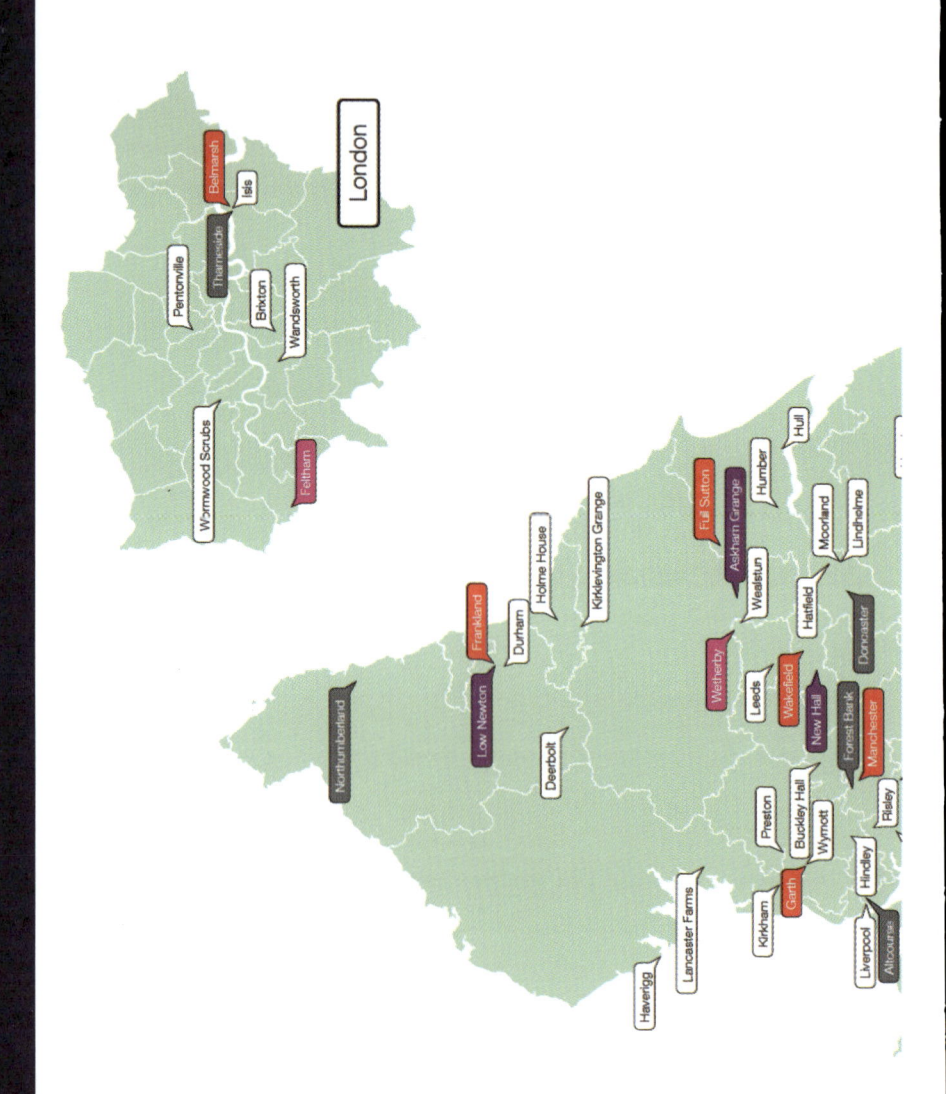

www.cellcompanion.uk

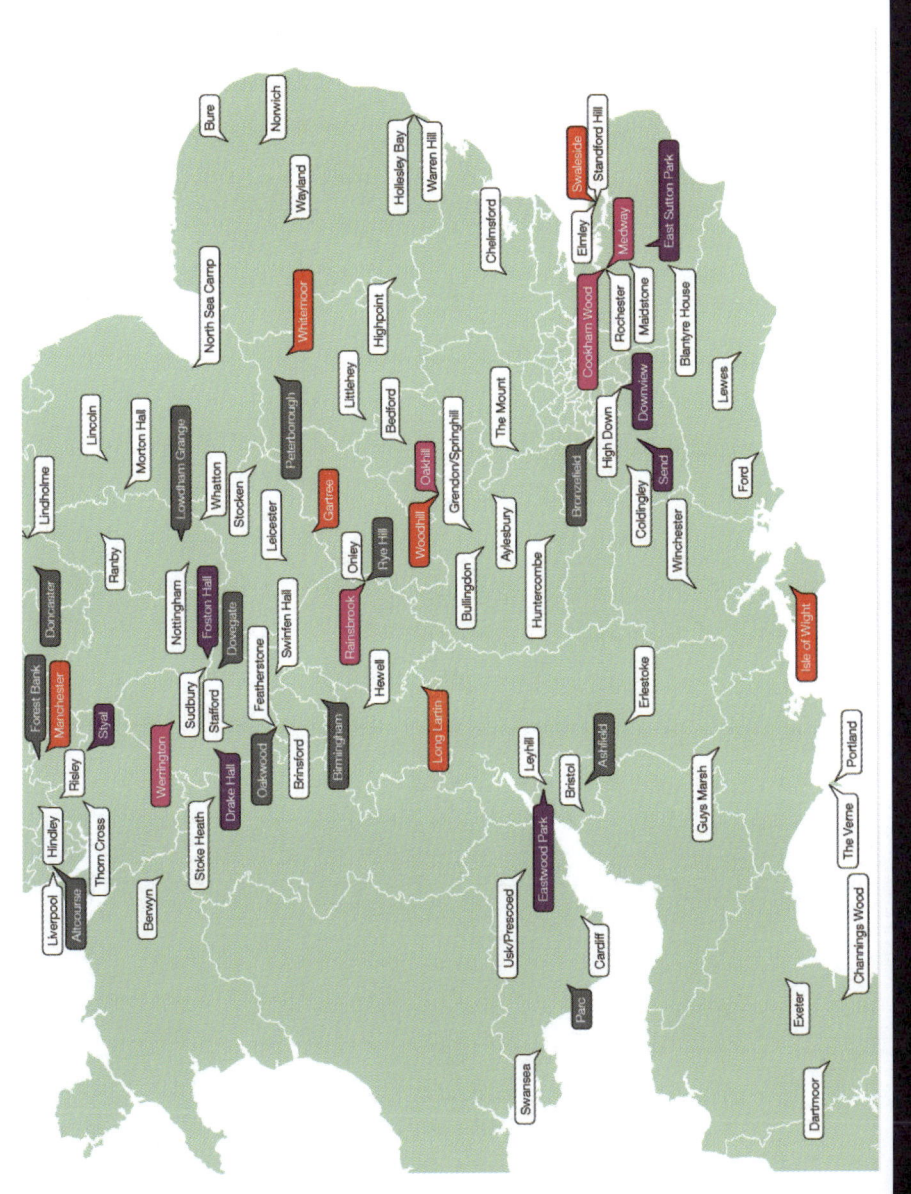

- 251 -

PRISON LAW *Index*

The Definitive A-Z Index to Prison Rules & Regulations

5th Edition Edited By Mark Leech

A-Z of 400 Prison Law Subjects Explained By Experts - from Access to Justice to Zoonotic Infections

www.PrisonOracle.com

2022

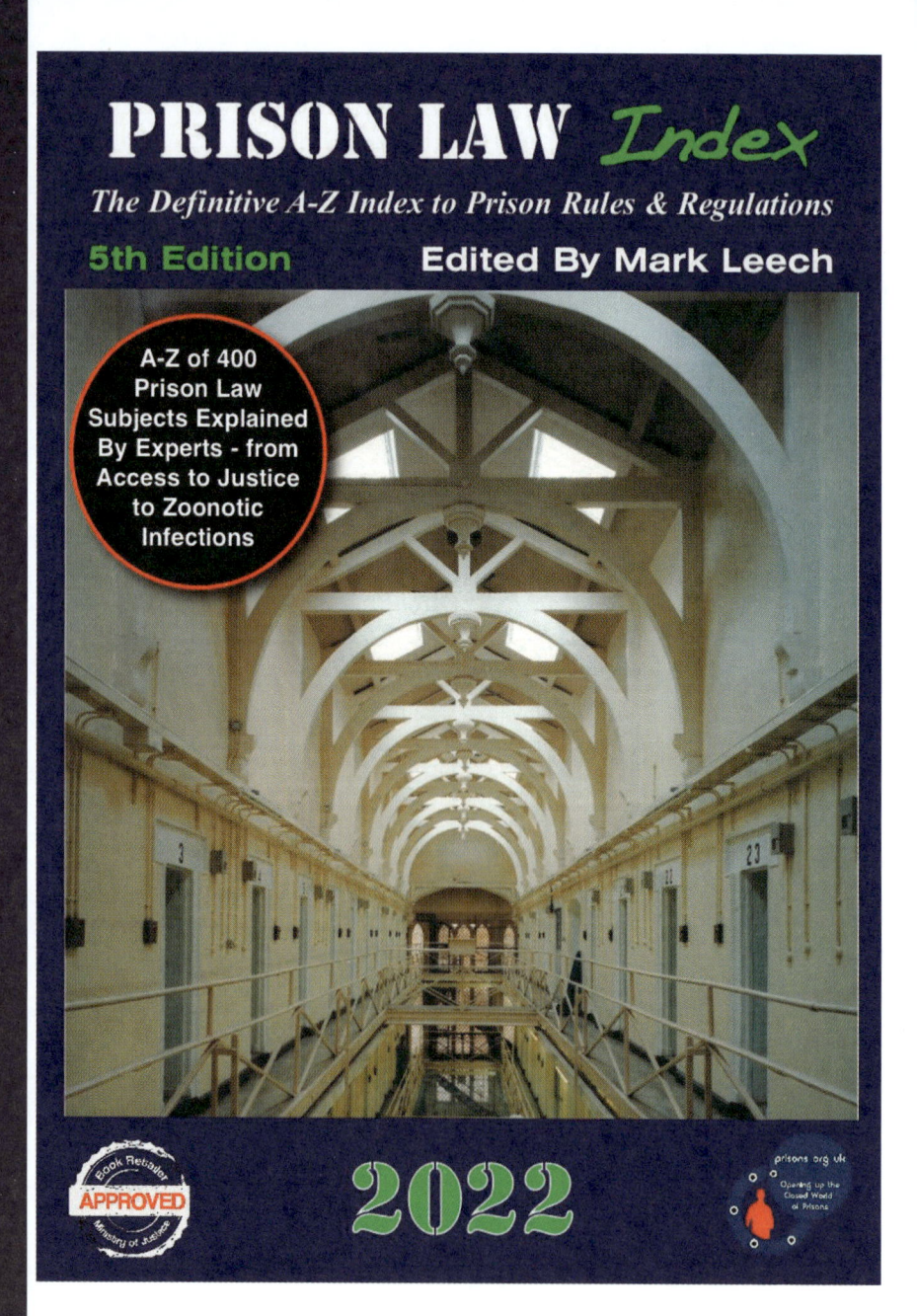

PURCHASE AT A DISCOUNT FROM
PRISONS.ORG.UK/PUBLICATIONS

£5,000
COMPENSATION
FOLLOWING WORKSHOP SLIP

Sean was working in the workshop without having been given any training when he fell and broke his left wrist. Our solicitors helped him claim £5,000.

Sean slipped on some loose plastic while breaking up window frames in the prison workshop. He landed on his left arm, breaking his left wrist. At the time of the accident, Sean was not wearing any Personal Protection Equipment and the trainers he was wearing were unsuitable for the area and the job he was doing. He'd also not been given any training or guidance from the prison staff about keeping the floor clear in the area he was working in.

His wrist injury caused Sean pain and discomfort for almost three years. The team at Prison Injury Lawyers helped him claim £5,000 in compensation for his injuries.

"WE UNDERSTAND PRISONERS AND PRISON INJURY CLAIMS. WE ARE THE UK'S LEADING PRISON INJURY LAWYERS AND WILL FIGHT FOR WHAT YOU DESERVE."

At Prison Injury Lawyers, we can help you claim for:

- Dental negligence
- Medical negligence
- Slips, trips and falls
- Workplace accidents
- Burns
- Assaults
- Bunk bed falls
- Transport accidents
- Accidents in the gym

STRICTLY CONFIDENTIAL · NO WIN NO FEE

0800 808 9577 | prisoninjurylawyers.co.uk
info@prisoninjurylawyers.co.uk

PRISON INJURY LAWYERS

The Triangle 8 Cross Street Altrincham
Cheshire WA14 1EQ

Prison Injury Lawyers is a trading name of Jefferies Solicitors Limited

www.prisons.org.uk

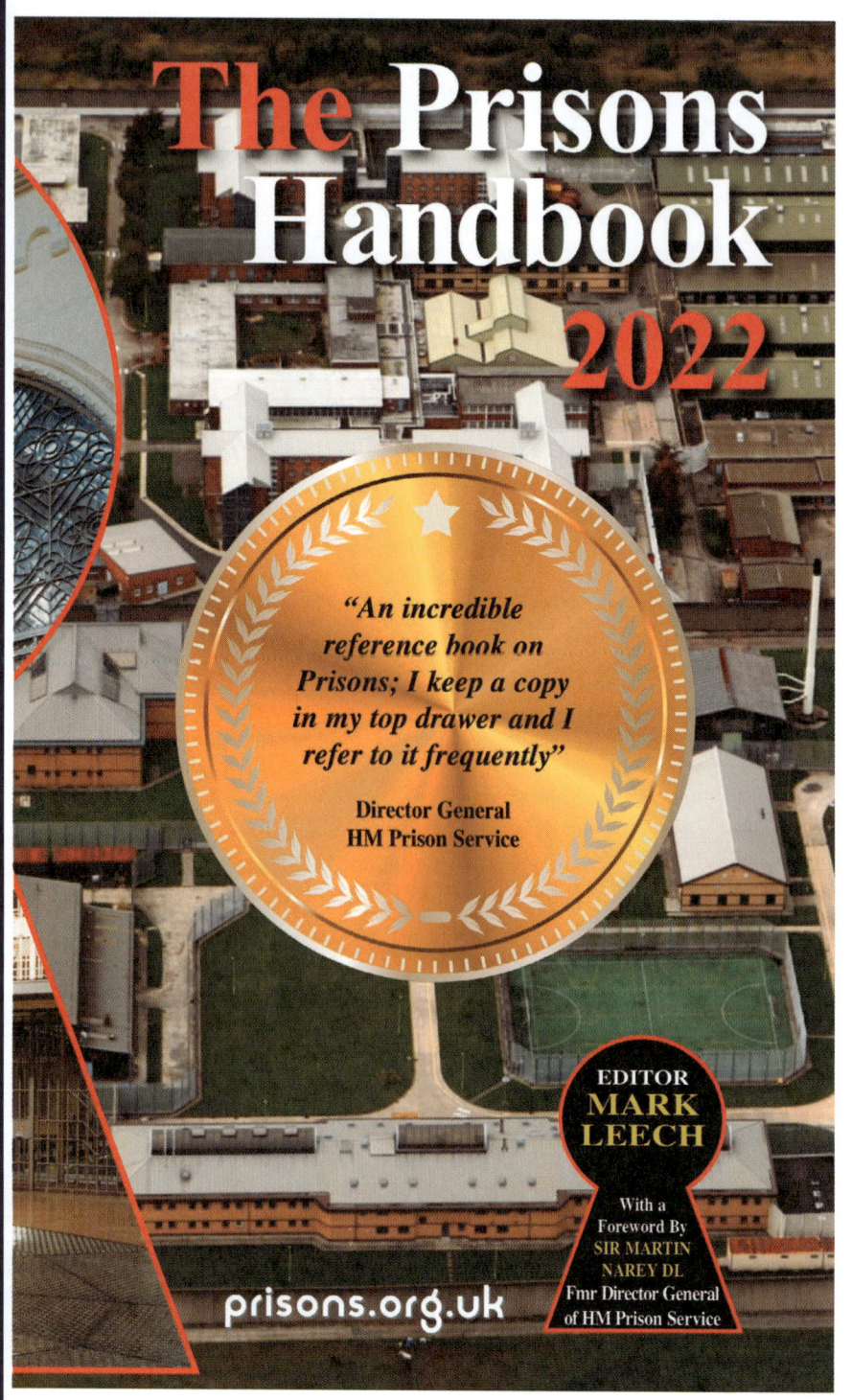

The Prisons Handbook 2022

"An incredible reference book on Prisons; I keep a copy in my top drawer and I refer to it frequently"

**Director General
HM Prison Service**

www.PrisonOracle.com

**EDITOR
MARK LEECH**

With a Foreword By
SIR MARTIN NAREY DL
Fmr Director General of HM Prison Service

prisons.org.uk

THE 2022 PRISONS HANDBOOK

For over 25 years it has been the definitive annual guide to the prison system of England and Wales. Buy it online at **HALF PRICE** for prisoners at:

WWW.PRISONS.ORG.UK

Tel: 0845 474 0013

www.prisons.org.uk

£35,000 COMPENSATION FOR MEDICAL NEGLIGENCE

After healthcare failed to diagnose Dave's wrist injury, he experienced prolonged pain and needed surgery. Our lawyers secured him £35,000.

Dave injured his wrist while playing football. He visited healthcare 3 times over 2 months because he was in significant pain. It was not until the third appointment that he was referred for x-rays and a fracture was diagnosed. Because healthcare failed to correctly examine Dave's wrist and diagnose his wrist fracture on two occasions, he experienced extended pain and suffering and ultimately required wrist surgery. After working with the medical negligence team at Prison Injury Lawyers Dave received £35,000.

"WE UNDERSTAND PRISONERS AND PRISON INJURY CLAIMS. WE ARE THE UK'S LEADING PRISON INJURY LAWYERS AND WILL FIGHT FOR WHAT YOU DESERVE."

At Prison Injury Lawyers, we can help you claim for:

- Dental negligence
- Medical negligence
- Slips, trips and falls
- Workplace accidents
- Burns
- Assaults
- Bunk bed falls
- Transport accidents
- Accidents in the gym

STRICTLY CONFIDENTIAL · NO WIN NO FEE

PRISON INJURY LAWYERS

0800 808 9577 | prisoninjurylawyers.co.uk
info@prisoninjurylawyers.co.uk

The Triangle 8 Cross Street Altrincham
Cheshire WA14 1EQ

Prison Injury Lawyers is a trading name of Jefferies Solicitors Limited

www.PrisonOracle.com